NEURAL NETWORKS
FOR
SIGNAL PROCESSING

Bart Kosko, Editor
University of Southern California

PRENTICE HALL, Englewood Cliffs, NJ 07632

Library of Congress Cataloging-in-Publication Data

Neural networks for signal processing / Bart Kosko, editor.
      p.   cm.
   Includes bibliographical references and index.
   ISBN 0-13-617390-X
   1. Signal processing--Digital techniques--Data processing.
   2. Neural networks (Computer science)   I. Kosko, Bart.
   TK5102.5.N44   1992
   621.382'2--dc20   91-21081
                                                        CIP

Acquisitions Editor: Pete Janzow
Production Editor: Joe Scordato
Copy Editor: Bob Lentz
Jacket Designer: Wanda Lubelska
Prepress Buyer: Linda Behrens
Manufacturing Buyer: Dave Dickey
Supplements Editor: Alice Dworkin
Editorial Assistant: Phyllis Morgan

The author and publisher of this book have used their best efforts in preparing this book. These efforts include the development, research, and testing of the theories and programs to determine their effectiveness. The author and publisher make no warranty of any kind, expressed or implied, with regard to these programs or the documentation contained in this book. The author and publisher shall not be liable in any event for incidental or consequential damages in connection with, or arising out of, the furnishing, performance, or use of these programs.

 © 1992 by Prentice-Hall, Inc.
A Simon & Schuster Company
Englewood Cliffs, New Jersey 07632

Printed in the United States of America

10 9 8 7 6 5 4 3 2

ISBN 0-13-617390-X

Prentice-Hall International (UK) Limited, *London*
Prentice-Hall of Australia Pty. Limited, *Sydney*
Prentice-Hall Canada Inc., *Toronto*
Prentice-Hall Hispanoamericana, S.A., *Mexico*
Prentice-Hall of India Private Limited, *New Delhi*
Prentice-Hall of Japan, Inc., *Tokyo*
Simon & Schuster Asia Pte. Ltd., *Singapore*
Editora Prentice-Hall do Brasil, Ltda., *Rio de Janiero*

To Gauss

CONTENTS

PREFACE

Neural networks approximate functions with raw sample data. A neural network's topology and dynamics define a black-box approximator from input to output. An unknown function $f\colon X \to Y$ produces the observed sample pairs (x_1, y_1), (x_2, y_2), (x_3, y_3), ... The sample data modify parameters in the neural estimator and bring the neural system's input-output responses closer to the input-output responses of the unknown estimand f. The approximation accuracy tends to increase as the sample size increases. In psychological terms, the neural system learns from experience.

Nowhere in the neural-estimation process need the neural engineer articulate, write down, or guess at the mathematical shape of the unknown function f. Neural estimation is *model-free*. Model-free estimation remains the central advantage of neurocomputing and accounts for its sense of mystery and beauty, a sense that underlies the field's recent interdisciplinary rebirth. Different neural engineers can estimate the same unknown function with the same sample data but with different neural models and still produce black boxes with similar input-output responses, as if they trimmed different shrubs to the same shape. The internal twigging differs and no one cares.

Model-freedom lifts from us the oldest burden of modern science—guessing at cause-and-effect relationships with functions, and with functions so simple and so tractable that our recently evolved brains can understand them and manipulate them in symbols. Should our psychology limit our engineering and science? The set of all "tractable" functions represents an infinitesimal point in the function space of all functions. Neural techniques allow us to estimate cause and effect with the vastly larger set of functions in some epsilon ball centered at our species-dependent point of tractability. Neural model-freedom represents a shift from scientific rationalism to scientific empiricism: Let the data tell their own story.

Most estimation procedures, from mean-squared linear estimation to nonlinear regression, require the analyst to write down a mathematical model of how outputs depend on inputs. This involves some question begging. If you already know the shape of the unknown function, why estimate it? At best you can adjust the parameters of the presumed function to bring it closer to the unknown function. But how close can a low-order polynomial come to the time-series footprints left by a chaotic system? The initial guess at the shape of the function tightly constrains the categories of functions we can estimate with it. Standard estimation theory works largely with linear or linearized systems. The Kalman filter behaves optimally in mean-squared and maximum-likelihood senses for linear state models. The extended Kalman filter offers no such optimality for nonlinear systems, and nonlinear systems represent the overwhelming proportion of the large-dimensional systems encountered in practice. Textbooks on estimation have over-represented model-based estimation because they focus on closed-form solutions and optimality theorems, especially the normal equations of least-squares. These texts have cast parameter and state estimation as a deductive science and not as the inductive, computer-intensive activity it has long since become.

Signal processing has depended almost exclusively on model-based techniques. Digital signal processing rests on the theory of linear time-invariant (LTI) systems, on mathematical convolutions. Adaptive signal processing builds on the LTI framework and often combines portions of it with iterative least-squares. Nonlinear signal processing techniques usually linearize nonlinear systems and then invoke standard LTI analysis. In many ways this dependence on linearity reflects the current state of mathematical knowledge in real analysis. We know a great deal about bounded linear functionals and almost nothing about bounded nonlinear functionals.

This volume explores nonlinear signal processing with neural networks. Most chapters assume a working knowledge of signal processing and pattern recognition techniques. The first chapter reviews many of these techniques and applies them to phoneme recognition. Each chapter includes review material and new research results. Each chapter also includes detailed homework problems to assist in classroom instruction. We wrote each chapter for a technical but interdisciplinary audience. I have edited this volume as a companion volume to my Prentice Hall textbook *Neural Networks and Fuzzy Systems* and refer the reader to that text for complete details on the supervised and unsupervised neural learning algorithms, global stability and convergence analysis, and the general perspective on computing with dynamical systems.

This volume covers sensory and cognitive signal processing and its electro-optical implementation. Chapters 1–5 apply neural networks to speech recognition, image processing, spectral estimation, and vision. Chapters 6 and 7 apply neural networks to robotics and control. Chapters 8 and 9 discuss new ways to implement neural networks in analog very-large-scale-integrated (VLSI) circuitry and in optical devices.

This volume arose from ongoing research in USC's Signal and Image Processing Institute (SIPI) and Center for Neural Engineering (CNE). All contributing faculty and graduate students belong directly or indirectly to SIPI and participate in its joint research efforts with the CNE. SIPI faculty were Rama Chellappa, Keith Jenkins, Bart Kosko, Jerry Mendel, Bing Sheu, and Armand Tanguay. CNE faculty were George Bekey, Sukhan Lee, and Christoph von der Malsburg.

ACKNOWLEDGMENTS

I would like to thank the USC faculty and graduate students who contributed sections and criticisms to this volume. I would like to thank Tim Bozik, Executive Editor at Prentice Hall, for his courage in instigating this volume and supporting its evolution and production. Most of all I want to thank Delsa Tan who processed the manuscript and tirelessly supervised its authors.

Bart Kosko
University of Southern California

PART ONE

SIGNAL AND IMAGE PROCESSING

DIFFERENTIAL COMPETITIVE LEARNING FOR PHONEME RECOGNITION

Seong-Gon Kong and Bart Kosko
Signal and Image Processing Institute
Department of Electrical Engineering–Systems
University of Southern California

ADAPTIVE VECTOR QUANTIZATION FOR PHONEME RECOGNITION

Phoneme recognition is a simple form of speech recognition. We can recognize a speech sample phoneme by phoneme. The phoneme-recognition system learns only a comparatively small set of minimal syllables or phonemes. More advanced systems learn and recognize words, phrases, or sentences, which are more numerous by orders of magnitude than phonemes. Words and phrases can also undergo more complex forms of distortion and time warping.

In principle we can recognize phonemes and speech with **vector-quantization** methods. These methods search for a small but representative set of prototypes, which we can then use to match sample patterns with nearest-neighbor techniques.

In neural-network phoneme recognition, a sequence of discrete phonemes from a continuous speech sample produces a series of neuronal responses. Kohonen's [1988b] supervised neural phoneme-recognition system successfully classifies 21 Finnish phonemes. This stochastic competitive-learning system behaves as an adaptive vector-quantization system.

Traditional vector-quantization systems may attempt to minimize a mean-squared-error or entropic performance measure. Formal minimization assumes knowledge of the sampled probability density function $p(\mathbf{x})$ and perhaps additional knowledge of how some parameters functionally depend on other parameters. The function $p(\mathbf{x})$ describes the continuous distribution of patterns in R^n. In general we do not know this probabilistic information. Instead we use learning algorithms to adaptively estimate $p(\mathbf{x})$ from sample realizations. This procedure often reduces to **stochastic approximation** [Robbins, 1951; Tsypkin, 1973].

Adaptive-vector-quantization (AVQ) systems adaptively quantize pattern clusters in R^n. Stochastic competitive-learning systems are neural AVQ systems. Neurons compete for the activation induced by randomly sampled patterns. The corresponding synaptic fan-in vectors adaptively quantize the pattern space R^n. The p synaptic vectors $\mathbf{m}_j$ define the p columns of the synaptic connection matrix M. M interconnects the n input or linear neurons in the input neuronal field F_X to the p competing nonlinear neurons in the output field F_Y.

In the simplest case the p synaptic vectors estimate centroids or modes of the sampled probability density function $p(\mathbf{x})$. The estimates are nonparametric. The user need not know or assume which probability density function $p(\mathbf{x})$ generates the training samples, the observed realizations of the underlying stochastic pattern process.

Pattern learning is **supervised** if the system uses pattern-class information. Suppose the k decision classes $\{D_j\}$ partition the pattern space R^n:

$$R^n \;=\; \bigcup_{j=1}^{k} D_j \quad \text{and} \quad D_i \cap D_j = \varnothing \quad \text{if} \quad i \neq j \tag{1-1}$$

The system knows and uses the class membership of each pattern $\mathbf{x}$. The system knows that $\mathbf{x} \in D_i$ and that $\mathbf{x} \notin D_j$ for all $j \neq i$. Pattern learning is **unsupervised** if the system does not know or use class-membership information. Unsupervised learning algorithms use **unlabelled** pattern samples.

Formally supervised learning depends on class **indicator functions** $\{I_{D_j}\}$:

$$I_{D_j}(\mathbf{x}) \;=\; \begin{cases} 1 & \text{if} \quad \mathbf{x} \in D_j \\ 0 & \text{if} \quad \mathbf{x} \notin D_j \end{cases} \tag{1-2}$$

I_{D_j} indicates whether pattern $\mathbf{x}$ belongs to decision class D_j. Unsupervised learning algorithms blindly cluster samples. They do not depend on class indicator functions. The random indicator functions define the **class probabilities** $P(D_1), \dots, P(D_k)$, since

$$P(D_j) \;=\; \int_{D_j} p(\mathbf{x})\,d\mathbf{x} \tag{1-3}$$

$$=\; \int_{R^n} I_{D_j}(\mathbf{x}) p(\mathbf{x})\,d\mathbf{x} \tag{1-4}$$

$$=\; E[I_{D_j}] \tag{1-5}$$

$E[x]$ denotes the mathematical expectation of scalar random variable x. The partition property and $P(R^n) = 1$ imply $P(D_1) + \cdots + P(D_k) = 1$.

Learning algorithms estimate the unknown probability density function $p(\mathbf{x})$. We need not learn if we know $p(\mathbf{x})$. Instead we could compute desired quantities with optimization, numerical-analytical, or calculus-of-variation techniques. For instance, we could directly compute the centroids $\bar{\mathbf{x}}_j$ of the pattern classes D_j. The centroids minimize the total mean-squared error of vector quantization.

Mean-squared error optimal learning drives synaptic vectors to the unknown centroids $\bar{\mathbf{x}}_j$ of the locally sampled pattern classes. More generally [Kosko, 1990c], $E[\mathbf{m}_j] = \bar{\mathbf{x}}_j$ holds asymptotically as the random synaptic vector $\mathbf{m}_j$ wanders in a Brownian motion about the centroid $\bar{\mathbf{x}}_j$. We observed this Brownian wandering in the simulations discussed below (Figure 1.8).

If there are exactly p distinct pattern classes or clusters, the p synaptic row vectors $\mathbf{m}_1(t), \ldots, \mathbf{m}_p(t)$ should asymptotically approach the centroid of a distinct pattern class. In general we do not know the number k of pattern classes. If there are fewer synaptic vectors than the number k of pattern classes, if $p < k$, the synaptic vectors should approach the centroids of the p most massive, most probable pattern clusters.

If $p > k$, the synaptic vectors should approximate the entire density function $p(\mathbf{x})$. More synaptic vectors should arrive at more probable regions. Where patterns x are dense or sparse, synaptic vectors $\mathbf{m}_j$ should be dense or sparse. The local count of synaptic vectors then gives an accurate nonparametric estimate of the volume probability $P(V)$ for volume $V \subset R^n$:

$$P(V) \quad = \quad \int_V p(\mathbf{x})\, \mathbf{dx} \tag{1-6}$$

$$\approx \quad \frac{\text{number of } \mathbf{m}_j \in V}{p} \tag{1-7}$$

In the extreme case that $V = R^n$, this approximation gives $P(V) = p/p = 1$. For small or improbable subsets V, $P(V) = 0/p = 0$.

Differential competitive learning (DCL) provides a new [Kosko, 1990b] unsupervised form of AVQ. DCL modifies stochastic synaptic vectors with a competing neuron's *change* in output signal. The neuronal signal velocity locally reinforces the synaptic vector. The time derivative's sign changes resemble the supervised sign changes in supervised-competitive-learning (SCL) algorithms. SCL systems use more information than DCL systems, since signal velocities do not depend on class-membership information. In particular, the DCL algorithm in (1-118) below does not use the class membership of the training sample x.

Both DCL-trained and SCL-trained synaptic vectors tend to rapidly converge to pattern-class centroids [Kosko, 1990b]. Our simulated DCL synaptic vectors converged faster to bipolar centroids—points in $\{-1, 1\}^n$—than did SCL synaptic vectors when, as in biological neural networks, a sigmoidal signal function nonlinearly transduced neuronal activations to bounded signals. DCL systems exploit a *win-rate* dependent sequence of learning coefficients. The faster the neuron wins or loses, the more the synaptic vector resembles or disresembles the sampled pattern. SCL systems ignore this instantaneous rate information.

In practice input neurons have linear signal functions: $S_i(x_i) = x_i$. The user presents the random sample x to the system as the *output* of the F_X neurons. In this case our simulated DCL and SCL synaptic vectors converged equally quickly. But the DCL-trained synaptic vectors wandered less about class centroids than did SCL-trained synaptic vectors.

Before we present and apply the competitive learning framework for phoneme recognition, we review the mathematical underpinnings of speech recognition in discrete linear systems theory and statistical pattern-recognition theory. This material can be found in any graduate curriculum in electrical engineering. Readers familiar with these subjects may wish to skip directly to the section below on competitive-learning AVQ algorithms.

DISCRETE LINEAR TIME-INVARIANT SYSTEMS

A **system** S is a mapping or transformation from an input space X to an output space Y. A **discrete system** $S: X \longrightarrow Y$ maps input *sequences* $\{x_n\} \in X$ of numbers to output *sequences* $\{y_n\} \in Y$ of numbers. So for each n,

$$S[x_n] = y_n \qquad (1\text{-}8)$$

A point in X or in Y defines a countably infinite sequence of real or complex numbers: $\dots, x_{-3}, x_{-2}, x_{-1}, x_0, x_1, x_2, x_3, \dots$. The subscript n is a time index. In general the time index ranges from negative infinity to positive infinity.

The set of all possible discrete systems is large. There are as many discrete systems as there are real numbers. (There are as many continuous systems as there are subsets of real numbers.) Most of these systems are incomprehensibly nonlinear. The equations describing how the output sequences $\{y_n\}$ depend on the input sequences $\{x_n\}$ through S could not be written down in a lifetime, indeed in a planet's lifetime. Worse, most discrete systems are time-varying. The defining parameters and coefficients of the systems vary nonlinearly with the time index n.

The simplest way to deal with such intractable nonlinearities and time variances is to ignore them. This is the approach of **linear systems theory**. Here we assume that systems are linear and time-invariant.

These two extreme assumptions have two advantages. First, they facilitate comparatively easy, and surprisingly comprehensive, mathematical analysis. For instance, they allow us to apply all the tools of linear algebra and linear transform theory. Second, we can accurately model many practical estimation and filtering problems as linear time-invariant digital systems. Many of these systems in turn are physically realizable and easy to compute.

We briefly review the theory of discrete linear time-invariant systems. We follow closely the popular Oppenheim-Schafer [1975, 1989] presentation of the theory.

The system $S: X \longrightarrow Y$ is **linear** if the output given a scaled sum equals the scaled sum of the outputs:

$$S[ax_n^1 + bx_n^2] = aS[x_n^1] + bS[x_n^2] \tag{1-9}$$

for any constants a and b and any two input sequences $\{x_n^1\}$ and $\{x_n^2\}$. The system S is **time-invariant** if shifts in the input sequence $\{x_n\}$ by some fixed value n_0 produce like shifts in the output sequence $\{y_n\}$:

$$S[x_{n-n_0}] = y_{n-n_0} \tag{1-10}$$

for all integers n_0. Intuitively the structure of a time-invariant system or filter does not change with time. The system $S: X \longrightarrow Y$ is a **linear time-invariant (LTI) system** if it is both linear and time-invariant.

LTI systems are completely characterized by their response to impulse inputs, by their **impulse-response function** $h_n = S[\delta_n]$, where δ_n is the **Kronecker delta** function:

$$\delta_n = \begin{cases} 1 & \text{if} \quad n = 0 \\ 0 & \text{if} \quad n \neq 0 \end{cases} \tag{1-11}$$

A **causal** system's output depends only on past inputs, not on future inputs. For a causal LTI system, $h_n = 0$ for $n < 0$.

A system is **bounded-input bounded-output (BIBO) stable** if the output sequence $\{y_n\}$ is bounded for every bounded input sequence $\{x_n\}$:

$$|x_n| \leq M < \infty \quad \text{implies} \quad |y_n| \leq N < \infty \tag{1-12}$$

for some fixed constants M and N. A necessary and sufficient condition for an LTI system to be stable is absolute summability of the impulse response function:

$$\sum_{n=-\infty}^{\infty} |h_n| < \infty \tag{1-13}$$

The Kronecker-delta structure of LTI systems implies that the output of a LTI system is the discrete **convolution** $x_n * h_n$ of the input sequence $\{x_n\}$ and the impulse response sequence $\{h_n\}$.

$$y_n = \sum_{k=-\infty}^{\infty} x_k h_{n-k} \tag{1-14}$$

$$= x_n * h_n \tag{1-15}$$

We define the **z-transform** $X(z)$ of a sequence $\{x_n\}$ as

$$X(z) = \sum_{n=-\infty}^{\infty} x_n z^{-n} \tag{1-16}$$

We call the z-transform $H(z)$ of the impulse response h_n the **system transfer function**. For an LTI system, applying (1-16) to (1-15) gives the z-transform of the convolution $x_n * h_n$ as the product of the z-transforms:

$$Y(z) = X(z)H(z) \tag{1-17}$$

The **discrete-time Fourier transform** of the discrete sequence $\{x_n\}$ equals the z-transform of $\{x_n\}$ evaluated on the unit circle (all complex z such that $|z| = 1$, or $z = e^{i\omega}$) of the z-plane:

$$X(e^{i\omega}) = X(z)|_{z=e^{i\omega}} \tag{1-18}$$

$$= \sum_{n=-\infty}^{\infty} x_n e^{-i\omega n} \tag{1-19}$$

The Fourier transform of the sequence $\{x_n\}$ exists if the sequence is **absolutely summable**:

$$\sum_{n=-\infty}^{\infty} |x_n| < \infty \tag{1-20}$$

Suppose the random sequence $\{x_n\}$ is **wide-sense stationary (WSS)**. Then its mean function is constant, and its covariance function is time-invariant. We can estimate the **autocorrelation** function $R_X(k)$ of a WSS (ergodic) random process by the time-average autocorrelation function from a long but finite segment of signal:

$$\hat{R}_X(k) = \frac{1}{N} \sum_{n=0}^{N-1-|k|} x_n x_{n+k} \tag{1-21}$$

for k values restricted to $0 \leq |k| \leq N - 1$. We estimate the **power spectral density** function $S_X(\omega)$ as

$$\hat{S}_X(\omega) = \sum_{k=-M}^{M} \hat{R}_X(k) w_k e^{-i\omega k} \tag{1-22}$$

where $\{w_k\}$ defines a window sequence of length $2M$.

The spectral properties of speech signals change little during short time intervals. But they do change slowly with time. We can accurately represent periodic or WSS random signals with standard Fourier transform representations. We cannot directly apply these representations to arbitrary time-varying speech signals.

To reflect the time-varying properties of speech waveforms, we can use a short-time Fourier transform. We call spectral analysis over a finite time interval, with a finite number of samples, **short-time spectral analysis**.

We define the **time-dependent Fourier transform** $X_n(e^{i\omega})$ of a sequence $\{x_n\}$ as

$$X_n(e^{i\omega}) = \sum_{k=-\infty}^{\infty} x_k w_{n-k} e^{-i\omega k} \tag{1-23}$$

where $\{w_{n-k}\}$ is a **window sequence**. $X_n(e^{i\omega})$ is a function of two variables: the discrete time index n and the continuous frequency index ω.

$X_n(e^{i\omega})$ has two interpretations. First, for fixed n, $X_n(e^{i\omega})$ equals the normal Fourier transform of the sequence $\{x_k w_{n-k}\}$ for $-\infty < k < \infty$. Second, for fixed ω, $X_n(e^{i\omega})$ defines a function of the time index n and equals the convolution relationship (1-23).

The window sequence $\{w_n\}$ maps integers to numbers. Usually the power spectra $W(\omega)$ of such functions have high-frequency resolution. They also tend to suffer from small spurious distortions when we compute the convolution with values outside the window's main lobe.

Some standard discrete-time window sequences of length N are as follows:

rectangular window:

$$w_n = 1 \quad \text{if} \quad 0 \le n \le N - 1$$

Bartlett window:

$$w_n = \begin{cases} \dfrac{2n}{N-1} & \text{if} \quad 0 \le n \le \dfrac{N-1}{2} \\[2mm] 2 - \dfrac{2n}{N-1} & \text{if} \quad \dfrac{N-1}{2} \le n \le N - 1 \end{cases}$$

Hamming window:

$$w_n = 0.54 - 0.46 \cos\left(\frac{2\pi n}{N-1}\right) \quad \text{if} \quad 0 \le n \le N - 1$$

If the window is short, spectral analysis can track the rapid time change of the spectrum, but at the expense of frequency resolution. If the window is long, then we obtain a high-frequency resolution for the average spectrum.

Figure 1.1(a) shows the time waveform of the pronounced English word $/six/$ as pronounced by a male. The fricative sound $/s/$ corresponds to the noiselike part of the waveform at the beginning of the utterance. The voiced sound $/i/$ corresponds to the quasi-periodic segment next to $/s/$. Such periodicity characterizes voiced sounds. Figure 1.1(b) shows the power spectral envelope of the time waveform 1.1(a) found by the time-dependent Fourier spectrum. We used a Hamming window with a 25.6-millisecond (ms) window width. Each windowed speech segment of 25.6 ms consisted of 256 samples with sampling frequency of 10 kilohertz (kHz).

We calculated the time-dependent Fourier transform of each windowed speech segment with the fast Fourier transform (FFT) algorithm. Each transformed segment is defined by 256 complex Fourier coefficients. The first 128 of these correspond to a frequency range of 0 Hz to 5 kHz. We computed the spectral envelope by calculating the average power of each windowed speech segment every 10 ms. As time passes, the phonemes transition in the order $/s/ \rightarrow /i/ \rightarrow /k/ \rightarrow /s/$. Note that most of the energy of the fricative sound $/s/$ resides in the high-frequency range of the spectrum. In contrast, most of the energy of the voiced sound $/i/$ resides in the low-frequency range.

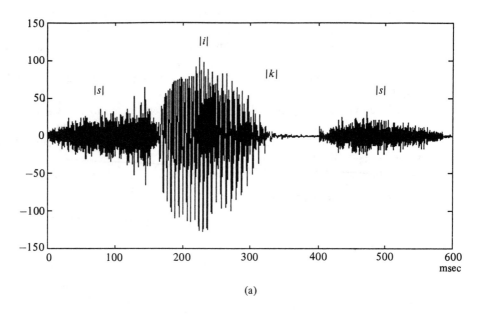

(a)

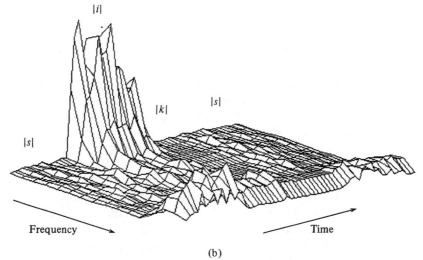

(b)

FIGURE 1.1 (a) Time waveform of the male-spoken word /*six*/. (b) Power spectral envelope of (a) computed with the time-dependent Fourier transform.

STATISTICAL PATTERN RECOGNITION

Statistical pattern-recognition systems map randomly sampled patterns $\mathbf{x} \in R^n$ to pattern **decision classes** $D_j \subset R^n$ or, more simply, to pattern class labels. The decision classes $\{D_j\}$ partition the pattern space R^n:

$$R^n = \bigcup_{j=1}^{k} D_j \quad \text{and} \quad D_i \cap D_j = \emptyset \qquad \text{if} \quad i \neq j \qquad (1\text{-}24)$$

Pattern recognition is **supervised** if the decision classes are known. The user knows, and the system uses, the class membership of each pattern $\mathbf{x}$. The user knows that $\mathbf{x} \in D_i$ but that $\mathbf{x} \notin D_j$ for all $j \neq i$. Pattern recognition is **unsupervised** if class memberships are unknown. Unsupervised pattern-recognition systems, such as the competitive-learning systems discussed below, are usually based on clustering algorithms. Unsupervised learning uses *unlabelled* samples.

The patterns $\mathbf{x} \in R^n$ are random or "statistical" in terms of their probability of selection when sampled. The probability density function $p(\mathbf{x})$ describes the probability distribution of the patterns in R^n. The function $p(\mathbf{x})\,dV$ measures the probability that pattern $\mathbf{x}$ is in the infinitesimal volume dV of the pattern sample space R^n.

In practice we must preprocess raw input data. This may involve numerical representation or dimension reduction. The processed data define the random sample patterns $\mathbf{x} \in R^n$. **Feature extraction** maps these input data to numerical pattern vectors. In this sense feature vectors and pattern vectors are synonymous. (Some treatments of the subject would call our pattern vectors x *feature vectors*, reserving the term *pattern vector* for the raw input patterns. This, though, forces a subject name change to *feature recognition*.) Phoneme-recognition matches feature vectors of preprocessed speech signals to stored phoneme pattern vectors or templates.

Pattern-recognition systems assume feature extraction preserves the structure of the raw input patterns. Presumably, if the unprocessed input patterns cluster into k clusters or classes, then these clusters correspond to the k decision classes $D_1, \ldots, D_k$.

SIMILARITY AS DISTANCE

Pattern-recognition systems further assume that the decision classes $\{D_j\}$ are similarity-relation meaningful. Usually patterns within a decision class D_i more resemble one another than they resemble patterns from classes D_i and D_j. This pattern-class similarity may hold only probabilistically. It inevitably breaks down at or near decision-class boundaries.

We metrically interpret *similarity* as a *distance measure* $d: R^n \times R^n \longrightarrow [0, \infty)$. We interpret close patterns as similar patterns. The **distance** $d(\mathbf{x}, \mathbf{y})$ between

n-vectors $\mathbf{x}$ and $\mathbf{y}$ obeys three metrical axioms:

$$\text{(i)} \quad d(\mathbf{x}, \mathbf{y}) \;=\; 0 \qquad\qquad\qquad \text{iff} \quad \mathbf{x} = \mathbf{y} \qquad (1\text{-}25)$$

$$\text{(ii)} \quad d(\mathbf{x}, \mathbf{y}) \;=\; d(\mathbf{y}, \mathbf{x}) \qquad\qquad\qquad\qquad (1\text{-}26)$$

$$\text{(iii)} \quad d(\mathbf{x}, \mathbf{y}) \;\leq\; d(\mathbf{x}, \mathbf{z}) + d(\mathbf{z}, \mathbf{y}) \quad \text{for all } \mathbf{z} \qquad (1\text{-}27)$$

Most distance measures, or metrics, are ℓ^p metrics:

$$\ell^p(\mathbf{x}, \mathbf{y}) \;=\; \left(\sum_{i=1}^{n} |x_i - y_i|^p \right)^{1/p} \qquad \text{for} \quad p \geq 1 \qquad (1\text{-}28)$$

If $p = 2$, we obtain classical **Euclidean distance**. We shall use the Euclidean or ℓ^2 metric as our default distance measure. Euclidean distance is **isotropic**, invariant under translation or rotation. So $d(T\mathbf{x}, T\mathbf{y}) = d(\mathbf{x}, \mathbf{y}) = d(R\mathbf{x}, R\mathbf{y})$ for any translation operator T and any rotation operator R. Euclidean distance is not invariant under linear transformation. Simple scalings can distort ℓ^2 distance relationships. If we multiplicatively scale the pattern vectors $\mathbf{x}$ and $\mathbf{y}$ with constant $c > 0$, then $d(c\mathbf{x}, c\mathbf{y}) = \ell^2(c\mathbf{x}, c\mathbf{y}) = c\, d(\mathbf{x}, \mathbf{y}) \neq d(\mathbf{x}, \mathbf{y})$ in general.

The cosine between two row vectors in R^n defines another metrical similarity measure:

$$d(\mathbf{x}, \mathbf{y}) \;=\; \frac{\mathbf{x}\mathbf{y}^T}{\|\mathbf{x}\|\|\mathbf{y}\|} \qquad (1\text{-}29)$$

This **cosine distance** is invariant under rotation and dilation.

A popular statistical distance measure is the **Mahalanobis distance**:

$$d_M(\mathbf{x}, \mathbf{y}) \;=\; (\mathbf{x} - \mathbf{y})\mathbf{K}^{-1}(\mathbf{x} - \mathbf{y})^T \qquad (1\text{-}30)$$

where

$$\mathbf{K} \;=\; E[(\mathbf{x} - \mathbf{m}_x)^T(\mathbf{x} - \mathbf{m}_x)] \qquad (1\text{-}31)$$

$$\mathbf{m}_x \;=\; E[\mathbf{x}] \qquad (1\text{-}32)$$

for random row vector $\mathbf{x}$. $\mathbf{K}$ denotes the positive-definite covariance matrix of the random vector $\mathbf{x}$; $\mathbf{m}_x$ denotes the mean vector of $\mathbf{x}$.

The Mahalanobis distance closely relates to the natural logarithm of the n-dimensional **Gaussian probability density** function,

$$p(\mathbf{x}) \;=\; \frac{1}{(2\pi)^{n/2}|\mathbf{K}|^{1/2}} \exp\left\{ -\frac{1}{2}(\mathbf{x} - \mathbf{m}_x)\mathbf{K}^{-1}(\mathbf{x} - \mathbf{m}_x)^T \right\} \qquad (1\text{-}33)$$

where $|\mathbf{K}|$ denotes the (positive) determinant of the covariance matrix $\mathbf{K}$. The Mahalanobis distance $d_M(\mathbf{x}, \mathbf{y})$ is useful for classifying Gaussian-distributed patterns.

The positive definiteness of $\mathbf{K}$ implies both that the matrix inverse $\mathbf{K}^{-1}$ exists and that it can be "square-root" decomposed:

$$\mathbf{K}^{-1} \;=\; \mathbf{P}\mathbf{P}^T \qquad (1\text{-}34)$$

The connection between Euclidean distance $\ell^2(\mathbf{x}, \mathbf{y})$ and Mahalanobis distance $d_M(\mathbf{x}, \mathbf{y})$ emerges when we view the "square-root" matrix $\mathbf{P}$ as a matrix transformation operator: $\mathbf{x}' = \mathbf{x}\mathbf{P}$ and $\mathbf{y}' = \mathbf{y}\mathbf{P}$. Then

$$
\begin{aligned}
d_M(\mathbf{x}, \mathbf{y}) &= (\mathbf{x} - \mathbf{y})\mathbf{K}^{-1}(\mathbf{x} - \mathbf{y})^T & (1\text{-}35) \\
&= (\mathbf{x} - \mathbf{y})\mathbf{P}\mathbf{P}^T(\mathbf{x} - \mathbf{y})^T & (1\text{-}36) \\
&= (\mathbf{x}\mathbf{P} - \mathbf{y}\mathbf{P})(\mathbf{x}\mathbf{P} - \mathbf{y}\mathbf{P})^T & (1\text{-}37) \\
&= (\mathbf{x}' - \mathbf{y}')(\mathbf{x}' - \mathbf{y}')^T & (1\text{-}38) \\
&= \ell^2(\mathbf{x}', \mathbf{y}') & (1\text{-}39)
\end{aligned}
$$

So the Mahalanobis distance between two vectors equals the Euclidean distance between the two square-root transformed vectors.

PATTERN CLASSIFICATION WITH DISCRIMINANT FUNCTIONS

A **discriminant function** $g_i\colon R^n \longrightarrow R$ [Duda, 1973] classifies patterns $\mathbf{x} \in R^n$ according to the decision rule

$$
\mathbf{x} \in D_i \qquad \text{iff} \quad g_i(\mathbf{x}) > g_j(\mathbf{x}) \quad \text{for all } j \neq i \qquad (1\text{-}40)
$$

A **linear discriminant function** has the form

$$
g_i(\mathbf{x}) = \mathbf{x}\mathbf{w}_i^T + w_{i0} \qquad (1\text{-}41)
$$

and behaves as a separating hyperplane in the pattern space R^n. $\mathbf{w}_i$ is a weight or synaptic vector and w_{i0} the threshold weight. The boundary between the two decision regions D_i and D_j defines the **decision surface**. We define the decision surface between D_i and D_j by all patterns $\mathbf{x}$ such that

$$
g_i(\mathbf{x}) = g_j(\mathbf{x}) \qquad (1\text{-}42)
$$

For a linear discriminant function, the decision surface is a hyperplane, as Figure 1.2 shows. Pattern classes D_i and D_j are **linearly separable** if $g_i(\mathbf{x}) > g_j(\mathbf{x})$ for all $\mathbf{x}$ in D_i and D_j. Then (1-42) defines a separating hyperplane between D_i and D_j.

For example, we define a two-class **nearest-neighbor decision** rule as

$$
\mathbf{x} \in D_1 \qquad \text{if} \quad d(\mathbf{x}, \mathbf{s}_1) < d(\mathbf{x}, \mathbf{s}_2) \qquad (1\text{-}43)
$$

$$
\mathbf{x} \in D_2 \qquad \text{if} \quad d(\mathbf{x}, \mathbf{s}_1) > d(\mathbf{x}, \mathbf{s}_2) \qquad (1\text{-}44)
$$

where $\mathbf{s}_1$ and $\mathbf{s}_2$ represent the reference or prototype vectors of the classes D_1 and D_2. Then we can define metrical discriminant functions as

$$
g_1(\mathbf{x}) = -d(\mathbf{x}, \mathbf{s}_1) \qquad (1\text{-}45)
$$

$$
g_2(\mathbf{x}) = -d(\mathbf{x}, \mathbf{s}_2) \qquad (1\text{-}46)
$$

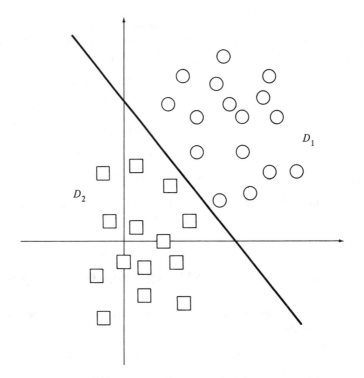

FIGURE 1.2 Linear discrimination of a two-class, two-dimensional pattern space.

Minimum-Distance-to-Class-Means Classifier

Suppose there are m pattern samples $\mathbf{y}$ in decision class $D_i \subset R^n$. Define $\bar{\mathbf{y}}_i$ as the *sample average* of the class D_i sample vectors:

$$\bar{\mathbf{y}}_i = \frac{1}{m} \sum_{k=1}^{m} \mathbf{y}_k \tag{1-47}$$

The **minimum-distance-to-class-means decision rule** assigns any input vector $\mathbf{x}$ to the pattern class D_i with mean vector $\bar{\mathbf{y}}_i$ closest to $\mathbf{x}$. Here we use Euclidean or ℓ^2 distance:

$$d(\mathbf{x}, \bar{\mathbf{y}}_i) = \ell^2(\mathbf{x}, \bar{\mathbf{y}}_i) \tag{1-48}$$

$$= (\mathbf{x} - \bar{\mathbf{y}}_i)(\mathbf{x} - \bar{\mathbf{y}}_i)^T \tag{1-49}$$

$$= \mathbf{x}\mathbf{x}^T - 2\mathbf{x}\bar{\mathbf{y}}_i^T + \bar{\mathbf{y}}_i\bar{\mathbf{y}}_i^T \tag{1-50}$$

The simplest form of the discriminant function is $g_i(\mathbf{x}) = -\ell^2(\mathbf{x}, \bar{\mathbf{y}}_i)$. Since $\mathbf{x}\mathbf{x}^T$

does not depend on the decision-class index i, the discriminant function becomes

$$g_i(\mathbf{x}) = \frac{1}{2}\left[\mathbf{x}\mathbf{x}^T - d(\mathbf{x}, \bar{\mathbf{y}}_i)\right] \tag{1-51}$$

$$= \mathbf{x}\bar{\mathbf{y}}_i^T - \frac{1}{2}\bar{\mathbf{y}}_i\bar{\mathbf{y}}_i^T \tag{1-52}$$

$$= \mathbf{x}\mathbf{w}_i^T + w_{i0} \tag{1-53}$$

for $\mathbf{w}_i = \bar{\mathbf{y}}_i$ and $w_{i0} = -\frac{1}{2}\bar{\mathbf{y}}_i\bar{\mathbf{y}}_i^T$ as in (1-41). The resulting decision surfaces define hyperplanes that perpendicularly bisect the n-dimensional lines that connect the class means.

Quadratic Discriminant Functions

Polynomial discriminant functions can sometimes separate linearly inseparable pattern classes. The simplest example is the **quadratic discriminant function**:

$$g_i(\mathbf{x}) = \mathbf{x}A_i\mathbf{x}^T + \mathbf{x}\mathbf{b}_i^T + w_0 \tag{1-54}$$

where A_i denotes an n-by-n matrix and $\mathbf{b}_i$ denotes a constant n-vector. The resulting decision boundary is nonlinear. A quadratic discriminant function in a suitably augmented space equals the linear discriminant function

$$g_i(\mathbf{x}) = \mathbf{h}\mathbf{w}_i^T + w_{m+1} \tag{1-55}$$

if

$$\mathbf{h} = [x_1^2, \ldots, x_n^2, x_1, \ldots, x_n, x_1x_2, x_1x_3, \ldots, x_{n-1}x_n] \tag{1-56}$$

$$= [h_1, \ldots, h_n, h_{n+1}, \ldots, h_{2n}, h_{2n+1}, \ldots, h_m] \tag{1-57}$$

PERCEPTRONS

The **perceptron** [Minsky, 1969] is a stochastic gradient-descent algorithm that attempts to linearly separate a set of n-dimensional training data. The popularity of the perceptron algorithm stems from the **perceptron convergence theorem**, which Rosenblatt [1962] first proved:

Perceptron Convergence Theorem. The perceptron algorithm finds a linear discriminant function $g_i(\mathbf{x}) = \mathbf{x}\mathbf{w}_i^T$ *in finite iterations* if the training set $\{x_1, \ldots, x_m\}$ is linearly separable.

Many perceptron training algorithms satisfy Rosenblatt's theorem. In general they update weight vector $\mathbf{w}_i$ at an iteration if the training sample $\mathbf{x} \in D_i$ produces $g_i(\mathbf{x}) = \mathbf{x}\mathbf{w}_i^T < 0$ — if the perceptron misclassifies $\mathbf{x}$. The perceptron finds a separating hyperplane when $g_i(\mathbf{x}) = \mathbf{x}\mathbf{w}_i^T > 0$ for all $\mathbf{x} \in D_i$, and $g_i(\mathbf{x}) = \mathbf{x}\mathbf{w}_i^T < 0$ for all $\mathbf{x} \notin D_i$.

The perceptron algorithm reduces to a simple form of stochastic approximation, as discussed in Chapter 5 of Kosko [1992]. We seek to minimize some expected criterion function $E[J(\mathbf{w})]$. An ideal **gradient-descent** learning law then takes the form

$$\mathbf{w}_{k+1} \quad = \quad \mathbf{w}_k - c_k \nabla_w E[J(\mathbf{w}_k)] \tag{1-58}$$

for some appropriate decreasing sequence of learning-rate parameters $\{c_k\}$.

The unknown probability density function $p(\mathbf{x})$ defines the deterministic expectation operator E. So we must estimate the gradient $\nabla_w E[J(\mathbf{w}_k)]$. Stochastic approximation [Robbins, 1951] estimates $E[J]$ as simply the random variable J, which depends only on the observed random realizations of the sampled random process.

Let $\mathcal{X}$ denote the observed set of misclassified training vectors (sample realizations). The perceptron algorithm measures classification performance with a linear misclassification function,

$$J(\mathbf{w}) \quad = \quad -\sum_{\mathbf{x} \in \mathcal{X}} \mathbf{x}\mathbf{w}^T \tag{1-59}$$

J is random since the $\mathbf{x}$ vectors are random. So we estimate the unobserved gradient $\nabla_w E[J]$ as the observed random gradient

$$\nabla_w J(\mathbf{w}) \quad = \quad -\sum_{\mathbf{x} \in \mathcal{X}} \mathbf{x} \tag{1-60}$$

Then the **perceptron algorithm** takes the general form

$$\mathbf{w}_{k+1} \quad = \quad \mathbf{w}_k + c_k \sum_{\mathbf{x} \in \mathcal{X}} \mathbf{x} \tag{1-61}$$

an estimated gradient-descent algorithm. The perceptron learns only if it misclassifies training samples.

We can restate the perceptron algorithm in two-class and multiclass versions.

Two-Class Perceptron Algorithm

If training sample $\mathbf{x} \in D_1$ yields $g_1(\mathbf{x}) = \mathbf{x}\mathbf{w}^T < 0$, then increase the weight vector at iteration $m + 1$:

$$\mathbf{w}_{m+1} \quad = \quad \mathbf{w}_m + c\,\mathbf{x} \tag{1-62}$$

If $\mathbf{x} \in D_2$ yields $\mathbf{x}\mathbf{w}^T > 0$, then decrease the weight vector:

$$\mathbf{w}_{m+1} \quad = \quad \mathbf{w}_m - c\mathbf{x} \tag{1-63}$$

where c is a constant. Repeat until $g_1(\mathbf{x}) = \mathbf{x}\mathbf{w}^T > 0$ for all $\mathbf{x} \in D_1$, and $g_2(\mathbf{x}) = -\mathbf{x}\mathbf{w}^T > 0$ for all $\mathbf{x} \in D_2$.

Multiclass Perceptron Algorithm

At iteration $m + 1$, if the perceptron classifies $\mathbf{x} \in D_i$ to the class D_j, $j \neq i$, then

$$\mathbf{w}_i(m+1) = \mathbf{w}_i(m) + c\,\mathbf{x} \qquad (1\text{-}64)$$

$$\mathbf{w}_j(m+1) = \mathbf{w}_j(m) - c\,\mathbf{x} \qquad (1\text{-}65)$$

$$\mathbf{w}_k(m+1) = \mathbf{w}_k(m) \quad \text{for all } k \neq i \text{ and } k \neq j \qquad (1\text{-}66)$$

If the perceptron correctly classifies $\mathbf{x}$, the algorithm does not update $\mathbf{w}$. In (1-64)–(1-66) subscripts refer to decision classes, not iteration steps.

BAYESIAN DECISION THEORY

Suppose we know only the **prior probabilities** $p(D_1)$ and $p(D_2)$ for a two-class problem. Then it seems reasonable to assign an unknown input vector $\mathbf{x}$ to the class with the larger probability of having generated $\mathbf{x}$. So the decision rule becomes $\mathbf{x} \in D_1$ iff $p(D_1) > p(D_2)$. Sometimes we know the conditional density functions $p(\mathbf{x} \mid D_1)$ and $p(\mathbf{x} \mid D_2)$ as well as the priori probabilities $p(D_1)$ and $p(D_2)$. Then we can calculate the converse or "posterior" probabilities using **Bayes' theorem**:

$$p(D_i \mid \mathbf{x}) = \frac{p(\mathbf{x} \mid D_i)p(D_i)}{p(\mathbf{x})} \qquad (1\text{-}67)$$

$$= \frac{p(\mathbf{x} \mid D_i)p(D_i)}{\displaystyle\sum_{j=1}^{2} p(\mathbf{x} \mid D_j)p(D_j)} \qquad (1\text{-}68)$$

Define the **error probability** as

$$p(\text{error} \mid \mathbf{x}) = \begin{cases} p(D_1 \mid \mathbf{x}) & \text{if } \mathbf{x} \in D_2 \\ p(D_2 \mid \mathbf{x}) & \text{if } \mathbf{x} \in D_1 \end{cases} \qquad (1\text{-}69)$$

Define the **average error probability** p_e as

$$p_e = \int_{R^n} p(\text{error} \mid \mathbf{x})p(\mathbf{x})\, d\mathbf{x} \qquad (1\text{-}70)$$

Define the **Bayes decision rule** for minimizing the average error probability as

$$\mathbf{x} \in D_1 \quad \text{if} \quad p(D_1 \mid \mathbf{x}) > p(D_2 \mid \mathbf{x}) \qquad (1\text{-}71)$$

$$\mathbf{x} \in D_2 \quad \text{if} \quad p(D_1 \mid \mathbf{x}) < p(D_2 \mid \mathbf{x}) \qquad (1\text{-}72)$$

where $p(D_1 | \mathbf{x})$ and $p(D_2 | \mathbf{x})$ denote the posterior probabilities. In general we cannot directly calculate the posterior probability distribution from measurements. So the decision rule reduces to the form:

$$\mathbf{x} \in D_1 \quad \text{if} \quad p(\mathbf{x} | D_1)p(D_1) > p(\mathbf{x} | D_2)p(D_2) \tag{1-73}$$

$$\mathbf{x} \in D_2 \quad \text{if} \quad p(\mathbf{x} | D_1)p(D_1) < p(\mathbf{x} | D_2)p(D_2) \tag{1-74}$$

In multiclass case,

$$\mathbf{x} \in D_i \quad \text{if} \quad p(\mathbf{x} | D_i) \, p(D_i) > p(\mathbf{x} | D_j) \, p(D_j) \quad \text{for all} \quad j \neq i \tag{1-75}$$

Then we can represent the discriminant functions as

$$g_i(\mathbf{x}) \; = \; p(\mathbf{x} | D_i) \, p(D_i) \tag{1-76}$$

Consider the problem of finding the decision boundary of the Bayes minimum-error classifier for Gaussian-distributed patterns $\mathbf{x} \sim N(\mathbf{m}_i, \mathbf{K}_i)$. We know the form of the Gaussian conditional probability density function,

$$p(\mathbf{x} | D_i) \; = \; \frac{1}{(2\pi)^{n/2}|\mathbf{K}_i|^{1/2}} \, \exp \left\{ -\frac{1}{2} \, (\mathbf{x} - \mathbf{m}_i)\mathbf{K}_i^{-1}(\mathbf{x} - \mathbf{m}_i)^T \right\} \tag{1-77}$$

where the covariance matrix $\mathbf{K}_i$ is diagonal, $\mathbf{K}_i = \sigma^2 \mathbf{I}$ and $\sigma^2 > 0$, and $\mathbf{m}_i = E[\mathbf{x}|D_i]$, the mean vector of pattern class D_i. Then we choose g_i as

$$g_i(\mathbf{x}) \; = \; \ln [\, p(\mathbf{x} | D_i)p(D_i) \,] \tag{1-78}$$

$$= \; \ln p(\mathbf{x}|D_i) + \ln p(D_i) \tag{1-79}$$

So

$$g_i(\mathbf{x}) \; = \; -\frac{1}{2} \ln |\mathbf{K}_i| - \frac{1}{2} \, (\mathbf{x} - \mathbf{m}_i)\mathbf{K}_i^{-1}(\mathbf{x} - \mathbf{m}_i)^T + \ln p(D_i) \tag{1-80}$$

$$\approx \; -\frac{1}{2\sigma^2} \, (\mathbf{x} - \mathbf{m}_i)(\mathbf{x} - \mathbf{m}_i)^T + \ln p(D_i) \tag{1-81}$$

$$\approx \; \frac{1}{2\sigma^2} \, (2\mathbf{x}\mathbf{m}_i^T - \mathbf{m}_i\mathbf{m}_i^T) + \ln p(D_i) \tag{1-82}$$

ignoring the class-independent scalar $\mathbf{x}\mathbf{x}^T$ in the last line. This reduces the Gaussian Bayes classifier to a linear discriminant function.

VECTOR QUANTIZATION

Quantization approximates continuous-amplitude signals with discrete-amplitude signals. When we jointly quantize a vector of parameters, we call the process **vector quantization**. Let $\mathbf{x} = (x_1, \ldots, x_n)$ denote an n-dimensional pattern vector whose elements are real, continuous-amplitude random variables. In vector quantization the vector $\mathbf{x}$ maps onto another real-valued, discrete-amplitude,

n-dimensional vector $\mathbf{y}$. The mapping $\mathbf{y} = Q(\mathbf{x})$ defines the vector-quantization process. Typically $\mathbf{y}$ takes one of a finite set of values $Y = [\, \mathbf{y}_1, \ldots, \mathbf{y}_k \,]$, where k denotes the number of classes $D_1, \ldots, D_k$. We call the $\mathbf{y}_i$ **reference vectors** or **templates**.

The centroids $\bar{\mathbf{x}}_i$ of the decision classes D_i minimize the **total mean-squared error of vector quantization** $\mathcal{E}$:

$$\bar{\mathbf{x}}_i \;=\; \frac{\displaystyle\int_{D_i} \mathbf{x}p(\mathbf{x})\,d\mathbf{x}}{\displaystyle\int_{D_i} p(\mathbf{x})\,d\mathbf{x}} \tag{1-83}$$

For the k decision classes $D_1, \ldots, D_k$ and the underlying pattern-space probability density function $p(\mathbf{x})$, we define $\mathcal{E}$ as

$$\mathcal{E} \;=\; \frac{1}{2}\sum_{j=1}^{k}\int_{D_j} \mathrm{TRACE}\,[\,(\mathbf{x} - \mathbf{m}_j)^T(\mathbf{x} - \mathbf{m}_j)]p(\mathbf{x})\,d\mathbf{x} \tag{1-84}$$

$$\;=\; \frac{1}{2}\sum_{j=1}^{k}\int_{D_j}\sum_{i=1}^{n}(x_i - m_{ij})^2 p(\mathbf{x})\,d\mathbf{x} \tag{1-85}$$

To find the $\mathcal{E}$-optimal quantized vector $\hat{\mathbf{m}}_j$, we vector-differentiate $\mathcal{E}$ and set this gradient equal to the null vector:

$$\mathbf{0} \;=\; \nabla_{m_j}\mathcal{E} = \left(\frac{\partial\mathcal{E}}{\partial m_{1j}} \cdots \frac{\partial\mathcal{E}}{\partial m_{nj}}\right)$$

$$\;=\; \left(\begin{array}{c} -\displaystyle\int_{D_j}(x_1 - \hat{m}_{1j})p(\mathbf{x})\,d\mathbf{x} \\ \vdots \\ -\displaystyle\int_{D_j}(x_n - \hat{m}_{nj})p(\mathbf{x})\,d\mathbf{x} \end{array}\right)^T$$

$$\;=\; -\int_{D_j}(\mathbf{x} - \hat{\mathbf{m}}_j)p(\mathbf{x})\,d\mathbf{x}$$

$$\;=\; -\int_{D_j}\mathbf{x}p(\mathbf{x})\,d\mathbf{x} + \hat{\mathbf{m}}_j\int_{D_j}p(\mathbf{x})\,d\mathbf{x} \tag{1-86}$$

when $\hat{\mathbf{m}}_j$ denotes the weight vector that minimizes the mean-squared error of vector quantization. (Second-order Hessian conditions ensure an error minimum, not maximum.) Solving for $\hat{\mathbf{m}}_j$ gives, as shown for competitive learning in Chapter 6 of Kosko [1992],

$$\hat{\mathbf{m}}_j = \frac{\int_{D_j} \mathbf{x} p(\mathbf{x}) \, \mathbf{dx}}{\int_{D_j} p(\mathbf{x}) \, \mathbf{dx}} \tag{1-87}$$

$$= \int_{D_j} \mathbf{x} \left(\frac{p(\mathbf{x})}{\int_{D_j} p(\mathbf{x}) \, \mathbf{dx}} \right) \mathbf{dx} \tag{1-88}$$

$$= \int_{D_j} \mathbf{x} p(\mathbf{x} \mid \mathbf{x} \in D_j) \, \mathbf{dx} \tag{1-89}$$

$$= E\left[\mathbf{x} \mid \mathbf{x} \in D_j\right] \tag{1-90}$$

$$= \bar{\mathbf{x}}_j \tag{1-91}$$

the centroid of pattern class D_j, as claimed.

STOCHASTIC COMPETITIVE-LEARNING ALGORITHMS

Autoassociative AVQ neural networks are two-layer feedforward networks trained with competitive learning. The input neuronal field F_X receives the sample data and passes it forward through synaptic connection matrix M to the p competing neurons in field F_Y. (Heteroassociative AVQ networks correspond to three-layer feedforward networks.) Synchronous feedforward flow obviates the neural interpretation. AVQ neural systems are simply signal-processing algorithms.

The metaphor of competing neurons reduces to nearest-neighbor classification. The system compares the current vector random sample $\mathbf{x}(t)$ in Euclidean distance to the p columns of the synaptic connection matrix M, to the p synaptic vectors $\mathbf{m}_1(t), \ldots, \mathbf{m}_p(t)$. If the jth synaptic vector $\mathbf{m}_j(t)$ is closest to $\mathbf{x}(t)$, then the jth neuron "wins" the competition for activation at time t.

Many within-field feedback dynamical systems approximate this nearest-neighbor, winner-take-all behavior. Mathematically the jth competing neuron should behave as a class indicator function: $S_j = I_{D_j}$. More generally the jth F_Y neuron only estimates I'_{D_j}. Then misclassification can still occur: $S_j(\mathbf{x}\mathbf{m}_j^T + f_j) = 1$ but $I_{D_j}(\mathbf{x}) = 0$ for row vectors $\mathbf{x}$ and $\mathbf{m}_j$, where f_j denotes the inhibitive within-field feedback the jth neuron receives.

We modify the nearest or "winning" synaptic vector $\mathbf{m}_j$ with a simple difference learning law. We add some scaled form of $\mathbf{x}(t) - \mathbf{m}_j(t)$ to $\mathbf{m}_j(t)$ to form

$\mathbf{m}_j(t + 1)$. We can also update near-neighbors of the winning neuron. In practice, and in the simulations below, we modify only one synaptic vector at a time. We do not modify "losers": $\mathbf{m}_i(t + 1) = \mathbf{m}_i(t)$.

The stochastic **unsupervised-competitive-learning** (UCL) algorithm represents the simplest competitive-learning algorithm. Pattern-recognition theorists first studied the UCL algorithm but called it **adaptive K-means clustering** [MacQueen, 1967]. Kohonen extended the UCL algorithm to two supervised versions, SCL1 [Kohonen, 1988a; 1988b] and SCL2 [Kohonen, 1988c]. The supervisor must know the class membership of each sample pattern $\mathbf{x}$. The SCL1 and SCL2 algorithms linearly "reward" correct classifications as in the UCL algorithm. They "punish" incorrect classifications with a sign change. We obtain all three algorithms from the following three-step algorithm if we replace the third step with the appropriate stochastic difference equation.

Competitive AVQ Algorithms

1. Initialize synaptic vectors: $\mathbf{m}_i(0) = \mathbf{x}(i)$, $i = 1, \ldots, p$. Sample-dependent initialization avoids many pathologies that can distort nearest-neighbor learning.

2. For random sample $\mathbf{x}(t)$, find the closest or "winning" synaptic vector $\mathbf{m}_j(t)$:

$$\|\mathbf{m}_j(t) - \mathbf{x}(t)\| = \min_i \|\mathbf{m}_i(t) - \mathbf{x}(t)\| \tag{1-92}$$

where $\|\mathbf{x}\|^2 = x_1^2 + \cdots + x_n^2$ defines the squared Euclidean vector norm of $\mathbf{x}$.

3. Update the winning synaptic vector $\mathbf{m}_j(t)$ with the UCL, SCL1, or SCL2 learning algorithm.

Unsupervised Competitive Learning (UCL)

$$\mathbf{m}_j(t + 1) = \mathbf{m}_j(t) + c_t \left[\mathbf{x}(t) - \mathbf{m}_j(t) \right] \tag{1-93}$$

$$\mathbf{m}_i(t + 1) = \mathbf{m}_i(t) \quad \text{if} \quad i \neq j \tag{1-94}$$

where $\{c_t\}$ denotes a slowly decreasing sequence of learning coefficients. In our simulations,

$$c_t = .1 \left(1 - \frac{t}{2000} \right)$$

for 2000 training samples. The UCL algorithm (1-93) restates the classical adaptive K-means clustering algorithm.

Stochastic approximation [Robbins, 1951] requires a decreasing gain sequence $\{c_t\}$ to suppress random disturbances and to guarantee convergence to local minima of mean-squared performance measures. The learning coefficients should decrease slowly,

$$\sum_{t=1}^{\infty} c_t = \infty \qquad (1\text{-}95)$$

but not too slowly,

$$\sum_{t=1}^{\infty} c_t^2 < \infty \qquad (1\text{-}96)$$

Harmonic-series coefficients, $c_t = 1/t$, satisfy these constraints. For fast *robust* [Huber, 1981] stochastic approximation, only the harmonic-series coefficients satisfy these constraints.

Supervised Competitive Learning 1 (SCL1)

$$\mathbf{m}_j(t+1) = \begin{cases} \mathbf{m}_j(t) + c_t\,[\,\mathbf{x}(t) - \mathbf{m}_j(t)\,] & \text{if} \quad \mathbf{x}(t) \in D_j \\ \mathbf{m}_j(t) - c_t\,[\,\mathbf{x}(t) - \mathbf{m}_j(t)\,] & \text{if} \quad \mathbf{x}(t) \notin D_j \end{cases} \qquad (1\text{-}97)$$

$$\mathbf{m}_i(t+1) = \mathbf{m}_i(t) \qquad \qquad \text{if} \quad i \neq j \qquad (1\text{-}98)$$

SCL1 supervises or reinforces synaptic modification. $\mathbf{m}_j$ learns positively if the system correctly classifies the random sample $\mathbf{x}$. $\mathbf{m}_j$ learns negatively, or forgets selectively, if the system misclassifies the random sample. Then $\mathbf{m}_j$ tends to move out of regions of misclassification in R^n. Tsypkin [1973] first derived the SCL1 algorithm as a special case of his adaptive Bayes classifier.

We can rewrite the SCL1 update equation (1-97) as

$$\mathbf{m}_j(t+1) = \mathbf{m}_j(t) + c_t r_j(\mathbf{x}(t))[\,\mathbf{x}(t) - \mathbf{m}_j(t)\,] \qquad (1\text{-}99)$$

if we define the supervised **reinforcement function** r_j as

$$r_j = I_{D_j} - \sum_{i \neq j} I_{D_i} \qquad (1\text{-}100)$$

r_j depends explicitly on class indicator functions. r_j rewards correct pattern classifications with $+1$ and punishes misclassifications with -1. We implicitly assume the jth neuron accurately estimates the jth indicator function: $S_j(\mathbf{x}\mathbf{m}_j^T + f_j) \approx I_{D_j}(\mathbf{x})$.

The SCL2 algorithm modifies slightly the SCL1 algorithm. The SCL2 algorithm better estimates the optimal Bayes decision-theoretic boundary in some cases. The Bayes decision boundary minimizes the misclassification error. It represents the crossing point of the unknown conditional densities $p(\mathbf{x} \mid D_i)$ and $p(\mathbf{x} \mid D_j)$.

The nearest-neighbor decision boundary corresponds to the hyperplane that bisects the line that connects the two class centroids. If the pattern distribution is asymmetric—if, for instance, local density functions with different variances generate different decision classes—then the SCL1 decision boundary may not resemble the Bayes decision boundary. Nearest-neighbor classification tends to perform better in the equal-variance case than in the unequal-variance case.

Supervised Competitive Learning 2 (SCL2)

$$\mathbf{m}_j(t+1) \;=\; \mathbf{m}_j(t) - c_t\,[\,\mathbf{x}(t) - \mathbf{m}_j(t)\,] \qquad (1\text{-}101)$$

$$\mathbf{m}_\ell(t+1) \;=\; \mathbf{m}_\ell(t) + c_t\,[\,\mathbf{x}(t) - \mathbf{m}_\ell(t)\,] \qquad (1\text{-}102)$$

if $\mathbf{x} \in D_\ell$ instead of $\mathbf{x} \in D_j$, and if $\mathbf{m}_j(t)$ is the nearest synaptic vector and $\mathbf{m}_\ell(t)$ is the next-to-nearest synaptic vector:

$$\|\mathbf{m}_j(t) - \mathbf{x}(t)\| \;<\; \|\mathbf{m}_\ell(t) - \mathbf{x}(t)\| \;=\; \min_{i \neq j}\|\mathbf{m}_i(t) - \mathbf{x}(t)\| \quad (1\text{-}103)$$

and if $\mathbf{x}(t)$ falls in a class-dependent "window." In all other cases

$$\mathbf{m}_i(t+1) \;=\; \mathbf{m}_i(t) \qquad (1\text{-}104)$$

The window defines a hyper-rectangle in R^n centered at the midpoint of the hyperline that connects the centroids of D_j and D_ℓ. If $\mathbf{x}(t)$ does not fall in the hyperwindow, we modify no synaptic vector. We defined the R^n window between D_j and D_ℓ as the n-dimensional hyperrectangle $[\bar{m}_1-d, \bar{m}_1+d] \times \cdots \times [\bar{m}_n-d, \bar{m}_n+d]$, where $\bar{\mathbf{m}}_{j\ell}$ denotes the midpoint $\bar{\mathbf{m}}_{j\ell} = (\bar{m}_1, \ldots, \bar{m}_n) = (\mathbf{m}_j + \mathbf{m}_\ell)/2$, and d denotes the window half-width. We put $d = 2.5$.

Differential Competitive Learning

The **differential competitive learning (DCL)** law [Kosko, 1990a] combines competitive and differential-Hebbian learning:

$$\dot{m}_{ij} \;=\; \dot{S}_j(y_j)[\,S_i(x_i) - m_{ij}\,] \qquad (1\text{-}105)$$

or in vector notation,

$$\dot{\mathbf{m}}_j \;=\; \dot{S}_j(y_j)[\,\mathbf{S}(\mathbf{x}) - \mathbf{m}_j\,] \qquad (1\text{-}106)$$

where $\mathbf{S}(\mathbf{x}) = (S_1(x_1), \ldots, S_n(x_n))$ and $\mathbf{m}_j = (m_{1j}, \ldots, m_{nj})$. m_{ij} denotes the synaptic weight between the ith neuron in input neuronal field F_X and the jth neuron in competitive field F_Y. Nonnegative **signal functions** S_i and S_j transduce the real-valued **activations** x_i and y_j into the bounded monotone-nondecreasing **signals** $S_i(x_i)$ and $S_j(y_j)$. $\dot{m}_{ij}$ and $\dot{S}_j(y_j)$ denote the time derivatives of m_{ij} and $S_j(y_j)$, synaptic and signal velocities.

The stochastic-calculus version of the DCL law relates random processes:

$$dm_{ij} \;=\; dS_j[\,S_i - m_{ij}\,] + dB_{ij} \qquad (1\text{-}107)$$

B_{ij} denotes a Brownian-motion diffusion process centered at the origin. We can rewrite (1-107) in "noise" notation as

$$\dot{m}_{ij} = \dot{S}_j[S_i - m_{ij}] + n_{ij} \qquad (1\text{-}108)$$

The "noise" process n_{ij} has zero mean, $E[n_{ij}] = 0$, and has finite variance, $V[n_{ij}] = \sigma^2_{ij} < \infty$. The random-sampling AVQ framework implicitly assumes that all competitive learning laws are stochastic differential or difference equations. Such stochastic synaptic vectors $\mathbf{m}_j$ tend to converge to pattern-class centroids, and converge exponentially quickly [Kosko, 1990b].

$S_j(y_j)$ measures the competitive status of the jth competing neuron in F_Y. Usually S_j approximates a binary threshold function. S_j may equal a steep binary logistic sigmoid,

$$S_j(y_j) = \frac{1}{1 + e^{-cy_j}} \qquad (1\text{-}109)$$

for some constant $c > 0$. The jth neuron wins the laterally inhibitive competition if $S_j = 1$, loses if $S_j = 0$.

In (1-105) $\mathbf{m}_j$ learns only if $S_j(y_j)$ changes. This contrasts with the classical competitive learning law

$$\dot{m}_{ij} = S_j(y_j)[S_i(x_i) - m_{ij}] \qquad (1\text{-}110)$$

which modulates the difference $\mathbf{S}(\mathbf{x}) - \mathbf{m}_j$ with the win-loss signal S_j, not its velocity $\dot{S}_j$. In (1-110) $\mathbf{m}_j$ learns only if the competitive signal S_j exceeds zero—only if the jth neuron "wins" the activation competition.

Real neurons transmit and receive pulse trains. Pulse-coded signal functions S_j reveal the connection between competitive and differential competitive learning. A pulse-coded signal function uses an exponentially fading window [Gluck, 1988] of sampled binary pulses:

$$S_j(t) = \int_{-\infty}^{t} y_j(s)e^{s-t}\, ds \qquad (1\text{-}111)$$

where $y_j(t) = 1$ if a pulse occurs at t, and $y_j(t) = 0$ if no pulse occurs at t. Then [Kosko, 1990c]

$$\dot{S}_j(t) = y_j(t) - S_j(t) \qquad (1\text{-}112)$$

So the DCL law (1-105) reduces to

$$\dot{m}_{ij} = y_j[S_i - m_{ij}] - S_j[S_i - m_{ij}] \qquad (1\text{-}113)$$

When the second term in (1-113) is sufficiently small, DCL reduces to competitive learning. This occurs when a losing neuron suddenly wins, for then $y_j = 1$ and $S_j \approx 0$. In the stochastic case, the *random* pulse function y_j represents an arbitrary random point process and converts (1-113) to a doubly stochastic model.

Similarly, the classical differential Hebbian law [Kosko, 1986]

$$\dot{m}_{ij} = -m_{ij} + \dot{S}_i\dot{S}_j \qquad (1\text{-}114)$$

reduces to signal Hebbian learning on average (in the absence of pulses):

$$\dot{m}_{ij} = -m_{ij} + \dot{S}_i \dot{S}_j \tag{1-115}$$

$$= -m_{ij} + S_i S_j + [x_i y_j - x_i S_j - y_j S_i] \tag{1-116}$$

$$\approx -m_{ij} + S_i S_j \tag{1-117}$$

on average. The approximation holds exactly if and only if no x_i or y_j pulses are present, a frequent event. Differential-Hebbian-learning synapses "fill in" with Hebbian learning when pulses are absent.

For discrete implementation, we use the DCL algorithm as a stochastic difference equation.

Differential Competitive Learning (DCL)

1. Initialize: $\mathbf{m}_i(0) = \mathbf{x}(i)$.

2. Find winning $\mathbf{m}_j(t)$: $\|\mathbf{m}_j(t) - \mathbf{x}(t)\| = \min_i \|\mathbf{m}_i(t) - \mathbf{x}(t)\|$.

3. Update winning $\mathbf{m}_j(t)$:

$$\mathbf{m}_j(t+1) = \mathbf{m}_j(t) + c_t \, \Delta S_j(y_j(t)) \, [\, S(\mathbf{x}(t)) - \mathbf{m}_j(t) \,]$$

$$\text{if the } j\text{th neuron wins} \tag{1-118}$$

$$\mathbf{m}_i(t+1) = \mathbf{m}_i(t) \qquad \text{if the } i\text{th neuron loses} \tag{1-119}$$

$\Delta S_j(y_j(t))$ denotes the time change of the jth neuron's competition signal $S_j(y_j)$ in the competition layer F_Y:

$$\Delta S_j(y_j(t)) = \text{sgn}\,[\, S_j(y_j(t+1)) - S_j(y_j(t)) \,] \tag{1-120}$$

We define the **signum operator**, sgn(x) as

$$\text{sgn}\,(x) = \begin{cases} 1 & \text{if } x > 0 \\ 0 & \text{if } x = 0 \\ -1 & \text{if } x < 0 \end{cases} \tag{1-121}$$

We update the F_Y neuronal activations y_j with the additive model

$$y_j(t+1) = y_j(t) + \sum_i^n S_i(x_i(t)) \, m_{ij}(t) + \sum_k^p S_k(y_k(t)) w_{kj} \tag{1-122}$$

In our simulations, the first sum in (1-122) reduced to

$$\sum_i^n x_i(t) m_{ij}(t) \tag{1-123}$$

when we did not transform the input patterns $\mathbf{x}$ with a nonlinear signal function S_i. Input or F_X neurons in feedforward networks usually behave linearly: $S_i(x_i) = x_i$.

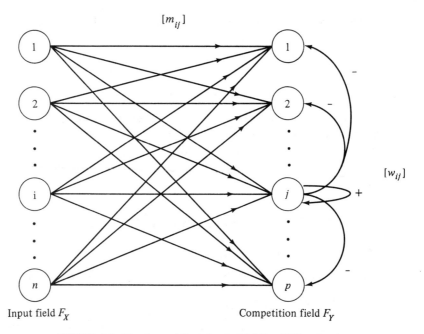

FIGURE 1.3 Topology of the laterally inhibitive DCL network.

For linear inputs we computed the second sum in (1-122) for linear signal functions S_k. Since we allowed only one winner per iteration, this sum reduced to a single term $y_k \, w_{kj}$, where k denotes the winning neuron.

The $p \times p$ matrix W defined the F_Y within-field synaptic connection strengths:

$$W \;=\; \begin{bmatrix} +2 & -1 & -1 & \dots & -1 \\ -1 & +2 & -1 & \dots & -1 \\ & & \vdots & & \\ -1 & -1 & -1 & \dots & +2 \end{bmatrix} \qquad (1\text{-}124)$$

Diagonal elements w_{ii} equaled 2; off-diagonal elements equaled -1. Figure 1.3 shows the connection topology of the laterally inhibitive DCL network.

Each neuron in F_Y codes for a specific pattern class. By (1-122) and the "cosine law,"

$$S(\mathbf{x}) \cdot \mathbf{m}_j \;=\; \|S(\mathbf{x})\| \|\mathbf{m}_j\| \cos\left(S(\mathbf{x}), \mathbf{m}_j\right) \qquad (1\text{-}125)$$

positive learning ($\dot{m}_{ij} > 0$) tends to occur when the system classifies $\mathbf{x}$ to the nearest pattern class D_j.

If we represent the F_X signal function S_i with the bipolar logistic function,

$$S_i(x_i) \;=\; \frac{2}{1 + e^{-cx_i}} - 1 \qquad (1\text{-}126)$$

$c > 0$, then the DCL algorithm (1-118) abstracts the corresponding bipolar pattern from the real-valued input. The unsupervised sign change ΔS_j in the DCL law (1-118) resembles the reward-punish sign change in the SCL1 and SCL2 algorithms. This suggests that we can meaningfully compare the algorithms' performance on the same training and test data.

If we choose $S_i(x_i)$ as a linear function of the input, if $S_i(x_i) = x_i$, then the discrete version of DCL resembles the UCL, SCL1, and SCL2 algorithms. We used both linear and nonlinear formulations to compare DCL with SCL1 and SCL2. The supervised SCL1 and SCL2 algorithms always outperformed the UCL algorithm. So we limited our DCL comparisons to SCL1 and SCL2 systems.

For most simulations we used linearly transformed data, $S_i(x_i) = x_i$. In these cases we approximated the signal difference ΔS_j as the activation difference Δy_j:

$$\Delta S_j(y_j(t)) \quad \approx \quad \Delta y_j(t) \tag{1-127}$$

$$= \quad \text{sgn}\left[\, y_j(t+1) - y_j(t) \,\right] \tag{1-128}$$

This approximation holds exactly over the linear part of a signal function's range. For then $S_j' = dS_j/dy_j = c$ for some constant $c > 0$. Then

$$\dot{S}_j \quad = \quad S_j' \, \dot{y}_j \tag{1-129}$$

$$= \quad c \, \dot{y}_j \tag{1-130}$$

The constant c does not affect the signum operator used in Δy_j.

Linear data often produce large activation sums $\sum_i^n x_i \, m_{ij}$ that saturate nonlinear signals S_j to extreme values. Then the signal difference ΔS_j equals zero and may not discriminate changes in competitive status. The activation difference Δy_j remains sensitive to these changes.

COMPARISON OF COMPETITIVE AND DIFFERENTIAL COMPETITIVE LEARNING FOR CENTROID ESTIMATION

We compared the DCL algorithm with the SCL1 and SCL2 algorithms for estimating centroids. All algorithms adaptively moved the synaptic vectors m_j to pattern-class centroids. They differed in how quickly the trained synaptic vectors reached the centroids and how much the synaptic vectors wandered about the centroids. The DCL algorithm moved the synaptic vectors to centroids at least as fast as did the SCL1 and SCL2 algorithms. Once the synaptic vectors reached the pattern-class centroids, the DCL-trained synaptic vectors wandered less about the centroids than did the SCL-trained synaptic vectors.

The DCL algorithm converged to centroids faster than the SCL1 and SCL2 algorithms. Convergence rates were the same for linear signal functions, $S_i(x_i) = x_i$.

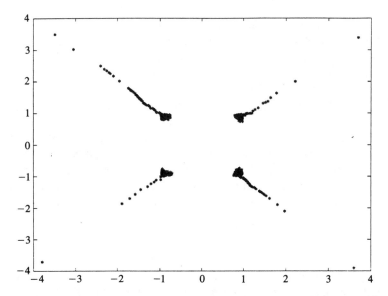

FIGURE 1.4 Convergence of DCL-trained synaptic vectors to bipolar centroids of four Gaussian clusters. Bipolar logistic signal functions $S_i(x_i)$ nonlinearly transduce the real-valued input vector **x** into a bipolar vector in $\{-1, 1\}^n$.

The pattern space consisted of 2000 two-dimensional Gaussian-distributed pattern vectors with variance 121 and with centroids or modes at $(20, 20)$, $(20, -20)$, $(-20, 20)$, and $(-20, -20)$. Figure 1.4 shows centroid convergence of DCL synaptic vectors with inputs transformed with bipolar signal functions. Figure 1.5 shows the slower convergence of the SCL1 algorithm with the same transformed Gaussian data. The symbol '$*$' denotes DCL synaptic vectors, and '$+$' denotes SCL1 synaptic vectors. Figures 1.6 and 1.7 show centroid convergence for the same Gaussian data when the sytems use linear signal functions.

DCL-trained synaptic vectors wandered with less mean-squared error about centroids than did SCL-trained synaptic vectors. Figure 1.8 shows mean-squared wandering about the Gaussian pattern-class centroid $(-20, 20)$. It represents several experiments with different Gaussian and non-Gaussian pattern distributions. Solid lines denote the convergence of the DCL synaptic vector; dashed lines, convergence of the SCL1 synaptic vector. We calculated the mean-squared error (MSE) of centroid wandering for the class centered at $(-20, 20)$ after 200 iterations. Other centroids produced comparable MSE of centroid wandering. In the first case we used 540 Gaussian samples with variance 25. Then for the DCL algorithm the MSE of centroid wandering equaled 0.48. For the SCL1 algorithm it equaled 1.48. In the second case we used 554 Gaussian samples with variance 121. Then for the DCL algorithm the MSE of centroid wandering equaled 4.0. For the SCL1 algorithm it equaled 7.11.

Next we compared the DCL system with the SCL1 and SCL2 systems for

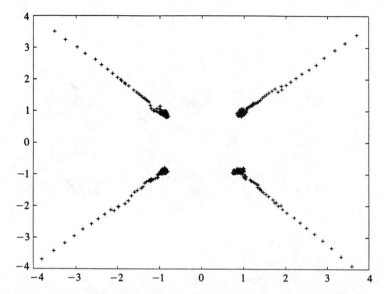

FIGURE 1.5 Centroid convergence of SCL1 synaptic vectors trained with the same patterns as in Figure 1.4. Bipolar logistic signal functions nonlinearly transduce real input patterns to bipolar patterns.

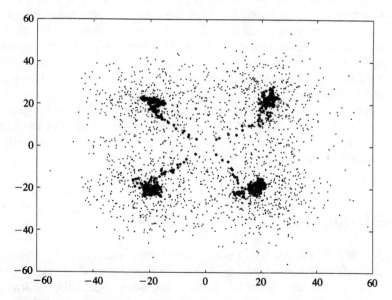

FIGURE 1.6 Convergence of DCL-trained synaptic vectors to Gaussian pattern-class centroids. Same pattern distribution as in Figures 1.4 and 1.5. Input data not transformed: $S_i(x_i) = x_i$.

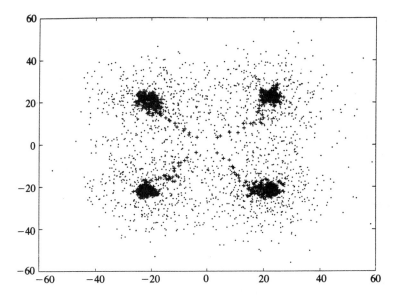

FIGURE 1.7 Convergence of SCL1-trained synaptic vectors to Gaussian pattern-class centroids for the same pattern distribution as in Figure 1.6.

pattern-classification accuracy. We trained each AVQ system with 500 Gaussian-distributed samples for each pattern class, and for each variance level centered about the same centroids $(-20, 0)$ and $(20, 0)$. We set variance levels at 20 units. For each variance level we tested each AVQ system with 1000 new Gaussian-distributed samples for each pattern class. Figure 1.9(a) shows the misclassification rates of the DCL, SCL1, and SCL2 systems for two representative Gaussian classes with equal variances. Figure 1.9(b) shows misclassification performance for each AVQ system when we repeated the simulation in Figure 1.9(a) for unequal variances. The pattern class with centroid $(20, 0)$ had twice the variance of the pattern class with centroid $(-20, 0)$. The three clustering algorithms behaved similarly for increasing variance values.

PHONEME-RECOGNITION SIMULATIONS

We obtained speech training samples from samples of continuous male speech with different English pronunciations. We used a time-dependent Fourier spectrum to extract features from the speech waveforms. An anti-alias low-pass filter pre-filtered the speech signals. We then digitized the signals to 8 bits with a 10-kHz sampling frequency. A Hamming window divided the digitized speech signal into 256 sample segments. The fast Fourier transform algorithm gave 256 complex Fourier coefficients for each of the 256 windowed sample segments. We divided

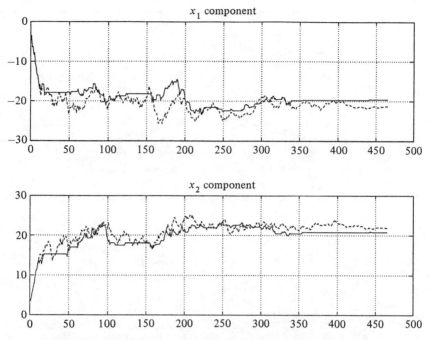

FIGURE 1.8 Trajectories of the synaptic vectors after reaching the Gaussian pattern-class centroid at $(-20, 20)$. Solid lines represent DCL-trained synaptic vectors; dashed lines, SCL1-trained synaptic vectors. The two graphs plot separately the m_1 and m_2 components of the synaptic vector $\mathbf{m} = (m_1, m_2)$.

the frequency range 200 Hz to 5 kHz into 16 regions. We divided the range 200 Hz to 3 kHz into 12 equal regions and the range 3 kHz to 5 kHz into four equal regions. Six Fourier coefficients represented each region in the range 200 Hz to 3 kHz. Thirteen Fourier coefficients represented each region in the range 3 kHz to 5 kHz. We calculated average power spectra over each region to form a 16-dimensional pattern vector. We produced 16-dimensional phoneme pattern vectors by repeatedly sliding the Hamming window by 100 samples.

The sample space consisted of real and artificial phonemes. The artificial phonemes were Gaussian random vectors with variance 9.0 centered at the real phoneme vectors. We generated these noisy phoneme samples to provide the AVQ systems with a statistically representative set of training samples.

The simulation compared the DCL, SCL1, and SCL2 learning systems for classification of nine representative English phonemes: five vowels $/a, e, i, o, u/$, two fricatives $/f, s/$, one nasal $/n/$, and one plosive sound $/t/$. Table 1.1 lists the misclassification rates. The AVQ systems tended to classify vowel and nasal sounds more accurately than fricative and plosive sounds.

We trained each competitive AVQ system with 1000 Gaussian-distributed random phoneme vectors clustered into nine pattern classes. Each pattern class was

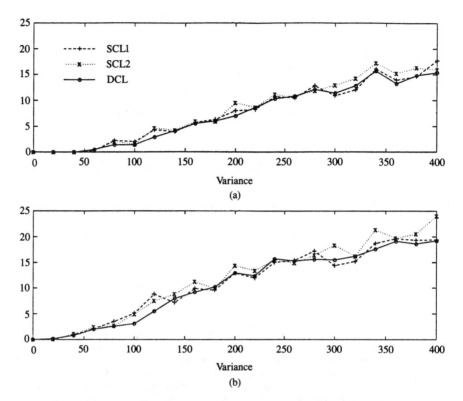

FIGURE 1.9 AVQ misclassification rates for two Gaussian clusters (a) with equal variance centered about the centroids $(-20,0)$ and $(20,0)$, and (b) with unequal variance. In (b), the pattern class centered about $(20,0)$ has twice the variance of the pattern class centered about $(-20,0)$.

TABLE 1.1 PERCENTAGE MISCLASSIFICATION RATES OF THE DCL, SCL1, AND SCL2 SYSTEMS FOR THE NINE ENGLISH PHONEMES $/A, E, I, O, U, F, S, N, T/$.

Phoneme	DCL	SCL1	SCL2
$/a/$	0	0	0
$/e/$	3	9	4
$/i/$	0	0	4
$/o/$	5	3	16
$/u/$	0	1	2
$/f/$	28	43	53
$/s/$	1	2	6
$/n/$	3	4	7
$/t/$	52	48	26

centered about the original spoken phoneme and radially distributed with variance $\sigma^2 = 9$. We randomly selected training data according to a uniform probability distribution to simulate nine equiprobable pattern classes. We tested each AVQ system with 100 new Gaussian-distributed phoneme samples for each phoneme type. Except for the two phonemes /o/ and /t/, the DCL system misclassified no more frequently than did the SCL systems.

CONCLUSIONS

The DCL system performed well in centroid estimation and phoneme recognition. DCL synaptic vectors converged faster to centroids than did SCL1 synaptic vectors when logistic bipolar signal functions transformed the input sample. DCL synaptic vectors wandered less about pattern-class centroids than did SCL synaptic vectors.

Our phoneme-recognition simulations were preliminary but agreed with our centroid-estimation simulations. The phoneme-recognition simulations suggest that unsupervised DCL systems will perform as well as supervised SCL1 and SCL2 systems in many pattern environments, even though DCL systems use less pattern-class information.

In general we do not know in advance whether $\mathbf{x} \in D_i$ for every training sample $\mathbf{x}$, and for every pattern class D_i, for an arbitrary classification, filtering, or estimation problem. We may not even know approximately the number or characteristics of the underlying decision classes. We can still apply DCL techniques in these cases and expect SCL-level performance. But we may never know how SCL systems would perform on the same data.

REFERENCES

Duda, R., and Hart, P., *Pattern Classification and Scene Analysis*, Wiley, New York, 1973.

Gluck, M., Parker, D., and Reifsnider, E., "Some Biological Implications of a Differential-Hebbian Learning Rule," *Psychobiology*, vol. 16, no. 3, 298–302, 1988.

Huber, P. J., *Robust Statistics*, Wiley, New York, 1981.

Kohonen, T., *Self-Organization and Associative Memory*, 2nd ed., Springer-Verlag, New York, 1988.

Kohonen, T., "The Neural 'Phonetic' Typewriter," *IEEE Computer Magazine*, 11–22, March 1988.

Kohonen, T., Barna, G., and Chrisley, R., "Statistical Pattern Recognition with Neural Networks: Benchmarking Studies," *Proceedings of International Conference on Neural Networks (ICNN-88)*, vol. I, 61–68, 1988.

Kosko, B., "Differential Hebbian Learning," *Proceedings of American Institute of Physics Conference: Neural Networks for Computing*, 277–282, April 1986.

Kosko, B., "Unsupervised Learning in Noise," *IEEE Transactions on Neural Networks*, vol. 1, no. 1, 44–57, March 1990.

Kosko, B., "Stochastic Competitive Learning," *Proceedings of the Summer 1990 International Joint Conference on Neural Networks (IJCNN-90)*, vol. II, 215–226, June 1990.

Kosko, B., *Neural Networks and Fuzzy Systems*, Prentice Hall, 1992.

MacQueen, J., "Some Methods for Classification and Analysis of Multivariate Observations," *Proceedings of the 5th Berkeley Symposium on Mathematical Statistics and Probability*, 281–297, 1967.

Minsky, M., and Papert, S., *Perceptrons: An Introduction to Computational Geometry*, 2nd ed., MIT Press, 1988.

Oppenheim, A. V., and Schafer, R. W., *Digital Signal Processing*, Prentice-Hall, Englewood Cliffs, NJ, 1975.

Oppenheim, A. V., and Schafer, R. W., *Discrete-Time Signal Processing*, Prentice-Hall, Englewood Cliffs, NJ, 1989.

Robbins, H., and Monro, S., "A Stochastic Approximation Method," *Annals of Mathematical Statistics*, vol. 22, 400–407, 1951.

Rosenblatt, F., *Principles of Neurodynamics*, Spartan Books, New York, 1962.

Tsypkin, Y. Z., *Foundations of the Theory of Learning Systems*, Academic Press, Orlando, FL, 1973.

PROBLEMS

1.1. Are the following systems linear? causal? time-invariant? BIBO stable?

    (a) $y_n = [x_{n-n_0} + 1]^2$.

    (b) $y_n = x_n \sin\left(\dfrac{\pi n}{3} + \dfrac{\pi}{5}\right)$.

    (c) $y_n = 1/x_n$.

    (d) $y_n = \displaystyle\sum_{m=-\infty}^{n} x_m$.

1.2. Show the following:

    (a) The z-transform of $\{x_{-n}\}$ is $X(z^{-1})$.

    (b) The z-transform of $\{nx_n\}$ is $-z\,\dfrac{dX(z)}{dz}$.

1.3. Find the z-transform of $\{x_n\}$ if

$$x_n = \begin{cases} na^n & \text{if } n \geq 0 \\ 0 & \text{if } n < 0 \end{cases}$$

1.4. Define the autocorrelation function of the *deterministic* sequence $\{x_n\}$ as

$$R_X(k) = \sum_{n=-\infty}^{\infty} x_n x_{n+k}$$

(a) Express $R_X(k)$ as the convolution of two sequences.

(b) Find the z-transform of $R_X(k)$ in terms of the z-transform of $\{x_n\}$.

1.5. Find the mean and variance of random variable x with uniform probability density function:

$$p(x) \;=\; \begin{cases} \dfrac{1}{b-a} & \text{if} \quad a \le x \le b \\[2mm] 0 & \text{otherwise} \end{cases}$$

1.6. Suppose $\{x_t\}$ is a wide-sense stationary Gaussian random process with power spectral density

$$S_x(f) \;=\; \begin{cases} \dfrac{N_o}{2}\left(1 - \dfrac{|f|}{f_o}\right) & \text{if} \quad |f| \le f_o \\[2mm] 0 & \text{otherwise} \end{cases}$$

Find the probability density function of the random variable x_t.

1.7. Suppose we pass a wide-sense stationary, zero-mean white-noise process $\{x_n\}$ through a linear filter. Show that the autocorrelation function of the output sequence $\{y_n\}$ is

$$R_Y(m) \;=\; \sigma_x^2 \sum_{k=-\infty}^{\infty} h_k h_{k+m}$$

where σ_x^2 is the variance of $\{x_n\}$, and $\{h_n\}$ is the impulse response sequence of the linear system.

1.8. Show that the Fourier transform of the rectangular window of size N,

$$w_n \;=\; \begin{cases} 1 & \text{if} \quad 0 \le n \le N-1 \\ 0 & \text{otherwise} \end{cases}$$

is

$$W(e^{i\omega}) \;=\; \frac{\sin(\omega N/2)}{\sin(\omega/2)} e^{-i\omega(N-1)/2}$$

1.9. Define the time-dependent Fourier transform of $\{x_n\}$ as

$$X_n(e^{i\omega}) \;=\; \sum_{k=-\infty}^{\infty} x_k w_{n-k} e^{-i\omega k}$$

Show

(a) If $z_n = x_n + y_n$, then $Z_n(e^{i\omega}) = X_n(e^{i\omega}) + Y_n(e^{i\omega})$.

(b) If $z_n = x_{n-n_0}$, then $Z_n(e^{i\omega}) = X_{n-n_0}(e^{i\omega}) e^{-i\omega n_0}$.

(c) If $z_n = \alpha x_n$, then $Z_n(e^{i\omega}) = \alpha X_n(e^{i\omega})$.

(d) If $z_n = \alpha^n x_n$, then $Z_n(e^{i\omega}) = X_n(\alpha^{-1} e^{i\omega})$.

1.10. Let $\mathbf{x}_1, \ldots, \mathbf{x}_m$ denote m n-dimensional row vectors. Let $\mathbf{P}$ denote any nonsingular n-by-n matrix. Show that the sample mean $\hat{\mathbf{x}}$,

$$\hat{\mathbf{x}} = \frac{1}{m} \sum_{k=1}^{m} \mathbf{x}_k$$

minimizes

$$\sum_{k=1}^{m} (\mathbf{x}_k - \hat{\mathbf{x}}) \mathbf{P}^{-1} (\mathbf{x}_k - \hat{\mathbf{x}})^T$$

1.11. Consider the following feature vectors:

$$\begin{aligned}
(1, \ 1) &\in D_1 \\
(1, -1) &\in D_2 \\
(-1, \ 1) &\in D_2 \\
(-1, -1) &\in D_1
\end{aligned}$$

   (a) Are they linearly separable in nonaugmented space?

   (b) Are they linearly separable in augmented space?

   (c) Are they separable by a quadratic polynomial discriminant function?

   (d) Assume they are separable by a quadratic discriminant function. Map this problem into a linearly separable problem of higher dimension. In augmented space, apply a one-at-a-time perceptron with $c = 1$, $\mathbf{w}_0 = \mathbf{1}$. Here $\mathbf{1}$ denotes the vector that has all elements equal to 1.

1.12. In a three-class problem, consider $p(\mathbf{x} \mid D_i)$ for the Gaussian pattern vector $\mathbf{x} \sim N(\mathbf{m}_i, \mathbf{K}_i)$, $i = 1, 2, 3$, and $\mathbf{K}_1 = \mathbf{K}_2 = \mathbf{K}_3 = \mathbf{K}$.

   (a) Find the discriminant functions for a Bayes minimum-error classifier.

   (b) Is this a linear Bayes minimum-error classifier?

   (c) Consider two-dimensional pattern vectors with

$$\mathbf{K} = \begin{bmatrix} \sigma_1^2 & 0 \\ 0 & \sigma_2^2 \end{bmatrix}, \qquad \sigma_1^2 > \sigma_2^2$$

and $\mathbf{m}_1 = (1, 0)$, $\mathbf{m}_2 = (-1, 0)$, $\mathbf{m}_3 = (0, 1)$. Draw the contours of constant probability density $p(\mathbf{x} \mid D_i)$ in the pattern space.

   (d) In addition to part (c), you know that $p(D_1) = p(D_2) = p(D_3) = 1/3$ and that

$$\mathbf{K} = \begin{bmatrix} 2 & 0 \\ 0 & 1 \end{bmatrix}$$

Find the discriminant functions for a Bayes minimum-error classifier.

   (e) In part (d), draw the resulting decision boundaries in pattern space and indicate each decision region.

1.13. Consider the two Gaussian pattern classes, D_1 and D_2, with $\mathbf{x} \sim N(\mathbf{m}_i, \mathbf{K}_i)$, $p(D_1) = p(D_2) = 1/2$, and

$$\mathbf{m}_1 \quad = \quad (1, 0), \qquad \mathbf{m}_2 \quad = \quad (-1, 0)$$

$$\mathbf{K}_1 \quad = \quad \mathbf{K}_2 \quad = \quad \begin{bmatrix} 1 & .5 \\ .5 & 1 \end{bmatrix}$$

    (a) Find the Bayes decision boundary that minimizes the error probability.

    (b) Repeat (a) for

$$\mathbf{K}_1 \quad = \quad \begin{bmatrix} 1 & .5 \\ .5 & 1 \end{bmatrix}, \qquad \mathbf{K}_2 \quad = \quad \begin{bmatrix} 1 & -.5 \\ -.5 & 1 \end{bmatrix}$$

1.14. Consider the two one-dimensional conditional densities $p(x \mid D_1)$ and $p(x \mid D_2)$ shown in the accompanying figure with $p(D_1) = p(D_2) = 1/2$. Assume infinitely many samples are available.

    (a) Find the minimum-error probability (p_e) Bayesian decision rule.

    (b) Find the minimum-achievable p_e using the Bayesian decision rule.

    (c) Find the exact p_e achieved in the limit as the number of samples goes to infinity when the nearest-neighbor decision rule is used.

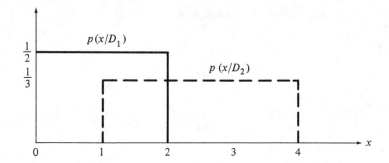

1.15. For a multiclass problem, if a single hyperplane separates every decision region D_k from all other regions D_j, the samples are *totally linearly separable* and we can separate them by decisions of the form D_k vs. not-D_k (D_k^c). Consider the discriminant functions

$$g_1(\mathbf{x}) \quad = \quad -x_1 + x_2$$
$$g_2(\mathbf{x}) \quad = \quad x_1 + x_2 - 5$$
$$g_3(\mathbf{x}) \quad = \quad -x_2 + 1$$

The decision rule is

$$\mathbf{x} \in D_i \quad \text{iff} \quad g_i(\mathbf{x}) > 0 \quad \text{and} \quad \mathbf{x} \in D_j^c, \qquad \text{for all } j \neq i$$

Draw the decision boundaries in pattern space. Label the classification of regions. Identify any indeterminant regions. Classify the samples $\mathbf{x}_1 = (6, 5)$, $\mathbf{x}_2 = (2.5, 2)$, $\mathbf{x}_3 = (3, 0)$.

1.16. Consider the two-class set of training vectors

$$D_1 = \{(2,2),\ (3,1),\ (3,3),\ (-1,-3),\ (4,2),\ (-2,-2)\}$$
$$D_2 = \{(7,1),\ (-2,2),\ (7,3),\ (-4,2),\ (-4,3),\ (8,3)\}$$

(a) Are the two decision regions linearly separable?

(b) Classify the patterns

$$\mathbf{y}_1 = (-1,-1)$$
$$\mathbf{y}_2 = (2,0)$$
$$\mathbf{y}_3 = (5,0)$$
$$\mathbf{y}_4 = (0,3)$$

using a minimum-distance classifier with respect to decision-region means. Draw the decision surfaces.

(c) Is the classifier in (b) linear?

1.17. There are three pattern classes, D_1, D_2, and D_3. Find linear discriminant functions with the perceptron algorithm, with fixed $c = 1$ in nonaugmented space, for the sample patterns

$$(0,1,-1,\ \ 2) \in D_1$$
$$(1,1,\ \ 1,\ \ 1) \in D_2$$
$$(-1,1,\ \ 0,-1) \in D_3$$

Initialize with $\mathbf{w}_k(0) = \mathbf{0}$ for all k.

2

TEXTURE SEGMENTATION WITH NEURAL NETWORKS[1]

R. Chellappa, B. S. Manjunath, and T. Simchony
Signal and Image Processing Institute
Department of Electrical Engineering–Systems
University of Southern California

NEURAL TEXTURE SEGMENTATION

In this chapter we consider the application of Markov random fields (MRF) in modeling texture data and discuss stochastic and deterministic relaxation algorithms for texture classification. We pose the segmentation process as an optimization problem and consider two different optimality criteria.

The first optimality criterion involves maximizing the posterior distribution of the intensity field given the label field (maximum a posteriori estimate (MAP)). The posterior distribution of the texture labels is derived by modeling the textures as Gaussian-Markov random field (GMRF) and characterizing the distribution of different texture labels by an Ising model. Fast, approximate solutions for MAP are obtained by using deterministic relaxation techniques implemented on an Amari-Hopfield neural network and are compared with a simulated annealing-based algorithm for obtaining the MAP estimate. A stochastic algorithm which introduces learning into the iterations of the Amari-Hopfield network is proposed. This iterated

---

[1]Partially supported by the ASFOR grant no. 86-0196.

hill-climbing algorithm combines the fast convergence of deterministic relaxation with the sustained exploration of the stochastic algorithms but is guaranteed to find only a local minimum.

The second optimality criterion requires minimizing the expected percentage of misclassification per pixel by maximizing the posterior marginal distribution, and the maximum posterior marginal algorithm is used to obtain the corresponding solution.

All these methods implemented on parallel networks can be easily extended for hierarchical segmentation, and we present results of the various schemes in classifying some real textured images.

IMAGE SEGMENTATION

Segmentation of image data is an important problem in computer vision, remote sensing, and image analysis. Most objects in the real world have textured surfaces. Segmentation based on texture information is possible even if there are no apparent intensity edges between the different regions. There are many existing methods for texture segmentation and classification, based on different types of statistics that can be obtained from the gray-level images.

Our approach uses Markov random field models for textures in an image. We assign two random variables for the observed pixel, one characterizing the underlying intensity and the other labelling the texture corresponding to the pixel location. We use the Gaussian-Markov Random Field model for the conditional density of the intensity field given the label field. Prior information about the texture label field is introduced using a discrete Markov distribution. The segmentation can then be formulated as an optimization problem involving minimization of a Gibbs energy function.

Exhaustive search for the optimum solution is not possible because of the large dimensionality of the search space. For example, even for the very simple case of segmenting a 128×128 image into two classes, there are $2^{2^{14}}$ possible label configurations. Derin and Elliott [1987] have investigated the use of dynamic programming for obtaining the maximum a posteriori estimate while Cohen and Cooper [1987] give a deterministic relaxation algorithm for the same problem. The optimal MAP solution can be obtained by using stochastic relaxation algorithms like simulated annealing [Geman, 1984].

Recently there has been considerable interest in using neural networks for solving computationally hard problems, and the main emphasis in this chapter is on developing parallel algorithms which can be implemented on such networks of simple processing elements.

The inherent parallelism of neural networks provides an interesting architecture for implementing many computer-vision algorithms [Poggio, 1985]. Some examples are image restoration [Zhou, 1988c], stereopsis [Zhou, 1988b] and computing optical flow ([Koch, 1987], [Zhou, 1988a], [Bulthoff, 1989]). Networks for solving combinatorially hard problems like the Traveling Salesman problem have received much attention in the neural network literature [Hopfield, 1985]. In all these cases the networks are designed to minimize an energy function defined by the network architecture. The parameters of the network are obtained in terms of the cost function it is designed to minimize, and it can be shown that [Hopfield, 1985] for networks having symmetric interconnections, the equilibrium states correspond to the local minima of the energy function. For practical purposes, networks with few interconnections are preferred because of the large number of processing units required in any image processing application. In this context Markov random field models for images play a useful role. They are typically characterized by local dependencies and symmetric interconnections which can be expressed in terms of energy functions using Gibbs-Markov equivalence [Geman, 1984].

We looked into two different optimality criteria for segmenting the image. The first corresponds to the label configuration which maximizes the posterior probability of the label array given the intensity array. As noted before, an exhaustive search for the optimal solution is practically impossible. An alternative is to use stochastic relaxation algorithms like simulated annealing [Geman, 1984], which asymptotically converge to the optimal solution. However the computational burden involved because of the theoretical requirements on the initial temperature and the impractical cooling schedules outweigh their advantages in many cases. Fast approximate solutions can be obtained by using a deterministic relaxation algorithm like the iterated conditional mode rule [Besag, 1986].

The energy function corresponding to this optimality criterion can be mapped into an Amari-Hopfield type network in a straightforward manner, and it can be shown that the network converges to an equilibrium state, which in general will be a local optimum. The solutions obtained using this method are sensitive to the initial configuration, and in many cases starting with a maximum-likelihood estimate is preferred.

Stochastic learning can be easily introduced into the network, and the overall system improves the performance by learning while searching. The learning algorithms used are derived from the theory of stochastic learning automata [Narendra, 1974 and 1989]. The stochastic nature of the system helps in preventing the algorithm from being trapped in a local minimum, and we observe that this improves the quality of the solutions obtained.

The second optimality criterion minimizes the expected percentage of classification error per pixel. This is equivalent to finding the pixel labels that maximize the marginal posterior probability given the intensity data [Grenander, 1981]. Since calculating the marginal posterior probability is very difficult, Marroquin [1985] suggested the maximum posterior marginal (MPM) algorithm that asymptotically computes the posterior marginal. Marroquin uses the algorithm for image restoration, stereo matching, and surface interpolation. Here we use this method to find the texture label that maximizes the marginal posterior probability for each pixel.

The organization of the chapter is as follows: the next section describes the image model. A neural network model for the relaxation algorithms is given in the section after the next along with a deterministic updating rule. The section following discusses the stochastic algorithms for segmentation and their parallel implementation on the network. A learning algorithm is then proposed, and the experimental results are provided.

MARKOV RANDOM FIELDS AND THE IMAGE MODEL

In modeling images consisting of more than one texture, we have to consider two random processes, one for the texture intensity distribution and the second for the label distribution. Various models have been proposed in the literature for textured images. In this section we discuss one such model based on Markov random fields.

In most image processing applications, the input image is a rectangular array of pixels taking values in the range 0–255. Let Ω denote such a set of grid points on an $M \times M$ lattice, i.e., $\Omega = \{(i,j),\ 1 \leq i,j \leq M\}$. Let $\{Y_s, s \in \Omega\ \}$ be a random process defined on this grid.

Definition. The process $\{Y_s\}$ is said to be strictly Markov if

$$P(Y_s \,|\, \text{all } Y_r,\ r \neq s) = P(Y_s \,|\, Y_r,\ r \text{ is a neighbor of } s) \qquad (2\text{-}1)$$

The neighborhood set of site s can be arbitrarily defined. However in many image-processing applications it is natural to consider neighbors which are also spatial neighbors of the site. The Markov process can further be classified as causal or noncausal, depending on the relationship of these neighbors with respect to the site. The use of MRF in image-processing applications has a long history (see, e.g., Chellappa [1985]), and MRFs have been used in applications such as image restoration, segmentation, etc. Cross and Jain [1983] provide a detailed discussion on the application of MRFs in modeling textured images. The GMRF model for the texture intensity process has been used by Derin [1987], Cohen [1987], and Chellappa [1985b]. The MRF is also used by Derin [1987] and Cohen [1987] to describe the label process. In the following we use $\{L_s, s \in \Omega\}$ to denote the label process and $\{Y_s, s \in \Omega\}$ for the zero mean intensity process.

Intensity process. We model the intensity process $\{Y_s\}$ by a Gaussian Markov random field. Depending on the neighborhood set, one can construct a hierarchy of GMRF models as shown in Figure 2.1. The numbers indicate the order of the GMRF model relative to the center location x. Note that this defines a symmetric neighborhood set. We have used the fourth-order model for the intensity process.

		7	6	7		
	5	4	3	4	5	
7	4	2	1	2	4	7
6	3	1	X	1	3	6
7	4	2	1	2	4	7
	5	4	3	4	5	
		7	6	7		

FIGURE 2.1 Structure of the GMRF model. The numbers indicate the order of the model relative to x [Cross, 1983].

Let N_s denote the symmetric fourth-order neighborhood of a site s. Let N^* be the set of one-sided shift vectors corresponding to the fourth-order neighborhood, i.e., N^* is the set of shift vectors corresponding to a fourth-order neighborhood system,

$$
\begin{aligned}
N^* &= \{\tau_1, \tau_2, \tau_3, \ldots, \tau_{10}\} \\
&= \{(-1,0), (0,1), (-1,1), (1,1), (-2,0), \\
&\qquad (0,2), (-1,2), (1,2), (-2,1), (2,1)\}
\end{aligned}
$$

and

$$
N_s = \{r: r = s \pm \tau, \tau \in N^*\} \tag{2-2}
$$

where $s + \tau$ is defined as

$$
s = (i, j), \quad \tau = (x, y), \quad s + \tau = (i + x, j + y)
$$

Assuming that all the neighbors of s also have the same label as that of s, the conditional density of the intensity at the pixel s is

$$
P(Y_s = y_s \mid Y_r = y_r, r \in N_s, L_s = l) = \frac{e^{-U(Y_s = y_s \mid Y_r = y_r, r \in N_s, L_s = l)}}{Z(l \mid y_r, r \in N_s)} \tag{2-3}
$$

$$
U(Y_s = y_s \mid Y_r = y_r, r \in N_s, L_s = l) = \frac{1}{2\sigma_l^2}\left(y_s^2 - 2\sum_{r \in N_s} \Theta_{s,r}^l y_s y_r\right) \tag{2-4}
$$

Equation (2-3) is a Gibbs distribution function. $U(.)$ is often referred to as a Gibbs measure, and $Z(l \mid y_r, r \in N_s)$ is called the partition function. In general any MRF can be expressed as in (2-3), and Geman and Geman [1984] provide a detailed discussion of the equivalence between MRF and Gibbs distributions. In particular if we are considering a GMRF, it is easy to write down an explicit expression for the Gibbs measure as in (2-4). In (2-4), σ_l and Θ^l are the GMRF model parameters of the lth texture class. A stationary GMRF model implies that the parameters satisfy $\Theta_{r,s}^l = \Theta_{r-s}^l = \Theta_{s-r}^l = \Theta_{\tau}^l$.

Estimation of the GMRF parameters.   There are several ways of estimating the GMRF parameters, and a comparison of different schemes can be found in Chellappa [1985a]. We have used the least-squares method in our experiments, and it is summarized below.

Let Ω be the lattice under consideration, and let Ω_I be the interior region of Ω, i.e.,

$$\Omega_I = \Omega - \Omega_B,$$

$$\Omega_B = \{s = (i,j), s \in \Omega \text{ and } s \pm \tau \notin \Omega \text{ for at least some } \tau \in N^*\} \quad (2\text{-}5)$$

Let

$$Q_s = [y_{s+\tau_1} + y_{s-\tau_1}, \ldots, y_{s+\tau_{10}} + y_{s-\tau_{10}}]^T \quad (2\text{-}6)$$

Then the least-squares estimates of the parameters are

$$\hat{\Theta} = [\sum_{\Omega_I} Q_s Q_s^T]^{-1} [\sum_{\Omega_I} Q_s y_s] \quad (2\text{-}7)$$

$$\hat{\sigma} = \frac{1}{M^2} \sum_{\Omega_I} [y_s - \Theta^T Q_s]^2 \quad (2\text{-}8)$$

We view the image intensity array as composed of a set of overlapping $k \times k$ windows W_s, centered at each pixel $s \in \Omega$. In each of these windows we assume that the texture label L_s is homogeneous (all the pixels in the window belong to the same texture) and models the intensity distribution in the window by a fourth-order stationary GMRF. Let $\mathbf{Y}_s^*$ denote the 2-D vector representing the zero mean intensity array in the window W_s. Using the Gibbs formulation and assuming a free boundary model, the joint probability density in the window W_s can be written as [Cohen, 1987]

$$P(\mathbf{Y}_s^* = \mathbf{y}_s^* \mid L_s = l) = \frac{e^{-U_1(\mathbf{y}_s^* \mid L_s = l)}}{Z_1(l)}$$

where $Z_1(l)$ is the partition function and

$$U_1(\mathbf{y}_s^* \mid L_s = l) = \frac{1}{2\sigma_l^2} \sum_{r \in W_s} \left\{ y_r^2 - \sum_{\tau \in N^* \mid r+\tau \in W_s} \Theta_\tau^l y_r (y_{r+\tau} + y_{r-\tau}) \right\} \quad (2\text{-}9)$$

Label process. The texture labels are assumed to obey a first- or second-order discrete Markov model with a single parameter β, which measures the amount of clustering between adjacent pixels. If $\hat{N}_s$ denotes the appropriate neighborhood for the label field, then we can write the distribution function for the texture label at site s conditioned on the labels of the neighboring sites as:

$$P(L_s \mid L_r, r \in \hat{N}_s) = \frac{e^{-U_2(L_s \mid L_r)}}{Z_2}$$

where Z_2 is a normalizing constant and

$$U_2(L_s \mid L_r, r \in \hat{N}_s) = -\beta \sum_{r \in \hat{N}_s} \delta(L_s - L_r), \qquad \beta > 0 \qquad (2\text{-}10)$$

In (2-10), β determines the degree of clustering, and $\delta(i - j)$ is the Kronecker delta. Using the Bayes rule, we can write

$$P(L_s \mid \mathbf{Y}_s^*, L_r, r \in \hat{N}_s) = \frac{P(\mathbf{Y}_s^* \mid L_s) P(L_s \mid L_r, r \in \hat{N}_s)}{P(\mathbf{Y}_s^*)} \qquad (2\text{-}11)$$

Since $\mathbf{Y}_s^*$ is known, the denominator in (2-11) is just a constant. The numerator is a product of two exponential functions and can be expressed as

$$P(L_s \mid \mathbf{Y}_s^*, L_r, r \in \hat{N}_s) = \frac{1}{Z_p} e^{-U_p(L_s \mid \mathbf{Y}_s^*, L_r, r \in \hat{N}_s)} \qquad (2\text{-}12)$$

where Z_p is the partition function and $U_p(.)$ is the posterior energy corresponding to (2-11). From (2-9) and (2-10) we can write

$$U_p(L_s \mid \mathbf{Y}_s^*, L_r, r \in \hat{N}_s) = w(L_s) + U_1(\mathbf{Y}_s^* \mid L_s) + U_2(L_s \mid L_r, r \in \hat{N}_s) \qquad (2\text{-}13)$$

Note that the second term in (2-13) relates the observed pixel intensities to the texture labels and the last term specifies the label distribution. The bias term $w(L_s) = \log Z_1(L_s)$ is dependent on the texture class, and it can be explicitly evaluated for the GMRF model considered here using the toroidal assumption. (The computations become very cumbersome if toroidal assumptions are not made.) An alternate approach is to estimate the bias from the histogram of the data as suggested by Geman and Graffigne [1987]. Finally, the posterior distribution of the texture labels for the entire image given the intensity array is

$$P(\mathbf{L} \mid \mathbf{Y}^*) = \frac{P(\mathbf{Y}^* \mid \mathbf{L}) P(\mathbf{L})}{P(\mathbf{Y}^*)} \qquad (2\text{-}14)$$

Maximizing (2-14) gives the optimal Bayesian estimate. Though it is possible in principle to compute the right-hand side of (2-14) and find the global optimum, the computational burden involved is so enormous that it is practically impossible to do so. However, we note that the stochastic relaxation algorithms discussed later in this chapter require only the computation of (2-12) to obtain the optimal solution. The deterministic relaxation algorithm given in the next section also uses these values, but in this case the solution is only an approximation to the MAP estimate.

A NEURAL NETWORK FOR TEXTURE CLASSIFICATION

We describe the network architecture used for segmentation and the implementation of deterministic relaxation algorithms. The energy function which the network minimizes is obtained from the image model discussed in the previous section. For convenience of notation, let $U_1(i,j,l) = U_1(\mathbf{Y}_s^*, L_s = l) + w(l)$, where $s = (i,j)$ denotes a pixel site, and $U_1(.)$ and $w(l)$ are as defined in (2-13). The network consists of K layers, each layer arranged as an $M \times M$ array, where K is the number of texture classes in the image and M is the dimension of the image. The elements (neurons) in the network are assumed to be binary and are indexed by (i,j,l), where $(i,j) = s$ refers to their position in the image and l refers to the layer. The (i,j,l)th neuron is said to be ON if its output V_{ijl} is 1, indicating that the corresponding site $s = (i,j)$ in the image has the texture label l. Let $T_{ijl;i'j'l'}$ be the connection strength between the neurons (i,j,l), and let (i',j',l') and let I_{ijl} be the input bias current. Then a general form for the energy of the network is [Hopfield, 1985]

$$E = -\frac{1}{2}\sum_{i=1}^{M}\sum_{j=1}^{M}\sum_{l=1}^{K}\sum_{i'=1}^{M}\sum_{j'=1}^{M}\sum_{l'=1}^{K} T_{ijl;i'j'l'}V_{ijl}V_{i'j'l'} - \frac{1}{2}\sum_{i=1}^{M}\sum_{j=1}^{M}\sum_{l=1}^{K} I_{ijl}V_{ijl} \quad (2\text{-}15)$$

From our earlier discussion, we note that a solution for the MAP estimate can be obtained by minimizing (2-14). Here we approximate the posterior energy by

$$P(\mathbf{Y}_s^* \mid L_s)P(L_s)U(\mathbf{L} \mid \mathbf{Y}^*) = \sum_s \{U(\mathbf{Y}_s^* \mid L_s) + w_{L_s} + U_2(L_s)\} \quad (2\text{-}16)$$

and the corresponding Gibbs energy to be minimized can be written as

$$E = \frac{1}{2}\sum_{i=1}^{M}\sum_{j=1}^{M}\sum_{l=1}^{K} U_1(i,j,l)V_{ijl} - \frac{\beta}{2}\sum_{l=1}^{K}\sum_{i=1}^{M}\sum_{j=1}^{M}\sum_{(i',j')\in\hat{N}_{ij}} V_{i'j'l}V_{ijl} \quad (2\text{-}17)$$

where $\hat{N}_{ij}$ is the neighborhood of site (i,j) (same as the $\hat{N}_s$ discussed earlier). In (2-17) it is implicitly assumed that each pixel site has a unique label, i.e., only one neuron is active in each column of the network. This constraint can be implemented in different ways. For the deterministic relaxation algorithm described below, a simple method is to use a *winner-takes-all* circuit for each column so that the neuron receiving the maximum input is turned on and the others are turned off. Alternately a penalty term can be introduced in (2-17) to represent the constraint as Hopfield does [1985]. From (2-15) and (2-17) we can identify the parameters for the network,

$$T_{ijl;i'j'l'} = \begin{cases} \beta & \text{if } (i',j')\in\hat{N}_{ij}, \quad \forall\, l = l' \\ 0 & \text{otherwise} \end{cases} \quad (2\text{-}18)$$

and the bias current,

$$I_{ijl} = -U_1(i,j,l) \quad (2\text{-}19)$$

Deterministic Relaxation

Equations (2-18) and (2-19) relate the parameters of the network to that of the image model. The connection matrix for the above network is symmetric, and there is no self-feedback, i.e., $T_{ijl;ijl} = 0, \forall\, i, j, l$. Let u_{ijl} be the potential of neuron (i, j, l). (Note that l is the layer number corresponding to texture class l.) Then

$$u_{ijl} \;=\; \sum_{i'=1}^{M}\sum_{j'=1}^{M}\sum_{l'=1}^{K} T_{ijl;\,i'j'l'}\; V_{i'j'l'} + I_{ijl} \qquad (2\text{-}20)$$

In order to minimize (2-17), we use the following updating rule:

$$V_{ijl} \;=\; \begin{cases} 1 & \text{if } u_{ijl} = \min_{l'}\{u_{ijl'}\} \\[2mm] 0 & \text{otherwise} \end{cases} \qquad (2\text{-}21)$$

This updating scheme ensures that at each stage the energy decreases. Since the energy is bounded, the convergence of the above system is assured, but the stable state will in general be a local optimum.

This network model is a version of the iterated conditional mode (ICM) algorithm of Besag [1986]. This algorithm maximizes the conditional probability $P(L_s = l\,|\,\mathbf{Y}_s^*, L_{s'}, s' \in \hat{N}_s)$ during each iteration. It is a local deterministic relaxation algorithm that is very easy to implement. We observe that in general any algorithm based on MRF models can be easily mapped onto neural networks with local interconnections. The main advantage of this deterministic relaxation algorithm is its simplicity. Often the solutions are reasonably good, and the algorithm usually converges within 20–30 iterations. In the next section we study two stochastic schemes which asymptotically converge to the global optimum of the respective criterion functions.

STOCHASTIC ALGORITHMS FOR TEXTURE SEGMENTATION

We look at two optimal solutions corresponding to different decision rules for determining the labels. The first one uses simulated annealing to obtain the optimum MAP estimate of the label configuration. The second algorithm minimizes the expected misclassification per pixel. The parallel network implementation of these algorithms has already been discussed.

Searching for MAP Solutions

The MAP rule [Geman, 1987] searches for the configuration L that maximizes the posterior probability distribution. This is equivalent to maximizing $P(\mathbf{Y}^*\,|\,\mathbf{L})P(\mathbf{L})$ since $P(\mathbf{Y}^*)$ is independent of the labels and $\mathbf{Y}^*$ is known. The right-hand side of (2-14) is a Gibbs distribution. To maximize (2-14) we use simulated annealing [Geman, 1984], a combinatorial optimization method which is based on sampling from varying Gibbs distribution functions

$$\frac{e^{-(1/T_k)U_p(L_s|\mathbf{Y}_s^*,L_r,r\in\hat{N}_s)}}{Z_{T_k}}$$

In order to maximize

$$\frac{e^{-U_p(\mathbf{L}|\mathbf{Y}^*)}}{Z}$$

T_k being the time-varying parameter referred to as the temperature, we used the following cooling schedule:

$$T_k = \frac{T_0}{1+\log_2 k} \qquad (2\text{-}22)$$

where k is the iteration number. When the temperature is high, the bond between adjacent pixels is loose and the distribution tends to behave like a uniform distribution over the possible texture labels. As T_k decreases, the distribution concentrates on the lower values of the energy function which correspond to points with higher probability. The process is bound to converge to a uniform distribution over the label configuration that corresponds to the MAP solution. Since the number of texture labels is finite, convergence of this algorithm follows from Geman [1984]. In our experiment, we realized that starting the iterations with $T_0 = 2$ did not guarantee convergence to the MAP solution. Since starting at a much higher temperature will slow the convergence of the algorithm significantly, we used an alternative approach, namely, cycling the temperature [Grenander, 1981]. We followed the annealing schedule until T_k reached a lower bound, then we reheated the system and started a new cooling process. By using only a few cycles, we obtained results better than those with a single cooling cycle. Parallel implementation of simulated annealing on the network has already been discussed. The results, which are presented later in the chapter, were obtained with two cycles.

Maximizing the Posterior Marginal Distribution

The choice of the objective function for optimal segmentation can significantly affect its result. The choice should be dependent upon the purpose of the classification. In many implementations the most reasonable objective function is the one that minimizes the expected percentage misclassification per pixel. The solution to the above objective function is also the one that maximizes the marginal posterior distribution of L_s given the observation $\mathbf{Y}^*$, for each pixel s.

$$P\{L_s = l_s \mid \mathbf{Y}^* = \mathbf{y}^*\} \propto \sum_{\mathbf{l}|L_s=l_s} P(\mathbf{Y}^* = \mathbf{y}^* \mid \mathbf{L} = \mathbf{l})\, P(\mathbf{L} = \mathbf{l})$$

The summation above extends over all possible label configurations, keeping the label at site s constant. This concept was thoroughly investigated by Marroquin

[1985a]. Marroquin [1985b] discusses this formulation in the context of image restoration and illustrates the performance on images with few gray levels. He also mentions the possibility of using this objective function for texture segmentation. In Besag [1986] the same objective function is mentioned in the context of image estimation.

To find the optimal solution, we used the stochastic algorithm suggested by Marroquin [1985a]. The algorithm samples out of the posterior distribution of the texture labels, given the intensity. Unlike the stochastic relaxation algorithm, samples are taken with a fixed temperature $T = 1$. The Markov chain associated with the sampling algorithm converges with probability one to the posterior distribution. We define new random variables $g_s^{l,t}$ for each pixel $(s \in \Omega)$:

$$g_s^{l,t}\{L_s^t\} = \begin{cases} 1, & L_s^t = l \\ 0, & \text{otherwise} \end{cases}$$

where L_s^t is the class of the s pixel, at time t, in the state vector of the Markov chain associated with the Gibbs sampler. We use the ergodic property of the Markov chain [Gidas, 1985] to calculate the expectations for these random variables using time averaging:

$$E\{g_s^{l,t}\} = \lim_{N \to \infty} \frac{1}{N} \sum_{t=1}^{N} g_s^{l,t} = P_s\{L_s = l \mid Y^*\}$$

where N is the number of iterations performed. To obtain the optimal class for each pixel, we simply chose the class that occurred more often than the others.

The MPM algorithm was implemented using the Gibbs sampler [Geman, 1984]. A much wider set of sampling algorithms such as Metropolis can be used for this purpose. The algorithms can be implemented sequentially or in parallel, with a deterministic or stochastic decision rule for the order of visiting the pixels. In order to avoid the dependence on the initial state of the Markov chain, we can ignore the first few iterations. In the experiments conducted, we obtained good results after 500 iterations. The algorithm does not suffer from the drawbacks of simulated annealing. For instance, we do not have to start the iterations with a high temperature to avoid local minima, and the performance is not badly affected by enlarging the state space.

Network Implementation of the Sampling Algorithms

All the stochastic algorithms described in the Gibbs formulation are based on sampling from a probability distribution. The probability distribution is constant in the MPM algorithm [Marroquin, 1985a] and is time varying in the case of annealing. The need for parallel implementation is due to the heavy computational load associated with their use.

The issue of parallel implementation in stochastic algorithms was first addressed by Geman and Geman [1984]. They show that the Gibbs sampler can be implemented by any deterministic or stochastic rule for choosing the order in which pixels are updated, as long as each pixel is visited infinitely often. An iteration is the time required to visit each pixel at least once (a full sweep). Note that the stochastic rules have a random period and allow us to visit a pixel more than once in a period. They consider the new Markov chain one obtains from the original by viewing it only after each iteration. Their proof is based on two essential elements. The first is the fact that the embedded Markov chain has a strictly positive transition probability p_{ij} for any possible states i, j, which proves that the chain will converge to a unique probability measure regardless of the initial state. The second is that the Gibbs measure is an invariant measure for the Gibbs sampler, so that the embedded chain converges to the Gibbs measure. The proof introduced by Geman [1984] can be applied to a much larger family of sampling algorithms satisfying the following properties [Gidas, 1985]:

1. The sampler produces a Markov chain with a positive transition probability p_{ij} for any choice of states i, j.

2. The Gibbs measure is invariant under the sampling algorithm.

The Metropolis and heat-bath algorithms are two such sampling methods. To see that the Metropolis algorithm satisfies Property 2, look at the following equation for updating a single pixel:

$$P^{n+1}(i) = \frac{1}{m} \sum_{\pi(j) < \pi(i)} P^n(j) + \frac{1}{m} \sum_{\pi(j) < \pi(i)} P^n(i) \frac{\pi(i) - \pi(j)}{\pi(i)}$$

$$+ \frac{1}{m} \sum_{\pi(j) \geq \pi(i)} P^n(j) \frac{\pi(i)}{\pi(j)}$$

where m is the number of values each pixel can take. The first term corresponds to the cases when the system was in state j and the new state i has higher probability. The second term corresponds to a system in state i and a new state j that has lower probability. The given probability is for staying in state i. The third term corresponds to a system in state j and a new state i with lower probability. If we now replace $P^{n+1}(i)$ and $P^n(i)$ by $\pi(i)$ and $P^n(j)$ by $\pi(j)$, we see that the equality holds, implying that the Gibbs measure is invariant under the Metropolis algorithm. The first property is also satisfied. Note that the states now correspond to the global configuration. To implement the algorithm in parallel, one can update pixels in parallel as long as neighboring pixels are not updated at the same time. A very clear discussion on this issue can be found in Marroquin [1985a].

We will now describe how these stochastic algorithms can be implemented on the network that has already been discussed. The only modification required for the simulated annealing rule is that the neurons in the network fire according to a time-dependent probabilistic rule. Using the same notation as described earlier, the probability that neuron (i, j, l) will fire during iteration k is

$$P(V_{ijl} = 1) \quad = \quad \frac{e^{-(1/T_k)u_{ijl}}}{Z_{T_k}} \qquad (2\text{-}23)$$

where u_{ijl} is as defined in (2-20) and T_k follows the cooling schedule (2-22).

The MPM algorithm uses the above selection rule with $T_k = 1$. In addition, each neuron in the network has a counter which is incremented every time the neuron fires. When the iterations are terminated, the neuron in each column of the network having the maximum count is selected to represent the label for the corresponding pixel site in the image.

We have noted before that for parallel implementation of the sampling algorithms, neighboring sites should not be updated simultaneously. Some additional observations are made later in this chapter.

STOCHASTIC LEARNING AND NEURAL NETWORKS

In the previous sections, purely deterministic and stochastic relaxation algorithms were discussed. Each has its own advantages and disadvantages. Now we will consider the possibility of combining the two methods using stochastic learning automata, and we will compare the results obtained by this new scheme with those of previous algorithms.

We will begin with a brief introduction to the stochastic learning automaton [Narendra, 1974]. An automaton is a decision maker operating in a random environment. A stochastic automaton can be defined by a quadruple (α, Q, T, R), where $\alpha = \{\alpha_1, \ldots, \alpha_N\}$ is the set of actions available to the automaton. The action selected at time t is denoted by $\alpha(t)$. $Q(t)$ is the state of the automaton at time t and consists of the action probability vector $\mathbf{p}(t) = [p_1(t), \ldots, p_N(t)]$, where $p_i(t) = \text{prob}\ (\alpha(t) = \alpha_i)$ and $\sum_i p_i(t) = 1\ \forall\ t$. The environment responds to the action $\alpha(t)$ with a $\lambda(t) \in R$, R being the set of the environment's responses. The state transitions of the automaton are governed by the learning algorithm T, $Q(t + 1) = T(Q(t), \alpha(t), \lambda(t))$. Without loss of generality, it can be assumed that $R = [0, 1]$; i.e., the responses are normalized to lie in the interval $[0, 1]$, '1' indicating a complete *success* and '0' total *failure*. The goal of the automaton is to converge to the optimal action, i.e., the action which results in the maximum expected reward. Again without loss of generality, let α_1 be the optimal action and $d_1 = E[\lambda(t)\,|\,\alpha_1] = \max_i \{E[\lambda(t)\,|\,\alpha_i]\}$. At present no learning algorithms exist which are optimal in the above sense. However, we can choose the parameters of certain learning algorithms in order to realize a response as close to the optimum as desired. This condition is called ϵ-optimality. If $M(t) \overset{\Delta}{=} E[\lambda(t)\,|\,p(t)]$, then a learning algorithm is said to be ϵ-optimal if it results in an $M(t)$ such that

$$\lim_{t \to \infty} E[M(t)] \quad > \quad d_1 - \epsilon \qquad (2\text{-}24)$$

for a suitable choice of parameters and for any $\epsilon > 0$. One of the simplest learning schemes is the linear reward-inaction rule, L_{R-I}. Suppose at time t we have $\alpha(t) = \alpha_i$ and $\lambda(t)$ is the response received. Then, according to the L_{R-I} rule,

$$
\begin{aligned}
p_i(t+1) &= p_i(t) + a\lambda(t)[1 - p_i(t)] \\
p_j(t+1) &= p_j(t)[1 - a\lambda(t)], \forall\, j \neq i
\end{aligned}
\tag{2-25}
$$

where a is a parameter of the algorithm controlling the learning rate. Typical values for a are in the range 0.01–0.1. It can be shown that this L_{R-I} rule is ϵ-optimal in all stationary environments, i.e., there exists a value for the parameter a so that condition (2-24) is satisfied. Some properties of this algorithm are explored in the exercises. For a detailed discussion on this and other nonlinear learning algorithms, we refer the reader to the book by Lakshmivarahan [1981].

Collective behavior of a group of automata has also been studied. Consider a team of N automata $A_i(i = 1, \ldots, N)$, each having r_i actions $\alpha^i = \{\alpha_1^i, \ldots, \alpha_{r_i}^i\}$. At any instant t each member of the team makes a decision $\alpha^i(t)$. The environment responds to this by sending a reinforcement signal $\lambda(t)$ to all the automata in the group. This situation represents a cooperative game among a team of automata with an identical payoff. All the automata update their action probability vectors according to (2-25) using the same learning rate, and the process repeats. Local convergence results can be obtained in case of stationary random environments. Variations of this rule have been applied to complex problems like decentralized control of Markov chains [Wheeler, 1986] and relaxation labelling [Thathachar, 1986].

The texture classification discussed in the previous sections can be treated as a relaxation labelling problem, and stochastic automata can be used to learn the labels (texture class) for the pixels. A learning automaton is assigned to each of the pixel sites in the image. The actions of the automata correspond to selecting a label for the pixel site to which it is assigned. Thus for a K class problem, each automaton has K actions and a probability distribution over this action set. Initially the labels are assigned randomly with equal probability. Since the number of automata involved is very large, it is not practical to update the action probability vector at each iteration. Instead we combine the iterations of the neural network described in the previous section with the stochastic learning algorithm. This results in an iterative hill-climbing type algorithm which combines the fast convergence of deterministic relaxation with the sustained exploration of the stochastic algorithm. The stochastic part prevents the algorithm from getting trapped in local minima and at the same time "learns" from the search by updating the state probabilities. However, unlike simulated annealing, we cannot guarantee convergence to the global optimum. Each cycle now has two phases. The first phase consists of the deterministic relaxation network's converging to a solution. The second phase consists of the learning network's updating its state, the new state being determined by the equilibrium state of the relaxation network. A new initial state is generated by the learning network, depending on its current state, and the cycle repeats. Thus relaxation and learning alternate with each other. After each iteration the probability of the more stable states increases, and, because of the stochastic nature of the algorithm, the possibility of getting trapped in bad local minima is reduced. The algorithm is summarized below.

Learning Algorithm

Let the pixel site be denoted by $s \in \Omega$ and the number of texture classes be K. Let A_s be the automaton assigned to site s and the action probability vector of A_s be $\mathbf{p}_s(t) = [p_{s,1}(t), \dots, p_{s,K}(t)]$ and $\sum_i p_{s,i}(t) = 1, \forall s, t$, where $p_{s,l}(t) = $ prob (label of site $s = l$). The steps in the algorithm are:

1. Initialize the action probability vectors of all the automata

$$ p_{s,l}(0) = \frac{1}{K}, \qquad \forall s, l $$

   Initialize the iteration counter to 0.

2. Choose an initial label configuration sampled from the distribution of these probability vectors.

3. Start the neural network explained earlier with this configuration.

4. Let l_s denote the label for site s at equilibrium. Let the current time (iteration number) be t. Then the action probabilities are updated as follows:

$$ p_{s,l_s}(t+1) = p_{s,l_s}(t) + a\lambda(t)[1 - p_{s,l_s}(t)] $$
$$ p_{s,j}(t+1) = p_{s,j}(t)[1 - a\lambda(t)], \qquad \forall j \neq l_s \text{ and } \forall s \qquad (2\text{-}26) $$

   The response $\lambda(t)$ is derived as follows: If the present label configuration resulted in a lower energy state compared to the previous one, then it results in a $\lambda(t) = \lambda_1$; if the energy increases, we have $\lambda(t) = \lambda_2$ with $\lambda_1 > \lambda_2$. In our simulations we used $\lambda_1 = 1$ and $\lambda_2 = 0.25$.

5. Generate a new configuration from these updated label probabilities, increment the iteration counter, and go to step 3.

Thus the system consists of two layers, one for relaxation and the other for learning. The relaxation network is similar to the one considered earlier, the only difference being that the initial state is decided by the learning network. The learning network consists of a team of automata, and learning takes place at a much lower speed than relaxation, with fewer updatings. The probabilities of the labels corresponding to the final state of the relaxation network are increased according to (2-26). Using these new probabilities, a new configuration is generated. Since the response does not depend on time, this corresponds to a stationary environment, and, as we have noted before, this L_{R-I} algorithm can be shown to converge to a stationary point, not necessarily to the global optimum.

TABLE 2.1 GMRF TEXTURE PARAMETERS

	Calf	Grass	Pigskin	Sand	Wool	Wood
θ_1	0.5689	0.5667	0.3795	0.5341	0.4341	0.5508
θ_2	0.2135	0.3780	0.4528	0.4135	0.2182	0.2498
θ_3	−0.1287	−0.2047	−0.1117	−0.1831	−0.0980	−0.1164
θ_4	−0.0574	−0.1920	−0.1548	−0.2050	−0.0006	−0.1405
θ_5	−0.1403	−0.1368	−0.0566	−0.1229	−0.0836	−0.0517
θ_6	−0.0063	−0.0387	−0.0494	−0.0432	0.0592	0.0139
θ_7	−0.0052	0.0158	−0.0037	0.0120	−0.0302	−0.0085
θ_8	−0.0153	0.0075	0.0098	0.0111	−0.0407	−0.0058
θ_9	0.0467	0.0505	0.0086	0.0362	0.0406	−0.0008
θ_{10}	0.0190	0.0496	0.0233	0.0442	−0.0001	0.0091
σ^2	217.08	474.72	79.33	91.44	126.22	14.44

EXPERIMENTAL RESULTS AND CONCLUSIONS

The segmentation results using the above algorithms are given in two examples. The parameters σ_l and Θ_l corresponding to the fourth-order GMRF for each texture class were precomputed from 64×64 images of the textures. The local mean (in an 11×11 window) was first subtracted to obtain the zero mean texture, and the least-squares estimates [Chellappa, 1985b] of the parameters were then computed from the interior of the image. The parameter values for the different textures used in our experiments are given in Table 2.1.

The first step in the segmentation process involves computing the Gibbs energies $U_1(\mathbf{Y}^*{}_s \mid L_s)$ in (2-9). This is done for each texture class, and the results are stored. For computational convenience, these $U_1(.)$ values are normalized by dividing by k^2, where k is the size of the window. To ignore the boundary effects, we set $U_1 = 0$ at the boundaries. We have experimented with different window sizes, and larger windows result in more homogeneous texture patches but the boundaries between the textures are distorted. The results reported here are based on windows of size 11×11 pixels. The bias term $w(l_s)$ can be estimated using the histogram of the image data [Geman, 1987], but we obtained these values by trial and error.

We observed earlier that neighboring pixel sites should not be updated simultaneously. This problem occurs only if digital implementation of the networks is considered, since the probability of this happening in an analog network is zero. When this simultaneous updating was tested for the deterministic case, it always converged to limit cycles of length 2. (In fact it can be shown that the system converges to limit cycles of length at most 2.)

The choice of β plays an important role in the segmentation process, and its value depends on the magnitude of the energy function $U_1(.)$. Various values of β ranging from 0.2–3.0 were used in the experiments. In the deterministic algorithm, it is preferable to start with a small β and increase it gradually. Large values of β

usually degrade the performance. We also observed that slowly increasing β during the iterations improves the results for the stochastic algorithms. It should be noted that using a larger value of β for the deterministic algorithm (compared to those used in the stochastic algorithms) does not improve the performance.

The nature of the segmentation results depends on the order of the label model. It is preferable to choose the first-order model for the stochastic algorithms if we know a priori that the boundaries are either horizontal or vertical. However, for the deterministic rule and the learning scheme the second-order model results in a more homogeneous classification.

The MPM algorithm requires the statistics obtained from the invariant measure of the Markov chain corresponding to the sampling algorithm. Hence it is preferable to ignore the first few hundred trials before starting to gather the statistics. The performance of the deterministic relaxation rule discussed earlier also depends on the initial state, and we have looked into two different initial conditions. The first one starts with a label configuration $\mathbf{L}$ such that $L_s = l_s$ if $U_1(\mathbf{Y}_s^* \mid l_s) = \min_{l_k}\{U_1(\mathbf{Y}_s^* \mid l_k)\}$. This corresponds to maximizing the probability $P(\mathbf{Y}^* \mid \mathbf{L})$ [Chatterjee, 1985]. The second choice for the initial configuration is a randomly generated label set. Results for both the cases are provided, and we observe that the random choice often leads to better results.

In the examples below, the following learning parameters were used: Learning rate $a = 0.05$ and reward/penalty parameters $\lambda_1 = 0.25$ and $\lambda_2 = 1.0$.

Example 2.1

This is a two-class problem consisting of grass and calf textures. The image is of size 128×128 and is shown in Figure 2.2(a). In Figure 2.2(b) the classification obtained by the deterministic algorithm already discussed is shown. The maximum likelihood estimate was the initial state for the network, and Figure 2.2(c) gives the result with random initial configuration. Notice that in this case the final result has fewer misclassified regions than in Figure 2.2(b), and this was observed to be true in general. Figures 2.2(d) and 2.2(e) give the MAP solution using simulated annealing and the MPM solution, respectively. The result of the learning algorithm is shown in Figure 2.2(f), and there are no misclassifications within the homogeneous regions. However, the boundary is not as good as those of the MAP or MPM solutions. In all the cases we used $\beta = 0.6$. ∎

Example 2.2

This is a 256×256 image (Figure 2.3(a)) having six textures: calf, grass, wool, wood, pigskin and sand. This is a difficult problem in the sense that three of the textures (wool, pigskin, and sand) have almost identical characteristics and are not easily distinguishable even by the human eye. The maximum-likelihood

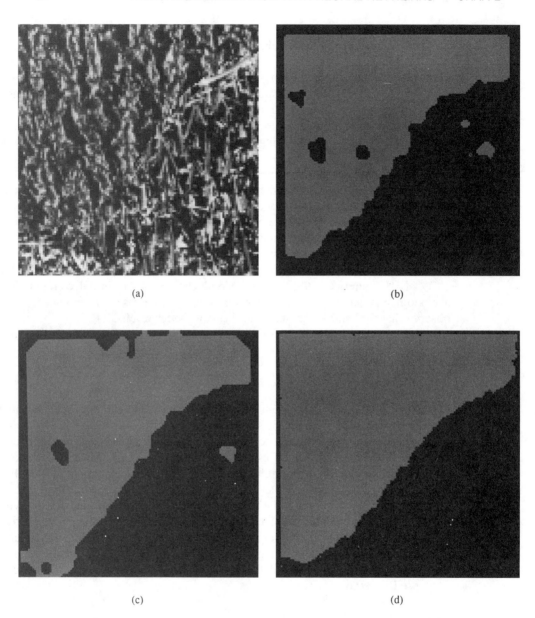

(a)

(b)

(c)

(d)

FIGURE 2.2 (a) Original image consisting of two textures. The classification using different algorithms is shown in (b)–(f) (The textures are coded by gray levels). (b) Deterministic relaxation with Maximum likelihood solution as initial condition and (c) with random initial condition. (d) MAP estimate using simulated annealing. (e) MPM solution. (f) Network with stochastic learning.

(e)   (f)

FIGURE 2.2   (contd.)

solution is shown in Figure 2.3(b), and Figure 2.3(c) is the solution obtained
by the deterministic relaxation network with the result in Figure 2.3(b) as the
initial condition. Figure 2.3(d) gives the result with random initial configuration. The MAP solution using simulated annealing is shown in Figure 2.3(e).
As was mentioned earlier, cycling of temperature improves the performance
of simulated annealing. The segmentation result was obtained by starting with
an initial temperature $T_0 = 2.0$ and cooling according to the schedule (2-22)
for 300 iterations. Then the system was reset to $T_0 = 1.5$, and the process
was repeated for 300 more iterations. In case of the MPM rule, the first 500
iterations were ignored and Figure 2.3(f) shows the result obtained using the
last 200 iterations. As in the previous example, the best results were obtained
by the simulated annealing and MPM algorithms. For the MPM case there
were no misclassifications within homogeneous regions but the boundaries
were not accurate, and, in fact, as indicated in Table 2.2, simulated annealing
has the lowest percentage error in classification. Introducing learning into deterministic relaxation considerably improves the performance (Figure 2.3(g)).
Table 2.2 gives the percentage classification error for the different cases.   ■

It is noted from the table that, although learning improves the performance of
the deterministic network algorithm, the best results were obtained by the simulated
annealing technique, which is to be expected.

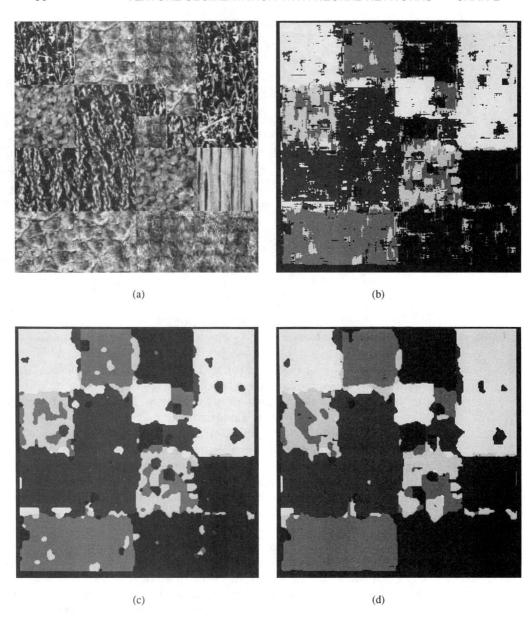

(a)   (b)

(c)   (d)

FIGURE 2.3 (a) Original image consisting of six textures. (b) Maximum likelihood solution. (c) Deterministic relaxation with (b) as initial condition and (d) with
random initial condition. (e) MAP estimate using simulated annealing. (f) MPM
solution. (g) Network with stochastic learning.

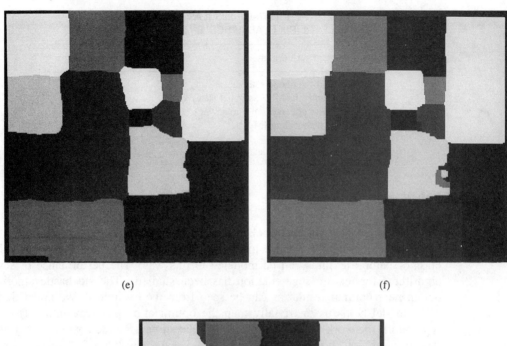

(e)   (f)

(g)

FIGURE 2.3   (contd.)

TABLE 2.2 PERCENTAGE MISCLASSIFICATION FOR
EXAMPLE 2.2 (SIX-CLASS PROBLEM)

Algorithm	Percentage error
Maximum-likelihood estimate	22.17
Neural network (MLE as initial state)	16.25
Neural network (random initial state)	14.74
Simulated annealing (MAP)	6.72
MPM algorithm	7.05
Neural network with learning	8.70

CONCLUSIONS

In this chapter we have looked into different texture segmentation algorithms based on modeling the texture intensities as a GMRF. We observed that a large class of natural textures can be modeled in this way. The performance of several algorithms for texture segmentation has been studied. The stochastic algorithms obtain near optimal results as can be seen from the examples. We noted that the MRF model helps us to trivially map the optimization problem onto a Hopfield-type neural network. This deterministic relaxation network converges extremely fast to a solution, typically in 20–30 iterations for the 256×256 image. Its performance, however, is sensitive to the initial state of the system and often is not very satisfactory. To overcome the disadvantages of the network, a new algorithm which introduces stochastic learning into the iterations of the network was proposed. This helps to maintain a sustained search of the solution space while learning from the past experience. This algorithm combines the advantages of deterministic and stochastic relaxation schemes, and it would be interesting to explore its performance in solving other computationally hard problems in computer vision.

REFERENCES

Besag, J., "On the Statistical Analysis of Dirty Pictures," *Journal of Royal Statistic Society B*, vol. 48, 259–302, 1986.

Bulthoff, H., Little, J., and Poggio, T., "A Parallel Algorithm for Real-Time Computation of Optical Flow," *Nature*, vol. 337, 549–553, February 1989.

Chatterjee, S., and Chellappa, R., "Maximum Likelihood Texture Segmentation Using Gaussian Markov Random Field Models," *Proceedings of Computer Vision and Pattern Recognition Conference*, San Francisco, June 1985.

Chellappa, R., "Two-Dimensional Discrete Gaussian-Markov Random Field Models for Image Processing," *Progress in Pattern Recognition 2*, L. N. Kanal and A. Rosenfeld (eds.), Elsevier Science Publishers, North-Holland, 79–112, 1985.

Chellappa, R., and Chatterjee, S., "Classification of Textures Using Gaussian-Markov Random Fields," *IEEE Trans. Acoust., Speech, Signal Process.*, vol. ASSP-33, 959–963, August 1985.

Cohen, F. S., and Cooper, D. B., "Simple Parallel Hierarchical and Relaxation Algorithms for Segmenting Noncausal Markovian Fields," *IEEE Trans. on Pattern Anal. Machine Intell.*, vol. PAMI-9, 195–219, March 1987.

Cross, G. R., and Jain, A. K., "Markov Random Field Texture Models," *IEEE Trans. on Pattern Anal. Machine Intell.*, vol. PAMI-5, 25–39, January 1983.

Derin, H., and Elliott, H., "Modeling and Segmentation of Noisy and Textured Images Using Gibbs Random Fields," *IEEE Trans. on Pattern Anal. Machine Intell.*, vol. PAMI-9, 39–55, January 1987.

Geman, S., and Geman, D., "Stochastic Relaxation, Gibbs Distributions, and Bayesian Restoration of Images," *IEEE Trans. on Pattern Anal. Machine Intell.*, vol. PAMI-6, 721–741, November 1984.

Geman, S., and Graffigne, C., "Markov Random Fields Image Models and Their Application to Computer Vision," *Proceedings of the International Congress of Mathematicians 1986*, A. M. Gleason (ed.), American Mathematical Society, Providence, 1987.

Gidas, B., "Non-Stationary Markov Chains and Convergence of the Annealing Algorithm," *Journal of Statistical Physics*, vol. 39, 73–131, 1985.

Grenander, U., *Lectures in Pattern Theory*, vols. I-III, Springer-Verlag, New York, 1981.

Hopfield, J. J., and Tank, D. W., "Neural Computation of Decisions in Optimization Problems," *Biological Cybernetics*, vol. 52, 114–152, 1985.

Koch, C., Luo, J., Mead, C., and Hutchinson, J., "Computation Motion Using Resistive Networks," *Proceedings of Neural Information Processing Systems*, D. Z. Anderson (ed.), Denver, 1987.

Lakshmivarahan, S., *Learning Algorithms Theory and Applications*, Springer-Verlag, New York, 1981.

Marroquin, J. L., *Probabilistic Solution of Inverse Problems*, Ph.D. thesis, M.I.T, Artificial Intelligence Laboratory, Cambridge, September 1985.

Marroquin, J., Mitter, S., and Poggio, T., "Probabilistic Solution of Ill-Posed Problems in Computer Vision," *Proceedings of the Image Understanding Workshop*, Miami Beach, 293–309, December 1985.

Narendra, K. S., and Thathachar, M. A. L., "Learning Automata—A Survey," *IEEE Trans. Syst., Man and Cybern.*, 323–334, July 1974.

Narendra, K. S., and Thathachar, M. A. L., *Learning Automata*, Prentice-Hall, New York, 1989.

Poggio, T., Torre, V., and Koch, C., "Computational Vision and Regularization Theory," *Nature*, vol. 317, 314–319, September 1985.

Thathachar, M. A. L., and Sastry, P. S., "Relaxation Labelling with Learning Automata," *IEEE Trans. Pattern Anal. Machine Intell.*, vol. PAMI-8, 256–268, March 1986.

Wheeler, R. M., Jr., and Narendra, K. S., "Decentralized Learning in Finite Markov Chains," *IEEE Trans. Automatic Control*, vol. AC-31, 519–526, June 1986.

Zhou, Y. T., and Chellappa, R., "Computation of Optical Flow Using a Neural Network," *Proceedings of the IEEE International Conference on Neural Networks*, vol. 2, San Diego, 71–78, July 1988.

Zhou, Y. T., and Chellappa, R., "Stereo Matching Using a Neural Network," *Proceedings of the IEEE International Conference on Acoustics, Speech and Signal Processing*, New York, 940–943, April 1988.

Zhou, Y. T., Chellappa, R., Vaid, A., and Jenkins, B. K., "Image Restoration Using a Neural Network," *IEEE Trans. Acoust., Speech and Signal Processing*, vol. ASSP-36, 1141–1151, July 1988.

PROBLEMS

2.1. (*Causal MRF*) Here we explore some properties of causal MRF.

(a) Consider the MRF $\{Y_s, s \in \Omega\}$, where Ω is a rectangular array of dimension $M \times M$. Let $s = (i, j)$, i being the row index and j the column index. Let $N_s = \{r: r = s + \tau, \tau \in N\}$, $N = \{\tau_1, \tau_2, \tau_3\} = \{(0, -1), (-1, 0), (-1, -1)\}$. Show that the joint probability $P(\mathbf{Y}) = \prod_s P(Y_s \mid Y_{s-\tau_1} Y_{s-\tau_2} Y_{s-\tau_3})$. Extend this to the case when $N_s = \{r = (p, q) : 1 \le p \le i$ and $1 \le q \le j\}$. This model is often called the Markov mesh random field. (*Hint:* Use induction.)

(b) Now consider a more general neighborhood set of site $s = (i, j)$, $N_s = \{r = (p, q), p < i$ or $p = i, q \le j\}$. In this case also we can write an expression for the joint distribution in terms of the conditional distributions. Show that the joint probability over the lattice $P(\mathbf{Y}) = \prod_s P(Y_s \mid Y_r, r \in N_s)$.

2.2. (*LS estimator*) An estimate $\hat{\Theta}$ of Θ is said to be asymptotically weakly consistent if it converges in mean square to the true value Θ. Show that the LS estimate of Θ as we have defined it is consistent. (*Hint:* Note that $Y_s = \sum_\tau \theta_\tau (Y_{s+\tau} + Y_{s-\tau}) + e_s$, where $\{e_s\}$ is stationary zero mean Gaussian process.)

2.3. (*Hopfield network*) Show that the neural network with the energy function $E = -\sum_{i,j,k,l} T_{ij:kl} V_{ij} V_{kl} - \sum_{i,j} I_{ij} V_{ij}$ and updating rule $V_{ij} = 1$ if $V_{ij} = \max_k V_{ik}$, with symmetric interconnections and $T_{ii:ii} = 0$, always converges. Can you relax the condition on $T_{ii:ii}$?

2.4. Consider an alternate NN implementation. The transfer function of the individual neurons is assumed to be monotonic and is the same for all the neurons. Also, the fact that each pixel can have only one label is expressed in terms of a cost function. Modify the NN discussed earlier to include these. What is the new energy function? Does this new network always converge? What are the new connection weights and the input bias currents?

2.5. (*Learning automata*) Here we consider some properties of the L_{R-I} learning rule. Let the automaton A have N actions and at instant t let its choice be treated as a success or failure depending on the response from the teacher. The teacher indicates this by setting λ to either 1 (success) or 0 (failure). Let the action probability vector be $\mathbf{p}(t) = [p_1(t), \ldots, p_N(t)]^T$. The automaton uses the following learning rule with $0 < a < 1$:

$$p_i(t+1) = p_i(t) + a\,\lambda(t)\,[1 - p_i(t)]$$
$$p_j(t+1) = p_j(t)[1 - a\,\lambda(t)], \forall\, j \neq i$$

where action α_i was chosen at time t. Let $d_i = \text{prob}(\lambda = 1 \mid \alpha_i)$. Assume that $d_l = \max d_j$ and $d_m = \min d_j$ are unique. Define the expected value of success at time t as $M(t) = \sum_j p_j(t)d_j$.

(a) A learning algorithm is said to be absolutely expedient if $E(M(t+1) \mid \mathbf{p}(t)) \geq M(t)$, with the equality only when one of the action probabilities is 1 and all others 0. Show that the above L_{R-I} algorithm is absolutely expedient.

(b) Show that this algorithm is also ϵ-optimal. Can you conclude that absolute expediency implies ϵ-optimality ?

(c) Extend the above results to the L_{R-I} rule where $\lambda(t)$ is a continuous variable, and conclude that in general these algorithms are ϵ-optimal in all stationary environments.

IMAGE RESTORATION WITH NEURAL NETWORKS

Y. T. Zhou and R. Chellappa
Signal and Image Processing Institute
Department of Electrical Engineering–Systems
University of Southern California

INTRODUCTION

Restoration of a high-quality image from a degraded recording is an important problem in early vision processing. Here *image* refers to a two-dimensional light-intensity function $x(a, b)$. Since light intensity is a real positive quantity and the maximum brightness of an image is also restricted by the practical imaging system, $x(a, b)$ is a finite, real, and nonnegative function:

$$0 \leq x(a, b) \leq A$$

where A is the maximum image brightness.

Figure 3.1 shows a **digital image-restoration system** containing three subsystems: an imaging system, image digitizer, and image-restoration system. The **imaging system**, which consists of an optical system and recording devices, is a major source of degradations. To enable processing by a computer, images are sampled and quantized by the **image digitizer**, which also introduces some degradations because of quantization error. The **image restoration system** uses some techniques

FIGURE 3.1   Digital image restoration system.

to remove (1) *deterministic degradations*, such as blur due to optical system aberrations, diffraction, motion, atmospheric turbulence, and film nonlinearities, and (2) *statistical degradations* such as noise due to electronic imaging sensors, film granularity and atmospheric light fluctuations. Hence the digital image-restoration system gives an estimate of the original image in some sense.

Over the last 20 years, various methods such as the inverse filter [Andrews and Hunt, 1977], Wiener filter [Andrews and Hunt, 1977], Kalman filter [Woods and Ingle, 1981], singular value decomposition (SVD) pseudoinverse [Andrews and Hunt, 1977; Pratt, 1978], and many other model-based approaches have been proposed for image restoration. A major drawback of most image-restoration algorithms is their computational complexity, so much so that many simplifying assumptions have been made, such as wide-sense stationarity (WSS) and availability of second-order image statistics, to obtain computationally feasible algorithms. The inverse-filter method works only for extremely high signal-to-noise-ratio images. The Wiener filter is usually implemented only after the WSS assumption has been made for images. Furthermore, knowledge of the power spectrum or correlation matrix of the undegraded image is required. Often additional assumptions regarding boundary conditions are made so that fast orthogonal transforms can be used. The Kalman-filter approach can be applied to a nonstationary image but is computationally very intensive. Similar statements can be made for the SVD pseudoinverse-filter method. Approaches based on noncausal models such as the noncausal autoregressive or Gaussian-Markov random-field models [Chellappa and Kashyap, 1982; Jinchi and Chellappa, 1986] also make assumptions such as WSS and periodic boundary conditions. It is desirable to develop a restoration algorithm that does not make WSS assumptions and can be implemented in a reasonable time. An artificial neural network system that can perform extremely rapid computations seems to be very attractive for image restoration in particular and for image processing and computer vision in general [Zhou, 1988; Zhou et al., 1988; Zhou and Chellappa, 1988a; Zhou and Chellappa, 1988b; Zhou and Chellappa, 1989].

In this chapter we present a neural-network algorithm for restoration of gray-level images degraded by a known space-invariant blur function and noise. It is based on the model described in [Hopfield and Tank, 1985; Hopfield, 1982; Amari, 1972] using a simple-sum number representation [Takeda and Goodman, 1986]. The image gray levels are represented by the simple sum of the neuron state variables, which take binary values of 1 or 0. The observed image is degraded by a space-invariant function and noise.

The restoration procedure consists of two stages: (1) estimation of the parameters of the neural-network model and (2) reconstruction of images. First, the parameters are estimated by comparing the energy function of the neural network with the constrained error function. Then the nonlinear restoration algorithm is implemented, using a dynamic iterative algorithm to minimize the energy function of the neural network. Owing to the model's fault-tolerant nature and computation capability, a high-quality image is obtained using this approach.

In order to reduce computational complexity a practical algorithm, which has equivalent results to the original one suggested above, is developed under the assumption that the neurons are sequentially visited. We illustrate the usefulness of this approach by using both synthetic and real images degraded by a known space-invariant blur function with or without noise. We also discuss the problem of choosing boundary values and introduce two methods to reduce the ringing effect. Comparisons with other restoration methods such as the SVD pseudoinverse filter, the minimum-mean-square-error (MMSE) filter, and the modified MMSE filter using the Gaussian Markov random-field model are given using real images. The advantages of the method presented in this chapter are that (1) WSS assumption is not required for the images, (2) the method can be implemented rapidly, and (3) it is fault tolerant.

The foregoing discussion assumes that the interconnection strengths of the neural network are known from the parameters of the image-degradation model and the smoothing constraints. The problem of learning the parameters for the image-degradation model from samples of original and degraded images is discussed in [Zhou et al., 1988].

The organization of the remainder of the chapter is as follows: First, a discrete linear, space-invariant image degradation model is given. Then a network model containing redundant neurons for image representation is described. A technique for parameter estimation is presented. Image generation using a dynamic algorithm is described. A practical algorithm with reduced computational complexity is developed. Computer-simulation results using synthetic and real degraded images are given. Choice of the boundary values is discussed. Comparisons to other methods are given. Conclusions and remarks are presented.

AN IMAGE-DEGRADATION MODEL

The effectiveness of restoration techniques mainly depends on the accuracy of the image modeling. Many image-degradation models have been developed based on different assumptions. Figure 3.2 shows a typical linear continuous image-degradation model. It is assumed that the image blur can be modeled as a super-position with an impulse response $h(\cdot)$ that may be space variant and its output is subject to an additive noise. In this case, the observed image is modeled by

$$y(a, b) = \int_{-\infty}^{\infty} \int_{-\infty}^{\infty} h(a, b; \alpha, \beta)x(\alpha, \beta)\, d\alpha\, d\beta + n(a, b) \qquad (3\text{-}1)$$

where $h(a, b; \alpha, \beta)$ is a blur (or impulse-response) function, $n(a, b)$ represents an additive noise, $x(\alpha, \beta)$ and $y(a, b)$ denote the original and degraded (or observed)

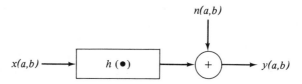

FIGURE 3.2 A typical linear continuous image degradation model.

images, respectively. If the system is space invariant, the blur function can be written as

$$h(a, b; \alpha, \beta) \quad = \quad h(a - \alpha, b - \beta)$$

As many types of degradations can be approximated by a space-invariant process, our attention will be focus on the linear space-invariant model. To measure image quality, the signal-to-noise ratio (SNR) defined in decibels (dB) is commonly used. The SNR is defined as

$$\text{SNR} \quad = \quad 10 \, \log_{10} \frac{\sigma_x^2}{\sigma_n^2} \tag{3-2}$$

where σ_x^2 and σ_n^2 are variances of original image and noise, respectively.

As shown in Figure 3.1, an image digitizer follows the imaging system. The output of the imaging system, i.e., the observed image, is first digitized both spatially and in the amplitude and then fed to the restoration system. For a discrete image-restoration system the object of the restoration is to produce a digital image (i.e., a two-dimensional array of samples) that is an estimate of the perfectly digitized original image. Hence, it is necessary to convert the continuous degradation model (3-1) into a discrete one. This can be accomplished by truncating and uniformly sampling the image and blur function to form two-dimensional arrays, provided that the sample rate satisfies the Nyquist rate and that truncation error is negligibly small. The image is commonly clipped to the intensity range 0 to M, where M is an integer, say $M = 255$.

When a space-invariant blur function $h(\cdot)$ can be written as a convolution over a small window $K \times K$ (K is an odd integer), the continuous model (3-1) can be written in discrete form as

$$
\begin{aligned}
y(i,j) \quad &= \quad x(i,j) * h(i,j) + n(i,j) \\
&= \quad \sum_{k=-\kappa}^{\kappa} \sum_{l=-\kappa}^{\kappa} x(i-k, j-l)h(k,l) + n(i,j)
\end{aligned}
\tag{3-3}
$$

where indices i and j take integer number, $*$ denotes the convolution operator, and $\kappa = (K - 1)/2$. It is often convenient to express the discrete degradation model (3-3) in terms of vector-matrix form [Wintz, 1977] as

$$\mathbf{Y} \quad = \quad H\mathbf{X} + \mathbf{N} \tag{3-4}$$

where H is the "blurring matrix" corresponding to a blur function, $\mathbf{N}$ is the signal-independent white noise, and $\mathbf{X}$ and $\mathbf{Y}$ are the original and degraded images, respectively. This is obtained by row scanning of the arrays. Furthermore, assuming that the dimension of the image array is $L \times L$, H and $\mathbf{N}$ can be represented as

$$H = \begin{bmatrix} h_{1,1} & h_{1,2} & \cdots & h_{1,L^2} \\ h_{2,1} & h_{2,2} & \cdots & h_{2,L^2} \\ \cdot & \cdot & & \cdot \\ \cdot & \cdot & & \cdot \\ \cdot & \cdot & & \cdot \\ h_{L^2,1} & h_{L^2,2} & \cdots & h_{L^2,L^2} \end{bmatrix} \tag{3-5}$$

and

$$\mathbf{N} = \begin{bmatrix} \mathbf{N}_1 \\ \mathbf{N}_2 \\ \cdot \\ \cdot \\ \cdot \\ \mathbf{N}_L \end{bmatrix} = \begin{bmatrix} n_1 \\ n_2 \\ \cdot \\ \cdot \\ \cdot \\ n_{L^2} \end{bmatrix}$$

$$\mathbf{N}_i = \begin{bmatrix} n(i,1) \\ n(i,2) \\ \cdot \\ \cdot \\ n(i,L) \end{bmatrix} = \begin{bmatrix} n_{(i-1)\times(L+1)} \\ n_{(i-1)\times(L+2)} \\ \cdot \\ \cdot \\ n_{i\times L} \end{bmatrix} \tag{3-6}$$

respectively. Vectors $\mathbf{X}$ and $\mathbf{Y}$ have representations similar to that of $\mathbf{N}$. Note that this expression is derived under the assumption of a linear, space-variant degradation model. Equation (3-4) is similar to the simultaneous-equations solution of [Takeda and Goodman, 1986], but differs in that it includes a noise term.

For instance, if the blur function takes the form

$$h(k, l) = \begin{cases} \frac{1}{2} & \text{if } k = 0, \, l = 0 \\ \frac{1}{16} & \text{if } |k|, \, |l| \leq 1, \, (k,l) \neq (0,0) \end{cases} \tag{3-7}$$

then the "blur matrix" H will be a block circulant or block Toeplitz matrix according to the boundary conditions. The general form of H corresponding to (3-7) is as follows

$$H = \begin{bmatrix} H_0 & H_1 & \mathbf{0} & \cdots & \mathbf{0} & H_c \\ H_1 & H_0 & H_1 & \cdots & \mathbf{0} & \mathbf{0} \\ \cdot & \cdot & \cdot & & \cdot & \cdot \\ \cdot & \cdot & \cdot & & \cdot & \cdot \\ \cdot & \cdot & \cdot & & \cdot & \cdot \\ H_c & \mathbf{0} & \mathbf{0} & \cdots & H_1 & H_0 \end{bmatrix} \tag{3-8}$$

where

$$H_0 = \begin{bmatrix} \tfrac{1}{2} & \tfrac{1}{16} & 0 & \cdots & 0 & h_c \\ \tfrac{1}{16} & \tfrac{1}{2} & \tfrac{1}{16} & \cdots & 0 & 0 \\ \cdot & & \cdot & & \cdot & \cdot \\ \cdot & & \cdot & & \cdot & \cdot \\ \cdot & & \cdot & & \cdot & \cdot \\ h_c & 0 & 0 & \cdots & \tfrac{1}{16} & \tfrac{1}{2} \end{bmatrix}$$

$$H_1 = \begin{bmatrix} \tfrac{1}{16} & \tfrac{1}{16} & 0 & \cdots & 0 & h_c \\ \tfrac{1}{16} & \tfrac{1}{16} & \tfrac{1}{16} & \cdots & 0 & 0 \\ \cdot & & \cdot & & \cdot & \cdot \\ \cdot & & \cdot & & \cdot & \cdot \\ \cdot & & \cdot & & \cdot & \cdot \\ h_c & 0 & 0 & \cdots & \tfrac{1}{16} & \tfrac{1}{16} \end{bmatrix} \tag{3-9}$$

and $\mathbf{0}$ is null matrix whose elements are all zeros. If the image has periodic boundaries, H becomes a block circulant matrix, i.e., $h_c = \tfrac{1}{16}$ and $H_c = H_1$. If the image boundaries are padded by zeros, H is then a block Toeplitz matrix with $h_c = 0$ and $H_c = \mathbf{0}$.

IMAGE REPRESENTATION

We use a neural network containing redundant neurons for representing the image gray levels. The model consists of $L^2 \times M$ mutually interconnected neurons, where L is the size of image and M is the maximum value of the gray-level function. The image is described by a finite set of gray-level functions $\{x(i,j),$ where $1 \leq i, j \leq L\}$ with $x(i,j)$ (positive integer number) denoting the gray level of the pixel (i,j). Let $V = \{v_{i,k},$ where $1 \leq i \leq L^2, 1 \leq k \leq M\}$ be a binary state set of the neural network with $v_{i,k}$ (1 for firing and 0 for resting) denoting the state of the (i,k)th neuron. The image gray-level function is represented by a simple sum of the neuron state variables as

$$x(i,j) = \sum_{k=1}^{M} v_{m,k} \tag{3-10}$$

where $m = (i-1) \times L + j$. Here the gray-level functions have degenerate representations. For instance, if a gray-level function is represented by M neurons and it takes a value of 10, then any 10 out of M neurons will fire and there are $M!/10!(M-10)!$ representations. This is a one-to-many mapping from an integer number space to a neuron state space. Note that any single misfiring neuron does not cause a large error in the number representation. It is interesting to see that the network using such a representation scheme has

$$\prod_{i=1}^{L} \prod_{i=1}^{L} \frac{M!}{x(i,j)!(M-x(i,j))!}$$

stable states for an $L \times L$ image! So many stable states offer the network more chances to reach a correct solution. Hence, use of this redundant number-representation scheme yields advantages such as fault tolerance and faster convergence to a solution [Takeda and Goodman, 1986].

In this model, each neuron (i,k) randomly and asynchronously receives inputs from all neurons and a bias input

$$u_{i,k} \;=\; \sum_{j}^{L^2} \sum_{l}^{M} T_{i,k;j,l} v_{j,l} + I_{i,k} \tag{3-11}$$

where $T_{i,k;j,l}$ denotes the strength (possibly negative) of the interconnection between neuron (i,k) and neuron (j,l) and $I_{i,k}$ is a bias input. We assume that the interconnection strength has the following properties:

$$T_{i,k;j,l} \;=\; T_{j,l;i,k}$$

and

$$T_{i,k;i,k} \;\neq\; 0$$

which means that the strengths are symmetric and neurons have self-feedback. Each $u_{i,k}$ is fed back to corresponding neurons after thresholding

$$v_{i,k} \;=\; g(u_{i,k}) \tag{3-12}$$

where $g(x)$ is a nonlinear function whose form can be taken as

$$g(x) \;=\; \begin{cases} 1 & \text{if } x \geq 0 \\ 0 & \text{if } x < 0 \end{cases} \tag{3-13}$$

In this model the state of each neuron is updated by using the latest information about other neurons.

ESTIMATION OF MODEL PARAMETERS

The neural model parameters, the interconnection strengths and bias inputs, can be determined in terms of the energy function of the neural network. As defined in [Hopfield and Tank, 1985], the energy function of the neural network can be written as

$$E \;=\; -\frac{1}{2} \sum_{i=1}^{L^2} \sum_{j=1}^{L^2} \sum_{k=1}^{M} \sum_{l=1}^{M} T_{i,k;j,l}\, v_{i,k}\, v_{j,l} - \sum_{i=1}^{L^2} \sum_{k=1}^{M} I_{i,k}\, v_{i,k} \tag{3-14}$$

In order to use the spontaneous energy-minimization process of the neural network, we reformulate the restoration problem as one of minimizing an error function with constraints defined as

$$E = \frac{1}{2}\|\mathbf{Y} - H\hat{\mathbf{X}}\|^2 + \frac{1}{2}\lambda\|D\hat{\mathbf{X}}\|^2 \tag{3-15}$$

where $\|\mathbf{Z}\|$ is the L_2 norm of $\mathbf{Z}$ and λ is a constant. An error function thus constrained is widely used in image-restoration problems [Andrews and Hunt, 1977] and is akin to the regularization techniques used in early vision problems [Poggio et al., 1985]. The first term in (3-15) is to seek an $\hat{\mathbf{X}}$ such that $H\hat{\mathbf{X}}$ approximates $\mathbf{Y}$ in a least-squares sense. Meanwhile, the second term is a smoothness constraint on the solution $\hat{\mathbf{X}}$. The constant λ determines their relative importance to achieve both noise suppression and ringing reduction.

In general, if H is a low-pass distortion, then D is a high-pass filter. A common choice of D is a second-order differential operator which can be approximated as a local window operator in the 2-D discrete case. For instance, if D is a Laplacian operator

$$\nabla = \frac{\partial^2}{\partial i^2} + \frac{\partial^2}{\partial j^2} \tag{3-16}$$

it can be approximated as a window operator

$$\frac{1}{6}\begin{bmatrix} 1 & 4 & 1 \\ 4 & -20 & 4 \\ 1 & 4 & 1 \end{bmatrix} \tag{3-17}$$

i.e.,

$$d(k,l) = \begin{cases} -\frac{10}{3} & \text{if } (k,l) = (0,0) \\ \frac{2}{3} & \text{if } (k,l) \in \{(-1,0),(0,-1),(0,1),(1,0)\} \\ \frac{1}{3} & \text{if } (k,l) \in \{(-1,-1),(-1,1),(1,-1),(1,1)\} \end{cases} \tag{3-18}$$

Then D will be a block matrix similar to (3-8).

Expanding (3-15) and then replacing x_i by (3-10), we have

$$E = \frac{1}{2}\sum_{p=1}^{L^2}(y_p - \sum_{i=1}^{L^2}h_{p,i}x_i)^2 + \frac{1}{2}\lambda\sum_{p=1}^{L^2}(\sum_{i=1}^{L^2}d_{p,i}x_i)^2$$

$$= \frac{1}{2}\sum_{i=1}^{L^2}\sum_{j=1}^{L^2}\sum_{k=1}^{M}\sum_{l=1}^{M}\sum_{p=1}^{L^2}h_{p,i}\,h_{p,j}\,v_{i,k}\,v_{j,l}$$

$$+ \frac{1}{2}\lambda\sum_{i=1}^{L^2}\sum_{j=1}^{L^2}\sum_{k=1}^{M}\sum_{l=1}^{M}\sum_{p=1}^{L^2}d_{p,i}\,d_{p,j}\,v_{i,k}\,v_{j,l}$$

$$- \sum_{i=1}^{L^2}\sum_{k=1}^{M}\sum_{p=1}^{L^2}y_p\,h_{p,i}\,v_{i,k} + \frac{1}{2}\sum_{p=1}^{L^2}y_p^2 \tag{3-19}$$

By comparing the terms in (3-19) with the corresponding terms in (3-14) and ignoring the constant term

$$\frac{1}{2} \sum_{p=1}^{L^2} y_p^2$$

we can determine the interconnection strengths and bias inputs as

$$T_{i,k;j,l} \quad = \quad -\sum_{p=1}^{L^2} h_{p,i}\, h_{p,j} - \lambda \sum_{p=1}^{L^2} d_{p,i}\, d_{p,j} \qquad (3\text{-}20)$$

and

$$I_{i,k} \quad = \quad \sum_{p=1}^{L^2} y_p\, h_{p,i} \qquad (3\text{-}21)$$

where $h_{i,j}$ and $d_{i,j}$ are the elements of the matrices H and D, respectively. Two interesting aspects of (3-20) and (3-21) should be pointed out: (1) the interconnection strengths are independent of subscripts k and l and the bias inputs are independent of subscript k, and (2) the self-connection $T_{i,k;i,k}$ is not equal to zero, which requires self-feedback for neurons.

From (3-20), one can see that the interconnection strengths are determined by the space-invariant blur function, differential operator, and constant λ. Hence, $T_{i,k;j,l}$ can be computed without error, provided the blur function is known. However, the bias inputs are functions of the observed degraded image. If the image is degraded by a space-invariant blur function only, then $I_{i,k}$ can be estimated perfectly. Otherwise, $I_{i,k}$ is affected by noise. The reasoning behind this statement is as follows. By replacing y_p by

$$\sum_{i=1}^{L^2} h_{p,i}\, x_i + n_p$$

we have

$$I_{i,k} \quad = \quad \sum_{p=1}^{L^2} (\sum_{i=1}^{L^2} h_{p,i}\, x_i + n_p)\, h_{p,i}$$

$$= \quad \sum_{p=1}^{L^2} \sum_{i=1}^{L^2} h_{p,i}\, x_i\, h_p + \sum_{p=1}^{L^2} n_p\, h_{p,i} \qquad (3\text{-}22)$$

The second term in (3-22) represents the effects of noise. If the SNR is low, then we have to choose a large λ to suppress effects due to noise. It seems that in the absence of noise, the parameters can be estimated perfectly, ensuring exact recovery of the image as error function E tends to zero. However, the problem is not so simple, as the performance of the restoration depends on both the parameters and blur function when a mean-square error or least-square error such as (3-15) is used. The effect of blur function is discussed in the concluding section of this chapter.

RESTORATION

Restoration is carried out by neuron evaluation and an image-construction procedure. Once the parameters $T_{i,k;j,l}$ and $I_{i,k}$ are obtained using (3-20) and (3-21), each neuron can randomly and asynchronously evaluate its state and readjust accordingly using (3-11) and (3-12). When one quasi-minimum energy point is reached, the image can be constructed using (3-10).

However, this neural network has self-feedback, i.e., $T_{i,k;i,k} \neq 0$. As a result the energy function E does not always decrease monotonically with a transition. This is explained below. Define the state change $\Delta v_{i,k}$ of neuron (i,k) and energy change ΔE as

$$\Delta v_{i,k} = v_{i,k}^{\text{new}} - v_{i,k}^{\text{old}} \qquad \text{and} \qquad \Delta E = E^{\text{new}} - E^{\text{old}}$$

Consider the energy function

$$E = -\frac{1}{2} \sum_{i=1}^{L^2} \sum_{j=1}^{L^2} \sum_{k=1}^{M} \sum_{l=1}^{M} T_{i,k;j,l}\, v_{i,k}\, v_{j,l} - \sum_{i=1}^{L^2} \sum_{k=1}^{M} I_{i,k}\, v_{i,k}, \qquad (3\text{-}23)$$

Then the change ΔE due to a change $\Delta v_{i,k}$ is given by

$$\Delta E = -\left(\sum_{j=1}^{L^2} \sum_{l=1}^{M} T_{i,k;j,l}\, v_{j,l} + I_{i,k} \right) \Delta v_{i,k} - \frac{1}{2} T_{i,k;i,k} (\Delta v_{i,k})^2 \qquad (3\text{-}24)$$

which is not always negative. For instance, if

$$v_{i,k}^{\text{old}} = 0, \qquad u_{i,k} = \sum_{j=1}^{L^2} \sum_{l=1}^{M} T_{i,k;j,l}\, v_{j,l} + I_{i,k} > 0$$

and the threshold function is as in (3-13), then $v_{i,k}^{\text{new}} = 1$ and $\Delta v_{i,k} > 0$. Thus, the first term in (3-24) is negative. But

$$T_{i,k;i,k} = -\sum_{p=1}^{L^2} h_{p,i}^2 - \lambda \sum_{p=1}^{L^2} d_{p,i}^2 < 0$$

with $\lambda > 0$ leading to

$$-\frac{1}{2} T_{i,k;i,k} (\Delta v_{i,k})^2 > 0$$

When the first term is less than the second term in (3-24), then $\Delta E > 0$ (we have observed this in our experiments), which means E is not a Lyapunov function. Consequently, the convergence of the network is not guaranteed [LaSalle, 1986].

Thus, depending on whether convergence to a local minimum or a global minimum is desired, we can design a deterministic or stochastic decision rule. The deterministic rule is to take a new state $v_{i,k}^{\text{new}}$ of neuron (i,k) if the energy change ΔE due to state change $\Delta v_{i,k}$ is less than zero. If ΔE due to state change is greater than 0, no state change is affected. One can also design a stochastic rule similar to the one used in simulated annealing techniques [Metropolis et al., 1953; Kirkpatrick et al., 1983]. The details of this stochastic scheme are given as follows:

Define an acceptance probability by

$$\mathbf{P}_T\{\text{accept}(v_{1,1}, ..., v_{i,k}^{\text{new}}, ..., v_{L^2,M})\} = \begin{cases} 1 & \text{if } \Delta E < 0 \\ e^{-\Delta E/T} & \text{if } \Delta E \geq 0 \end{cases} \quad (3\text{-}25)$$

where ΔE is the energy change and T is the parameter that acts like temperature. A new state $v_{i,k}^{\text{new}}$ is taken if

$$\mathbf{P}_T\{\text{accept}(v_{1,1}, ..., v_{i,k}^{\text{new}}, ..., v_{L^2,M})\} = 1$$

or

$$\xi \leq \mathbf{P}_T\{\text{accept}(v_{1,1}, ..., v_{i,k}^{\text{new}}, ..., v_{L^2,M}\} < 1$$

where ξ is a random number uniformly distributed in the interval [0,1]. The speed of convergence of the algorithm depends on the choice of the temperature T and the number of transitions generated at each temperature T.

The restoration algorithm is summarized as below.

Algorithm 3.1

1. Set the initial state of the neurons.

2. Update the state of all neurons randomly and asynchronously according to the decision rule.

3. Check the energy function; if energy does not change, go to step 4; otherwise, go back to step 2.

4. Construct an image using (3-10).

A PRACTICAL ALGORITHM

The algorithm described above is difficult to simulate on a conventional computer, owing to high computational complexity even for images of reasonable size. For instance, if we have an $L \times L$ image with M gray levels, then $L^2 M$ neurons and $\frac{1}{2}L^4 M^2$ interconnections are required and $L^4 M^2$ additions and multiplications are needed at each iteration. Therefore, the space and time complexities are $O(L^4 M^2)$ and $O(L^4 M^2 K)$, respectively, where K, typically 10–100, is the number of iterations. Usually, L and M are 256–1024 and 256, respectively. However, simplification is possible if the neurons are sequentially updated.

In order to simplify the algorithm, we begin by reconsidering (3-11) and (3-12) of the neural network. As noted earlier, the interconnection strengths given in (3-20) are independent of subscripts k and l and the bias inputs given in (3-21) are independent of subscript k; the M neurons used to represent the same image gray-level function have the same interconnection strengths and bias inputs. Hence, one set of interconnection strengths and one bias input are sufficient for every gray-level function; i.e., the dimensions of the interconnection matrix T and bias input matrix I can be reduced by a factor of M^2. From (3-11) all inputs received by a neuron, say, the (i,k)th neuron, can be written as

$$
\begin{aligned}
u_{i,k} &= \sum_j^{L^2} T_{i,\cdot;j,\cdot} \left(\sum_l^M v_{j,l} \right) + I_{i,\cdot} \\
&= \sum_j^{L^2} T_{i,\cdot;j,\cdot} \, x_j + I_{i,\cdot} \quad\quad\quad (3\text{-}26)
\end{aligned}
$$

where we have used (3-10) and x_j is the gray-level function of the jth image pixel. The symbol "$\cdot$" in the subscripts means that the $T_{i,\cdot;j,\cdot}$ and $I_{i,\cdot}$ are independent of k. Equation (3-26) suggests that we can use a multivalue number to replace the simple-sum number. Since the interconnection strengths are determined by the blur function, the differential operator, and the constant λ as shown in (3-20), it is easy to see that if the blur function is local, then most interconnection strengths are zeros and the neurons are locally connected. Therefore, most elements of the interconnection matrix T are zeros. If the blur function is space-invariant, taking the form in (3-7), and the image boundaries are padded by zeros, then the interconnection matrix is block Toeplitz, so that only a few elements need to be stored. Based on the value of inputs $u_{i,k}$, the state of the (i,k)th neuron is updated by applying a decision rule. The state change of the (i,k)th neuron in turn causes the gray-level function x_i to change

$$
x_i^{\text{new}} = \begin{cases} x_i^{\text{old}} & \text{if } \Delta v_{i,k} = 0 \\ x_i^{\text{old}} + 1 & \text{if } \Delta v_{i,k} = 1 \\ x_i^{\text{old}} - 1 & \text{if } \Delta v_{i,k} = -1 \end{cases} \quad\quad (3\text{-}27)
$$

where $\Delta v_{i,k} = v_{i,k}^{\text{new}} - v_{i,k}^{\text{old}}$ is the state change of the (i,k)th neuron. The superscripts "new" and "old" are for after and before updating, respectively. We use x_i to represent the gray-level value as well as the output of M neurons representing x_i. Assuming that the neurons of the network are sequentially visited, it is straightforward to show that the updating procedure can be reformulated as

$$
u_{i,k} = \sum_j^{L^2} T_{i,\cdot;j,\cdot} \, x_j + I_{i,\cdot} \quad\quad\quad (3\text{-}28)
$$

$$
\Delta v_{i,k} = g(u_{i,k}) = \begin{cases} \Delta v_{i,k} = 0 & \text{if } u_{i,k} = 0 \\ \Delta v_{i,k} = 1 & \text{if } u_{i,k} > 0 \\ \Delta v_{i,k} = -1 & \text{if } u_{i,k} < 0 \end{cases} \quad\quad (3\text{-}29)
$$

$$x_i^{\text{new}} = \begin{cases} x_i^{\text{old}} + \Delta v_{i,k} & \text{if } \Delta E < 0 \\ x_i^{\text{old}} & \text{if } \Delta E \geq 0 \end{cases} \tag{3-30}$$

Note that the stochastic decision rule can also be used in (3-30). In order to limit the gray-level function to the range 0–255 after each updating step, we have to check the value of the gray-level function x_i^{new}. Equations (3-28), (3-29) and (3-30) give a much simpler algorithm. This algorithm is summarized below.

Algorithm 3.2

1. Take the degraded image as the initial value.

2. Sequentially visit all numbers (image pixels). For each number, use (3-28), (3-29) and (3-30) to update it repeatedly until no further change occurs; i.e., if $\Delta v_{i,k} = 0$ or $\Delta E \geq 0$, then move to next one.

3. Check the energy function. If energy does not change any more, a restored image is obtained; otherwise, go back to step 2 for another iteration.

The calculations of the inputs $u_{i,k}$ of the (i, k)th neuron and the energy change ΔE can be simplified. When we update the same image gray-level function repeatedly, the input received by the current neuron (i, k) can be computed by making use of the previous result

$$u_{i,k} = u_{i,k-1} + \Delta v_{i,k-1} \, T_{i,.;i,.} \tag{3-31}$$

where $u_{i,k-1}$ is the inputs received by the $(i, k-1)$th neuron. The energy change ΔE due to the state change of the (i, k)th neuron can be calculated as

$$\Delta E = -u_{i,k} \, \Delta v_{i,k} - \frac{1}{2} T_{i,.;i,.} (\Delta v_{i,k})^2 \tag{3-32}$$

If the blur function is space invariant, all these simplifications reduce the space and time complexities significantly from $O(L^4 M^2)$ and $O(L^4 M^2 K)$ to $O(L^2)$ and $O(M L^2 K)$, respectively. Since every gray-level function needs only a few updating steps after the first iteration, the computation at each iteration is $O(L^2)$. The resulting algorithm can be easily simulated on minicomputers for images as large as 512×512.

COMPUTER SIMULATIONS

The practical algorithm described in the previous section was applied to synthetic and real images on a Sun-3/160 Workstation. In all cases only the deterministic decision rule was used. The results are summarized in Figures 3.3 and 3.4.

Figure 3.3 shows the results for a synthetic image. The original image, shown in Figure 3.3(a), is of size 32×32 with three gray levels. The image was degraded by convolving with a 3×3 blur function as in (3-7) using circulant boundary

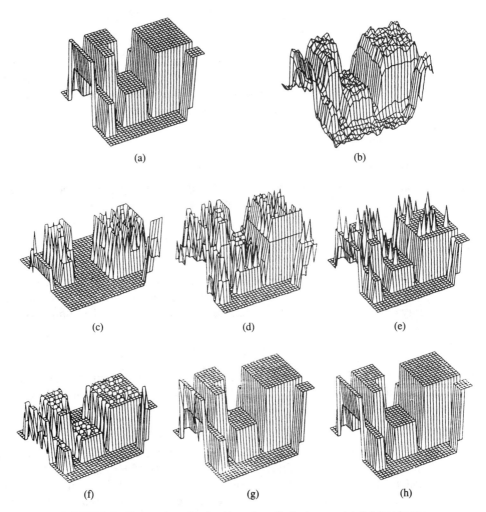

FIGURE 3.3 Restoration of noisy blurred synthetic image. (a) Original image. (b) Degraded image. (c) The first iteration. (d) The second iteration. (e) The third iteration. (f) The fourth iteration. (g) The fifth iteration. (h) The sixth iteration.

conditions; 22 dB white Gaussian noise was added after convolution. Figure 3.3(b) shows the degraded image. A perfect image, shown in Figure 3.3(h), was obtained after six iterations without preprocessing. For illustration, the intermediate results are also shown in Figure 3.3(c)–(g). We set the initial state of all neurons to equal 1, i.e., firing, and chose $\lambda = 0$ owing to the well conditioning of the blur function.

Figure 3.4(a) shows the original girl image. The original image is of size 256×256 with 256 gray levels. The variance of the original image is 2797.141. It was degraded by a 5×5 uniform blur function, i.e.,

$$h(k, l) \ = \ \frac{1}{25} \quad \text{for } |k|, \ |l| \leq 2 \tag{3-33}$$

A small amount of quantization noise was introduced by quantizing the convolution results to 8 bits. The noisy blurred image is shown in Figure 3.4(b). For comparison purposes, Figure 3.4(c) shows the output of an inverse filter [Pratt et al., 1978], completely overridden by the amplified noise and the ringing effects due to the ill-conditioned blur matrix H. Since the blur matrix H corresponding to the 5×5 uniform blur function (3-33) is not singular, the pseudoinverse filter [Pratt et al., 1978] and the inverse filter have the same output. The restored image by using our approach is shown in Figure 3.4(d). In order to avoid the ringing effects, due to the boundary conditions, we took 4-pixel-wide boundaries, i.e., the first and last four rows and columns, from the original image and updated the interior region (248×248) of the image only. The noisy blurred image was used as an initial condition for accelerating the convergence. The constant λ was set to zero because of small noise and good boundary values. The restored image in Figure 3.4(d) was obtained after 213 iterations. The square error (i.e., energy function) defined in (3-15) is 0.02543, and the square error between the original and the restored image is 66.5027.

CHOOSING BOUNDARY VALUES

As mentioned in [Woods et al., 1985], choosing boundary values is a common problem for techniques ranging from deterministic inverse-filter algorithms to stochastic Kalman filters. In these algorithms boundary values determine the entire solution when the blur is uniform [Sondhi, 1972]. The same problem occurs in the neural-network approach. Since the 5×5 uniform blur function is ill conditioned, improper boundary values may cause ringing which may affect the restored image completely. For example, appending zeros to the image as boundary values introduces a sharp edge at the image border and triggers ringing in the restored image even if the image has zero mean. Another procedure is to assume a periodic boundary. When the left (top) and right (bottom) borders of the image are different, a sharp edge is formed and ringing results even though the degraded image has been formed by blurring with periodic boundary conditions. The drawbacks of these two assumptions for boundary values were reported in [Woods et al., 1985; Woods and Ingle, 1981; Biemond et al., 1983] for the 2-D Kalman filtering technique. We also tested our algorithm using these two assumptions for boundary values; the results indicate the restored images were seriously affected by ringing.

In the last section, to avoid the ringing effect we took 4-pixel-wide borders from the original image as boundary values for restoration. Since the original image is not always available in practice, an alternative to eliminate the ringing

(a)

(b)

(c)

(d)

FIGURE 3.4 Restoration of noisy blurred real image. (a) Original girl image. (b) Image degraded by a 5×5 uniform blur and quantization noise. (c) The restored image using inverse filter. (d) The restored image using our approach.

effect caused by sharp false edges is to use the blurred noisy boundaries from the degraded image. Figure 3.5(a) shows the restored image using the first and last four rows and columns of the blurred noisy image in Figure 3.4(b) as boundary values. In the restored image there still exists some ringing due to the naturally occurring sharp edges in the region near the borders in the original image, but not due to boundary values. A typical cut of the restored image to illustrate ringing near the borders is shown in Figure 3.6. To remove the ringing near the borders caused by naturally occurring sharp edges in the original image, we suggest the following techniques.

First, divide the image into three regions: border, subborder, and interior region, as shown in Figure 3.7. For 5×5 uniform blur case, the border region will be 4 pixels wide, owing to the boundary effect of the bias input $I_{i,k}$ in (3-21), and the subborder region will be 4 or 8 pixels wide. In fact, the width of subborder region will be image dependent. If the regions near the border are smooth, then the width of subborder region will be small or even zero. If the border contains many sharp edges, the width will be large. For the real girl image, we chose the width of the subborder region to be 8 pixels.

We suggest using one of the following two methods.

Method 1. In the case of small noise, such as quantization-error noise, the blurred image is usually smooth. Therefore, we restricted the difference between the restored and blurred image in the subborder region to a certain range to reduce the ringing effect. Mathematically, this constraint can be written as

$$\|\hat{x}_i - y_i\| \ \leq \ T \qquad \text{for } i \in \text{subborder region} \qquad (3\text{-}34)$$

where T is a threshold and $\hat{x}_i$ is the restored-image gray value. Figure 3.5(b) shows the result of using this method with $T = 10$.

Method 2. This method simply sets λ in (3-15) to zero in the interior region and nonzero in the subborder region, respectively. Figure 3.5(c) shows the result of using this method with $\lambda = 0.09$. In this case, D was a Laplacian operator.

Owing to checking all restored-image gray values in the subborder region, method 1 needs more computation than method 2. However, method 2 is very sensitive to the parameter λ, while method 1 is not. Experimental results show that both methods 1 and 2 reduce the ringing effect significantly by using the suboptimal blurred boundary values.

COMPARISON OF RESTORATION METHODS

Comparing the performance of different restoration methods needs some quality measures, which are difficult to define owing to the lack of knowledge about the human visual system. The word "optimal" used in the restoration techniques usually refers only to a mathematical concept and is not related to response of the

(a)

(b)

(c)

FIGURE 3.5 Results using blurred noisy boundaries. (a) Blurred noisy boundaries. (b) Method 1. (c) Method 2.

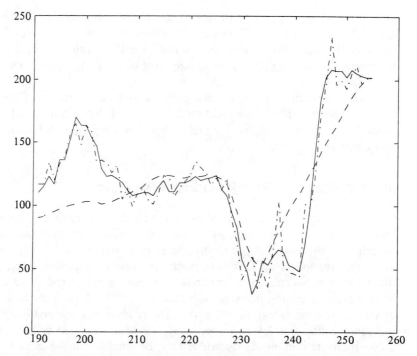

FIGURE 3.6 One typical cut of the restored image using the blurred noisy boundaries. Solid line is for original image, dashed line for blurred noisy image, and dashed and dotted line for restored image.

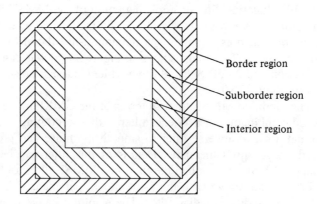

FIGURE 3.7 Border, subborder, and interior regions of the image.

human visual system. For instance, when the blur function is ill conditioned and the SNR is low, the MMSE method improves the SNR, but the resulting image is not visually good. We believe that human objective evaluation is the best ultimate judgment. Meanwhile, the mean-square error or least-square error can be used as a reference.

For comparison purposes, we give the outputs of inverse filter, SVD pseudoinverse filter, MMSE filter, and modified MMSE filter in terms of the Gaussian-Markov random-field (GMRF) model parameters [Chellappa and Jinchi, 1985; Jinchi and Chellappa, 1986].

Inverse Filter and SVD Pseudoinverse Filter

An inverse filter can be used to restore an image degraded by a space-invariant blur function with high signal-to-noise ratio. When the blur function has some singular points, an SVD pseudoinverse filter is needed; however, both filters are very sensitive to noise. This is because the noise is amplified in the same way as the signal components to be restored. The inverse filter and SVD pseudoinverse filter were applied to an image degraded by the 5×5 uniform blur function and quantization noise (about 40 dB SNR). The blurred and restored images are shown in Figure 3.4(b) and 3.4(c), respectively. As we mentioned before, the outputs of these filters are completely overridden by the amplified noise and ringing effects.

MMSE and Modified MMSE Filters

The MMSE filter is also known as the **Wiener filter** (in frequency domain). Under the assumption that the original image obeys a GMRF model, the MMSE filter (or Wiener filter) can be represented in terms of the GMRF model parameters and the blur function. In our implementation of the MMSE filter we used a known blur function, unknown noise variance, and the GMRF model parameters estimated from the blurred noisy image by a maximum-likelihood (ML) method [Chellappa and Jinchi, 1985]. The image shown in Figure 3.8(a) was degraded by 5×5 uniform blur function and 20 dB SNR additive white Gaussian noise. The restored image is shown in Figure 3.8(b).

The modified MMSE filter in terms of the GMRF model parameters is a linear weighted combination of a Wiener filter with a smoothing operator (such as median filter) and a pseudoinverse filter to smooth the noise and preserve the edge of the restored image simultaneously. Details of this filter can be found in [Jinchi and Chellappa, 1986]. We applied the modified MMSE filter to the same image used in the MMSE filter above with the same model parameters. The smoothing operator is a 9×9 cross-shape median filter. The resulting image is shown in Figure 3.8(c).

The result of our method is also shown in Figure 3.8(d). The D we used in (3-15) was a Laplacian operator as in (3-16). We chose $\lambda = 0.0625$ and used 4-pixel-wide blurred noisy boundaries for restoration. The total number of iterations

(a)

(b)

(c)

(d)

FIGURE 3.8 Comparison of restoration methods. (a) Image degraded by 5×5 uniform blur and 20 dB SNR additive white Gaussian noise. (b) The restored image using the MMSE filter. (c) The restored image using the modified MMSE filter. (d) The restored image using our approach.

TABLE 3.1 MEAN-SQUARE ERROR IMPROVEMENT.

Method	MMSE	MMSE(o)	Modified MMSE	Neural network
Mean-square error	1.384 dB	2.139 dB	1.893 dB	1.682 dB

was 20. The improvement of mean-square error between the restored image and the original image for each method is shown in Table 3.1. In the table the "MMSE(o)" denotes that the parameters were estimated from the original image. The restored image using "MMSE(o)" is very similar to Figure 3.8(a). As we mentioned before, the comparison of the outputs of the different restoration methods is a difficult problem. The MMSE filter visually gives the worst output which has the smallest mean-square error for MMSE(o) case. The result of our method is smoother than that of the MMSE filter. Although the output of the modified MMSE filter is smooth in flat regions, it contains some artifacts and snake effects at the edges, owing to the use of a large-sized median filter.

CONCLUSION

This chapter has introduced a new approach for the restoration of gray-level images degraded by a space-invariant blur function and additive noise. The restoration procedure consists of two steps: parameter estimation and image reconstruction. In order to reduce computational complexity, a practical algorithm (Algorithm 3.2), which has equivalent results to the original one (Algorithm 3.1), is developed under the assumption that the neurons are sequentially visited. The image is generated iteratively by updating the neurons representing the image gray levels via a simple-sum scheme. As no matrices are inverted, the serious problems of ringing due to the ill-conditioned blur matrix H and noise overriding caused by inverse filter or pseudoinverse filter are avoided by using suboptimal boundary conditions. For the case of a 2-D uniform blur plus small noise, the neural-network-based approach gives high-quality images compared to some of the existing methods. We see from the experimental results that the error defined by (3-15) is small, while the error between the original image and the restored image is relatively large. This is because the neural network decreases energy according to (3-15) only. Another reason is that when the blur matrix is singular or ill conditioned, the mapping from X to Y is not one-to-one; therefore, the error measure (3-15) is no longer reliable. In our experiments, when the window size of a uniform blur function was 3×3, the ringing effect was eliminated by using blurred noisy boundary values without any smoothing constraint. When the window size was 5×5, ringing effect was reduced with the help of the smoothing constraint and suboptimal boundary conditions.

REFERENCES

Andrews, H. C., and Hunt, B. R., *Digital Image Restoration*, Prentice-Hall, Englewood Cliffs, NJ, 1977.

Amari, S., "Learning Patterns and Pattern Sequences by Self-Organizing Nets of Threshold Elements," *IEEE Trans. on Computers*, vol. C-21, 1197–1206, November 1972.

Biemond, J., Rieske, J., and Gerbrand, J., "A Fast Kalman Filter for Images Degraded by Both Blur and Noise," *IEEE Trans. Accoust., Speech, Signal Processing*, vol. ASSP-31, 1248–1256, October 1983.

Chellappa, R., and Jinchi, H., "A Nonrecursive Filter for Edge Preserving Image Restoration," in *Proc. Intl. Conf. on Acoustics, Speech, and Signal Processing*, 652–655, Tampa, March 1985.

Chellappa, R., and Kashyap, R. L., "Digital Image Restoration Using Spatial Interaction Models," *IEEE Trans. Acoust., Speech, Signal Processing*, vol. ASSP-30, 461–472, June 1982.

Hopfield, J. J., "Neural Networks and Physical Systems with Emergent Collective Computational Abilities," *Proc. Natl. Acad. Sci. USA*, vol. 79, 2554–2558, April 1982.

Hopfield, J. J., and Tank, D. W., "Neural Computation of Decisions in Optimization Problems," *Biological Cybernetics*, vol. 52, 141–152, 1985.

Jinchi, H., and Chellappa, R., "Restoration of Blurred and Noisy Images Using Gaussian Markov Random Field Models," in *Proc. Conf. on Information Science and Systems*, 34–39, Princeton University, NJ, 1986.

Kirkpatrick, S., Gelatt, C. D., and Vecchi, M. P., "Optimization by Stimulated Annealing," *Science*, vol. 220, 671–680, 1983.

LaSalle, J. P., *The Stability and Control of Discrete Processes*, Springer-Verlag, New York, 1986.

Metropolis, N., Rosenbluth, A. W., Rosenbluth, M. N., Teller, A. H., and Teller, E., "Equations of State Calculations by Fast Computing Machines," *J. Chem. Phys.*, vol. 21, 1087–1091, 1953.

Pratt, W. K., Faugeras, O. D., and Gagalowicz, A., "Visual Discrimination of Stochastic Texture Fields," *IEEE Trans. Syst., Man, Cybern.*, vol. SMC-8, 796–814, November 1978.

Pratt, W. K., *Digital Image Processing*, Wiley, New York, 1978.

Poggio, T., Torre, V., and Koch, C., "Computational Vision and Regularization Theory," *Nature*, vol. 317, 314–319, September 1985.

Sondhi, M. M., "The Removal of Spatially Invariant Degradations," *Proc. of IEEE*, vol. 60, 842–853, July 1972.

Takeda, M., and Goodman, J. W., "Neural Networks for Computation: Number Representations and Programing Complexity," *Applied Optics*, vol. 25, no. 18, 3033–3046, September 1986.

Woods, J. W., Riemond, J., and Tekalp, A. M., "Boundary Value Problem in Image Restoration," in *Proc. Intl. Conf. on Acoustics, Speech, and Signal Processing*, 692–695, Tampa, March 1985.

Woods, J. W., and Ingle, V. K., "Kalman Filtering in Two Dimensions: Further Results," *IEEE Trans. Acoustics, Speech, Signal Processing*, vol. ASSP-29, 188–197, April, 1981.

Wintz, P., *Digital Image Processing*, Addison-Wesley, Reading, MA, 1977.

Zhou, Y. T., and Chellappa, R., "Computation of Optical Flow Using a Neural Network," in *Proc. IEEE Intl. Conf. on Neural Networks*, vol. 2, 71–78, San Diego, July 1988a.

Zhou, Y. T., and Chellappa, R., "Stereo Matching Using a Neural Network," in *Proc. Intl. Conf. on Acoustics, Speech, and Signal Processing*, 940–943, New York, April 1988b.

Zhou, Y. T., and Chellappa, R., "Neural Network Algorithms for Motion Stereo," in *Proc. Intl. Joint Conf. on Neural Networks*, vol. 2, 251–258, Washington, DC, June 1989.

Zhou, Y. T., Chellappa, R., Vaid, A., and Jenkins, B. K., "Image Restoration Using a Neural Network," *IEEE Trans. Acoustics, Speech, Signal Processing*, vol. 36, 1141–1151, July 1988.

Zhou, Y. T., *Artificial Neural Network Algorithms for Some Computer Vision Problems*, Ph.D. thesis, University of Southern California, Los Angeles, November 1988.

PROBLEMS

3.1. Assuming that the image variance is σ_s^2 and the value of the SNR is 10 dB, determine the noise variance.

3.2. An image with gray values ranging from 0.0 to 100.0 is uniformly quantized to 256 levels.

(a) Find the mean and variance of the quantization error. The error is assumed to be uniformly distributed.

(b) Find the SNR. Assume the image variance to be 25.

3.3. Consider a linear, space-invariant system. Assume that $x(i,j)$, which is zero outside $0 \leq i, j \leq 3$, is given by

$$\begin{bmatrix} 2 & 8 & 5 & 1 \\ 3 & 1 & 9 & 4 \\ 6 & 7 & 3 & 2 \\ 8 & 2 & 2 & 6 \end{bmatrix}$$

and $h(i,j)$, which is zero outside $-1 \leq i, j \leq 1$, is given by

$$\begin{bmatrix} 0 & -1 & 0 \\ -1 & 4 & -1 \\ 0 & -1 & 0 \end{bmatrix}$$

Determine the output

$$y(i, j) \;=\; \sum_{m=0}^{2} \sum_{n=0}^{2} h(i - m, j - n) x(m, n) \qquad \text{for } 0 \leq i, j \leq 3$$

using

(a) Periodic boundaries.

(b) Zero padding boundaries.

3.4. To model aberrations in a lens with finite aperture, the Gaussian-shaped blur function is commonly used. This function is defined by

$$h(m, n) \;\; = \;\; \beta e^{-\alpha(m^2 + n^2)}, \qquad -\kappa \leq m, n \leq \kappa$$

where α, β, and κ are constants. If $\alpha = 0.001$ and $\kappa = 2$, find β such that

$$\sum_{m=-\kappa}^{\kappa} \sum_{n=-\kappa}^{\kappa} h(m, n) \;\; = \;\; 1$$

3.5. Assume that the blur function with periodic boundary conditions is a Gaussian-shaped function given in Problem 3.4 with $\alpha = 0.001$ and $\kappa = 1$. For the Laplacian operator given by (3-17), find all nonzero interconnection strengths $T_{i,k;j,l}$ defined in (3-20).

3.6. Find the blur matrix H corresponding to a 5×5 uniform blur function with

  (a) Periodic boundary conditions.

  (b) Zero padding boundary conditions.

  The input and output images are assumed to be of size $L \times L$.

3.7. The two-dimensional discrete Fourier transform (2-D DFT) of $x(m, n)$ is defined as

$$X(k, l) \;\; = \;\; \sum_{m=0}^{N-1} \sum_{n=0}^{N-1} x(m, n) e^{-j2\pi(mk + nl)/N} \qquad \text{for } k, l = 0, \ldots, N-1$$

where $x(m, n)$ is an $N \times N$ area sequence. For simplicity of notation, we use $\mathcal{F}_{2-D}\{x(m,n)\}$ to denote the Fourier transform of $x(m,n)$. Find the 2-D DFT of the following finite-area sequences with support were $N \times N$ array.

  (a) $x(m, n) \;\; = \;\; \delta(m, n)$.

  (b) $x(m, n) \;\; = \;\; \begin{cases} 1, & 0 \leq m, n \leq K \leq N - 1 \\ 0, & \text{otherwise} \end{cases}$

3.8. Assuming that an $L \times L$ image is written in vector form by row scanning, let the Fourier kernel matrix be

$$F \;\; = \;\; W \otimes W$$

where

$$W \;\; = \;\; \begin{bmatrix} 1 & 1 & \ldots & 1 \\ 1 & w & \ldots & w^{L-1} \\ \cdot & \cdot & & \cdot \\ \cdot & \cdot & & \cdot \\ \cdot & \cdot & & \cdot \\ 1 & w^{L-1} & \ldots & w^{(L-1)^2} \end{bmatrix}$$

$w = e^{-j2\pi/L}$, and $\otimes$ is the direct product. Show that the 2-D DFT of the image is given by

$$\mathcal{F}_{2-D}\{\mathbf{X}\} \;\; = \;\; F\mathbf{X}$$

3.9. (*Inverse filtering*) Consider a linear, space-invariant degradation model

$$\mathbf{Y} \;=\; H\mathbf{X}$$

with periodic boundary conditions. Assume that the blur matrix H is nonsingular and the images are of size $L \times L$. Let F be the Fourier kernel matrix, D a diagonal matrix, and $F-1$ and D^{-1} their inverses, respectively. Show that the image can be restored by

$$\mathbf{X} \;=\; F^{-1}D^{-1}F\mathbf{Y}$$

$F^{-1}D^{-1}F$ is called inverse filter, which can also be written as $1/H(k,l)$, where $H(k,l)$ is the 2-D DFT of the blur function $h(m,n)$. (*Hint:* A block circulant matrix can be diagonalized by the 2-D DFT.)

3.10. The Wiener filter is given by

$$\frac{H^{*}(k,\,l)S_{xx}(k,\,l)}{|H(k,\,l)|^{2}S_{xx}(k,\,l) + S_{nn}(k,\,l)}$$

where $H(k,l)$ is the 2-D DFT of the blur function $h(m,n)$, $*$ denotes the conjugate, and $S_{xx}(k,l)$ and $S_{nn}(k,l)$ are the power spectral densities of the original image and noise, respectively. State when the Wiener filter can be identical to the following filters:

(a) The Wiener smoothing filter

$$\frac{S_{xx}(k,\,l)}{S_{xx}(k,\,l) + S_{nn}(k,\,l)}$$

(b) The inverse filter

$$\frac{1}{H(k,\,l)}$$

(c) The pseudoinverse filter

$$\begin{cases} \dfrac{1}{H(k,l)}, & H(k,l) \neq 0 \\ 0, & H(k,l) = 0 \end{cases}$$

3.11. Consider the simple-sum number representation

$$x \;=\; \sum_{i-1}^{M} v_{i}$$

Show that the number of possible representations is $M!/(M-n)!n!$ for a given value $x = n$.

3.12. Let $n_{i,j}$ denote the image gray value at pixel (i,j). Assume that the image is of size $L \times L$ and that M neurons are used for each pixel. Show that the number of possible representations is

$$\prod_{i=1}^{L} \prod_{j=1}^{L} \frac{M!}{(M-n)!n_{i,j}!}$$

3.13. Let $\mathbf{V}$ be a vector of $0-1$ binary variables

$$\mathbf{V} \quad = \quad \left[V_{1,1}, \ldots, V_{1,M}, V_{2,1}, \ldots, V_{2,M}, \ldots, V_{L^2,1}, \ldots, V_{L^2,M} \right]$$

S be a set of all states of $\mathbf{V}$, S_{opt} be a set of the states corresponding to optimal solutions, and E_v be an energy function corresponding to a typical state $\mathbf{V} = v$. Assume that the gray-level function of an $L \times L$ image is represented by a simple sum of binary variables and that the equilibrium distribution of the vector $\mathbf{V}$ is defined as

$$\mathbf{P}_T(\mathbf{V} = v) \quad = \quad \frac{e^{-E_v/T}}{\sum_{u \in S} e^{-E_u/T}}$$

where T is the temperature.

(a) Show that

$$\lim_{T \downarrow 0} \mathbf{P}_T(\mathbf{V} = v) \quad = \quad \frac{1}{N_{\mathrm{opt}} \mathcal{X}_{\mathrm{opt}}(v)}$$

where N is the number of optimal solutions

$$N_{\mathrm{opt}} \quad = \quad \prod_{i=1}^{L} \prod_{j=1}^{L} \frac{M!}{(M - n_{i,j})! n_{i,j}!}$$

and $\mathcal{X}_{\mathrm{opt}}(v)$ is a characteristic function: $\mathcal{X}_{\mathrm{opt}}(v) = 1$ if $v \in S_{\mathrm{opt}}$, and $\mathcal{X}_{\mathrm{opt}}(x) = 0$ otherwise.

(b) Show that

$$\lim_{T \downarrow 0} \mathbf{E}_T\{E\} \quad = \quad E_{v_{\mathrm{opt}}}$$

where $\mathbf{E}$ is an expectation and $E_{v_{\mathrm{opt}}}$ an energy function corresponding to an optimal solution.

3.14. Show that the energy change ΔE due to a state change $\Delta v_{i,k}$ can be written as

$$\Delta E \quad = \quad - \left(\sum_{j=1}^{L^2} \sum_{l=1}^{M} T_{i,k;j,l} v_{j,l}^{\mathrm{old}} + I_{i,k} \right) \Delta v_{i,k} - \frac{1}{2} T_{i,k;i,k} (\Delta v_{i,k})^2$$

3.15. Show that if the neurons are sequentially visited, the updating schemes given in Algorithms 3.1 and 3.2 are equivalent.

IDENTIFICATION OF MOVING-AVERAGE SYSTEMS USING HIGHER-ORDER STATISTICS AND LEARNING

Jerry M. Mendel and Li-Xing Wang
Signal and Image Processing Institute
Department of Electrical Engineering–Systems
University of Southern California

NEURAL NETWORKS AND HIGHER-ORDER STATISTICS

Neural networks and **cumulant-based system identification** (Nikias and Raghuveer, 1987; Mendel, 1988) are two emerging technologies. Neural networks provide the potential for massive parallel computing architectures which have many computational advantages over traditional algorithm-based methods (Lippmann, 1987). Studies of cumulant-based system identification have shown that **cumulants**, i.e., higher-order statistics, are powerful tools for identifying systems that may be nonminimum phase, whose inputs are non-Gaussian, or whose output measurements are corrupted by additive colored noise. In this chapter we shall develop a two-level, three-layer neural network which provides the parameters of a moving-average (MA) dynamical system. These parameters will be obtained by training the neural network using both second- and third-order statistics.

To begin, we provide the reader with background information about higher-order statistics and their applications to moving-average [i.e., finite-impulse response (FIR)] dynamical systems.

CUMULANTS*

Let $\mathbf{v} = \mathrm{col}(v_1, v_2, \ldots, v_k)$ and let $\mathbf{x} = \mathrm{col}(x_0, x_1, \ldots, x_{k-1})$, where $(x_0, x_1, \ldots, x_{k-1})$ denote a collection of random variables. The kth-order **cumulant** of these random variables is defined (Priestley, 1981) as the coefficient of $(v_1 v_2 \cdots v_k)$ in the Taylor series expansion of the cumulant-generating function

$$K(\mathbf{v}) = \ln \mathbf{E}\{\exp(j\mathbf{v}'\mathbf{x})\} \tag{4-1}$$

The kth-order cumulant is therefore defined in terms of its joint moments of orders up to k.

For zero-mean random variables, the second-, third- and fourth-order cumulants are given by

$$\mathrm{cum}(x_0, x_1) = \mathbf{E}\{x_0 x_1\} \tag{4-2}$$

$$\mathrm{cum}(x_0, x_1, x_2) = \mathbf{E}\{x_0 x_1 x_2\} \tag{4-3}$$

$$\mathrm{cum}(x_0, x_1, x_2, x_3) = \mathbf{E}\{x_0 x_1 x_2 x_3\} - \mathbf{E}\{x_0 x_1\}\mathbf{E}\{x_1 x_2\}$$
$$- \mathbf{E}\{x_0 x_2\}\mathbf{E}\{x_3 x_1\} - \mathbf{E}\{x_0 x_3\}\mathbf{E}\{x_1 x_2\} \tag{4-4}$$

Let $\{x(t)\}$ be a zero-mean kth-order **stationary** random process. The kth-order cumulant of this process, denoted $C_{k,x}(\tau_1, \tau_2, \ldots, \tau_{k-1})$, is defined as the joint kth-order cumulant of the random variables $x(t), x(t + \tau_1), \ldots, x(t + \tau_{k-1})$. Because of stationarity, the kth-order cumulant is only a function of the $k-1$ lags $\tau_1, \tau_2, \ldots, \tau_{k-1}$. Note that cumulants can also be defined for periodic signals, transient signals, and nonstationary random processes. In this chapter we are not interested in such signals, so we focus our attention only on cumulants of stationary random processes.

For a zero-mean stationary random process, and for $k = 3, 4$, the kth-order cumulant of $\{x(t)\}$ can also be defined as

$$C_{k,x}(\tau_1, \tau_2, \ldots, \tau_{k-1}) = \mathbf{E}\{x(0)x(\tau_1)\cdots x(\tau_{k-1})\} - \mathbf{E}\{g(0)g(\tau_1)\cdots g(\tau_{k-1})\} \tag{4-5}$$

where $\{g(t)\}$ is a Gaussian random process with the same second-order statistics as $\{x(t)\}$. Cumulants, therefore, not only display the amount of higher-order correlation, but also provide a measure of the distance of the random process from Gaussianity. Clearly, if $x(t)$ is Gaussian, then the cumulants are all zero; this is true not only for $k = 3$ and 4 but for all k.

The second-, third- and fourth-order cumulants of zero-mean stationary random process $x(t)$ are:

$$C_{2,x}(\tau) = \mathbf{E}\{x(t)x(t + \tau)\} \tag{4-6}$$

$$C_{3,x}(\tau_1, \tau_2) = \mathbf{E}\{x(t)x(t + \tau_1)x(t + \tau_2)\} \tag{4-7}$$

$$C_{4,x}(\tau_1, \tau_2, \tau_3) = \mathbf{E}\{x(t)x(t + \tau_1)x(t + \tau_2)x(t + \tau_3)\}$$
$$- C_{2,x}(\tau_1)C_{2,x}(\tau_2 - \tau_3) - C_{2,x}(\tau_2)C_{2,x}(\tau_3 - \tau_1)$$
$$- C_{2,x}(\tau_3)C_{2,x}(\tau_1 - \tau_2) \tag{4-8}$$

---

*The material in this section is taken, for the most part, from Swami (1988).

where $C_{2,x}(\tau)$ is just the usual correlation functon. A **1-D slice** of the kth-order cumulant is obtained by freezing $(k-2)$ of its $k-1$ indexes. A **diagonal slice** is obtained by setting $\tau_i = \tau, i = 1, 2, \ldots, k-1$.

Assuming that $C_{k,x}(\tau_1, \tau_2 \ldots, \tau_{k-1})$ is absolutely summable, the kth-order **polyspectrum** is defined as the $(k-1)$-dimensional Fourier transform of the kth-order cumulant, i.e.,

$S_{k,x}(\omega_1, \omega_2, \ldots, \omega_{k-1})$

$$= \sum_{\tau_1 = -\infty}^{\infty} \cdots \sum_{\tau_{k-1} = -\infty}^{\infty} C_{k,x}(\tau_1, \tau_2, \ldots, \tau_{k-1}) \exp[-j \sum_{i=1}^{k-1} \omega_i \tau_i] \quad (4\text{-}9)$$

$S_{3,x}(\omega_1, \omega_2)$ is known as the **bispectrum**, whereas $S_{4,x}(\omega_1, \omega_2, \omega_3)$ is known as the **trispectrum**.

Many symmetries (Brillinger and Rosenblatt, 1967) exist in the arguments of $C_{k,x}(\tau_1, \tau_2, \ldots, \tau_{k-1})$ and $S_{k,x}(\omega_1, \omega_2, \ldots, \omega_{k-1})$ which make their calculations manageable. The same is not true for cumulants in the nonstationary case. For example, in the stationary case

$$C_{3,x}(\tau_1, \tau_2) = C_{3,x}(\tau_2, \tau_1) \qquad (4\text{-}10)$$

$$C_{3,x}(\tau_1, \tau_2) = C_{3,x}(-\tau_1, \tau_2 - \tau_1) = C_{3,x}(-\tau_2, \tau_1 - \tau_2) \qquad (4\text{-}11)$$

$$C_{3,x}(\tau_1, \tau_2) = C_{3,x}(\tau_2 - \tau_1, -\tau_1) = C_{3,x}(\tau_1 - \tau_2, -\tau_2) \qquad (4\text{-}12)$$

Following are some important properties of cumulants, which are useful in theoretical developments (Rosenblatt, 1985):

1. If $\lambda_i, i = 1, \ldots, k$, are constants, and $x_i, i = 1, \ldots, k$, are random variables, then

$$\text{cum}(\lambda_1 x_1, \ldots, \lambda_k x_k) = (\prod_{i=1}^{k} \lambda_i)[\text{cum}(x_1, \ldots, x_k)] \qquad (4\text{-}13)$$

2. Cumulants are symmetric in their arguments, i.e.,

$$\text{cum}(x_1, \ldots, x_k) = \text{cum}(x_{j+1}, \ldots, x_k, x_1, \ldots x_j) \qquad (4\text{-}14)$$

3. Cumulants are additive in their arguments, i.e.,

$$\text{cum}(x_0 + y_0, z_1, \ldots, z_k) = \text{cum}(x_0, z_1, \ldots, z_k) + \text{cum}(y_0, z_1, \ldots, z_k) \qquad (4\text{-}15)$$

4. If α is a constant, then

$$\text{cum}(\alpha + z_1, z_2, \ldots, z_k) = \text{cum}(z_1, \ldots, z_k) \qquad (4\text{-}16)$$

5. If the random variables $\{x_i\}$ are independent of the random variables $\{y_i\}$, $i = 1, 2, \ldots, k$, then

$$\text{cum}(x_1 + y_1, \ldots, x_k + y_k) = \text{cum}(x_1, \ldots, x_k) + \text{cum}(y_1, \ldots, y_k) \qquad (4\text{-}17)$$

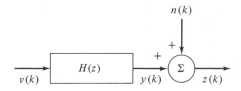

FIGURE 4.1 Single-channel linear time-invariant system.

6. If a subset of the k random variables $\{x_i\}$ is independent of the rest, then

$$\text{cum}(x_1, \ldots, x_k) = 0 \qquad (4\text{-}18)$$

Cumulants of an independent, identically distributed (i.i.d.) random process are delta functions (the same is not true for joint moments, which is one of the main reasons for working with cumulants instead of moments). That is, if $w(t)$ is an i.i.d. process, then $C_{k,w}(\tau_1, \tau_2, \ldots, \tau_{k-1}) = \gamma_{k,w}\delta_{\tau_1,\ldots,\tau_{k-1}}$, where $\gamma_{k,w}$ is the kth-order cumulant of the random variable w.

Suppose $z(n) = y(n) + v(n)$, where $y(n)$ and $v(n)$ are independent. Then, from Property 5, we see that

$$C_{k,z}(\tau_1, \tau_2, \ldots, \tau_{k-1}) = C_{k,y}(\tau_1, \tau_2, \ldots, \tau_{k-1}) + C_{k,v}(\tau_1, \tau_2, \ldots, \tau_{k-1}) \qquad (4\text{-}19)$$

If $v(n)$ is Gaussian (colored or white) and $k \geq 3$, then $C_{k,z}(\tau_1, \tau_2, \ldots, \tau_{k-1}) = C_{k,y}(\tau_1, \tau_2, \ldots, \tau_{k-1})$, whereas $C_{2,z}(\tau) \neq C_{2,y}(\tau)$. *This makes the higher-order statistics more robust to additive measurement noise than correlation, even if that noise is colored.*

CUMULANT-POLYSPECTRA FORMULAS FOR LINEAR SYSTEMS

A familiar starting point for many problems in signal processing is the single-input single-output (SISO) model depicted in Figure 4.1, in which $v(k)$ is white Gaussian noise with variance σ_v^2, $H(z)[h(k)]$ is causal and stable, and $n(k)$ is also white Gaussian noise with variance σ_n^2. Letting $r(\cdot)$ and $S(\cdot)$ denote correlation [in the rest of this chapter, we use the more traditional notation for correlation, namely $r_y(l)$ instead of $C_{2,y}(l)$] and Fourier transform of correlation (i.e., spectrum), respectively, then it is well known that (e.g., Papoulis, 1984):

$$r_z(k) = r_y(k) + r_n(k) = \sigma_v^2 \sum_{i=0}^{\infty} h(i)h(i+k) + \sigma_n^2\delta(k) \qquad (4\text{-}20)$$

$$S_z(\omega) = \sigma_v^2|H(\omega)|^2 + \sigma_n^2 \qquad (4\text{-}21)$$

$$r_{vz}(k) = \sigma_v^2 h(k) \qquad (4\text{-}22)$$

From (4-21) we see that all phase information has been lost in the spectrum (or in the autocorrelation); hence, we say that *correlations or spectra are phase blind*.

In 1946 Bartlett established a major generalization to equations (4-20) and (4-21). In his case the system in Figure 4.1 is assumed to be exponentially stable, and $\{v(i)\}$ is assumed to be independent, identically distributed, and **non-Gaussian**, i.e.,

$$
C_{k,v}(\tau_1, \tau_2, \ldots, \tau_{k-1}) = \begin{cases} \gamma_{k,v} & \text{if } \tau_1 = \tau_2 = \ldots = \tau_{k-1} = 0 \\ 0 & \text{otherwise} \end{cases} \tag{4-23}
$$

where $\gamma_{k,v}$ denotes the kth-order cumulant of $v(i)$. Additive noise $n(k)$ is assumed to be Gaussian, but need not be white. His generalizations to equations (4-20) and (4-21) are:

$$
C_{k,z}(\tau_1, \tau_2, \ldots, \tau_{k-1}) = \gamma_{k,v} \sum_{n=0}^{\infty} h(n)h(n + \tau_1) \cdots h(n + \tau_{k-1}) \tag{4-24}
$$

and

$$
S_{k,z}(\omega_1, \omega_2, \ldots, \omega_{k-1})
$$
$$
= \gamma_{k,v} H(\omega_1)H(\omega_2) \cdots H(\omega_{k-1})H(-\sum_{i=1}^{k-1} \omega_i) \tag{4-25}
$$

Observe that when $k = 2$, (4-24) and (4-25) reduce to (4-20) [subject to the addition of $\sigma_n^2 \delta(k)$] and (4-21).

MOVING-AVERAGE SYSTEMS

Single-input single-output systems come in many guises. Those that have only zeros are called **moving-average (MA) systems**; those that have only poles are called **autoregressive (AR) systems**; and those that have both poles and zeros are called **autoregressive moving-average (ARMA) systems**. In this chapter we shall focus our attention on MA systems. See Mendel (1988) for discussions on how cumulants have been used to identify AR and ARMA systems.

The MA model is

$$
\sum_{i=0}^{q} b(i)v(k - i) = y(k) \tag{4-26}
$$

where $v(k)$ is zero-mean, i.i.d., non-Gaussian, and stationary with unity variance and nonzero third-order cumulant $\gamma_{3,v}$ [if $v(k)$ is symmetrically distributed, so that its third-order cumulant equals zero, then we must use fourth-order cumulants; we shall assume that $\gamma_{3,v} \neq 0$]. The MA parameters are $b(0), b(1), \ldots, b(q)$, where q is the order of the MA model. We have assumed that σ_v^2 equals unity in order to resolve

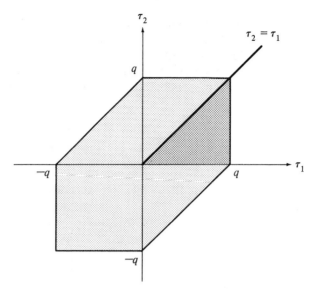

FIGURE 4.2 Domain of support for $C_{3,y}(\tau_1, \tau_2)$ of an MA system. The dark-shaded triangular region is the key region.

the scale ambiguity that exists between the MA coefficients and the input noise $v(k)$. When all the zeros of the MA system lie inside the unit circle in the complex z-domain, the system is said to be **minimum phase** (Oppenheim and Schafer, 1975); when all the zeros lie outside the unit circle, the system is said to be **maximum phase**; and when some of the zeros lie either inside or outside the unit circle, the system is said to be **mixed phase**. The latter situation, also called **nonminimum phase**, is the one we are interested in, because minimum-phase systems can be identified from second-order statistics, whereas nonminimum-phase systems cannot.

It is well known that for a causal (i.e., a system that does not respond before its input is applied) MA model

$$h(i) \quad = \quad b(i), \qquad i = 0, 1, \ldots, q \tag{4-27}$$

hence, an MA system is also known as a finite impulse response (FIR) system. As a consequence of (4-27), we see, from (4-24), that

$$C_{3,y}(\tau_1, \tau_2) \quad = \quad \gamma_{3,v} \sum_{n=0}^{q} b(n)b(n + \tau_1)b(n + \tau_2) \tag{4-28}$$

A comparable formula exists for $C_{4,y}(\tau_1, \tau_2, \tau_3)$.

Observe, from (4-28), that $C_{3,y}(\tau_1, \tau_2)$ is a three-dimensional function. The **domain of support** for $C_{3,y}(\tau_1, \tau_2)$ includes those values of τ_1 and τ_2 for which $C_{3,y}(\tau_1, \tau_2)$ exists. It is depicted in Figure 4.2. From the symmetry conditions in Equations (4-10)–(4-12), it follows that $C_{3,y}(\tau_1, \tau_2)$ can be computed over its entire domain of support just by computing its values in the darkly shaded triangular region $0 \le \tau_2 \le \tau_1 \le q$.

A number of different identification problems can now be formulated for the MA system when we only have access to output measurements. This situation is quite common, for example, in reflection seismology and channel equalization. These problems are:

1. Given $y(1), y(2), \ldots, y(N)$ and knowledge of the MA order q, determine the MA parameters $b(0), b(1), \ldots, b(q)$.

2. Same as 1, except we are given noisy values of $\{y(i)\}$, i.e., $z(i) = y(i) + n(i)$, $i = 1, 2, \ldots, N$.

3. Same as 1 or 2, except MA order q is unknown.

DETERMINING MA COEFFICIENTS USING CUMULANTS

Until the recent application of cumulants to MA parameter identification nothing really new had occurred regarding its solution in quite a few years. Trying to determine MA coefficients from just second-order statistics can usually be accomplished only via mathematical programming (e.g., Box and Jenkins, 1970). As mentioned above, second-order statistics are phase blind; hence, they can only retrieve the coefficients of minimum-phase MA processes. Not only have cumulants led to some closed-form solutions for MA parameters, but they have also led to a wide range of new and innovative methods for obtaining these coefficients. This section gives a brief survey of some of these methods. For a more comprehensive survey, see Mendel (1988).

First, let us address the existence question of whether or not MA coefficients can indeed be recovered from cumulants. Giannakis (1987) was the first to show that the IR of a qth-order MA system can be calculated just from the system's output cumulants, as

$$
\begin{aligned}
h(k) &= \frac{C_{3,y}(q,k)}{C_{3,y}(-q,-q)} \\
&= \frac{C_{3,y}(q,k)}{C_{3,y}(q,0)}, \qquad k = 0, 1, \ldots, q
\end{aligned}
\tag{4-29}
$$

Note that $C_{3,y}(-q,-q) = C_{3,y}(q,0)$ follows from symmetry properties of the third-order cumulant. Equation (4-29) expresses $h(k)$ in terms of third-order cumulants. Comparable results for fourth-order cumulants are:

$$
\begin{aligned}
h(k) &= \frac{C_{4,y}(q,q,k)}{C_{4,y}(-q,-q,-q)} \\
&= \frac{C_{4,y}(q,q,k)}{C_{4,y}(q,0,0)}, \qquad k = 0, 1, \ldots, q
\end{aligned}
\tag{4-30}
$$

The generalization of these results to arbitrary-order cumulants is obvious [see, e.g., Swami and Mendel (1988), equation (4-24)]. These equations, which are quite remarkable, are the "output-only" counterparts to (4-22).

Equation (4-29) [or (4-30)] is often referred to as the "$C(q,k)$ formula." Lohmann et al. (1983) provide a nonrigorous derivation of the $C(q,k)$ formula for 1-D and 2-D continuous-time processes. If the system's input is not symmetrically distributed, so that $\gamma_{3,v} \neq 0$, we use (4-29) to compute $h(k)$; however, if it is symmetrically distributed, so that $\gamma_{3,v} = 0$, but $\gamma_{4,v} \neq 0$, then we must use (4-30) (or comparable formulas that involve higher-order cumulants) to compute $h(k)$. Note that (4-29) and (4-30) use only 1-D slices of the output cumulant. Note, also, that they require exact knowledge of MA order q. They are interesting and important from a theoretical point of view but impractical for actual computation. This is because, in practice, the output cumulant must be estimated, and (4-29) and (4-30) do not provide any filtering to reduce the effects of cumulant estimation errors.

A byproduct of the derivation of the $C(q,k)$ formula is the following formula for $\gamma_{3,v}$:

$$\gamma_{3,v} \;=\; \frac{C_{3,y}(0,0)}{\displaystyle\sum_{k=0}^{q}\left[\frac{C_{3,y}(q,k)}{C_{3,y}(q,0)}\right]^{3}} \tag{4-31}$$

A comparable result exists for $\gamma_{4,v}$.

Let $C_{3,y}(\tau)$ denote the diagonal slice of the 3rd-order cumulant, i.e., $C_{3,y}(\tau) = C_{3,y}(\tau_1 = \tau, \tau_2 = \tau)$. Its z-transform is denoted $S_{3,y}(z)$. In Giannakis (1987) and Giannakis and Mendel (1989) it is shown that

$$S_{3,y}(\omega) \;=\; \left(\frac{1}{2\pi}\right)\int_{-\pi}^{\pi} S_{3,y}(-\omega,\,\phi)\,d\phi \tag{4-32}$$

where $S_{3,y}(-\omega,\phi)$ is the bispectrum. $S_{3,y}(\omega)$ is referred to by Giannakis and Mendel as the "$1\tfrac{1}{2}$-D spectrum." Let

$$H_2(z) \;=\; H(z)*H(z) \tag{4-33}$$

where $*$ denotes complex convolution; then Giannakis and Mendel have also shown that

$$H_2(z)S_y(z) \;=\; \left(\frac{\sigma_v^2}{\gamma_{3,v}}\right)H(z)S_{3,y}(z) \tag{4-34}$$

This interesting equation links the usual spectrum of $y(k)$ to its $1\tfrac{1}{2}$-D spectrum. Its extension to higher-than-third-order polyspectra is

$$H_k(z)S_y(z) \;=\; \left(\frac{\sigma_v^2}{\gamma_{k,v}}\right)H(z)S_{k,y}(z) \tag{4-35}$$

where

$$H_k(z) \;=\; H(z)*H(z)*\ldots*H(z) \qquad (k-1 \text{ complex convolutions}) \tag{4-36}$$

and $S_{k,y}(z)$ is the z-transform of $C_{k,y}(\tau) = C_{k,y}(\tau_1 = \tau, \tau_2 = \tau, \ldots, \tau_{k-1} = \tau)$.

Variations of the results in (4-34) can be developed by working with $C_{3,y}(\tau_1 = \tau, \tau_2 = \tau + m)$ instead of $C_{3,y}(\tau_1 = \tau, \tau_2 = \tau)$ (e.g., Friedlander and Porat, 1990).

Thus far equation (4-35) has found widespread applicability only in the MA case (e.g., Giannakis, 1987; Giannakis and Mendel, 1989; Friedlander and Porat, 1989, 1990; and Porat and Friedlander, 1987; Friedlander and Porat refer to it as the "GM equation"), for which

$$H(z) \quad = \quad \sum_{k=0}^{q} b(k) z^{-k} \tag{4-37}$$

In this case the time-domain version of (4-34) is

$$\sum_{k=0}^{q} b^2(k) r_y(m-k) \quad = \quad \left(\frac{\sigma_v^2}{\gamma_{3,v}}\right) \sum_{k=0}^{q} b(k) C_{3,y}(m-k, m-k) \tag{4-38}$$

where $m = 1, 2, \ldots$. The counterpart of this equation for fourth-order cumulants is

$$\sum_{k=0}^{q} b^3(k) r_y(m-k) \quad = \quad \left(\frac{\sigma_v^2}{\gamma_{4,v}}\right) \sum_{k=0}^{q} b(k) C_{4,y}(m-k, m-k, m-k) \tag{4-39}$$

where $m = 1, 2, \ldots$. These formulas, especially (4-38), have been used to estimate the MA coefficients, $b(0), b(1), \ldots, b(q)$, using least-squares or adaptive algorithms. Observe, in (4-38) for example, that both $b(k)$ and $b^2(k)$ appear. After $b(k)$ and $b^2(k)$ are computed by concatenating (4-38) and using least squares, the estimates of $b(k)$ and $b^2(k)$ are combined to provide a final estimate of $b(k)$.

Lii and Rosenblatt (1982) have suggested two schemes for estimation of MA parameters. In their first method, the output correlation is used to obtain the spectrally equivalent minimum-phase (SEMP) MA process. The MA polynomial is then factorized and a maximum of 2^q competing models are obtained by reflection of one or more of the minimum-phase zeros to reciprocal locations outside of the unit circle. The theoretical cumulant values for each of these models is computed using the IR summation formula in (4-28). The model whose cumulant best matches, in a least-squares sense, the output cumulant sequence is then deemed to be the true model.

Their second approach involves nonlinear optimization. The MA parameter set is chosen to be the one that minimizes the sum of the squared differences between the observed cumulant and the cumulant of the proposed model. Although they never implemented either approach, Tugnait (1986, 1987) did, but for ARMA models. Because our neural-network approach to determining the MA parameters is quite close to Lii and Rosenblatt's second approach, let us explain how it is accomplished in more detail. We do this for the perfect-measurement case when q is known.

To begin, we are given time-limited data $y(1), y(2), \ldots, y(N)$. Third-order cumulants must be estimated from this data [i.e., we can't evaluate the expectation in (4-7) because we don't know the probability density function of $\{y(i)\}$]. As usual, we replace the expectation by the sample average, i.e., $C_{3,y}(m,n)$ is estimated as $\hat{C}_{3,y}(m,n)$, where

$$\hat{C}_{3,y}(m,\,n) \;\;=\;\; \frac{1}{N}\sum_{k=0}^{N} y(k)y(k+m)y(k+n) \qquad (4\text{-}40)$$

Using the symmetry conditions for the third-order cumulant, as well as its domain of support for a MA process (see the dark-shaded triangular region in Figure 4.2), we compute $\hat{C}_{3,y}(0,0)$, $\hat{C}_{3,y}(1,0)$, $\hat{C}_{3,y}(1,1)$, $\hat{C}_{3,y}(2,0)$, $\hat{C}_{3,y}(2,1)$, $\hat{C}_{3,y}(2,2),\ldots,\hat{C}_{3,y}(q,0)$, $\hat{C}_{3,y}(q,1),\ldots$, $\hat{C}_{3,y}(q,q)$. Next, we collect all the unknown parameters into a parameter vector θ, i.e., $\theta = \mathrm{col}[b(0),b(1),\ldots,b(q)]$. We let $\hat{\theta}$ denote the estimate of θ. The following squared-error cost function is then established:

$$J(\theta) \;\;=\;\; \frac{1}{2}\sum_{0\le n\le m\le q}\left[\sum_{k=0}^{q} b(k)b(k+m)b(k+n) - \hat{C}_{3,y}(m,n)\right]^{2} \qquad (4\text{-}41)$$

Note that the outer sum covers all nonredundant values of $\hat{C}_{3,y}(m,n)$ (see the dark-shaded triangular region of Figure 4.2). Finally, $\hat{\theta}$ is obtained by minimizing $J(\theta)$ with respect to θ. To do this a mathematical programming algorithm must be used, such as steepest descent, Newton's method, the Marquardt-Levenberg algorithm, or the like.

To illustrate such an algorithm, because we will need it later, we give the **steepest-descent algorithm**:

$$b_{i+1}(k) = b_i(k) - \rho\left[\frac{\partial J(\theta)}{\partial b(k)}|_i\right], \qquad k = 0,\,1,\,\ldots,\,q \qquad (4\text{-}42)$$

where $b_i(k)$ denotes the estimate of $b(k)$ at the ith step; $[\partial J(\theta)/\partial b(k)|_i]$ means that after we obtain the partial derivative $\partial J(\theta)/\partial b(k)$, we evaluate it at $\theta = \hat{\theta}_i$; and ρ is a step size (acceleration constant) that must be prespecified. We leave it as an exercise for the reader to show that

$$\frac{\partial J(\theta)}{\partial b(l)} \;\;=\;\; \sum_{0\le n\le m\le q}\left[\sum_{k=0}^{q} b(k)b(k+m)b(k+n) - \hat{C}_{3,y}(m,n)\right]$$

$$[b(\ell+m)b(\ell+n) + b(\ell-m)b(\ell-m+n)$$

$$+ b(\ell-n)b(\ell-n+m)], \quad \ell = 0,1,\ldots,q \qquad (4\text{-}43)$$

Other methods for determining MA coefficients from cumulants can be found in Pan and Nikias (1988), Nikias (1988), and Friedlander and Porat (1987, 1989).

PROBLEM STATEMENT

In the preceding optimization approach for obtaining the MA coefficients, all the data was used at one time and the MA coefficients were chosen to fit all the data simultaneously in a minimum-squared-error sense. In the rest of this chapter we take a different approach to obtaining the MA parameters. Our approach is motivated by the preceding optimization approach and by the well-known pattern-recognition procedure of "training with a teacher."

We shall view each nonzero and nonredundant value of $r_y(\ell)$ and $C_{3,y}(m,n)$ as a **pattern** to be learned by a neural network. We shall develop a neural network and an associated training algorithm such that after all the patterns have been learned, the MA coefficients can be obtained from the neural-network weights. In practice, because the true second- and third-order statistics are not available, we shall use their estimated values as the patterns to be learned. The estimated value of $C_{3,y}(m,n), \hat{C}_{3,y}(m,n)$, is given in (4-40), whereas the estimated value of $r_y(\ell)$, denoted $\hat{r}_y(\ell)$, is given as

$$\hat{r}_y(\ell) \;=\; \frac{1}{N} \sum_{k=0}^{N} y(i)y(i+\ell) \tag{4-44}$$

NEURAL-NETWORK ARCHITECTURE

We shall now develop a two-level, three-layer neural network which obtains the MA parameters using second- and third-order statistics. The first level is composed of some random-access-memory (RAM) units which are used to control the synaptic connectivities of the second-level neurons. A similar idea, i.e., using RAM units to control the synaptic connections of neurons, is used in Graf et al. (1988) to determine whether a synaptic connection between two neurons is excitatory or inhibitory. As pointed out in that reference, this strategy is very easy to realize by VLSI techniques.

The second level is a three-layer neural network. The neurons of this network are of the linear-weighted-sum variety, i.e., the output of a neuron equals the weighted sum of its inputs. We shall see that the number of neuron weights equals the number of MA coefficients that we want to estimate, and each neuron weight represents an MA parameter. The synaptic connectivities of these neurons will be controlled by the first-level RAMs in such a way that the outputs of the second-level neural network will equal the estimated second- or third-order statistics of the MA system's output if the neurons' weights equal their corresponding true MA parameter values. Three layers are needed because the third-order cumulant can be represented as third-order functions of the MA parameters [see (4-28)]. This two-level neural network can be viewed as a **structure-controllable network**.

Figure 4.3 depicts the structure of the basic neuron used in our neural network. Observe that the weights are labeled as the MA coefficients. Our goal is to connect

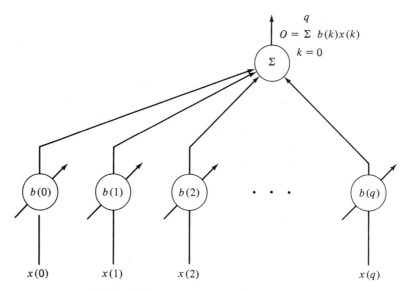

FIGURE 4.3 Basic neuron. "O" denotes output.

these neurons into a network whose outputs are $C_{3,y}(m,n)$ and $r_y(\ell)$ for given values of m, n, and ℓ. We will obtain the MA parameter estimates by training the neural network to match $\hat{C}_{3,y}(m,n)$, for $0 \leq n \leq m \leq q$, and $\hat{r}_y(\ell)$ for $0 \leq \ell \leq q$.

Our structure-controllable neural network is depicted in Figure 4.4 for the $q = 2$ case. Observe that the first and second layers each contain $q + 1$ neurons. The inputs to each neuron are controlled by a switch. The third layer contains one neuron and one simple summing unit. The neurons in the first two layers are interconnected in the following way:

1. The output of the first-left (i.e., the most-left) neuron in the first layer is connected to the inputs of the $q + 1$ second-layer neurons which correspond to $b(0)$.

2. The output of the second-left neuron in the first layer is connected to the inputs of the $q + 1$ second-layer neurons which correspond to $b(1)$.

q. The output of the qth neuron in the first layer is connected to the inputs of the $q + 1$ second-layer neurons which correspond to $b(q)$.

The connections between the second and third layers are obvious.

As mentioned above, there is a switch to each of the inputs to the first and second layers' $2(q+1)$ neurons. When a switch is "on," the corresponding synaptic line is connected and the synaptic strength is determined by the corresponding weight parameter. When a switch is "off," the corresponding input equals zero. The states of these switches are controlled by the RAM units, as illustrated in Figure 4.5. The RAM units form the first level of the whole neural network.

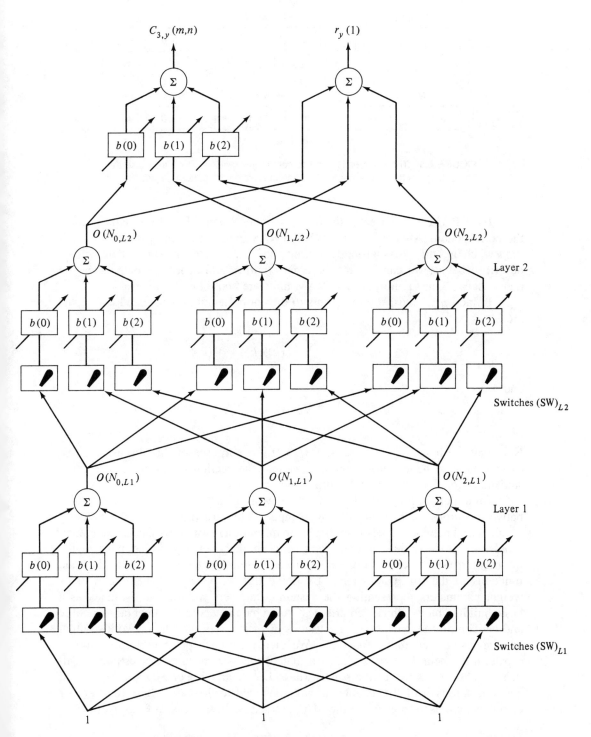

FIGURE 4.4 Three-layer neural network for the $q = 2$ case. The switches are controlled by the RAMs depicted in Figure 4.5.

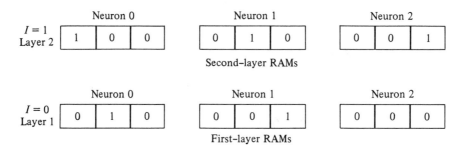

FIGURE 4.5 The RAM units used to control the switches (SW) in Figure 4.4. The settings in this figure are for the case of learning the pattern $C_{3,y}(0,1)$.

Each RAM unit corresponds to one switch. When a RAM unit equals unity, the corresponding switch is "on." When a RAM unit equals zero, the corresponding switch is "off." By properly setting the RAM units, in a way that will be described below, we can control the connectivities, and hence the outputs, of the neural network in Figure 4.4. The RAM units are controlled by m, n, and ℓ.

In fact m, n, and ℓ are the inputs to the entire neural network, and its outputs are

$$C_{3,y}(m,n) \;=\; \sum_{k=0}^{q} b(k)b(k+m)b(k+n)$$

and

$$r_y(\ell) \;=\; \sum_{k=0}^{q} b(k)b(k+\ell)$$

Note that we have set $\gamma_{3,v} = 1$ and $\sigma_v^2 = 1$ for purposes of this discussion. We explain how to handle the nonunity cases in the section on extensions to input statistic estimation and order determination.

An important property of this neural network is that the synaptic connectivities between neurons can be controlled by its inputs. This structure-controllable property of our neural network makes it applicable to many other system-parameter estimation problems. In fact, this approach can be generalized to any problem where the information used to estimate the system parameters can be expressed as algebraic functions of the true parameters. By doing this we view each neuron, with its weight parameters representing the system parameters we want to estimate, as a basic building block which "contributes" some parameters to the algebraic function, and we control the synaptic connectivities in such a way that the network's output will be just the algebraic function. We then view each piece of information as a pattern the neural network needs to match; the system parameter estimates will then be obtained when all the patterns have been learned. For example, the neural network approach of this chapter can be extended to the case where fourth-order cumulants are used to estimate the MA parameters. In this case a four-layer neural network is needed, because the fourth-order cumulant can be expressed as in (4-8) and (4-24).

In order to set the RAM units we need an address system. Here we use a three-number address, (I, J, K), where:

1. I indicates whether a RAM unit coresponds to a first-layer switch ($I = 0$) or to a second-layer switch ($I = 1$);

2. J refers to the neuron number in each layer ($J = 0, 1, \ldots, q$), where $J = 0$ refers to the leftmost neuron, etc.; and

3. K refers to the specific switch number within a neuron ($K = 0, 1, \ldots, q$), where $K = 0$ refers to the leftmost switch.

A careful analysis reveals that in order for the network's output to be $C_{3,y}(m, n)$ we must set the RAM units addressed $(0, m, n)$, $(0, m+1, n+1)$, $(0, m+2, n+2)$, $\ldots$, $(0, m+q, n+q)$, and $(1, 0, m)$, $(1, 1, m+1)$, $(1, 2, m+2)$, $\ldots$, $(1, q, m+q)$ equal to unity. All other RAM units are set equal to zero. If for some values of m and n there are no units for these addresses, we ignore the address. Additionally, in order for the network's output to be $r_y(\ell)$, we must set the RAM units addressed $(0, 0, \ell)$, $(0, 1, \ell+1)$, $(0, 2, \ell+2)$, $\ldots$, $(0, q, \ell+q)$, and $(1, 0, 0)$, $(1, 1, 1)$, $(1, 2, 2)$, $\ldots$, $(1, q, q)$ equal to unity. All other RAM units are set equal to zero. If for some values of ℓ there are no units for these addresses, we ignore the address.

In order to quantify the preceding discussion, we introduce the following notation (see Figure 4.4): $O(N_{J,L1} \mid m, n)$ denotes the output of neuron J in Layer 1 conditioned on cumulant inputs m and n; $O(N_{J,L1} \mid \ell)$ denotes the output of neuron J in Layer 1 conditioned on correlation input ℓ; $O(N_{J,L2} \mid m, n)$ denotes the output of neuron J in Layer 2 conditioned on cumulant inputs m and n; $O(N_{J,L2} \mid \ell)$ denotes the output of neuron J in Layer 2 conditioned on correlation input ℓ; $SW_{L1}(J, K \mid m, n)$ denotes the output of the Kth switch at the input to the Jth neuron of Layer 1 conditioned on the cumulant inputs m and n; $SW_{L1}(J, K \mid \ell)$ denotes the output of the Kth switch at the input to the Jth neuron of Layer 1 conditioned on the correlation input ℓ; $SW_{L2}(J, K \mid m, n)$ denotes the output of the Kth switch at the input to the Jth neuron of Layer 2 conditioned on the cumulant inputs m and n; and $SW_{L2}(J, K \mid \ell)$ denotes the output of the Kth switch at the input to the Jth neuron of Layer 2 conditioned on the correlation input ℓ.

Using this notation, we see from Figure 4.4 that

$$O(N_{J,L1} \mid m, n) = \sum_{K=0}^{q} b(K) SW_{L1}(J, K \mid m, n) \quad J = 0, 1, \ldots, q \quad (4\text{-}45)$$

$$O(N_{J,L2} \mid m, n) = \sum_{K=0}^{q} b(K) O(N_{K,L1} \mid m, n) SW_{L2}(J, K \mid m, n)$$

$$J = 0, 1, \ldots, q \quad (4\text{-}46)$$

TABLE 4.1 $SW_{L1}(J, K \mid M, N)^*$

		K				
		n	$n+1$	$n+2$	...	$n+q$
	m	1	0	0	...	0
	$m+1$	0	1	0	...	0
J	$m+2$	0	0	1	...	0
	...					
	$m+q$	0	0	0	...	1

$^*SW_{L1}(J, K \mid m, n) = 0$ if J or $K \notin [0, 1, \ldots, q]$

TABLE 4.2 $SW_{L2}(J, K \mid M, N)^*$

		K				
		m	$m+1$	$m+2$	...	$m+q$
	0	1	0	0	...	0
	1	0	1	0	...	0
J	2	0	0	1	...	0
	...					
	q	0	0	0	...	1

$^*SW_{L2}(J, K \mid m, n) = 0$ if K or $K \notin [0, 1, \ldots, q]$

$$O(N_{J,L1} \mid \ell) = \sum_{K=0}^{q} b(K) SW_{L1}(J, K \mid \ell) \qquad J = 0, 1, \ldots, q \quad (4\text{-}47)$$

$$O(N_{J,L2} \mid \ell) = \sum_{K=0}^{q} b(K) O(N_{K,L1}) \mid \ell) SW_{L2}(J, K \mid \ell)$$
$$J = 0, 1, \ldots, q \quad (4\text{-}48)$$

$$C_{3,y}(m, n) = \sum_{J=0}^{q} b(J) O(N_{J,L2} \mid m, n) \qquad (4\text{-}49)$$

$$r_y(\ell) = \sum_{J=0}^{q} O(N_{J,L2} \mid \ell) \qquad (4\text{-}50)$$

where the switching functions are specified in Tables 4.1 through 4.4.

In order to illustrate how one uses these equations and tables, consider the formation of $C_{3,y}(1, 2)$ for a fourth-order MA system. In this case $q = 4$, $m = 1$, and $n = 2$. Observe, from Table 4.1, that the nonzero entries occur at the (J, K) pairs $(1, 2)$, $(2, 3)$, and $(3, 4)$; $SW_{L1}(J, K \mid 1, 2) = 0$ for all other pairs of J and K. Consequently, from (4-45), we find that $O(N_{0,L1} \mid 1, 2) = 0$, $O(N_{1,L1} \mid 1, 2) = b(2)$, $O(N_{2,L1} \mid 1, 2) = b(3)$, $O(N_{3,L1} \mid 1, 2) = b(4)$ and $O(N_{4,L1} \mid 1, 2) = 0$. From Table 4.2, we observe that the nonzero entries occur at the (J, K) pairs $(0, 1)$, $(1, 2)$, $(2, 3)$, and $(3, 4)$; $SW_{L2}(J, K \mid 1, 2) = 0$ for all other pairs of J and K. Consequently, from (4-46) and the just-computed values of $O(N_{K,L1} \mid 1, 2)$, we find that $O(N_{0,L2} \mid 1, 2) =$

TABLE 4.3 $SW_{L1}(J, K \mid \ell)$

			K		
	l	$l+1$	$l+2$	...	$l+q$
0	1	0	0	...	0
1	0	1	0	...	0
J 2	0	0	1	...	0
...					
q	0	0	0	...	1

$^*SW_{L1}(J, K \mid l) = 0$ if K or $K \notin [0, 1, \ldots, q]$

TABLE 4.4 $SW_{L2}(J, K \mid \ell)$

			K		
	0	1	2	...	q
0	1	0	0	...	0
1	0	1	0	...	0
J 2	0	0	1	...	0
...					
q	0	0	0	...	1

$b(1)b(2)$, $O(N_{1,L2} \mid 1, 2) = b(2)b(3)$, $O(N_{2,L2} \mid 1, 2) = b(3)b(4)$, $O(N_{3,L2} \mid 1, 2) = 0$, and $O(N_{4,L2} \mid 1, 2) = 0$. Finally, substituting these values of $O(N_{J,L2} \mid 1, 2)$ into (4-49), we find that $C_{3,y}(1, 2) = b(0)b(1)b(2) + b(1)b(2)b(3) + b(2)b(3)b(4)$, which is exactly what we get from (4-28).

TRAINING ALGORITHM

We see, from Figure 4.4 and its associated discussions, that there is a special requirement for training our neural network: the weight parameters of different neurons which represent the same MA parameters must change in the same fashion in order for the network's outputs to have a proper meaning. This constraint actually makes it easier to realize the training algorithm.

The difficulty in training a multilayer network (e.g., Rumelhart and McCleland, 1986) is in training the hidden-layer neurons, because the dependence of the outputs on the weight parameters of the hidden-layer neurons is usually very complicated. For our neural network, however, the dependence of its outputs on the weight parameters of different neurons is the same; hence, we can train all the neurons, in whichever layer the neurons belong to, toward the same goal [matching the neural network's output to $C_{3,y}(m, n)$ and $r_y(\ell)$] and in the same fashion.

We define the errors

$$e_i^2(m, n) = \left[\sum_{k=0}^{q} b_i(k)b_i(k+m)b_i(k+n) - \hat{C}_{3,y}(m, n) \right]^2 \quad (4\text{-}51)$$

and

$$e_i^2(\ell) \;=\; \left[\sum_{k=0}^{q} b_i(k)b_i(k+\ell) - \hat{r}_y(\ell)\right]^2 \tag{4-52}$$

where $b_i(k)$ denotes the estimate of $b(k)$ at the ith instant of training. Various training algorithms could be used. We tried backpropagation and steepest-descent algorithms. Better results were obtained for the latter. Specifically, our steepest-descent algorithm is:

$$b_{i+1}(k) \;=\; b_i(k) - \rho_1\left[\frac{\partial e_i^2(m,n)}{\partial b(k)}\big|_i\right], \qquad k = 0, 1, \ldots, q \tag{4-53}$$

for patterns $\hat{C}_{3,y}(m,n)$, where $0 \le n \le m \le q$, and ρ_1 is an acceleration constant; and

$$b_{i+1}(k) \;=\; b_i(k) - \rho_2\left[\partial e_i^2(\ell)/\partial b(k)|_i\right], \qquad k = 0, 1, \ldots, q \tag{4-54}$$

for patterns $\hat{r}_y(\ell)$, where $0 \le \ell \le q$, and ρ_2 is also an acceleration constant. With a little bit of analysis, it is straightforward to show that (4-53) and (4-54) can be expressed as:

$$\begin{aligned} b_{i+1}(k) \;=\; & b_i(k) + 2\rho_1 e_i(m,n)[b_i(\ell+m)b_i(\ell+n) \\ & + b_i(\ell-m)b_i(\ell-m+n) + b_i(\ell-n)b_i(\ell-n+m)] \end{aligned} \tag{4-55}$$

for patterns $\hat{C}_{3,y}(m,n)$, where $0 \le n \le m \le q$, and

$$b_{i+1}(k) \;=\; b_i(k) + 2\rho_2 e_i(\ell)[b_i(k+\ell) + b_i(k-\ell)] \tag{4-56}$$

for patterns $\hat{r}_y(\ell)$, where $0 \le \ell \le q$. Equations (4-55) and (4-56) are easy to realize because $e_i(m,n)$ and $e_i(\ell)$ are just the errors of the neural network's outputs; these quantities are easily fed back to every neuron.

Our training algorithm consists of the following five steps:

1. Set the initial weight parameters $b_0(k)(k = 0, 1, \ldots, q)$ at some small random values; choose the acceleration constants ρ_1 and ρ_2; and start from any pattern $\hat{C}_{3,y}(m,n)$ or $\hat{r}_y(\ell)$ where $0 \le n \le m \le q$ and $0 \le \ell \le q$.

2. For a given pattern $\hat{C}_{3,y}(m,n)$ or $\hat{r}_y(\ell)$, input m, n, or ℓ to the two-level neural network, and use (4-55) or (4-56) to update the weight parameters of all the neurons until the error $e_i(m,n)$ or $e_i(\ell)$ is less than a prespecified threshold.

3. Input a new pattern, and use the converged weight parameters of the previous learned pattern as the initial parameters for the new pattern; then use (4-55) or (4-56) to update the weight parameters until the error $e_i(m,n)$ or $e_i(\ell)$ is less than a prespecified threshold.

4. Repeat by going to step 2 until all patterns $\hat{C}_{3,y}(m,n)$ and $\hat{r}_y(\ell)$ (where $0 \le n \le m \le q$ and $0 \le \ell \le q$) have been learned.

5. If the parameter estimates are not good enough, return to step 2 to learn the patterns again until acceptable estimates are obtained.

Step 1 is the weight-initialization step. Instead of using random values for the initial weights, we could use MA estimate values obtained from any one of the methods described in the section on determining MA coefficients using cumulants. In step 2 we train the network on a single cumulant or correlation pattern. Training continues until the network has done its very best to learn that pattern. In steps 3 and 4 we repeat step 2, but for all the cumulant and correlation patterns. These patterns can be presented in a fixed order or in a randomized order. Step 5 requires a test. Our test is to present all the cumulant and correlation patterns to the network one last time and accumulate all their errors. If the accumulated errors are too large, we retrain. If not, we stop.

There are four fundamental questions about this training algorithm: (1) For a given pattern is the algorithm convergent? (2) Does there exist a set of weight parameters $b^*(0), b^*(1), \ldots, b^*(q)$ for which all the patterns will be matched? In other words, is there an optimal "state" of the neural network such that when the network falls into this "state," all the patterns will never be forgotten? (3) Is this "state" stable? In other words, when the patterns are learned again and again, and the neural network is already in the optimal "state," does the "state" of the neural network change? (4) Does our training algorithm lead the neural network into the stable optimal "state" if such a "state" exists?

The answer to the first question is "yes," because it is equivalent to the question, "Is the steepest descent algorithm convergent?"—a question that has been extensively studied in the literature (e.g., Widrow and Stearns, 1985). The answers to the second and third questions are "Yes, but under certain conditions." The details are very technical. The fourth question remains unanswered. We simulated our training algorithm for many examples (two of which are presented in the section after the next), and in all cases the MA parameter estimates converged to their true values.

EXTENSIONS TO INPUT STATISTIC ESTIMATION AND ORDER DETERMINATION

In the section on moving-average systems we assumed that $b(0)$ is unknown, in which case $v(k)$ has its variance fixed at unity, which resolves the scale ambiguity that exists between the MA coefficients and the input noise. In the section on neural-network architecture we also assumed that $\gamma_{3,v} = 1$. In practice we cannot fix both the variance and third-order cumulant of $v(k)$ at unity. Additionally, in many publications (e.g., Giannakis and Mendel, 1989) $b(0)$ is assumed equal to unity, in which case the variance of $v(k)$ must be estimated. We demonstrate next that even if we assume that $b(0) = 1$, the preceding approach is valid, subject to some simple modifications.

When σ_v^2 and $\gamma_{3,v}$ are unknown, we can proceed as follows:

1. Train the neural network only with $\hat{C}_{3,y}(m,n)$ values to ultimately obtain estimates of $b(1), b(2), \ldots, b(q)$ and $\gamma_{3,v}$. In this case, we first reexpress $\hat{C}_{3,y}(m,n)$, our measured value of $C_{3,y}(m,n)$, using (4-24), as

$$\hat{C}_{3,y}(m,n) \simeq \gamma_{3,v} \sum_{i=0}^{q} b(i)b(i+m)b(i+n)$$

$$= \sum_{i=0}^{q} b'(i)b'(i+m)b'(i+n) \qquad (4\text{-}57)$$

where

$$b'(i) = (\gamma_{3,v})^{1/3} b(i), \qquad i = 0, 1, \ldots, q \qquad (4\text{-}58)$$

The right-hand side of (4-57) fits our earlier model that was the basis for our neural network in Figure 4.4. We train the neural network to obtain $\hat{b}'(i)$, $i = 0, 1, \ldots, q$; from these values we then find $\hat{\gamma}_{3,v}$ and $\hat{b}(i)$, $i = 1, 2, \ldots, q$, since

$$\hat{\gamma}_{3,v} = [\hat{b}'(0)]^3 \qquad (4\text{-}59)$$

because $b(0) = 1$, and

$$\hat{b}(i) = \frac{\hat{b}'(i)}{\hat{b}'(0)}, \qquad i = 1, 2, \ldots, q \qquad (4\text{-}60)$$

2. Estimate σ_v^2 from

$$\hat{\sigma}_v^2 = \frac{\hat{r}_y(0)}{\displaystyle\sum_{i=0}^{q} \hat{b}^2(i)} \qquad (4\text{-}61)$$

This equation was obtained by setting $\ell = 0$ in $r_y(\ell)$. To evaluate (4-61) we must compute $\hat{r}_y(0)$ from the data. In the case of noisy measurements, for which (4-20) applies, (4-61) must be modified to

$$\hat{\sigma}_v^2 = \frac{\hat{r}_z(\ell)}{\displaystyle\sum_{i=0}^{q} \hat{b}(i)\hat{b}(i+\ell)}, \qquad \ell \neq 0 \qquad (4\text{-}62)$$

For nonzero ℓ, the additive-noise variance term is not present in (4-20).

3. Normalize $\hat{C}_{3,y}(m,n)$ by $\hat{\gamma}_{3,v}$ and $\hat{r}_y(\ell)$ by $\hat{\sigma}_v^2$. Train the neural network to learn both $\hat{C}_{3,y}(m,n)$ and $\hat{r}_y(\ell)$. This provides us with a new set of $\hat{b}(i), i = 0, 1, \ldots, q$.

4. Reestimate $\hat{\gamma}_{3,v}$ from

$$\hat{\gamma}_{3,v} = \frac{\hat{C}_{3,y}(0,0)}{\sum_{i=0}^{q} \hat{b}^3(i)} \tag{4-63}$$

and reestimate σ_v^2 from (4-61). Equation (4-63) follows from (4-28).

5. Repeat steps 3 and 4 until there are no appreciable differences in the estimated MA coefficient values.

Our neural network approach to MA parameter estimation can also be used to perform **order determination** (e.g., Giannakis, 1986 and Giannakis and Mendel, 1989) in the following straightforward way. First, choose the number of weight parameters as $\bar{q}$, where $\bar{q}$ is large enough so that the true system order, q, is certainly less than $\bar{q}$. Then train the neural network to obtain $\bar{q}$ weight parameters. Finally, perform a statistical test on the MA coefficients to find a q such that $\hat{C}_{3,y}(q,q) \neq 0$ and $\hat{C}_{3,y}(q+1,q+1) = 0$. This means that q can be determined as the lag of the last nonzero cumulant sample. A statistical test has to be used because the data is random.

SIMULATIONS

In this section we present two examples, the data for which was obtained by using the following four-step procedure:

1. Generate 640 samples of a zero-mean, i.i.d., non-Gaussian input $v(k)$ for which $\sigma_v^2 = 1/4^{1/3}$ and $\gamma_{3,v} = 1$. This was done (Papoulis, 1984) by first generating an independent exponentially distributed random process $x(k)(k = 1, 2, \ldots, 640)$, where the probability density function of $x(k)$ is $p(x) = 2^{1/3} \exp(-2^{1/3}x)$. Then we obtained $v(k)$ as $v(k) = x(k) - 1/2^{1/3}$, for which it is easy to show that $E\{v(k)\} = 0, E\{v^2(k)\} = 1/4^{1/3}$, and $E\{v^3(k)\} = 1$. To generate $x(k)$ we first generated a sequence of uniformly distributed random numbers $U(k)$ over $(0, 1)$, and then obtained $x(k)$ as $x(k) = -(1/2)\ln[U(k)]$.

2. Obtain 640 samples of $y(k)$ using the specific model equations in each of the examples that is described below.

3. Calculate $\hat{C}_{3,y}(m,n)$ and $\hat{r}_y(\ell)$ using (4-40) and (4-44), respectively.

4. Run our neural network training procedure for the patterns obtained in step 4 until convergence occurs.

We performed 15 Monte Carlo runs for each example and plotted the estimates of MA parameter $b(i)$ (for different values of i) for all 15 runs on the same plot. The mean value of the estimates can be obtained by visualizing the average of the 15 curves; the "thickness" of the overlaid 15 curves provides a sense of the standard deviation of the parameter estimates. For both examples there is no measurement

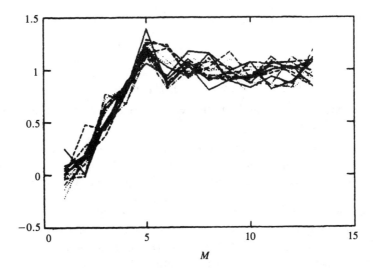

FIGURE 4.6 Estimates of $b(0)$ for Example 4.1.

noise and we assume that the variance and third-order cumulant of the input noise are known; hence, our results should be indicative of the best performance that can be obtained using the training procedure for the relatively short data record of 640 measurements.

Example 4.1

This first example is for the following MA(2) model:

$$y(k) = v(k) - 2.333v(k-1) + 0.667v(k-2) \qquad (4\text{-}64)$$

This MA system is nonminimum phase, because its two zeros are at $z = 2$ and $z = 1/3$; the zero at 2 lies outside the unit circle. We assume that the MA order, q, is known, i.e., $q = 2$.

Estimates of $b(0), b(1)$ and $b(2)$ are depicted in Figures 4.6, 4.7, and 4.8, respectively. On these figures the vertical axis represents the values of the parameter estimates, whereas the horizontal axis represents the patterns which have been learned. Specifically, $M = 1, 2, \ldots, 9$; $10, 11, \ldots$ correspond to the learning of the ordered patterns $\hat{C}_{3,y}(0,0), \hat{C}_{3,y}(1,0), \hat{C}_{3,y}(1,1), \hat{C}_{3,y}(2,0),$ $\hat{C}_{3,y}(2,1), \hat{C}_{3,y}(2,2), \hat{r}_y(0), \hat{r}_y(1), \hat{r}_y(2)$; $\hat{C}_{3,y}(0,0), \hat{C}_{3,y}(1,0), \ldots$; and the parameter estimate at $M = i$ denotes the parameter estimate after the patterns corresponding to $M = 1, 2, \ldots, i$ have been learned. The acceleration constants [see (4-55) and (4-56)] for this example were both set equal to 0.02. Observe, from these figures, that convergence does occur (in some probabilistic sense) in a very dynamic way; i.e., the plot of $b(i)$ first has a transient phase and then reaches a steady state, after which additional training does no good. For this

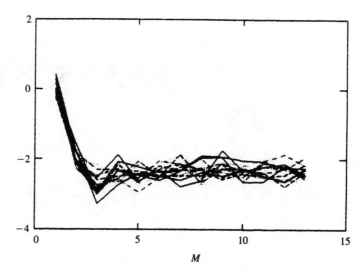

FIGURE 4.7 Estimates of $b(1)$ for Example 4.1.

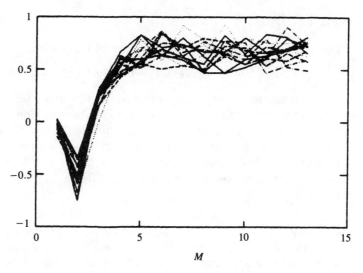

FIGURE 4.8 Estimates of $b(2)$ for Example 4.1.

example, steady state appears to be reached just from the cumulant subset of the nine training samples. This is not that surprising, because the cumulants contain the correct phase information about the MA process, whereas the correlation values do not.

Additional experiments demonstrated that the ordering of the training samples had no influence on the final results.   ■

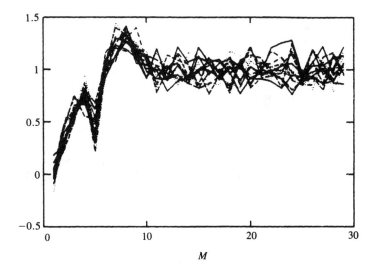

FIGURE 4.9   Estimates of $b(0)$ for Example 4.2.

Example 4.2

Our second example is for the following MA(3) model:

$$y(k) \quad = \quad v(k) + 0.9v(k-1) + 0.385v(k-2) - 0.771v(k-3) \qquad (4\text{-}65)$$

It is also nonminimum phase, with zeros at 0.6, and $-0.75 \pm j0.85$. For this example we assumed that the MA order is unknown. Consequently, we chose $\bar{q} = 5$, so that six parameters had to be estimated. Plots of these six estimates, which are analogous to the plots for Example 4.1, are depicted in Figures 4.9 through 4.14. In this case, however, $M = 1, 2, \ldots, 26; 27, 28, \ldots$ correspond to the learning of the ordered patterns $\hat{C}_{3,y}(0,0), \hat{C}_{3,y}(1,0), \hat{C}_{3,y}(1,1), \hat{C}_{3,y}(2,0),$ $\hat{C}_{3,y}(2,1), \hat{C}_{3,y}(2,2), \ldots, \hat{C}_{3,y}(5,0), \hat{C}_{3,y}(5,1), \hat{C}_{3,y}(5,2), \hat{C}_{3,y}(5,3), \hat{C}_{3,y}(5,4),$ $\hat{C}_{3,y}(5,5), \hat{r}_y(0), \hat{r}_y(1), \hat{r}_y(2), \ldots, \hat{r}_y(5); \hat{C}_{3,y}(0,0), \hat{C}_{3,y}(1,0), \ldots$. Both acceleration constants were set equal to 0.03. As in the figures for Example 4.1, each of the plots clearly demonstrates a dynamical behavior indicative of learning. Once again, convergence occurs, and for a relatively small number of training samples. The most interesting behavior is for parameters $b(4)$ and $b(5)$; observe their convergence, in some probabilistic sense to zero. These plots demonstrate that our training procedure does have the capability to estimate the correct order of the MA model.   ∎

Of course, much more testing needs to be done on these and other examples before final conclusions can be drawn; however, our results are quite encouraging. When measurement noise is included, we can assuredly expect the results to become worse; however, it is well known that by using longer data records we can offset

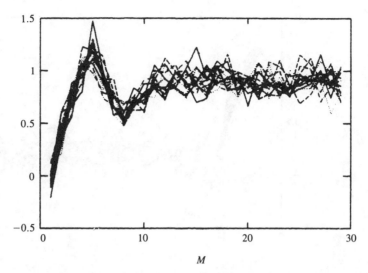

FIGURE 4.10   Estimates of $b(1)$ for Example 4.2.

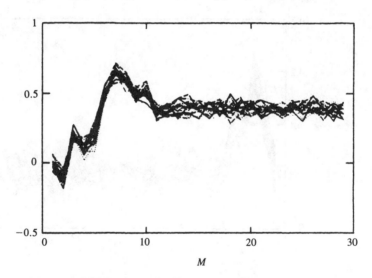

FIGURE 4.11   Estimates of $b(2)$ for Example 4.2.

the effects of measurement noise (see the examples in Pan and Nikias, 1988, for example). Our use of 640 samples represents a short data length compared to the lengths that are reported in similar experiments. When the input-noise variance and its cumulant are unknown, then we need to use a method such as the one described in the preceding section. Finally, we need to study the effects of initializing the training procedure with MA parameter values obtained by one of the methods described in the section on determining MA coefficients using cumulants.

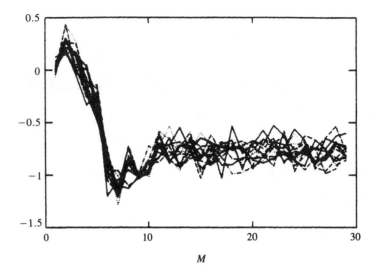

FIGURE 4.12 Estimates of $b(3)$ for Example 4.2.

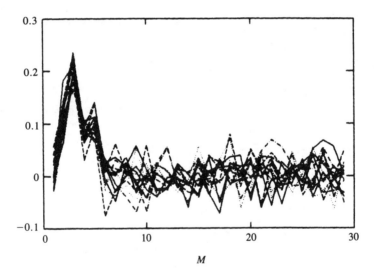

FIGURE 4.13 Estimates of $b(4)$ for Example 4.2.

CONCLUSIONS

The key points of this chapter are threefold: (1) a structure-controllable neural network was proposed which, in principle, can be generalized to any parameter-estimation problem, if the information used to estimate the parameters can be expressed as algebraic functions of the true parameters; (2) the idea of interpreting each cumulant and correlation as a "pattern" the neural network needs to learn was

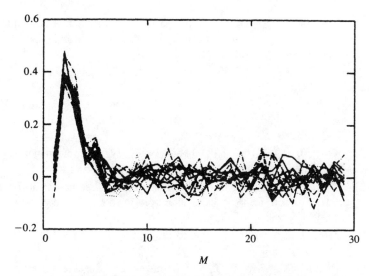

FIGURE 4.14   Estimates of $b(5)$ for Example 4.2.

proposed and evaluated; and (3) an equal-neuron steepest-descent training algorithm was proposed and tested via simulations.

We believe that the ideas of this paper can be extended to estimating parameters in AR and ARMA models.

Finally, while it is true that we never used the neural-network architecture depicted in Figure 4.4 to implement the training procedure for our two examples, if, in the future, the linear weighted-sum neurons can be realized by hardware or microsoftware techniques, we can use these hardware neurons to realize our network. When parallel hardware becomes available, we believe the neural-network architecture will be needed.

REFERENCES

Box, G. E., and Jenkins, G. H., *Time Series Analysis: Forecasting and Control*. Holden-Day, San Francisco.

Brillinger, D. R., and Rosenblatt, M., "Asymptotic Theory of Estimates of kth Order Spectra," in *Spectral Analysis of Time Series*, B. Harris (ed.), Wiley, New York, 1967, 153–188.

Friedlander, B., and Porat, B., "Adaptive IIR Algorithms Based on Higher-Order Statistics," *IEEE Trans. on Acoustics, Speech, and Signal Processing*, vol. 37, 485–495, 1989.

Friedlander, B., and Porat, B., "Asymptotically Optimal Estimation of MA and ARMA Parameters of Non-Gaussian Processes from Higher-Order Moments," *IEEE Trans. on Automatic Control*, vol. 35, 1990.

Giannakis, G. B., "Signal Processing via Higher-Order Statistics," Ph.D. Dissertation, Dept. of Electrical Engineering, University of Southern California, July 1986. Also Signal and Image Processing Institute Report No. 104.

Giannakis, G. B., "Cumulants: A Powerful Tool in Signal Processing," *Proc. IEEE*, vol. 75, 1333–1334, 1987.

Giannakis, G. B., and Mendel, J. M., "Identification of Nonminimum Phase Systems Using Higher-Order Statistics," *IEEE Trans. on Acoustics, Speech, and Signal Processing*, vol. 37, 360–377, 1989.

Graf, H. P., Jackel, L. D., and Hubbard, W. E., "VLSI Implementation of a Neural Network Model," *Computer* 41–49, March 1988.

Lii, K-S., and Rosenblatt, M., "Deconvolution and Estimation of Transfer Function Phase and Coefficients for NonGaussian Linear Processes," *The Annals of Statistics*, vol. 10, 1195–1208, 1982.

Lippmann, R. P., "An Introduction to Computing with Neural Nets," *IEEE ASSP Magazine*, 36–54, April 1987.

Lohmann, A. W., Weigelt, G., and Wirnitzer, B., "Speckle Masking in Astronomy: Triple Correlation Theory and Applications," *Applied Optics*, vol. 22, 4028–4037, 1983.

Mendel, J. M., "Use of Higher-Order Statistics in Signal Processing and System Theory: An Update," *Proc. SPIE Conf. on Advanced Algorithms and Architectures for Signal Processing III*, 126–144, San Diego, 1988.

Nikias, C. L., "ARMA Bispectrum Approach to Nonminimum Phase System Identification," *IEEE Trans. on Acoustics, Speech, and Signal Processing*, vol. 36, 513–524, 1988.

Nikias, C. L., and Raghuveer, M. R., "Bispectrum Estimation: A Digital Signal Processing Framework," *Proc. IEEE*, vol. 75, 869–891, July 1987.

Oppenheim, A. V., and Schafer, R. W., *Digital Signal Processing*, Prentice-Hall, Englewood Cliffs, NJ, 1975.

Pan, R., and Nikias, C. L., "The Complex Spectrum of Higher Order Cumulants and Nonminimum Phase System Identification," *IEEE Trans. on Acoustics, Speech and Signal Processing*, vol. 36, 186–205, 1988.

Papoulis, A., *Probability, Random Variables, and Stochastic Processes*. McGraw-Hill, New York, 1984.

Porat, B., and Friedlander, B., "Performance Analysis of Parameter Estimation Algorithms Based on Higher-Order Statistics," submitted for publication, December 1987.

Priestley, M. B., *Spectral Analysis and Time Series*. Academic Press, London, 1981.

Rosenblatt, M., *Stationary Sequences and Random Processes*. Birkhauser, Boston, 1985.

Rumelhart, D. E., and McCleland, J. L., *Parallel Distributed Processing*, I. MIT Press, Cambridge, MA, 1986.

Swami, A., "System Identification Using Cumulants," Ph.D. Dissertation, Dept. of Electrical Engineering, University of Southern California, 1988. Also Signal and Image Processing Institute Report No. 140.

Swami, A., and Mendel, J. M., "ARMA Parameter Estimation Using Only Output Cumulants," *Proc. 4th IEEE ASSP Workshop on Spectrum Estimation and Modeling*, 193–198, Minneapolis, 1988.

Tugnait, J. K., "Identification of Nonminimum Phase Linear Stochastic Systems," *Automatica*, vol. 22, 457–464, 1986.

Tugnait, J. K., "Identification of Linear Stochastic Systems via Second- and Fourth-Order Cumulant Matching," *IEEE Trans. Info. Theory*, vol. IT-33, 393–407, 1987.

Widrow, B., and Stearns, S. D., *Adaptive Signal Processing*. Prentice-Hall, Englewood Cliffs, NJ, 1985.

PROBLEMS

4.1. Suppose x is a Gaussian random variable. Prove that its third- and fourth-order cumulants equal zero.

4.2. Prove the truth of the symmetry conditions for the third-order cumulants, which are stated in (4-10), (4-11) and (4-12).

4.3. Using the five equations in (4-10), (4-11) and (4-12), show that the $\tau_1 - \tau_2$ plane can be divided into the six regions depicted in the figure below. Then show that by knowing $C_{3,x}(\tau_1, \tau_2)$ in any one of the six regions, the third-order cumulant can be determined in the other five regions by virtue of the symmetry relationships.

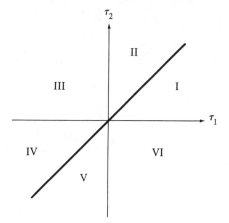

4.4. Verify cumulant properties [1]–[6] for third-order cumulants of zero-mean random variables.

4.5. Derive correlation equation (4-20) and cross-correlation equation (4-22).

4.6. Derive equations (4-24) and (4-25) for zero-mean random processes.

4.7. Using (4-21), explain why nonminimum phase systems cannot be identified from second-order statistics of the output of a dynamical system.

4.8. Derive the impulse response results for an MA system that are given in (4-27).

4.9. Derive the domain of support for $C_{3,y}(\tau_1, \tau_2)$, for the MA(q) system depicted in Figure 4.2.

4.10. Derive the $C(q, k)$ formula in (4-29) and the formula for $\gamma_{3,v}$ in (4-31).

4.11. Derive (4-34), which links the spectrum and the $1\frac{1}{2}$-D spectrum.

4.12. For an MA(q) system, show that the time-domain version of (4-34) is given by (4-38).

4.13. Derive the equation for $\partial J(\theta)/\partial b(\ell)$ given in (4-43).

4.14. Confirm that the settings in Figure 4.5 are correctly shown for the pattern $C_{3,y}(0, 1)$.

4.15. Develop the counterparts to Figure 4.5 for an MA(4) system for the following patterns: (a) $C_{3,y}(1,3)$, (b) $C_{3,y}(4,2)$, (c) $r_y(2)$, and (d) $r_y(3)$.

4.16. (*Project*) Develop a four-layer network that is structure-controllable for using fourth-order cumulants to estimate MA parameters. Provide the same level of detail as is done in the chapter for third-order cumulants.

4.17. Show that (4-53) and (4-54) can be expressed as in (4-55) and (4-56), respectively.

4.18. (*Project*) Choose an MA model and repeat Examples 4.1 and 4.2. Then use the method that is described in the chapter to handle the case of unknown noise statistics.

5

OBJECT RECOGNITION WITH GABOR FUNCTIONS IN THE DYNAMIC LINK ARCHITECTURE[*]
PARALLEL IMPLEMENTATION ON A TRANSPUTER NETWORK

Joachim Buhmann[†] and Jörg Lange
Center for Neural Engineering
Department of Computer Science
University of Southern California

Christoph von der Malsburg
Center for Neural Engineering
Departments of Computer Science and Biology
University of Southern California

Jan C. Vorbrüggen and Rolf P. Würtz
Max-Planck-Institut für Hirnforschung
Frankfurt, Germany

OBJECT RECOGNITION IN THE DYNAMIC LINK ARCHITECTURE

This chapter describes a neural object-recognition system based on a new neural information-processing concept, the dynamic link architecture [von der Malsburg, 1981, 1983, 1985]. This architecture was first proposed in 1981 as an attempt to solve certain conceptual problems of conventional neural networks. Prominent

---

[*]Supported by grants from the German Ministry for Science and Technology (ITR-8800-H1) and from the AFOSR (88-0274).
[†]Supported by NATO grant DAAD 300/402/513/9.

among these problems is the expression of syntactical relationships in neural networks. Owing to the development of the dynamic link architecture, various ambitious applications are now becoming accessible, such as distortion-invariant object recognition, sensory segmentation, and scene analysis. This may soon lead to massively parallel and fault-tolerant technical applications as well as to new insights into brain function. The dynamic link architecture is revolutionary in utilizing synaptic plasticity already on the fast time scale of information processing and not only for memory acquisition. In this way it is possible to instantly bind sets of neurons and to treat such sets as higher symbolic units. Conventional neural systems do not provide this grouping ability, simultaneous activity in several groups of neurons inevitably leading to their merging into one structureless global assembly. Whereas the conventional scheme is very successful with small, tightly predefined problem spaces, it doesn't cope well with complex problems, especially when flexibility is required.

The power of the dynamic link architecture is best demonstrated when applied to a complex problem like position- and distortion-invariant object recognition, the subject of this chapter. We chose the problem of face discrimination to demonstrate the performance of our system, which, however, is in no way specialized to that application. The recognition of faces is a particularly taxing problem, because their images can vary profoundly owing to perspective distortion and change in expression. Although our system is able to cope with these difficulties successfully, it is of utmost simplicity and generality. It has been implemented several times (on VAX, Sun, and transputers, and in Fortran, C, and OCCAM), sometimes within a few weeks, once by two students as a class project. The version we are describing here is to be regarded as a relatively primitive first step in the construction of a comprehensive model for the visual system.

This chapter on face recognition has the goal of enabling the reader to write his own first implementation of the dynamic link architecture, which may then form the basis for direct applications and for further developments.

The Problem of Invariant Pattern Recognition

Visual recognition of objects invariant with respect to viewing conditions is a major scientific issue. An artificial neural system demonstrating it convincingly under realistic constraints will very likely contain many of the architectural ingredients necessary for an understanding of the brain. A key element has to be the ability to associate two structures (image and stored object, for instance) on the basis of their structural relations, not just on the basis of their previously learned pairing. More specifically, an object should be recognized in any position on the retina after a brief examination. The challenge is to find a general way of discarding irrelevant information (about position, perspective, etc.), at the same time keeping relevant structure (especially the spatial relations within an object).

This is extremely difficult to achieve in conventional neural architecture, essentially because in that architecture, relations between neurons have to be encoded by more neurons. Since relations generally are object specific, it is difficult to build a visual architecture with intrinsic generalization over object position. The dynamic link architecture [von der Malsburg, 1981, 1983, 1985] has been developed specifically to overcome this difficulty. Structural, or more general, syntactical relationships are represented without requiring specialized neurons to do so. Feature cells that want to express the existence of a relationship (referring, for instance, to neighborhood in an object) do so by correlating their activity in time. This representation of relations is "cheap," because it requires no extra hardware. It is ubiquitously available for any order of relation (*order* meaning number of neurons involved) but is "expensive" in that it forces the system into a sequential mode and thus requires time. Correlated activity patterns are naturally produced in the nervous system by connectivity patterns (like short-range connections in the image domain), and they are interpreted by other neurons or circuits which act as coincidence detectors. The temporal activity patterns posited in the dynamic link architecture are discussed in the experimental literature as temporally shifting focal attention [Treisman and Gelade, 1980; Crick, 1984] or as temporal oscillations in local field potentials [Gray et al., 1989; Freeman, 1975; Eckhorn et al., 1988]. More comprehensive correlation patterns can be created and stabilized in a network with the help of rapid synaptic plasticity [McNaughton, 1982], which is discussed in the literature as short-term potentiation (STP) or as augmentation.

The positive feedback loop between signal correlation patterns and short-term activated connectivity patterns stabilizes certain organized connectivity patterns. Among these are two-dimensional topological networks, which are ideal for the representation of images of objects, and relational graphs between homeomorphic connectivity patterns, ideal for the implementation of attributed graph matching and pattern correlation [von der Malsburg, 1981, 1985; Buhmann et al., 1989; von der Malsburg and Bienenstock, 1986].

A neural system able to represent the binding of groups of cells into composite entities on demand and to handle these composite entities as temporary units is much more powerful than a conventional neural system. In particular, this ability frees the system from the necessity to form specialized feature detectors before it can represent new objects.

INVARIANT OBJECT RECOGNITION IN THE DYNAMIC LINK ARCHITECTURE

The specific implementation of invariant object recognition in the dynamic link architecture described in the next section is optimized for ease of implementation. In this section we give the basic idea in qualitative form. The reader interested only in the implementation may skip to the next section, which can be read independently.

Although object representation and object recognition eventually will have to be implemented in a multilevel structure, we will introduce here the basic idea based on just two levels, as shown in Figure 5.1. We will refer to the two levels as the image domain I and the object domain O. (Sometimes we want to distinguish the whole image domain $\bar{I}$ from that part I that is occupied by a specific object; likewise the whole object domain $\bar{O}$ from a single stored object O.)

The image domain is a two-dimensional sheet of neurons. Each position x of the sheet is occupied by a set of feature detectors. Such a set is called a **node**. Let us denote it by $S_x^I = \{(x, \alpha) \,|\, \alpha = 1, \dots, F\}$, where F is the number of feature types. In principle, feature cells could just be local light detectors [Bienenstock and von der Malsburg, 1987], but a slightly more sophisticated feature set is desirable; see below and [Buhmann et al., 1989].

The image domain is coupled to a light-sensor array (an eye or a camera). An image shone into the sensor array leads to the activation of a subset of the neurons in each node (or to the activation of all of the neurons in a graded fashion, depending on whether neurons are binary or analog in their output signal). The resulting signal of neuron (x, α) will be called $s_{x,\alpha}^I$, and we will refer to the vector $J_x^I = \{s_{x,\alpha}^I \,|\, \alpha = 1, \dots, F\}$ of activities in a location x of the image domain as a **jet**.

Let us denote by $T_{x,\alpha;\,y,\beta}^I$ the connection in the image domain between neuron (x, α) and neuron (y, β). These connections have to serve two purposes. They are necessary for low-level vision, that is, for the cooperative computation of the cellular signals $s_{x,\alpha}^I$. And they are necessary to encode neighborhood relations in the form of correlated signal fluctuations; see below. For our present purposes it is enough to assume that once a set of neurons has been activated by low-level vision mechanisms, the connections between neurons of this set are excitatory and of short range.

After these preparations we can see that an image is represented in the image domain as an attributed graph. Its nodes are what we already have called nodes. Its attributes are vectors of activity of local feature detectors in nodes, which we called jets. And its links are the connections $T_{x,\alpha;\,y,\beta}^I$ for $x \neq y$.[1] A particular object is represented by that part of the image domain which is affected by the object.

The object domain is an associative memory in which attributed graphs can be stored and from which they can be retrieved. Individual stored graphs are idealized copies of graphs in the image domain. Various versions of an associative memory for graph structures have been implemented [von der Malsburg, 1985, 1988; von der Malsburg and Bienenstock, 1987], but details don't matter here.

To summarize so far, patterns in both the image domain and in the object domain are represented by attributed graphs. The nodes of the graphs refer to points in two-dimensional images of objects. Attributes are constituted by jets, that is, feature vectors which describe local patterns around the points referred to by the

---

[1] An alternative (almost equivalent) view would consider individual feature detectors as nodes, their activities as attributes, and all T^I connections as links.

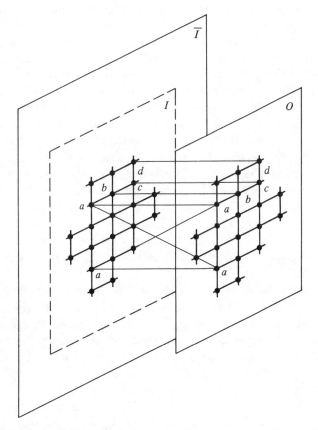

FIGURE 5.1 Matching graphs in image domain and object domain. Within the object domain (designated $\bar{O}$, not shown) there is a subgraph O that is *isomorphic* to a subgraph I in the image domain $\bar{I}$: I and O contain the same feature types $(a, b, c, \ldots)$ in the same arrangement (only one feature type shown per node, for simplicity). In both domains, neurons in neighboring nodes (and within nodes, not shown) are connected. Connections between domains are feature-type preserving, but not position specific (for example, all a-detectors in I are connected to all a-detectors in O). Owing to isomorphy, all connections between corresponding points exist. Graph dynamics is a positive feedback loop: signal correlations favor activation of links, active links produce correlations. Locally, graph dynamics favors richly connected blocks of neurons—here, blocks are formed out of neighboring cells in I and neighboring cells in O, in corresponding positions. More globally, dynamic attractors are optimal combinations of local blocks—here, the graph composed of subgraph I of $\bar{I}$, subgraph O of $\bar{O}$, and connections between corresponding nodes. Other objects in $\bar{O}$ lose the competition; they have a different arrangement of feature types, and there isn't a complete system of one-to-one connections to I.

nodes. Links of the graphs connect neighboring points in the patterns. The problem of object identification is then the problem of attributed graph matching.

What machinery is necessary to perform this attributed graph matching? The basis must be a signal code which allows to send information on attributes and links from the image domain to the object domain. This has to be done without automatically sending information on position within the image domain to achieve our goal of separating position information from relational information.

Here is a signal code which does just that. We assume that the actual output signal $\sigma_{x,\alpha}^I(t)$ of neuron (x,α) in I fluctuates rapidly in time. The structure of the signal $\sigma_{x,\alpha}^I(t)$ is determined by three factors: the input image, random spontaneous excitation within neurons, and interaction with other cells of the same or neighboring nodes in the image domain, using connections $T_{x,\alpha;y,\beta}^I$. The actual attribute values can be read off the fluctuating signals as time averages, $s_{x,\alpha}^I = \langle \sigma_{x,\alpha}(t) \rangle_t$, where the average $\langle \cdot \rangle_t$ is taken over a time interval shorter than the presentation time of the image. The neighborhood relationships between neurons can be read off the correlations $C_{x,\alpha;y,\beta}^I = \langle \sigma_{x,\alpha}^I \sigma_{y,\beta}^I \rangle_t$, these correlations being induced by the excitatory connections within I.

The correlations $C_{x,\alpha;y,\beta}^I$ encode two types of information. The correlations $C_{x,\alpha;x,\beta}^I$ within a node bind the components of a jet to each other; the correlations between cells in different nodes, a decreasing function of distance due to decreasing connection strengths, encode neighborhood relationships between jets.

A second requirement for attributed graph matching between the image domain and the object domain is the existence of physical connections. These have the form of feature-preserving connections between cells in the image domain and cells in the object domain: two neurons, one in the image domain, one in the object domain, have a connection between them if and only if they belong to the same feature type. There is no condition on the position within the image domain—there couldn't be, since the object and its features could appear in any part of the image domain.

After a segment of the image domain has been selected as a possible candidate for recognition as an object, the attributed graph-matching process has to identify a matching graph in the object domain. As part of this job it has to identify nodes in the image domain with nodes in the object domain. This identification is based on two types of evidence. One type talks about the similarity of attributes in image and object. This evidence leaves ambiguities, depending on the level of specificity of attributes. The other type of evidence is based on the graph structure and can be formulated as the requirement of mapping neighboring nodes in the image to neighboring nodes in the object.

Attributed graph matching has often been discussed in the context of object recognition. Many authors feel, though, that its computational complexity is prohibitive. It is known that subgraph matching is NP-complete in the general case [Garey and Johnson, 1979]. There are, however, specific kinds of graphs for which there are efficient algorithms (e.g., [Miller, 1980]). The graphs we are dealing with in visual object recognition are special in that they all have the same basic structure, based on the topology of the two-dimensional plane. In addition, the existence of labels or attributes reduces the complexity of the problem further. It is likely that the complexity of the problem is logarithmic in the size of the graphs, given parallel hardware.

We will give here a qualitative description of the particular process by which attributed graph matching is implemented in the dynamic link architecture. This implementation is based on rapidly modifiable synaptic connections. The underlying mechanism works in the following way. A connection between two neurons i and j is characterized by two numbers, T_{ij} and J_{ij}. The former describes the "permanent" weight of the connection, which may be changed slowly by long-term synaptic plasticity. The latter, J_{ij}, changes rapidly, is constrained by T_{ij} (for instance as $0 \leq J_{ij} \leq T_{ij}$), and is the synaptic weight responsible for coupling signals between neurons. The short-term weights J_{ij} are controlled by signal correlations $C_{ij} = \langle \sigma_i \sigma_j \rangle_t$ between neurons i and j. Negative C_{ij} leads to decrease, positive C_{ij} leads to increase of J_{ij}. In the absence of controlling signals in the two neurons, J_{ij} slowly returns to some resting value J_{ij}^o, a fixed fraction of T_{ij}.

The dynamic link architecture replaces the mere spread of activity in conventional neural networks by a rapid process of self-organization. This process is based on the following loop of interactions. A network with a given set of connectivity variables J_{ij} supports an activity process from which correlations can be read off. These correlations control changes in connectivity values. The modified network then supports a modified activity process, closing the loop. This loop creates a runaway situation which can profoundly change the structure of the connectivity J_{ij}. Certain connectivity patterns, though, are stabilized by the organization loop. Let us reserve the term **connectivity pattern** for them. There is a universe of connectivity patterns, determined in their structure largely by the nature of the loop of organization described. Of particular importance here is the fact that this universe contains the two-dimensional topological graphs necessary to represent objects as well as the composite graphs formed when matching image to object in one-to-one mappings.

In our particular application, both the connections from the image domain to the object domain, and the connections within the object domain, are short-term modifiable. (There is no need here for the connections in the image domain to be modifiable, although this may be important for image segmentation.) The process of graph matching now takes the following form. When an image is presented to the unprimed system, activity is pumped into a subgraph of the complete system. This subgraph contains the neurons activated in $\bar{I}$ (the image domain), those neurons in $\bar{O}$ with feature types which are active somewhere in $\bar{I}$, and all connections between active cells in $\bar{I}$ and $\bar{O}$. If there is a stored object graph O that is isomorphic to a part I of the image, then graph dynamics has to find and selectively activate the subgraph composed of I, O, and the one-to-one connections between corresponding points in I and O. This dynamic process has three aspects to it—identification and selective activation of I, identification and selective activation of O, and switching off of all J_{ij} between noncorresponding points in $\bar{I}$ and $\bar{O}$.

The first of these processes amounts to figure-ground separation. Part of it can already be done without reference to $\bar{O}$, on the basis of low-level information. The basic principle is this. Pairs of nodes that are close to each other in image space and that describe similar local quality (expressed by similarity of the vectors $s^I_{x,\alpha}$ and $s^I_{x',\alpha}$) are strongly coupled to each other and tend to synchronize their activity. This is likely to happen within parts of the image corresponding to one object. On the other hand, pairs of nodes that describe different local quality are coupled less strongly and have a weaker tendency to synchronize. This principle can be exploited to break the dynamic links between segments and to strengthen them within segments, as has been shown in simulations [von der Malsburg and Schneider, 1986; Schneider, 1986].

The second of these processes, retrieval of a graph from an associative memory for graphs, has been demonstrated before [von der Malsburg, 1985, 1988; von der Malsburg and Bienenstock, 1987]. Different degrees of cellwise overlap between stored objects have been realized in those studies. They ranged from 100% [von der Malsburg, 1985; von der Malsburg and Bienenstock, 1987] over a fraction [von der Malsburg, 1988] to disjoint objects [Buhmann et al., 1989].

The last process, reduction of the $I \leftrightarrow O$ connections to a one-to-one projection between nodes, is analogous (on a different time scale) to the ontogenetic problem of establishing topological fiber projections. The process is driven by an elementary event in which a cluster of cells fires, and all connections within the cluster are strengthened at the expense of competing connections. About half of the cluster is part of the image domain, the other half lying in the object domain. Each of the halves is likely to comprise cells contiguous in the image or in the object, because such sets of cells are tightly coupled by the topological connections within those domains. The two halves of a cluster preferentially lie in corresponding positions in the image and in an object structurally related to part of the image, because only then are a large number of feature-specific $I \leftrightarrow O$ connections guaranteed to exist.

This process of paring down many-to-many connections between topological connectivity patterns to one-to-one connections has been studied extensively, both in computer simulations [Willshaw and von der Malsburg, 1976, 1979] and analytically [Häussler and von der Malsburg, 1983]. The latter study, especially, shows that for the particular graphs of interest here the reduction of a many-to-many connection pattern to a one-to-one connection pattern can be achieved without backtracking as a deterministic, hierarchically structured sequence. In early stages of the process large parts of the input graph are selectively connected to large parts of the output graph; in later stages the process is applied on a smaller scale and in parallel to the mapping of subparts to subparts.

In a first implementation [Bienenstock and von der Malsburg, 1987] of the whole process of attributed graph matching just described, the image domain I was a regular grid of nodes, each containing just two feature types, a black pixel and a white pixel. The object domain O contained a superposition of several graphs, each describing a different arrangement of black and white pixels. All of the stored graphs were formed out of the same set of 100 cells, 50 black, 50 white, in permuted order. In simulations on a Cray XMP it was possible to demonstrate position- and distortion-invariant pattern identification. The system was based on a graph-mutation process which optimized the number of cycles of length 4 (formed, for instance, by two neighboring cells in I and two neighboring cells in O). An apparent weakness of the implementation was its excessive time requirement: recognition of a letter took the Cray about 5 minutes. This was due to three factors: the small number (two) of feature types, the 100% cellwise overlap between stored graphs, and an optimization process based on too-small clusters (comprising only four cells). The small number of feature types leads to immense ambiguity in the $I \leftrightarrow O$ connections, one cell connecting to half of all the cells in the other structure.

In a second study [von der Malsburg, 1988], much faster object identification was possible. The system was based on 50 types of distinguishable features, one feature type per position in I (synthetic data), on a process of matching clusters of 9 cells in I to clusters of about 9 cells in O, and on small overlap between objects. After only a few cluster activations it was usually possible to identify the correct object.

SPECIFIC IMPLEMENTATION

As our application domain we chose camera-derived grey-level images of the format 128×128 pixels. The system is in no way specialized to a specific type of object, but we decided to exercise it with human portrait images. We have also tried it with infrared images of vehicles taken with varying perspective, with satisfactory results [von der Malsburg et al., 1988]. In our implementation we put emphasis on simplicity rather than detailed neural style. The overall process management is done in conventional algorithmic fashion. Image coding is based on Morlet wavelets, which correspond well with what we know about receptive field types in the visual cortex [Marčelja, 1980; Jones and Palmer, 1987].

Image Coding

Gabor and wavelet transform. In an abstract sense, any (linear) transformation of an image represents the image by its scalar products with functions taken from a fixed family. The properties of the transform follow inevitably from the properties of the function family. The reader will know at least two possible image representations. The simplest one consists simply of local samples of grey value. You might not consider that a transform, but it corresponds to forming the scalar product with the set of functions that are 1 for a specific pixel and 0 elsewhere. In the ideal case of infinite resolution, these functions are known as δ functions. They can be visualized as extremely sharp and high peaks and thought of as instruments to measure values at specific locations in (two-dimensional) space.

The other representation is given by the Fourier transform of the image. In terms of function families, this corresponds to the scalar product with a set of sines and cosines which can be combined to functions of the form e^{ikx}. They measure the spatial periodicity belonging to a given frequency.

These two transformations or representations are extreme opposites in the sense that δ functions are localized in ordinary space, whereas sines and cosines are localized in frequency space. Each of them is excellent at measuring what it is designed to measure and perfectly unable to do the task of the other one. It is common knowledge that δ functions contain *all* frequencies, and it is obvious that sines and cosines are spread out over the entire plane.

For many reasons, e.g., to get rid of high-frequency noise and to become insensitive to global distortions, it is desirable to find a compromise between these extremes, i.e., to have a family of functions which are localized both in space (making them good local detectors) *and* in the frequency domain (making them good frequency detectors). In the context of modeling brain function, there is good evidence that so-called simple cells in the visual cortex have both properties [Marčelja, 1980; Jones and Palmer, 1987].

The degree to which a filter function can simultaneously attain precision in the spatial domain and in the frequency domain is limited by an uncertainty principle which directly results from a mathematical property of the Fourier transform, the Cauchy-Schwartz inequality. (In the context of quantum mechanics, the principle is named after Heisenberg.) It states that for any function the product of the widths in the spatial domain and in the frequency domain cannot be arbitrarily small, and there is a well-defined minimum (which in physics corresponds to Planck's constant and generally depends on the units of measurement for space and frequency).

To achieve optimal system behavior, it seems a good idea to use functions which indeed achieve that minimum uncertainty (see Problem 5.1). In 1946 D. Gabor introduced a new transform into signal analysis [Gabor, 1946]. The idea is related to that of the Fourier transform and differs from it by the introduction of a narrow window that restricts the transform functions in the spatial domain.

There still is freedom in the choice of the window function, but a minimum uncertainty product can only be attained by Gaussian windows. Gabor's functions have the following form:

$$\gamma_k \;=\; a_{k,\sigma}\, \exp\left(-\frac{x^2}{2\sigma^2}\right)\exp\left(ikx\right) \qquad (5\text{-}1)$$

where the constant $a_{k,\sigma}$ is a normalization constant to ensure $\|\psi_k\| = 1$. We will use a family of functions related to (5-1) which describe an object at different frequency scales or levels of resolution. In the last couple of years much work has been done on families of transform functions which are self-similar at different scales. They have been named **wavelets** [Combes et al., 1989]. Wavelets are self-similar in the sense that members of the family are all identical in shape, being related by shift and dilation (i.e., scaling in the space variable). In the case of Gabor functions this obviously implies that the wavelength of the oscillation has to be in a fixed proportion to the width of the window. This gives us the following formula for wavelets based on Gabor functions:

$$\psi_k = b_{k,\sigma} \exp\left(-\frac{k^2 x^2}{2\sigma^2}\right) \exp\left(ikx\right) \tag{5-2}$$

Honoring J. Morlet, who first studied these functions, they are called **Morlet wavelets**.[2] For any fixed frequency they are identical to Gabor functions. Note that (5-2) differs from (5-1) only by the factor k^2 in the Gaussian window. Of course, optimality with respect to the uncertainty principle is preserved. These families of functions have stimulated a lot of research in recent years. This is due to their beautiful mathematical properties (see, e.g., [Daubechies et al., 1986]), their appropriateness for signal-processing applications, and their biological relevance.

In order to adapt (5-2) for application to two-dimensional images, we replace the variables k and x by vectors and interpret the products as scalar products in two-dimensional vector space:

$$\psi_{\mathbf{k}} := n_{k,\sigma} \exp\left(\frac{-\mathbf{k}^2 \mathbf{x}^2}{2\sigma^2}\right) \exp\left(i\mathbf{k}\mathbf{x}\right) \tag{5-3}$$

Here, $k = |\mathbf{k}|$, and $n_{k,\sigma}$ again is a normalization constant. As demonstrated in Figure 5.2, this leads to a set of functions which are shifted, scaled or *rotated* versions of each other. The continuous Fourier transform of $\psi_{\mathbf{k}}$ is (the proof is left to the reader as an exercise; see Problems 5.1 and 5.9):

$$(\mathcal{F}\psi_{\mathbf{k}})(\boldsymbol{\omega}) = m_{k,\sigma} \exp\left(-\frac{\sigma^2(\boldsymbol{\omega} - \mathbf{k})^2}{2k^2}\right) \tag{5-4}$$

Unlike the sines and cosines of the Fourier transform, wavelets are localized in space. Correspondingly, that the Morlet transform still contains a position variable:

$$(\mathcal{W}I)(\mathbf{k}, \mathbf{x}_0) := \int \psi_{\mathbf{k}}(\mathbf{x}_0 - \mathbf{x})I(\mathbf{x})\, d^2 x \tag{5-5}$$

where $\mathbf{x}_0$ ranges over the image plane and $\mathbf{k}$ ranges over the frequency plane. Equation (5-5) can be interpreted as the scalar product of the intensity function $I(\mathbf{x})$ with a shifted version of $\psi_{\mathbf{k}}$, which was our above intention, or as a *convolution* with $\psi_{\mathbf{k}}$. Owing to the latter interpretation, wavelets (or Gabor functions) may be considered as transformation *kernels*. We will switch back and forth between these interpretations whenever it seems convenient.

The properties of the two-dimensional wavelet transforms are not as well known as they are in one dimension, but research is in progress [Murenzi, 1989] and will (hopefully very soon) provide a better theoretical foundation for our algorithm.

---

[2]To really meet the definition of a wavelet, a slight correction term would have to be added to make the function "admissible," i.e., of integral 0. The correction is negligible in practice for the values of σ we are considering here [Grossmann and Morlet, 1985].

 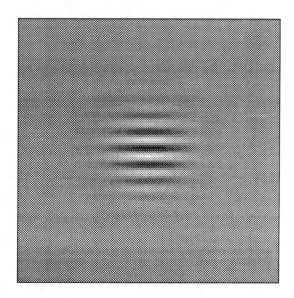

FIGURE 5.2 Bird's-eye view of two different wavelets. On the left-hand side the real part (cosine phase) of the wavelet for $|\mathbf{k}| = 0.55$, $\phi = 45°$, on the right the imaginary part (sine phase) of the wavelet for $|\mathbf{k}| = 0.78$, $\phi = 90°$.

Jets.   We have defined the wavelet transform as a linear operator on the space of all possible images. We will now drop the property of linearity by introducing two nonlinear distortions of the wavelet transform. In return we obtain a set of feature values that measure intensity gradients on various scales of resolution. If you look at the convolution of a sharp intensity edge with a Morlet kernel (Problem 5.2), you will realize that $(\mathcal{W}I)(\mathbf{k}, \mathbf{x}_0)$ is a rapidly oscillating function of $\mathbf{x}_0$ with a wavelength of $2\pi/k$, due to the oscillatory part of (5-3). This implies that the presence of an edge is signaled by large positive and negative numbers.

Here are our nonlinearities. Instead of using the convolution result directly to encode image properties, we take the modulus of the transform, which varies smoothly across an intensity variation and thus greatly alleviates jet matching (see below). A second nonlinearity is introduced to let receptive fields of all sizes contribute about equally to the matching procedure. In many grey-level images the low-frequency coefficients are considerably larger than those for high frequency, although important structure is encoded in the latter. We normalize the different frequency scales by dividing the transform by the average modulus of all components at fixed k. Our final formula for the jet formed for image I at position $\mathbf{x}_0$ is:

$$\mathcal{J}I(\mathbf{k}, \mathbf{x}_0) \quad = \quad \frac{|\mathcal{W}I|}{\int |\mathcal{W}I|\, d^2x\, d\phi} \tag{5-6}$$

where ϕ is the orientation of $\mathbf{k}$ in the frequency plane.

The nonlinearities just introduced save us a lot of trouble when matching input images to stored images. On the other hand they cause theoretical problems about information content and render image reconstruction difficult. It is not clear whether the loss of information incurred when abolishing phases and normalizing magnitudes in (5-6) leaves intact those aspects of image structure that are essential for object recognition.

Frequency sampling.   The Morlet transform (5-5) can be seen as a form of local Fourier transform. Its output is a function on the four-dimensional space spanned by the two spatial coordinates x_0 and the two frequency coordinates k. There are many ways of placing samples in this space. For this placement it is important to know about the dependence between values in different points of (x_0, k)-space. On the x_0 dependence we will comment below, in connection with discussion of the method of transformation. The transform (5-5), taken as a function of k, is a low-pass filtered version of the full Fourier transform of the image. The width of the filter kernel is k/σ; see (5-4). This relationship dictates the density of samples in k-space. A reasonable way to implement the sampling is to subdivide frequency space into a sequence of rings with widths proportional to k/σ (where k is the middle radius), and each ring into sectors of equal size. This cuts the k-space into frequency bands which correspond to the orientation detectors found in the visual cortex [Jones and Palmer, 1987; Hubel and Wiesel, 1962]. Our particular way of sampling the frequency domain is described in a later section (see also Problem 5.3). As a result of discrete frequency sampling, our jet (5-6) is turned into a vector with as many components as there are frequency bands.

Implementation of the image transform.   This section contains some technical details on the image transform we are using. Readers who consider this trivial or are not writing their own implementation may proceed to the next section.

For a given frequency k the Morlet transform takes the form of a convolution, as was mentioned before. An efficient way to implement a convolution is to first calculate the fast Fourier transform (FFT) of image and kernel, then their (complex) pointwise product in the frequency domain, and finally the inverse FFT of the product back into the spatial domain. This procedure is summarized by the formula:

$$f * g \;=\; \mathcal{F}^{-1}((\mathcal{F}f) \cdot (\mathcal{F}g)) \tag{5-7}$$

In general, this method is suboptimal (see, e.g., [Nussbaumer, 1982]), but in our special case there are several circumstances which further recommend it.

- The *same* data is to be convolved with many different filters (in our case one for each value of k), so the forward FFT of the data has to be done only once.

- The Fourier transform of the kernels can be calculated analytically (5-4), which means that no numerical FFT of the kernels has to be performed.

- Calculation of kernels is cheaper in the frequency domain than in the spatial domain, because only one transcendental function (the exponential) is required instead of three (exponential, sine, and cosine).

- As the Fourier transforms of our kernels are *real*, the complex multiplication reduces to two real ones.

On the other hand, this method works just "the wrong way round." Because we think of our jets to be local descriptors of points, we would like to have a (preferably fast) algorithm that could calculate the jets for selected points—in other words, the Morlet transform for fixed x_0 instead of for fixed $\mathbf{k}$. Unfortunately, our integral (5-5) in that case no longer has the form of a convolution, and we don't have an algorithm of complexity $O(n \log n)$ to calculate it. The argument can be put quantitatively, and it turns out that the FFT implementation is faster than the direct integral if more jets are required than twice the number of filters in the transform. This, however, will certainly be true when we try to match our object with part of the image domain. As a consequence, we have to store the *complete* Morlet transform of the image, which may require a huge amount of memory. With our standard set of parameters (described in a later section), this adds up to $128^2 \cdot 6 \cdot 8$ complex numbers of four bytes each, or 6.29 Mbytes, but is cut in half by the fact that we only keep the modulus of the complex numbers.

Now there are several ways to handle the problem, but remember that there is always a tradeoff between memory requirement and computation time. (This is due to the "law of conservation of trouble," which limits the simultaneous optimization of the use of both resources—of course it does not prevent algorithms from behaving arbitrarily badly in either respect.)

- **Brute Cash Method:** If you have sufficient RAM at hand, just use it and don't bother. This method has no theoretical drawbacks. If your RAM is distributed in a parallel system, you pay in terms of some "bureaucratic overhead," but you will gain insight in parallel programming.

- **Nyquist's Method:** As our kernels can be regarded as bandpass filters, the results will be band-limited in a predictable way. The sampling theorem then gives a lower bound on the number of samples to be kept without losing information. This certainly is less than the original size of the image if your frequency bands don't span the full range. The result is a resolution pyramid. But now the information, although not lost, will be harder to retrieve. To obtain the jet for an arbitrary point would require interpolation, and consequently time.

- **Accuracy Method:** Remember that numerical accuracy is not the name of the game in our pattern-recognition concept, and certainly it makes no sense to store the transformed image with a higher accuracy than the original data. The typical accuracy of camera pictures is 1 byte/pixel, so by just rescaling the four-byte floating-point numbers to the range $[0, 255]$ and converting them to single bytes, one can roughly save 75% of the memory required. (Actually it is a bit less than that, because the scaling factors must be kept as well.) Theoretically, the accuracy could be cut further this way, but this is not very practical in high-level programming languages that usually do not provide efficient access to data items smaller than one byte.

- Finally, if RAM is really limited, one has to give up the FFT method and calculate the integrals directly. As in such a case the CPU is probably the limiting factor, this cannot be recommended.

Before we discuss the calculation of $\mathcal{F}\psi_k$, it should be mentioned that the lion's share of computation time is consumed by the convolution, so that if this is well optimized, the rest won't probably be worth your effort. Anyway, we will give some brief comments on how we did it.

The factor $m_{k,\sigma}$ in front of the transformed kernel (see (5-4)) is constant within frequency levels (that is, within sets of k with constant length k—don't confuse this with the frequency bands mentioned earlier). Provided that the transform is rescaled by the average value over a frequency level (or something else which depends only on $|\mathbf{k}|$), this factor will be modified anyway, and there is no point in including it in the computation of the kernel.

The next thing to be noted is that all kernels at a given frequency level (fixed k) are just shifted versions of each other, or of a standard generic one. A shift in the indices of a matrix is computationally very cheap. The simplest way to produce such a "generic kernel" is by putting $\mathbf{k} = 0$ in the numerator (but obviously not the denominator) of the exponent of (5-4). To move between frequency levels requires only raising the given kernel to a certain power. If the frequency steps happen to be half octaves, as described in [Buhmann et al., 1989], walking down one step is equivalent to squaring the generic kernel, which is very fast compared to computing the transcendental functions. Although this sounds good theoretically, one has to take rounding and discretization errors into account. The fact that we don't need very high accuracy somewhat alleviates the problem, but it still needs close attention.

The discrete Fourier transform is only an approximation. One consequence is that the data is assumed to be cyclic; in other words, the natural domain will be a torus rather than a square. Although it is no problem to "glue" the appropriate sides of the square together, this usually leads to artificial intensity discontinuities at the borderlines, and, as a result of the wrap-around operation, we get large wavelet coefficients. We chose to smooth our images at the edges, which means replacing the actual values at a frame of, say, 1 to 5 pixels by an interpolation of the values on opposite edges.

Object Domain

The image coding is the hardest part of the implementation, in terms of computational resources as well as of programming effort. Now let's briefly review what our object recognition will be like.

According to our general scheme introduced earlier, the object domain $\overline{O}$ is formed by a collection of attributed graphs, one for each stored object. We chose to store each object as a separate data set, without paying too much attention to detailed neural style. For a given object we shall denote the vertex set by V, the edge set by E, and an edge connecting vertices i and j by (i, j). The *vertices* correspond to positions within the object and are labeled by the jets defined above. All *edges* carry as label the vector connecting the two vertices. This is needed for the constraint to preserve the topological arrangement of points between the image domain and the object domain.

For each object to be stored, a labeled graph is created by picking jets from a grid of points centered at the object and noting the position vectors of these points. At present we are using a regular grid of points in the image space and we are centering it on the object by hand. In future versions, the selection of jets should be automatic by picking salient points in the image in a reproducible way. We ran promising preliminary simulations based on a saliency measure in terms of the length of jets or of their low-frequency part. For face recognition salient points were located around the eyes, the nose, the mouth, and near the borderline between the face and the background. A theoretically sound way to generate the graph would be to measure the information content per jet and to select image points with a large information content, provided they cover the whole object and do not lump together in one location. More work is required here.

Object Recognition by Graph Matching

Outline.   Now we are ready to do object recognition. Each object in memory is selected in turn and attempts a match to part of the image. The matching operation amounts to the creation of a composite graph, consisting of the object graph just described, an image graph, and links between vertices corresponding to each other in the two graphs. We simplify the process by selecting exactly one vertex in the image for each vertex in the object and by creating exactly one link in the image graph for each link in the object graph. Attributes are formed by noting (or forming, depending on implementation details) the image jet at the location of an image vertex, and by noting the position vector. The total graph thus created is now optimized by moving the image vertices around in a diffusion process. Optimization is done by minimizing some cost function that characterizes the total graph. The cost function contains two terms, one measuring resemblance between object jets and corresponding image jets, the other comparing image links to object links. An object is recognized by comparing the minimal costs achieved for each stored object and picking the best. Subsequent statistical analysis of the values allows us to estimate the reliabiltiy of the identification.

Picking an initial image graph.   The procedure of graph matching is started by picking an initial image graph. In our implementation the vertices of the object graphs all lie on a rectangular grid. The simplest way to initialize the image graph is to pick a grid of image points of identical arrangement, in a location selected by hand. This is what we do at present. This is cheating, to be sure, since the whole process should be automatic and shouldn't rely on human intervention, and we will have to return to this point later.

Cost function. Resemblance between jets is measured by means of a similarity function $\mathcal{S}(\mathcal{J}^O, \mathcal{J}^I)$, to which we will return in a moment. Similarities are added up over all pairs of corresponding points in the two graphs, yielding a "jet cost function":

$$C_{\text{jet}} \quad := \quad \sum_{i \in V} \mathcal{S}(\mathcal{J}_i^O, \mathcal{J}_i^I) \tag{5-8}$$

If this term were minimized on its own, a topologically scrambled projection between image domain and object domain would result. We therefore introduce a *penalty for image graph deformation* or "topological cost function":

$$C_{\text{top}} \quad := \quad \sum_{(i,j) \in E} (\Delta_{(i,j)}^I - \Delta_{(i,j)}^O)^2 \tag{5-9}$$

Obviously a good match will be one where both these costs are minimized concurrently. We merge them into one cost function:

$$C_{\text{total}} \quad := \quad \lambda C_{\text{top}} + C_{\text{jet}} \tag{5-10}$$

The factor λ serves a double purpose. It adapts the different units of measure for topological and jet costs, and its variation controls the degree of rigidity with which the shape of the object graph is reproduced in the image graph.

Now we have a cost function (for economists) or a Hamiltonian (for physicists) at hand, which can be minimized by a suitable algorithm. The reader is invited to choose his favorite one, but we will describe ours in the next section. Before we do that we still have to specify two things: the edge set E for the object and the image graph (the graph topology), and the similarity function $\mathcal{S}$ to compare jets. Both of them certainly influence the discriminatory power of the system. It is not easy to define criteria for choosing their structure, so we let simplicity dictate our choice—which, however, cannot be the last word.

For graph topology we chose a *complete* graph; every pair of vertices from either the image or the object graph is connected by an edge. We also tried nearest-neighbor edges, with slightly different results; in this case the graph deforms like an elastic sheet.

Ignoring the fact that jets represent functions on a radially sampled frequency plane, we simply regard them as vectors in a high-dimensional Euclidean vector space (the dimensionality being the number of samples taken in the frequency domain). In this space we can calculate the angle of two elements (or rather the cosine of that angle) using the scalar product, normalized by vector length. This function has the nice property that it is always less than or equal to 1, and the equality holds

 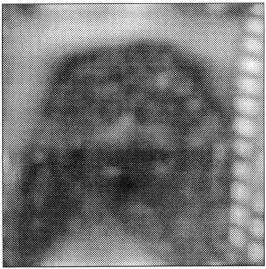

FIGURE 5.3 A jet centered on the tip of Rolf's nose is compared with all other jets and the results are coded as grey values (black is the best match). This gives an impression of the "force field" controlling vertex diffusion.

if and only if the vectors have the same direction. We want the cost to be minimal for equal jets, which requires a negative sign:

$$\mathcal{S}(\mathcal{J}_1, \mathcal{J}_2) \quad := \quad -\frac{\mathcal{J}_1 \cdot \mathcal{J}_2}{\|\mathcal{J}_1\| \, \|\mathcal{J}_2\|} \qquad (5\text{-}11)$$

Although these choices may not be optimal, we have achieved satisfactory results with them. A different choice for the similarity measure is described in [Buhmann et al., 1989]. There, two additional factors are included in $\mathcal{S}$ which favor equal lengths for the two jets compared and which emphasize the importance of long jets. Our comparison of the two similarity functions is not yet conclusive.

Vertex diffusion.   The optimization of the cost function is done by an off-the-shelf Monte Carlo method known as the **Metropolis algorithm**. It starts with our initial guess for the image graph. This graph is compared to the object graph in terms of the total cost (5-11). To improve this value, we choose a random vertex in the image graph and shift it by a random displacement vector (of suitably restricted length). Then the total cost value is recalculated. If the new value is lower, the displacement is accepted and made permanent. Otherwise the old position is kept for that point. This process of vertex diffusion is repeated until the cost value doesn't improve any longer. For examples of resulting graphs, see Figure 5.5. Our break-off criterion was chosen again for its simplicity—we stop the process when more than

 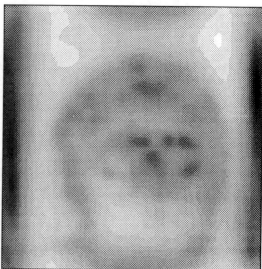

FIGURE 5.4 This figure shows Jan's face and the Euclidean lengths of all the jets (coded again as grey values, with the largest values in black). These lengths provide some sort of saliency measure.

a preset number of consecutive trials have failed. It should be mentioned that the Metropolis algorithm in its original form contained an additional parameter, called "temperature." Positive values of it help to avoid local minima in the optimization. Our version amounts to "simulated annealing at temperature 0," which is simpler (and faster!) and proved sufficient for our purpose.

To gain further insight into the diffusion dynamics, it is instructive to plot the similarity function $\mathcal{S}(\mathcal{J}_0^O, \mathcal{J}_x^I)$ of a preselected object jet $\mathcal{J}_0^O$ with all jets in the image domain; see Figure 5.3. The resulting two-dimensional function can be interpreted as a potential, the gradient of which is a force acting on vertex diffusion. In case the potential contains only one broad minimum, the zero-temperature Monte-Carlo method will find it. On the other hand, if the potential has local minima, the algorithm has to allow occasional ascent. This can be done with simulated annealing, a method that has proved to be of very general applicability. We therefore feel confident that our diffusion algorithm, especially when used at finite temperature, will be able to give robust results for a large class of object types and imaging processes.

The sequence of updates of position x^I for given x^O can be formalized as a Markov process, and the position of x^I in image space can be desribed by a probability distribution that evolves in time. In the limit of many iteration steps and of high image resolution, time and space can be approximated as continuous variables, and this evolution is described by a partial differential equation, which

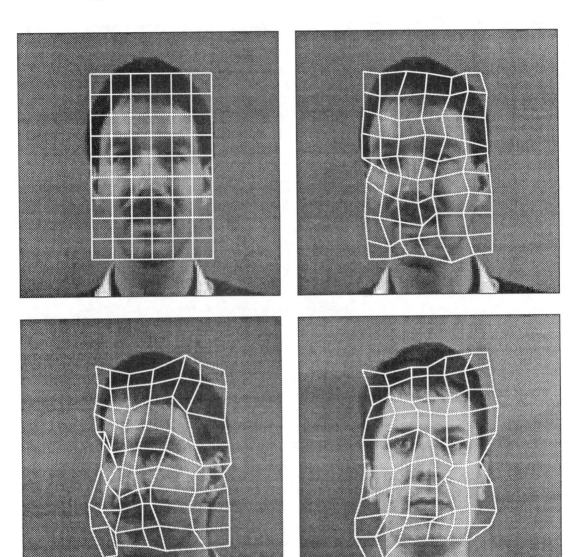

FIGURE 5.5 *Upper left picture:* Joachim's face with a rectangular grid as an example of a stored "object." The other pictures show different views of his and Jörg's faces and the image graphs that best match the object graph. All edges of the graph are shown: in this particular set of runs only neighbors contributed to the topology term in Equation (5-10).

is called a **Fokker-Planck equation (FPE)**. The gradient of the cost function C_{total} in Equation (5-10) enters the FPE as a drift term, whereas the stochastic update with finite temperature gives a diffusion term. In Problems 5.5 and 5.6 the reader is encouraged to derive FPEs for simple Markov processes, free one-dimensional diffusion, and diffusion in a quadratic potential.

Automatic determination of the initial graph. Let us come back here to the issue of selecting the initial image graph, which in the version we gave so far needed human intervention. The problem is really that of selecting an image region as the object to be recognized. A mature visual system needs complicated management structure to select a region of interest and to segment it from the background. In our tests we made sure that the image domain contained only one interesting object against a rather unstructured backdrop.

A naive guess for an initial vertex set for the image graph may be a random set of points. Unfortunately it is extremely hard for the diffusion process to unscramble a garbled graph, owing to many local minima. The next best guess is a topologically correct graph in a random (or some standard) position. But now each single point, in groping for a better match in the image, has to work against the topology constraint, which keeps it near its (so far undisplaced) neighbors. As a consequence, the grid can only move extremely slowly. Fortunately, there's an easy way out of this difficulty. If moving around single points is too expensive, then why not move the whole graph? And indeed, choosing a single displacement vector and then moving *all the points* by this same vector makes the arbitrary initial graph move (undeformed) over the image and settle in a position where it covers the object. After this procedure has converged, the system switches to the previously described mode of individual point diffusion. The initial location of the image graph could be done once, for the first trial object, and could then be employed as a starting point for all consecutive objects.

Recognition statistics. Some simple statistics have been applied to check the significance of recognition. When the image is compared with all objects, the final result of the matching algorithm will be an array with as many entries as there are objects. The entry with minimal cost value corresponds to the recognized object. We will refer to this array as **final cost values**. Clearly, the recognition is only reliable if these values differ significantly. In order to get a measure for the quality of matches, we currently assume that the set of all final cost values *excluding the minimum* form a normal distribution. We calculate the mean and the standard deviation and divide the distance of the maximum from the mean by the standard deviation. Applying an inverse *erf* function yields a number that can be interpreted as a probability for the recognition to be incorrect. The results of this method seem to correspond well with the subjective quality of the match. The only drawback for our recognition statistics is that we cannot really justify the assumption of a normal distribution.

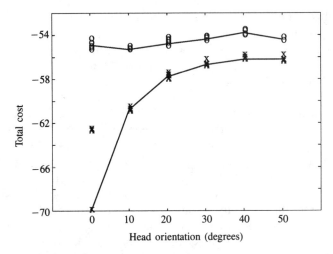

FIGURE 5.6 Matching of one image (of Rolf, looking straight ahead, no glasses) with a number of other images ("objects"). Each match has been repeated with different random-number seeds, yielding local clusters of points. *Lower curve*: Rolf, taken at different angles of head orientation, no glasses. The lowest value, −70 at 0°, corresponds to the image compared to itself. *Isolated cluster*: The object is Rolf, looking straight ahead, wearing glasses. *Upper curve*: Jan, wearing glasses, at different head orientations.

Object-Recognition Performance

Apart from some successful trials on infrared images of vehicles [von der Malsburg et al., 1988] we tried our system on human-face images. Since our main interest is in further development of our system to overcome its limitations (see the discussion section), we didn't invest much effort in a systematic evaluation of recognition performance. We acquired a picture gallery by just taking snapshots of occasional visitors to our lab. As our system does not have mechanisms for figure-ground separation and for computing object data from image data, we should have used rigidly standardized viewing conditions, controlling lighting, distance, head posture, and facial expression. Instead we allowed subjects to freely control those variables.

In spite of these variations the system is surprisingly successful in picking out the correct photo from the picture gallery, which fluctuates in size around 30 portraits. About 80 percent of all recognition attempts identify the correct portrait from the gallery. About half of the remaining attempts give very low significance values (as defined in the section on recognition statistics). Thus, the number of false positives—wrong identifications claimed to have high confidence—was only about 10 percent. Many of these false positives can easily be explained by the known deficiencies of our system, and can be suppressed in future versions.

Figures 5.5 and 5.6 show some typical runs. They demonstrate that the system is able to deal with perspective distortion, in addition to the translation invariance which is intrinsic to it. If the image is taken with rotated perspective, the image graph deforms accordingly in order to place its jets in positions corresponding to those in the stored object. Figure 5.5 was produced with a version that had only nearest-neighbor interactions in its topology term, Equation (5-10). In this case the image graph behaves somewhat like an elastic membrane. In Figure 5.6 graphs in object and image were complete. In this case the topology term of (5-10) pays more attention to the global form of the image graph than to its local structure. Both versions gave good results. As Figure 5.6 shows, the quality of fit is reduced gradually with head rotation angle when comparing two portraits of Rolf. At all rotation angles, the correct pairing gives better values than comparison with a different face. With a larger picture gallery, angular differences beyond 10 degrees may already lead to false identifications, and different views of the same person have to be stored in the gallery. The one isolated cluster of points in Figure 5.6 compares two head-on portraits of Rolf, one with glasses, one without. The cost value is strongly increased, owing to the system's inability to treat composite objects in a sophisticated way. In spite of this, the match is still better than with any of Jan's portraits.

A shortcoming in the present system is its insistence upon finding a match for each stored object jet. In rotated views of an object, some jets would correspond to hidden parts of the surface. A similar situation arises with partial occlusion (as with glasses). In a more mature version, provision has to be made for this by allowing object jets to give up. This will reduce image graph distortion and the optimal cost value.

Parallel Implementation on a Transputer Network

We implemented the algorithms on a network of T800 transputers. **Transputers** are a family of microprocessors designed with parallel distributed processing in mind. They consist of a RISC-style processor with microcoded support for communicating parallel processes (the CSP model; see [Hoare, 1978, 1989]). Transputers communicate among themselves using bidirectional, serial links running at 20 Mbaud. Each processor has four of these, which can transfer data independently of the processor, and some fast on-chip RAM (typically 4 Kb). The T800 adds a fast floating-point unit. It also has support for bit reversal and 2-D block moves, which improve the performance of the FFT significantly.

Our system (*paracom* Inc., Batavia) consists of a crate which can hold up to 15 boards. We are using one board with one T800 processor and 4 Mb of memory, and a number of boards with two T800 processors having 2 Mb each. Processors are connected manually by cables on a switchboard. Pictures are acquired using a frame-grabber board, controlled by a transputer, which can digitize a video signal of 640×512 pixels with 256 grey levels. The same board can also be used as a graphics display. A PC/AT compatible is used as I/O server. We developed our program under the MultiTool[3] development system, using the OCCAM language [INMOS, 1989]. OCCAM enables us to exploit the parallel programming features of transputers to their fullest, while allowing easy development of numerical code.

General-purpose farm software.   The first thing to decide is the way we parallelize our algorithms. All of them can be easily divided into a number of similar tasks which operate on a subset of the data. This type of job is well suited to parallelization as a **farm**: *one* "controller" hands out the tasks (with their data) to *any number* of identical, anonymous "workers" and collects the results of their computations. As long as the individual tasks take long compared to communication times in the network and the controller doesn't become a bottleneck, near-optimal speedup can be expected for any number of processors.

The typical chain of events when using a farm is as follows:

- The controller conducts a dialog with the user to determine what is to be done next.

- It sends out the global (read-only) data required for the job. At the same time, the workers can be asked to compute any tables, etc., that will be needed; this is often more efficient than having the controller compute and then distribute them. This step is supported by the ability of the underlying routing system (described later) to broadcast to all workers.

- Now a "run" is started. This consists of a set of tasks that can be performed in parallel. Each worker is handed a task; when it has returned the results, it is given a new one, until there are no more tasks available. At this point, the controller waits for any remaining results to come in.

OCCAM makes it easy for both the user and the farm to perform these two activities of the controller in parallel, thus increasing performance. It also makes it easy to ensure proper synchronization at the end of a run, when the program can proceed only after all results have been collected.

This sequence is repeated until the program is terminated. Note that one user-requested action may require a number of runs by the farm (an example is given in a later section).

To make the job easier for the application developer, we designed a set of routines which implement a general-purpose farm. The user provides two routines (one for the controller, one for the workers) which use a simple and safe interface to the farm via OCCAM channels. On the controller, the farm software takes care of distributing tasks to the workers and collecting the results, routing messages as necessary. It also gives the user control of acquisition and display of performance data (described in a subsequent section on performance figures). On the worker processors, the farm software provides an interface to the routing system and handles the read-out of monitoring data. It also allows the reception and buffering of the

---

[3]This is a slightly modified version of INMOS's TDS.

next command from the router while the previous one is being worked on; thus, an optimal overlap of computation and communication is achieved.

The major problem not yet handled by the farm software stems from the fact that the communications network can handle messages only up to a fixed maximum buffer size. Thus, long messages have to be broken into smaller pieces by the sender and reassembled at their destination. Currently, this has to be handled by the user explicitly. A further restriction, which would be quite difficult to remove, is that task packets are limited in length to that maximum buffer size. All other packets, including results produced by a worker, can use the multimessage technique just described.

Network Topology and Routing Software

The next thing to settle is the topology of the network. As the controller has a unique role, it should also have a unique place in the network. Suited to the structure of a farm, then, will be some sort of tree structure, with the controller at its root. Because a transputer has four links, a ternary tree will make maximal use of the available hardware. However, in order to achieve increased flexibility, the router system supports any treelike structure.[4]

This flexibility is made possible by the initialization part of the router. When the transputer network is loaded, each router waits for a message to come in on any of its "down" links (toward the leaves of the tree), while sending (in parallel) a message on its "up" link (toward the root). The information gathered from the "down" links is then forwarded up the tree. Thus, every node in the tree is informed of the availability of processors on its branch. A reconfiguration therefore necessitates changes in the description of the network only to the network loader, not to the software. This description also assigns to every processor an address (a small integer); this is used when packets have to be routed (see below).

After initialization is complete, each router runs two parallel processes. The up process receives messages coming in from all active "down" links and from the local worker process. It then sends these messages on its "up" link. The up process on the controller hands all incoming messages to the farm software, which passes them on to the user. The down process receives message from the "up" link (or from the farm software, in case of the controller processor). It examines the address field of every message and then passes it on either to the local worker or, after examining its routing table, to the appropriate "down" link. If the address has the reserved value 0, it is a broadcast packet and is sent down all active links and to the local worker.

---

[4]In fact, because of the overhead of OCCAM'S ALT construct, for eight processors a linear chain is about 1 percent faster than the equivalent ternary tree. For a larger system, the tree is expected to be faster because of its smaller radius and therefore lower latency.

Parallelization of the two-dimensional FFT. The parallelization of the FFT works in two stages. First, the workers are notified that an FFT run will be started and are informed whether this is to be a forward or an inverse FFT. Then, a run is started in which the tasks are the one-dimensional FFTs of the rows of the data matrix. The results are collected into the same matrix, and a similar run is started for the column FFTs.

Parallelization of the Morlet transform. The Morlet transform first uses the parallel two-dimensional FFT just described to compute the Fourier transform of the picture. The result of this operation is sent as global data to all workers, which are also instructed to calculate the Morlet kernels. Then, a run is started in which the tasks are the convolution with one of the kernels. This requires the multiplication of the transformed image with the kernel and the inverse FFT of the result. The result is converted to byte values, and these are sent to the controller, together with the scaling parameters and the average (as described in an earler section). The controller sorts the results into an array and normalizes the scaling parameters for every value of k (see Equation 5-6).

Parallelization of the recognition. The tasks for the recognition are the comparisons between the image and one of the objects in the database. In this case, the global data is the complete set of image jets. Then, the object database is loaded from disk into the controller. The controller starts a run, sending as task data one of the object graphs (described earlier). The results returned by the workers are the optimized values of the various cost functions and some performance data. After all comparisons have been completed, the controller sorts the results and displays the 15 best matches on the graphics screen, together with a table of pertinent values on the terminal.

Actual parameters used. Our images have the size of 128×128 pixels. They are acquired by first cutting camera pictures of 640×512 pixels to square format and then averaging over 16 pixels to shrink them to their final size. The grey values have one byte of precision and are converted to floating-point numbers for the transform, the result of which is again rescaled to fit into one byte.

The parameter σ in the Morlet transform was chosen as 2π. The frequency space is sampled radially, which makes it reasonable to write **k** in polar coordinates as (k, ϕ). The angles then are:

$$\phi \in \{\frac{\mu\pi}{N} \mid \mu = 0, 1, ..., N-1\} \tag{5-12}$$

Our choice for N is 8. The sizes of the frequency vectors are sampled in half octaves, the highest frequency being π:

$$k \in \{\pi\sqrt{2}^{-\mu} \mid \mu = 0, 1, ..., M-1\} \tag{5-13}$$

For M the value 6 proved suitable.

The graphs describing the objects are rectangular grids with 7 points horizontally and 10 points vertically. The distance between two neighboring points (in either direction) is 11 pixels.

For the optimization we chose $\lambda = 10^{-5}$, the maximum allowed displacement is 10 pixels, and the process is stopped once 100 consecutive trials have failed. It should be noted that the values of these parameters depend on the graph topology and the similarity function described above. Once these are changed, the parameters have to be adjusted as well, especially λ.

Performance Figures

To evaluate the performance of the program, we used two methods:

- The user is mainly interested in the elapsed (wall-clock) time. OCCAM gives easy access to the timer of the transputer, which has a resolution of $64\,\mu s$ and negligible overhead. This time is reported in the tables of the following section as "elapsed time" and includes the time to broadcast global data and the sequential sections between runs. In addition, these times allow the calculation of the serial part of the program, which ultimately limits the usefulness of an increase in processor number. This is done by fitting the first few data points on a n^{-1}–t diagram to a line; the t intercept corresponds to an infinite number of processors and is the serial part of the program.

- To get an impression of the load on individual transputers and the amount of communication, we implemented a simple monitor. It exploits the fact that transputers can run processes at two priorities, low and high. Any high-priority process wanting to execute will preempt a running low-priority process. The controller, worker, and farm processes all run at low priority, while the router processes run at high priority. The monitor process is also started at high priority. It then "sleeps" for a user-selectable amount of time. When it wakes up, it checks to see whether it has interrupted a low-priority process. If so, a counter is incremented. It also checks whether any links are actively transferring data; then it goes to sleep for another interval. This statistical sampling technique may seem very crude, but it gives quite a good impression of the load balancing on a network and indicates the bottlenecks while having negligible overhead. As pointed out above, in a farm system the controller tends to be such a bottleneck. This is borne out by the utilization data gathered with this method in the tables of the next section.

Performance on FFT and on Morlet transform.   Tables 5.1 and 5.2 summarize the performance data for the FFT and Morlet transforms. For details on conditions during the measurements, see the table legends. The relative speedup is calculated as $(n \times t_n - t_1)/t_1$, where n is the number of processors and t_i denotes the elapsed time with i processors. It should be noted that in some cases the number of

TABLE 5.1 PERFORMANCE OF PARALLEL FFT
IMPLEMENTATION

Number of processors	Elapsed time (s)	Utilization of controller (%)	Relative speedup
1	4.975	8.2	1.00
2	2.489	16.4	1.00
4	1.285	32.2	0.97
6	0.884	44.8	0.93
8	0.689	56.7	0.89
12	0.558	76.9	0.65

Times given are for the transformation of a vertical-stripe pattern 128×128 pixels in size; both the forward and inverse FFT were computed. The serial part is calculated as 0.08 second. A sampling interval of 3 ms was used; this has an overhead of less than 1 percent. Note the impact of increased controller utilization on the relative speedup, especially for 12 processors. This limits the useful network size to about 16 processors.

TABLE 5.2 PERFORMANCE OF PARALLEL MORLET
TRANSFORM

Number of processors	Elapsed time (s)	Utilization of controller (%)	Relative speedup
1	153.05	2.5	1.00
2	76.53	4.9	1.00
4	38.95	9.8	0.98
6	26.66	14.6	0.95
8	20.70	18.8	0.92
12	15.47	26.0	0.79
14	14.33	28.1	0.69

Times given are for a white 64×64 pixel square centered in a black field of 128×128 pixels, and include the time to perform the forward FFT of the data. Measurement conditions are as in Table 5.1. The serial part is calculated as 1.37 seconds. In this case, the bottleneck is the communication of the results from the workers to the controller.

(worker) processors is not a divisor of the number of tasks (128 for the FFT, 48 for the Morlet transform). Because of this, at the end of a run, for some processors there is no work left and they will be idle, which decreases the speedup.

Performance of recognition.   The time to compare one object to the image is very data-dependent. In addition, the size of the object database changes very often, as new objects are added and old ones deleted. The tasks and results to be distributed are quite small and burden the controller and the communications system only lightly. It therefore does not make much sense to give a table as in the previous section. As a figure of reference, we will mention that a single iteration of the diffusion process takes about 2.5 ms, and a comparison takes from 2500 to 5000 iterations, of which about 10 percent improve the cost function.

DISCUSSION

This chapter aims to help the reader understand and reimplement our neural system for object recognition. This system has been created to demonstrate the potential of a new architecture. The dynamic link architecture derives its power from a data format based on syntactically linked structures. This capability has been exploited here on three levels.

First, when an image is formed in the image domain, the local feature detectors centered on one of its points can be bundled to form a composite feature detector, an entity we called a **jet**. A composite feature detector can be shipped to the object domain and can be compared as a whole to composite feature detectors there. This frees the system from the necessity to train new individual neurons as detectors for complex features before new object classes can be recognized, a major burden on conventional layered systems.

Second, links are used to represent neighborhood relationships within the image domain and within the object domain. Neural objects thereby acquire internal structure, and their communication can now be constrained to combinations with matched syntactical structure. This forms the basis for graph matching.

Finally, the dynamical formation and representation of the binding structures between matched graphs constitute a third level in a hierarchy, which in the future can be extended to more complex dynamical data objects.

The most mature application of neural networks has been to low-level vision. The current roadblock to further development of this application is the inability of conventional neural networks to represent high-level objects. It is obvious that this roadblock can and will be removed with the help of a neural data-and-process architecture capable of dynamically forming hierarchically structured composite objects. The dynamic link architecture has the potential to do this.

This chapter actually gives two versions of the system for object recognition in the dynamic link architecture. One is fully neural and is described in qualitative form to convey the idea. The other is optimized for ease of implementation in current digital hardware, and is formulated in full detail. The concrete implementation falls short of being fully neural in detail—floating-point numbers are used to represent feature values, digital addresses are used to represent links, and, most important, different special algorithms are used to replace network dynamics. There were various motives for this corruption of neural style. For instance, representation of continuous numbers in sets of neurons is possible and has been demonstrated, with, say, the help of the thermometer code, but it would be extremely expensive to simulate on a digital processor, and this number representation would waste the power of the 32-bit parallel floating-point unit of our transputers. The price paid here for the nonneural style of implementation is its rigid restriction to the exact process implemented—it wouldn't be possible to have the same system learn an improved similarity function or to combine parts of existing objects into a new one. The advantage of our conventional style of implementation is computing efficiency and the avoidance of the complexities of nonlinear dynamics. A full-blown implementation of the dynamic link architecture will require specifically optimized hardware and the development of sophisticated methods of process control.

Whatever the details of implementation, the system proposed here is distinguished by utmost simplicity. It is based on a completely general set of feature types, Morlet wavelets in the specific implementation, and on a very general system of high-level object representation. Although we exercised the system on portrait photographs, nothing is specialized to this application. This style is to be compared to classical AI, in which object recognition is traditionally based on extensive algorithms and data structures specifically created to deal with a given object class. Our system is so simple it can easily be reimplemented within a few weeks by a moderately experienced programmer.

This conceptual simplicity of our system shifts the balance between cost of processing and cost of implementation, much needed in a time of exploding software costs and declining hardware costs. Our object-recognition system admittedly is processing intensive. Most of the time is spent on image transformation and on optimizing the map between the image and individual stored objects. The first expense is unavoidable in a general system, and cheaper feature sets would limit the system to specific applications. The second expense would cause serious problems if the necessary graph-matching costs grew explosively with graph size. As has been remarked before, however, this is not the case, owing to the topological structure of the graphs and to the existence of potent specific attributes. In the present system, processing demands beyond image transformation grow linearly with the size of the picture gallery. This wouldn't slow a system with fully parallel hardware, but it would still be expensive. This expense can easily be reduced in future systems by arranging objects in a decision tree and by searching this tree in a sequential fashion. The strategy would reduce the processing costs in the search at least to a scale logarithmic in the number of objects. Moreover, early identification of object classes could serve to relabel image points in terms of object-class specific attributes and could thus enormously speed up later matches.

It has been objected that the dynamic link architecture, being inherently sequential owing to its foundation in temporal correlations, would degrade the full parallelity of neural architecture. This objection is not a serious one. Our nervous system certainly has processing times far beyond simple signal-propagation delays, and as soon as multiple bindings are to be sorted out processing times vastly increase (see, for instance, [Treisman and Gelade, 1980]), testifying to sequential action. As for technical implementations, these have to play off their millionfold superior switching speeds against the vast number of processing elements of the brain and will therefore continue to process sequentially even in the presence of massive concurrency.

Our particular choice of feature detectors, Morlet wavelets, has been motivated from two sides. One motivation we have already given: feature detectors have to be robust with respect to image variations such as perspective distortion, changes in illumination, and noise. This consideration speaks for feature detectors that are localized both in the space and in the frequency domain. The advantage of Morlet wavelets over Gabor functions lies in the fact that image dilations affect all Morlet components to the same degree, whereas Gabor components are much more sensitive at high frequencies, where the fixed window spans more oscillations.

The other source of motivation for Morlet wavelets is biology. Neurophysiology ([Marčelja, 1980; Jones and Palmer, 1987]) has shown that receptive fields of simple cells in the visual cortex approximate symmetric (cosine) and antisymmetric (sine) Morlet wavelets. Their frequency width is about one octave. Complex cells respond to light bars and edges independent of exact position within the receptive field, and they may correspond to the magnitude of the complex Morlet components, and thus to the components of our jets. Psychophysical work makes it likely that our visual system analyzes images in terms of frequency bands about an octave wide [Wilson et al., 1983]. Newer psychophysical results indicate that receptive fields tend to come in pairs of even and odd symmetry (just like the real and imaginary parts of our wavelets). Burr, Morrone, and Spinelli in [Morrone and Burr, 1988] built a vision model based on the squared sum of these pairs of cells and provide psychophysical evidence that some of human vision actually could work that way [Burr et al., 1989].

Our specific implementation inherently generalizes over object position, but it doesn't do so over orientation or size. This is due to the structure of the feature-specific connections between the image domain and the object domain. It would in principle be possible to let these connections also generalize over size and orientation, but then the number of distinguishable feature types would be unduly reduced, and attributed graph matching would become difficult. It is interesting to note that reaction times of our visual system grow for objects in unexpected orientations. This may apply also to size invariance, which anyway works only over a limited range. This suggests that our visual system does not have invariance to orientation (and possibly to size) to the same degree to which it has translation invariance.

Here is a way our system could deal with these invariances. First, estimate size and orientation of an object to be recognized. There usually is a solid basis for this estimate, owing to the existence of a gravity field, knowledge about object distance, and information available after image segmentation. Use these estimates to transform features into standard size and orientation. Attempt object recognition and use the result for a better estimate of the original parameters. Iterate if necessary. If composite feature similarity behaves smoothly over reasonable ranges of orientation and size, this strategy is bound to succeed. Morlet wavelets are designed to be robust with respect to small distortions, including changes in size and in orientation.

A somewhat more complex issue is invariance with respect to perspective movement. Our system is based on two-dimensional representation. Essentially different views of a three-dimensional object have to be recognized with the help of multiple views (possibly merged into one coherent two-dimensional representation). It is, however, mandatory that recognition be robust with respect to small changes in perspective. A system based on Morlet wavelets and topological mapping is ideally suited for this, as demonstrated here.

Our system in its present form has some serious shortcomings. There is no provision for segmentation in the image domain, there are no general mechanisms for determination of object properties from image data, and there isn't the possibility to represent composite objects as such. However, all these aspects can naturally be implemented in a fully neural realization of the dynamic link architecture. The graph-matching system described here would just form an element of a more mature system. This would have a multi-layered hierarchical structure, which would be supported by a layered anatomy similar to the one described in [Fukushima, 1980; Marko and Giebel, 1970]. Between each pair of layers connections would be restricted to relatively small distances within the image plane.[5] The anatomical hierarchy of this layered system would reflect a hierarchy of computations to be performed.

Segmentation based on low-level data [von der Malsburg and Schneider, 1986; Schneider, 1986] resides in the lower levels of the hierarchy. As described earlier, segmentation can be based on temporal correlations between all neurons in the image domain that are hit by the same object. This is possible with the help of preexisting connections that encode the likelihood for a pair of neurons to belong to the same segment. In a simple version [Schneider, 1986], connections run only between neurons within nodes, and between neurons for different positions but the same local quality (state of movement, texture, stereo depth). Signals from neurons in the same segment become correlated and can cooperate with each other in graph matching. Signals from neurons in different segments become anticorrelated and cannot interact. The correlations relevant for segmentation would be measured on a time scale coarser than that of the correlations encoding neighborhood relationships within a segment. Segmentation based on high-level knowledge has been demonstrated in [DeLiang et al., 1989].

Determination of object properties from image data is to be performed with the help of detectors for object primitives. Local shapes, for instance, have as their signature characteristic arrays of grey-level values, edges, and highlights, which can be detected by locally residing network patterns, matched as graphs to small pieces

---

[5]This anatomy would alleviate the biologically unrealistic feature of our simple system to require anatomical connections between all parts of the image domain and of the object domain. In a technical implementation this isn't a problem, since those connections can be replaced by a simple bus with as many connections as there are feature types.

of the image. Such object-primitive detectors would, for the purpose of ascending connections, carry labels referring to object shape. On lower levels the system would have multiple copies of shape primitives, to avoid their overloading when many instantiations are required in complex scenes.

On higher levels, composite objects would be formed as graphs whose "nodes" are smaller graphs themselves. (In fact, our present system already conforms to this style: objects are represented as topological network patterns with nodes in the form of jets, which can be seen as primitive subgraphs.) A full hierarchy could include many levels: local feature detectors, local object descriptors, object primitives, individual objects, object schemes of several levels of complexity and abstraction (e.g., "human shape" or "vehicle"), and finally scene descriptions. The full scene representation would be afforded by hierarchically structured connectivity patterns, produced by a continuous graph-dynamical process.

A last feature missing from our system but required in a mature version is the ability to absorb structure from examples. Learning is realized in the dynamic link architecture by synaptic plasticity similar to the one in conventional neural networks. More specifically, a permanent T_{ij} connection is increased in strength when the fluid weight J_{ij} is forced to maximal value by a strong correlation C_{ij}. Very few of the pairs of neurons active in a given scene will actually be bound to each other by active links; the majority of pairs will be kept from strengthening their fluid weights and hence their permanent weights. As a consequence, only meaningful and significant connections will be strengthened. This leads to enormous reductions in learning time. The elementary learning process would be implemented in our system as a sequence of steps. The first step is an attempt to recognize the object. If this succeeds, the object-representing connectivity pattern can be modified, both within individual nodes and in the connections between nodes. If recognition fails, a copy of the object is formed in the object domain, and the copy is stored by strengthening connections between neighboring cells. After some learning the system will always be able to represent new objects as arrays of shape primitives. New objects can thus be stored by knitting overlapping or contiguous shape primitives together.

Acknowledgments.   We would like to thank Wolf Singer for generously extending his hospitality to us and for providing excellent working conditions in Frankfurt. Peter König contributed to this project through many helpful and inspiring discussions.

REFERENCES

Bienenstock, E., and von der Malsburg, C., "A Neural Network for Invariant Pattern Recognition," *Europhysics Letters*, vol. 4, 121–126, 1987.

Buhmann, J., Lange, J., and von der Malsburg, C., "Distortion Invariant Object Recognition by Matching Hierarchically Labeled Graphs," In *IJCNN International Conference on Neural Networks, Washington*, I 155–159, IEEE, 1989.

Burr, D. C., Morrone, M. C., and Spinelli, D., "Evidence for Edge and Bar Detectors in Human Vision," *Vision Research*, vol. 29, no. 4, 419–431, 1989.

Combes, J. M., Grossmann, A., and Tchamitchian, Ph., (eds.), "Wavelets, Time-Frequency Methods and Phase Space," *Proceedings of the International Conference, Marseille, France, December 14–18, 1987*, Springer, Berlin, Heidelberg, New York, 1989.

Crick, F., "Function of the Thalamic Reticular Complex: The Searchlight Hypothesis," *Proceedings of the National Academy of Sciences, USA*, vol. 81, 4568–4590, 1984.

Daubechies, I., Grossmann, A., and Meyer, Y., "Painless Nonorthogonal Expansions," *Journal of Mathematical Physics*, vol. 27, no. 5, 1271–1283, 1986.

DeLiang, W., Buhmann, J., and von der Malsburg, C., "A Syntactically Structured Associative Memory," Submitted to *Neural Computation*, 1989.

Eckhorn, R., Bauer, R., Jordan, W., Brosch, M., Kruse, W., Munk, M., and Reitboeck, H. J., "Coherent Oscillations: A Mechanism of Feature Linking in the Visual Cortex?" *Biological Cybernetics*, vol. 60, 121–130, 1988.

Freeman, W. J., *Mass Action in the Nervous System*, Academic Press, New York, 1975.

Fukushima, K., "Neocognitron: A Self-Organizing Neural Network Model for a Mechanism of Pattern Recognition Unaffected by Shift in Position," *Biological Cybernetics*, vol. 36, 193–202, 1980.

Gabor, D., "Theory of Communication," *J. Inst. Elec. Eng. (London)*, vol. 93, 429–457, 1946.

Garey, M. R., and Johnson, D. S., *Computers and Intractability*, W. H. Freeman, New York, 1979.

Gray, C. M., König, P., Engel, A. K., and Singer, W., "Oscillatory Responses in Cat Visual Cortex Exhibit Intercolumnar Synchronization Which Reflects Global Stimulus Properties," *Nature*, vol. 338, 334–337, 1989.

Grossmann, A., and Morlet, J., "Decomposition of Functions into Wavelets of Constant Shape, and Related Transforms," In *Mathematics and Physics, Lecture on Recent Results*, World Scientific Publishing, Singapore, 1985.

Häussler, A. F., and von der Malsburg, C., "Development of Retinotopic Projections—An Analytical Treatment," *Journal of Theoretical Neurobiology*, vol. 2, 47–73, 1983.

Hoare, C. A. R., "Communicating Sequential Processes," *Commun. ACM*, vol. 21, no. 8, 666–677, 1978.

Hoare, C. A. R., *Communicating Sequential Processes*, Prentice Hall International, Hemel Hempstead, 1989.

Hubel, D. H., and Wiesel, T. N., "Receptive Fields, Binocular Interaction and Functional Architecture in the Cat's Visual Cortex," *J. Physiology (London)*, vol. 160, 106–154, 1962.

Jones, J. P., and Palmer, L. A., "An Evaluation of the Two-Dimensional Gabor Filter Model of Simple Receptive Fields in Cat Striate Cortex," *Journal of Neurophysiology*, 1233–1258, 1987.

INMOS Limited, OCCAM 2 *Reference Manual*, Prentice Hall International, Hemel Hempstead, 1989.

Marko, H., and Giebel, H., "Recognition of Handwritten Characters with a System of Homogeneous Layers," *Nachrichtentechnische Zeitschrift*, vol. 9, 455–459, 1970.

Marčelja, S., "Mathematical Description of the Responses of Simple Cortical Cells," *Journal of the Optical Society of America*, vol. A 70, no. 11, 1297–1300, 1980.

McNaughton, B. L., "Long-term Synaptic Enhancement and Short-Term Potentiation in Rat Fascia Dentata Act through Different Mechanisms," *J. Physiology*, vol. 324, 249–262, 1982.

Miller, G., "Isomorphism Testing for Graphs of Bounded Genus," In *Proc. 12th ACM STOC Symp.*, 218–224, 1980.

Morrone, M. C., and Burr, D. C., "Feature Detection in Human Vision: A Phase-Dependent Energy Model," *Proceedings of the Royal Society London*, vol. B 235, 221–245, 1988.

Murenzi, R., "Wavelet Transforms Associated to the n-Dimensional Euclidean Group with Dilations: Signals in More Than One Dimension," In *Wavelets, Time-Frequency Methods and Phase Space*, 239–246, Springer, Berlin, Heidelberg, New York, 1989.

Nussbaumer, H. J., *Fast Fourier Transform and Convolution Algorithms*, 2nd ed., Springer Series in Information Sciences, Springer, Berlin, Heidelberg, New York, 1982.

Press, W. H., Flannery, B. P., Teukolsky, S. A., and Vetterling, W. T., *Numerical Recipes in C—The Art of Scientific Programmming*, Cambridge University Press, New York, 1988.

Schneider, W., "Anwendung der Korrelationstheorie der Hirnfunktion auf das akustische Figur-Hintergrund-Problem (Cocktailparty-Effekt)," Ph.D. thesis, Universität Göttingen, 3400 Göttingen, F.R.G., 1986.

Treisman, A. M., and Gelade, G., "A Feature Integration Theory of Attention," *Cognitive Psychology*, vol. 12, 97–136, 1980.

von der Malsburg, C., Buhmann, J., Flaton, K., and Lange, J., "Vehicle Identification in IR Images, Based on Labeled Graph Matching," Project report, Hughes Aircraft Co., El Segundo, CA, 1988.

von der Malsburg, C., and Schneider, W., "A Neural Cocktail-Party Processor," *Biological Cybernetics*, vol. 54, 29–40, 1986.

von der Malsburg, C., "The Correlation Theory of Brain Function," Technical report, Max-Planck-Institute for Biophysical Chemistry, Postfach 2841, Göttingen, FRG, 1981.

von der Malsburg, C., "How Are Nervous Structures Organized?," in Başar, E., Flohr, H., Haken, H., and Mandell, A. J., (eds.), *Synergetics of the Brain, Proceedings of the International Symposium on Synergetics*, 238–249. Springer, Berlin, Heidelberg, New York, 1983.

von der Malsburg, C., "Nervous Structures with Dynamical Links," *Ber. Bunsenges. Phys. Chem.*, vol. 89, 703–710, 1985.

von der Malsburg, C., "Pattern Recognition by Labeled Graph Matching," *Neural Networks*, vol. 1, 141–148, 1988.

von der Malsburg, C., and Bienenstock, E., "Statistical Coding and Short-Term Synaptic Plasticity: A Scheme for Knowledge Representation in the Brain," In Bienenstock, E., Fogelman, F., and Weisbuch, G., (eds.), *Disordered Systems and Biological Organization, NATO Advanced Research Workshop*, 247–272, Springer, Berlin, Heidelberg, New York, 1986.

von der Malsburg, C., and Bienenstock, E., "A Neural Network for the Retrieval of Super-imposed Connection Patterns," *Europhysics Letters*, vol. 3, 1243–1249, 1987.

Willshaw, D. J., and von der Malsburg, C., "How Patterned Neural Connections Can Be Set Up by Self-Organization," *Proceedings of the Royal Society, London*, vol. B 194, 431–445, 1976.

Willshaw, D. J., and von der Malsburg, C., "A Marker Induction Mechanism for the Establishment of Ordered Neural Mappings," *Philosophical Transactions of the Royal Society, London*, vol. B 287, 203–243, 1979.

Wilson, H. R., MacFarlane, D. A., and Phillips, G. C., "Spatial Frequency Tuning of Orientation Selective Units Estimated by Oblique Masking," *Vision Research*, vol. 23, 873–882, 1983.

PROBLEMS

5.1. (Fourier Transform of the One-dimensional Gabor Function) The Gabor function is defined as

$$G_{k,x_0}(x) = \frac{1}{N}\exp\left(ik(x-x_0)\right)\exp\left(-\frac{k^2(x-x_0)^2}{2\sigma^2}\right)$$

(a) Compute the normalization constant N such that

$$\int_{-\infty}^{+\infty} G_{k,x_0}^*(x)\,G_{k,x_0}(x)\,dx = 1$$

where the asterisk denotes complex conjugation.

(b) Calculate the Fourier transform $\mathcal{F}(G)$ of the Gabor function.

(c) Show that the Gabor functions fulfill the uncertainty relationship $\Delta x\Delta k = 1/2$, where Δx and Δk are the mean square deviations of $G_{k,0}(x)$ and of its Fourier transform, respectively.

5.2. (Sinusoidal Grating) The Gabor convolution is defined as

$$g_k(x_0) = \frac{1}{N}\int_{-\infty}^{+\infty}\exp\left(ikx\right)\exp\left(-\frac{k^2x^2}{2\sigma^2}\right)I(x_0-x)\,dx$$

(a) Compute the Gabor convolution of the intensity profile $I(x) = 1 + \cos(\Omega x)$.

(b) Plot $g_k(x_0)$ in the limit $\sigma^2/2 \gg 1$ as a function of the parameter Ω.

(c) Compute numerically the absolute value of the Gabor convolution $|g_k(x_0)|$ for the intensity profile $I(x) = \Theta(x-a)$, where $\Theta(x)$ is the step function

$$\Theta(x) = \begin{cases} 1, & \text{if } x > 0 \\ 0, & \text{otherwise} \end{cases}$$

(d) Find approximations of $|g_k(x_0)|$ for the three different cases $x_0 \gg a$, $x_0 \ll a$, and $x_0 \approx a$.

5.3. (Wavelet Pyramid) The two-dimensional Gabor function is given by (N_2: two-dimensional normalization constant)

$$G_{\mathbf{k}}(\mathbf{x}) \;=\; \frac{1}{N_2}\,\exp\left(i\mathbf{k}\cdot\mathbf{x}\right)\,\exp\left(-\frac{\mathbf{k}\cdot\mathbf{k}\,\mathbf{x}\cdot\mathbf{x}}{2\sigma^2}\right)$$

A family of functions can be generated from $G_{\mathbf{k}}(\mathbf{x})$ by dilation, rotation, and translation. Assume that you have an image of size $N \times N$ pixels. Construct a multiresolution pyramid with two-dimensional Gabor functions in the following way. Frequency space is sampled in octaves by restricting the length of $\mathbf{k}$ to the set

$$k \;\equiv\; \|\mathbf{k}\| \;=\; \frac{2\pi}{N}2^{\nu} \qquad \text{with } \nu \in \{0, \dots, (\log_2 N) - 1\}$$

and by employing six different orientations, i.e.,

$$\mathbf{k} \;=\; k\begin{pmatrix}\cos\phi \\ \sin\phi\end{pmatrix} \qquad \text{with } \phi = \mu\frac{\pi}{6},\ \mu \in \{0, \dots, 5\}$$

(a) Calculate the relative distance $\Delta x k/\sigma$ between two different Gabor functions such that N^2 Gabor coefficients are obtained.

(b) Calculate the overlap between two Gabor functions of the same size and orientation shifted by Δx (as calculated in (a)) in the direction of the wave vector $\mathbf{k}$.

5.4. (Angle between Two High-Dimensional Random Vectors) $\mathbf{x} = (x_1, x_2, \dots, x_n)$ and $\mathbf{y} = (y_1, y_2, \dots, y_n)$ are two n-dimensional vectors with random, positive components. The components are distributed as

$$P(x_i) \;=\; \frac{1}{\sqrt{2\pi}\sigma}\,\exp\left(-\frac{x_i{}^2}{2\sigma^2}\right)\,\Theta(x_i)$$

$\Theta(x)$ is the threshold function defined in Problem 5.2. Compute $\langle \mathbf{x}\cdot\mathbf{y}\rangle / \langle|\mathbf{x}|\rangle\langle|\mathbf{y}|\rangle$ which approximates the expectation value of the cosine of the angle between the two vectors. [*Hint*: The surface of the segment of the n-dimensional sphere where all components are positive is given by

$$S_n \;=\; \frac{n\pi^{n/2}}{2^n\,(n/2)!}\,r^{n-1}$$

(Restrict yourself to even values of n, unless you know the *Gamma* function!)]

5.5. (Free One-Dimensional Diffusion (Wiener Process)) Assume you have an infinite one-dimensional chain and an ant sitting initially (time $t = 0$) at site $x = 0$. The ant crawls with equal probability to site $x + \delta$ or $x - \delta$.

(a) Derive the rate equation for the probability distribution $p(x, t + \tau)$ that the ant is at site x after one time step τ if the distribution at time t was $p(x, t)$.

(b) Approximate the difference equation for $p(x,t)$ derived in (a) by a first-order differential equation in time t. This equation is called a **master equation**.

(c) Derive a partial differential equation which continues in time and space from the master equation calculated in (b), by considering the limit $\delta \to 0$. This equation is called a **Fokker–Planck equation**. [*Hint*: Make a Taylor expansion of the difference equation and keep only the leading terms in $O(\tau)$ and $O(\delta)$.]

(d) Compute the conditional probability $p(x,t\,|\,0,0)$ that the ant is at site x at time t. $p(x,t\,|\,0,0)$ is called the *Greens function* for the diffusion equation.

5.6. (One-Dimensional Diffusion in a Force Field (Ornstein–Uhlenbeck Process)) You have the same situation as in the previous problem, but the probability for crawling left or right depends on x:

$$P(x \to x') \;=\; \left(1 + \exp\left(\frac{H(x') - H(x)}{T}\right)\right)^{-1}$$

(a) Compute the master equation and the Fokker–Planck equation as in Problem 5.5.

(b) For the potential $H(x) = x^2/2$ (linear drift force) and initial position x_0, compute the conditional probability $p(x,t\,|\,x_0,0)$ of finding the ant at position x at time t.

5.7. (Implementation of a One-Dimensional Convolution)

(a) Implement a one-dimensional convolution

- directly, using the equation:

$$(f * g)(n) \;=\; \sum_{\nu=0}^{N-1} f(\nu)g(\nu - n)$$

  If $\nu - n$ leaves the range $[0, N)$, "wrap it around" in a cylic manner.
- by exploiting Equation (5-7). (Use an FFT routine from a numerical library, if you can. Otherwise, refer to [Press et al., 1988].)

(b) Measure the computation times for different values of N in both implementations and compare them.

(c) Give a brief (!) explanation in your own words why the FFT deserves its first F.

5.8. (Implementation of a Two-Dimensional Fast Fourier Transformation) A two-dimensional FFT is implemented by first executing one-dimensional FFTs on all the rows of the matrix and then on all the columns.

(a) Why?

(b) How would the results be different if the columns were transformed before the rows?

5.9. (Fourier Transform of Two-Dimensional Wavelets)

(a) Prove Equation (5-4). If you don't like that, proceed directly to (b).

(b) Implement the Morlet wavelets straightforwardly in the space domain.

(c) Implement them by using Equation (5-4) and applying an inverse FFT.

(d) Compare (as a relative error) the results of (b) and (c) for several values of **k** and try to explain them. [*Hint*: Check for proper normalization factors of the kernel *and* the inverse FFT.]

PART TWO

ROBOTICS
AND CONTROL

6

ROBOTICS AND NEURAL NETWORKS

George A. Bekey
Center for Neural Engineering
Departments of Computer Science and Electrical Engineering–Systems
University of Southern California

THE NEED FOR NEURAL-NETWORK MODEL-FREE ESTIMATION IN ROBOTICS

The field of robotics concerns the design and application of articulated mechanical systems to manipulate and transfer objects, to perform mechanical tasks with versatility approaching that of human arms, and to provide mobility. A variety of autonomous and semiautonomous systems are termed "robots" if they involve processing of sensory inputs from the environment and some mechanical interaction with it.

Since robot manipulators (or legs) are open-chain kinematic mechanisms, their control is difficult. Clearly there is coupling between motions of individual segments. Furthermore, the parameters of a manipulator depend upon its configuration, and the governing equations are highly nonlinear. The control of robots is particularly difficult, since the desired trajectory of the endpoint of the arms (or legs) is normally specified in Cartesian space, while motions are actually obtained from actuators located at the joints. The transformation from Cartesian to joint coordinates is a computationally intensive problem, the accurate solution of which depends both on the algorithms used and on precise knowledge of robot parameters.

Living organisms with articulated extremities perform the transformation from goal space to actuator (muscle) coordinates whenever they move. While some aspects of this transformation appear to be preprogrammed in the genes (thus enabling animals to move almost immediately after birth), other aspects appear to be learned from experience. This aspect of motion control in biological systems has provided a model for the application of connectionist approaches to robot control, since neural networks can, in principle, be trained to approximate relations between variables regardless of their analytical dependency [Rummelhart et al., 1986]. Hence, it is appealing to attempt to solve various aspects of the robot-control problem without accurate knowledge of the governing equations or parameters with *model-free estimation* systems—by using neural networks trained by a sufficiently large number of examples.

ROBOTICS PROBLEMS

The control of a robot manipulator involves three fundamental problems: task planning, trajectory planning, and motion control. In the **task-planning** phase, high-level planners manage and coordinate information concerning the job to be performed. **Trajectory planning** involves finding the sequence of points through which the manipulator end point must pass, given initial and goal coordinates, intermediate (or via) points, and appropriate constraints. Such constraints may include limits on velocity and acceleration or the need to avoid obstacles. Given such a trajectory, the **motion-control** problem consists of finding the joint torques which will cause the arm to follow it while satisfying the constraints.

Artificial neural networks find applications in all three of the problem areas indicated above. However, since most of the useful work to date has been done in trajectory planning and motion control, we shall discuss these two areas first.

There are two approaches to the trajectory-planning problem, which are referred to as **joint-space planning** and **Cartesian-space planning**. Since trajectory constraints are generally specified in Cartesian space, planning a trajectory in joint space requires that the location of the end points and via points be transformed to their corresponding joint-space coordinates. A smooth trajectory can then be obtained (say by fitting a polynomial to these points) [Craig, 1986]. Alternatively, the path planning can be done in Cartesian coordinates and then each path point converted into its corresponding joint-space values for control. Clearly, the key to trajectory planning is the transformation of information from Cartesian to joint coordinates, which we consider next.

Inverse Kinematics

The joint coordinates θ are related to the Cartesian coordinates $\mathbf{x}$ by the kinematic equation

$$\mathbf{x} \;=\; \mathbf{f}(\theta) \tag{6-1}$$

For a six-degree-of-freedom system, both θ and $\mathbf{x}$ are six-dimensional vectors. When path planning is done in Cartesian coordinates, the required trajectory is obtained by the planning algorithm and then transformed to joint space by solving Equation (6-1). Since this solution requires inverting Equation (6-1), the approach is termed **position-based inverse kinematic control**. In many cases, the trajectory specification includes velocity constraints, in which case the forward kinematic equation is obtained by differentiating Equation (6-1):

$$\dot{\mathbf{x}} = \mathbf{J}(\theta)\dot{\theta} \tag{6-2}$$

where the elements of the Jacobian matrix $\mathbf{J}$ are the partial derivatives

$$\frac{\partial x_i}{\partial \theta_j} \quad \forall\, i,\, j$$

Solution of Equation (6-2) yields the inverse relation

$$\dot{\theta} = \mathbf{J}^{-1}(\theta)\dot{\mathbf{x}} \tag{6-3}$$

At any joint position θ the planner now computes the velocity $\dot{\mathbf{x}}$ that causes the manipulator end point to move toward the next via point or end point. Thus, trajectory planning based on (6-3) is referred to as **velocity-based inverse kinematic control** (or **inverse Jacobian control**). Clearly, for this method to be feasible, one must assume that the Jacobian is invertible at each point. In practice, the Jacobian matrix is well behaved, except near singularity points [Craig, 1986]. Since efficient inversion of the Jacobian is evidently the key to successful application of this method, a number of algorithms have been proposed, e.g. [Leahy et al., 1987; Chang and Lee, 1989].

It should be noted that success of the inverse kinematic method depends not only on efficient inversion of the Jacobian but also on accurate knowledge of the robot kinematic parameters. In the absence of such knowledge, it may be necessary to use system-identification techniques to obtain parameter estimates before trajectory planning can begin. Since neural-network approaches do not depend on accurate a priori knowledge, they are attractive alternatives to the inverse Jacobian method.

Review of Prior Work

One of the earliest connectionist approaches to robot control is due to Albus [1975]. His **Cerebellar Model Articulation Controller (CMAC)** uses a three-layer network, the first set of connections being random while the second employs adjustable weights. The network has no advance knowledge of the structure of the system being controlled and thus can be trained to accomplish the robot-control task, provided there are sufficient adjustable and random connections. The basic idea of CMAC is to compute control commands by look-up tables rather than by solving control equations analytically. The table is organized in a distributed fashion, so that the function value for any point in the input space is derived by summing the contents over a number of memory locations. While Albus pioneered the application of neural networks to robotics, he did not attempt to model the structural characteristics of networks of neurons, as did later investigators.

Kuperstein [1987] concerned himself with models of visual motor coordination in robots. While he did not explicitly address the inverse-kinematics problem, his work did in fact use neural networks to obtain the transformation needed to convert desired hand coordinates in Cartesian space into the appropriate joint coordinates. The work is based on that of Grossberg and Kuperstein [1986] on adaptive sensory-motor control. The system was designed to teach a two-joint robot arm to move to a point in three-dimensional Cartesian space as located by a vision system. Neither kinematic relationships nor the calibration of joint angles to actuator signals were known a priori. The architecture of the system consisted of an input layer fed by a stereo camera, whose outputs are connected to three arrays which convert the visual inputs into distributions. These distributions are connected to a target map with adjustable weights.

The strategy followed by Kuperstein is the following. First, a random generator activates the target map, which orients the robot arm into random positions. These positions are sensed by means of the camera and registered on the input map. The outputs of this map are then correlated with the desired or target locations. At the same time the network receives the visual activation corresponding to the end of the arm and determines an activation pattern which is compared with the actual pattern. Errors are used to adjust weights in the network by means of Hebb's rule [Rummelhart et al., 1986]. Basically, this is a **circular sensory-motor reaction** [Grossberg and Kuperstein, 1986] in which a spatial representation is formed based on signals used to orient and move in the space. Inverse kinematic control has also been studied by a number of other investigators, e.g., Elsley [1988], Guez and Ahmad [1988], Josin et al. [1988] and Psaltis et al. [1987], using the backpropagation algorithm for learning. All the papers cited above have demonstrated the algorithms on robots with either 2 or 3 degrees of freedom (DOF). Attempts to apply backpropagation directly to systems with more DOF have not been very successful, since these systems typically exhibit high-order nonlinearities and hence very slow learning rates. In order to achieve reasonable convergence time in learning, it appears to be necessary to decompose the systems into smaller subsystems that have better scale-up properties. One approach to this problem is discussed in the section that follows on context-sensitive networks.

Inverse Dynamics

Once the desired kinematic relationships have been established, it is still necessary to compute the joint torques required to achieve the desired motion. This computation is considerably more complex than the kinematic computation, since it involves such dynamic parameters as friction in the joints and the inertia of the moving arm segments. We shall consider the inverse-kinematics problem first.

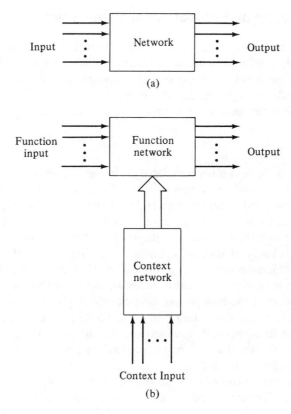

FIGURE 6.1 Structure of conventional and context-dependent networks.

CONTEXT-SENSITIVE NETWORKS

The usual way to represent a general computation unit by means of neural networks is shown in Figure 6.1(a), where the box labelled "Network" contains the required number of input and output units and at least two hidden layers. For the inverse-kinematics problem, θ and $\dot{x}$ from Equation (6-3) are used as the input, while $\dot{\theta}$ is the output of the network. A 6-DOF robot requires 12 input and 6 output units. The mapping is highly nonlinear, since the transformation depends on the location of the system in the coordinate frame. It is well known that learning in highly nonlinear mappings may be very time-consuming. As shown by Yeung [Yeung and Bekey, 1989; Yeung, 1989], the set of input variables can be partitioned into two groups (Figure 6.1(b)). One set is used as the input to the network which approximates the basic mathematical operations being represented (the function network), while the second set determines the setting or context within which the function is determined. In the robotics case, the context is the spatial location of the manipulator.

Architecture and Properties of Context Networks

We now consider context-sensitive networks of the feedforward type, such as commonly used with with the backpropagation algorithm. Suppose w_{ij} is a weight in either the function or the context network, connecting unit i in one layer with unit j in the next layer. Let the inputs be denoted by x and the outputs by y as usual. Then the total input to unit j can be written as

$$x_j \;=\; \sum_i w_{ji} y_i + b_j \tag{6-4}$$

where b_j is the bias term associated with unit j. The output y_j is related to the input through a sigmoid activation function $f_i(\cdot)$. Since the output units of the context network are used to set up the weights in the function network, the context network has as many output units as there are weights in the function network. Since this number can be very large, it is desirable that the function network be as simple as possible; ideally, it should be linear. The discussion that follows will concentrate on linear function networks; clearly, other choices are possible.

Learning in feedforward context-sensitive networks can be accomplished by an extension of the backpropagation algorithm [Yeung and Bekey, 1989]. Consider Figure 6.2, which shows unit k in the last hidden layer of the context network being connected to output unit l, which sets up the weight w_{ji} in the function network. It can be shown that the required gradient components can be computed using backpropagation in the function network.

It is interesting to note the nature of the coupling. Consider the weight w_{ji} in Figure 6.2. The total input to unit j can be expressed as

$$x_j \;=\; \sum_i w_{ji} y_i \;=\; \sum_i g_l(y_l) y_i \tag{6-5}$$

where $g(\cdot)$ is the coupling function between unit l of the context network and weight w_{ji} of the function network. For the special case when g is a linear function, i.e., $g(x) = a_l x$ for some constant $a_l \neq 0$, we have

$$x_j \;=\; \sum_i a_l y_l y_i \tag{6-6}$$

Thus, in this case the total input to unit j is a quadratic function of the activation values of other units, as opposed to the usual form of being a linear function. Such mutiplicative units have been discussed by Hinton [1981].

Context-Sensitive Architecture for Learning Inverse Models

The issue of choosing an appropriate set of input variables for the context input depends on the specific problem. If possible, the context should be chosen in such a way that the function network now represents a linear function, or at least one of reduced complexity. In the case of robot kinematics, it is natural to choose the configuration of the arm (as given by the joint state vector θ) as the context

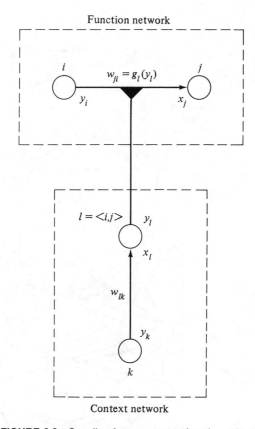

FIGURE 6.2 Coupling from context to function network.

input and $\mathbf{x}$ as the function input. For a given context θ, the joint velocity vector $\dot{\theta}$ and the Cartesian coordinates $\mathbf{x}$ are linearly related. Thus the function network need only represent linear functions with no constant terms.

An n-DOF arm requires a function network with n input and n output units, as shown in Figure 6.3. The output units have no bias terms, and their activation functions are just the identity function $f(x) = x$. The network has n^2 weights, which correspond to the entries in the inverse Jacobian matrix $\mathbf{J}^{-1}(\theta)$ evaluated at θ. The context network consists of n^2 decoupled learning subnetworks (Figure 6.3), each of which is responsible for learning a single scalar function corresponding to one entry in the matrix. The n input units are common to all the subnetworks, each of which has two hidden layers. Generally, both the hidden and output units will be chosen with sigmoid activation functions. Note that decoupling an n-to-n^2 mapping into n^2 n-to-1 functions simplifies the learning problem, since the role of each hidden unit is much clearer. Furthermore, the functions can be learned in parallel. Increasing the number of degrees of freedom n only increases the number of functions to be learned.

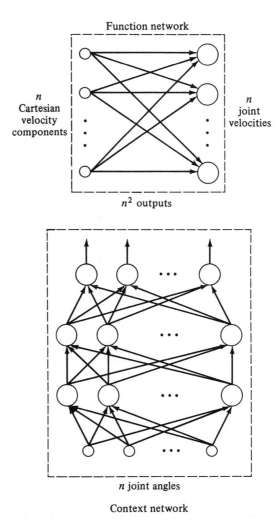

FIGURE 6.3 Context network for robot inverse kinematics.

Simulation of a 2-DOF Planar Arm

A 2-degree-of-freedom arm is shown in Figure 6.4. The two links are of length d_1 and d_2 respectively. The Cartesian coordinates of the end effector are related to the joint angles by the kinematic equations

$$\begin{bmatrix} x \\ y \end{bmatrix} = \begin{bmatrix} d_1 \cos \theta_1 + d_2 \cos (\theta_1 + \theta_2) \\ d_1 \sin \theta_1 + d_2 \sin (\theta_1 + \theta_2) \end{bmatrix} \tag{6-7}$$

The corresponding equations for velocity-based control are obtained by differ-

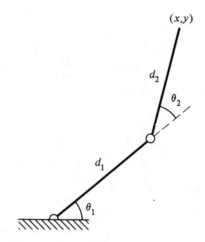

FIGURE 6.4   Two-degree-of-freedom arm.

entiating (6-7) with respect to time to obtain

$$
\begin{bmatrix} \dot{x} \\ \dot{y} \end{bmatrix} = \begin{bmatrix} -d_1 \sin\theta_1 - d_2 \sin(\theta_1 + \theta_2) & -d_2 \sin(\theta_1 + \theta_2) \\ d_1 \cos\theta_1 + d_2 \cos(\theta_1 + \theta_2) & d_2 \cos(\theta_1 + \theta_2) \end{bmatrix} \begin{bmatrix} \dot{\theta}_1 \\ \dot{\theta}_2 \end{bmatrix} \quad (6\text{-}8)
$$

In this simple case, the inverse kinematic equations can be obtained analytically:

$$
\begin{bmatrix} \dot{\theta}_1 \\ \dot{\theta}_2 \end{bmatrix} = \begin{bmatrix} \dfrac{\cos(\theta_1 + \theta_2)}{d_1 \sin\theta_2} & \dfrac{\sin(\theta_1 + \theta_2)}{d_1 \sin\theta_2} \\ -\dfrac{\cos\theta_1}{d_2 \sin\theta_2} - \dfrac{\cos(\theta_1 - \theta_2)}{d_1 \sin\theta_2} & -\dfrac{\sin\theta_1}{d_2 \sin\theta_2} - \dfrac{\sin(\theta_1 - \theta_2)}{d_1 \sin\theta_2} \end{bmatrix} \begin{bmatrix} \dot{x} \\ \dot{y} \end{bmatrix}
$$

$$(6\text{-}9)$$

During off-line learning of the inverse model, the training set consisted of examples generated by solving the above equations for 400 random contexts $(\theta_1, \theta_2)^T$.
For each context, four input-output pairs representing the Cartesian and joint velocity
components were generated for the function network. The context- and function-
network input variables were linearly scaled from their actual values to the range
$[-1, 1]$. The segment lengths were both set to 0.5. The context network we used
had 20 units in the first hidden layer and 10 units in the second (selected by exper-
imentation). The simulation was compared to a standard, "naive" neural network
architecture as shown in Figure 6.5, both being run with identical numbers of hidden units, learning rate, and momentum factor. The mean-squared output error,
averaged over 100 trials, for both the standard and the context-sensitive networks,
is shown in Figure 6.6. An **epoch** corresponds to cycling through the entire set
of training examples once. It is evident that the context-sensitive architecture exhibits dramatically faster convergence than the standard network, for this simple
inverse-kinematics problem.

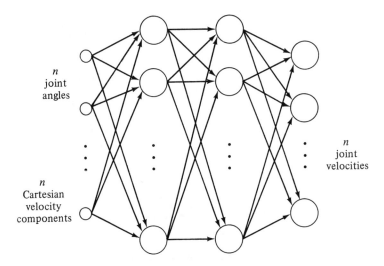

FIGURE 6.5   "Naive" neural-network architecture for inverse kinematics.

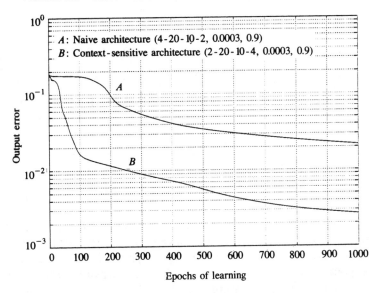

FIGURE 6.6   Learning curves for standard and context-sensitive networks.

Simulation of 3-DOF PUMA Kinematics

The example above, while encouraging, was restricted to 2 degrees of freedom. In order to validate the context-network techniques, it was necessary to apply the method to a more realistic problem. We have applied context-sensitive networks to inverse kinematics computation in both 3-DOF and 6-DOF problems using models of the Unimation PUMA robot, a standard industrial manipulator. The PUMA 560

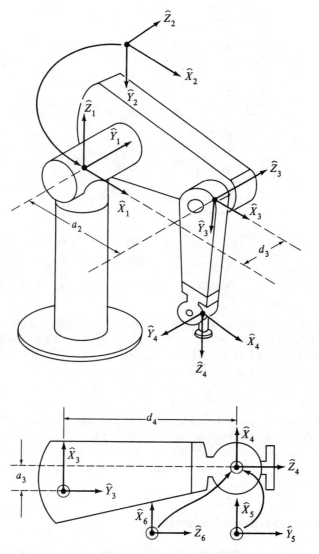

FIGURE 6.7 Some kinematic parameters and frame assignments for PUMA 560.

arm has 6 DOF. However, by careful choice of coordinate frame assignments (as in Figure 6.7) it is possible to reduce some of the elements of the Jacobian to zero, thus producing a system with only 3 DOF [Craig, 1986].

The training set used in off-line learning of the feedforward model for the 3-DOF PUMA arm consisted of examples corresponding to 400 randomly generated contexts or joint configurations. The details of the simulation are given by Yeung [1989]. For simplicity, the context network was implemented as a single multi-

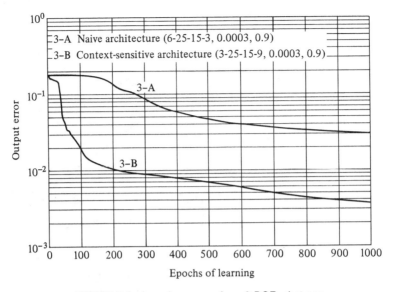

FIGURE 6.8 Learning curves for a 3-DOF robot arm.

layer network. Using decoupled subnetworks, as in Figure 6.3, would be expected to further improve performance. The context network had 20 units in the first hidden layer and 15 units in the second. As before, the learning rate was compared with that of a standard network using the same parameters (same number of hidden layers, number of units in each layer, learning rate, and momentum factor). The corresponding learning curves are shown in Figure 6.8. It can be seen from the results that the performance of the context-sensitive network is significantly better than that of a standard-architecture network. After learning for 1000 epochs, the rms errors of the standard and the context-sensitive network decreased to 0.0301 and 0.0036, respectively. The rate of improvement is particularly dramatic during the first 200 training epochs.

Inverse Jacobian Control

Having described the network architecture and the learning procedure, we now consider the use of the neural network in a feedback control system for arm control. Figure 6.9 shows the block diagram of such a system, which is sometimes referred to as **inverse Jacobian control**. The box labelled "Neural network controller" solves the inverse-kinematics problem by computing the joint velocity $\dot{\theta}$ from the context input θ and the Cartesian velocity $\dot{x}$. The arm is then controlled with the given joint velocity. Sensors on the arm provide the feedback signals θ and x. The current position x and the next target location x_g are used to estimate the velocity $\dot{x}$. It is important to note that the control scheme of Figure 6.9 does not take system dynamics into account. Furthermore, there are other ways in which feedforward

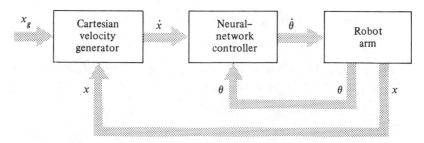

FIGURE 6.9 Inverse Jacobian control for robot manipulators.

models and feedback information can be combined for control purposes. One such approach, due to Kawato et al. [1987], will be discussed below in conjunction with dynamics problems.

THE INVERSE-DYNAMICS PROBLEM

The foregoing discussion has focused on the problem of transforming the representation of manipulator position from Cartesian to joint coordinates. (Such a transformation probably also occurs in the position control of human arms and the legs or wings of animals, since they must also transform points in the external world to their equivalent skeletal joint angles.) Given the desired joint configuration, it is now necessary to compute the torques to be applied at the joints to drive the arms, legs, or robot manipulators to the desired orientation. Generally, the desired motions will be subject to constraints or performance criteria, such as minimum overshoot, minimum energy, or minimum time. The computation of the necessary torques requires consideration of such parameters as inertia and damping. In view of the fact that the arm segments are coupled, the inertia matrix is not diagonal and the dynamical equations are highly nonlinear. Gravitational and Coriolis forces must also be considered.

The Simplified Equations

The general form of the dynamics equation can be expressed as [Craig, 1986]:

$$\tau = \mathbf{M}(\theta)\ddot{\theta} + \tau_v(\theta, \dot{\theta}) + \tau_g(\theta) + \tau_f(\theta, \dot{\theta}) \qquad (6\text{-}10)$$

where τ is the torque vector, $\mathbf{M}(\theta)$ is the mass matrix, $\tau_v(\theta, \dot{\theta})$ is a vector of centrifugal and Coriolis terms, $\tau_g(\theta)$ is a vector of gravity terms, and $\tau_f(\theta, \dot{\theta})$ is a vector of friction terms. The acceleration is often specified in Cartesian coordinates. In order to relate the Cartesian acceleration to the joint acceleration, we return to the kinematic relationship

$$\mathbf{x} = \mathbf{f}(\theta)$$

and differentiate it twice with respect to time, obtaining

$$\ddot{\mathbf{x}} = \mathbf{J}(\theta)\ddot{\theta} + \mathbf{H}(\theta)\dot{\theta} \tag{6-11}$$

where $\mathbf{H}(\theta)$, the matrix of second derivative, is known as the Hessian. Solving this expression for the joint acceleration and substituting in (6-10), we obtain

$$\tau = \mathbf{M}(\theta)\mathbf{J}^{-1}(\theta)\ddot{\mathbf{x}} - \mathbf{M}(\theta)\mathbf{J}^{-1}(\theta)\mathbf{H}(\theta)\dot{\theta} + \tau_v(\theta,\dot{\theta}) + \tau_g(\theta) + \tau_f(\theta,\dot{\theta}) \tag{6-12}$$

For small values of angular velocity and neglecting the effects of gravity, the torque can be approximated by the first term on the right-hand side of Equation (6-12), i.e.,

$$\tau_x = \mathbf{M}(\theta)\mathbf{J}^{-1}(\theta)\ddot{\mathbf{x}} \tag{6-13}$$

Note the analogy between this expression and the inverse kinematic relation,

$$\dot{\theta} = \mathbf{J}^{-1}(\theta)\dot{\mathbf{x}}$$

Again, we have a linear relationship between two variables, for a given spatial orientation of the robot, as given by the vector θ. Hence the matrix $\mathbf{M}(\theta)\mathbf{J}^{-1}(\theta)$ represents the context, and the linear expression can be obtained using a function network. Clearly, the discussion on context-sensitive networks applies to this simplified version of the inverse-dynamics problem. Using Equation (6-13) for inverse dynamic control poses a requirement for fast computation of the inverse Jacobian matrix.

Review of Prior Work

While considerable work has been done on the applications of neural networks to kinematic control, considerably less work has been reported in the general area of dynamic control. In spite of the analogy between the inverse problems, the inverse-dynamics problem presents considerably greater difficulty, owing to nonlinearity, coupling between variables, and lack of knowledge of the plant. Traditional proportional-integral-derivative (PID) controllers are not satisfactory for robot control, since they assume fixed plant parameters. Robot parameters are dependent on the joint configuration. This difficulty can be overcome by using some form of adaptive control based on identification of the robot parameters and consequent adjustment of controller gains. While this technique is feasible, it is complex and may be too slow for real-time applications. Hence, techniques based on learning without accurate knowledge of the parameters are very appealing.

The question of control architecture arises quickly, since the most popular learning algorithms for neural networks (such as backpropagation) are useful only with feedforward networks. The question of control architecture was addressed by Psaltis et al. [1987], who proposed two configurations termed **specialized learning architecture** and **generalized learning architecture**, respectively, as illustrated in

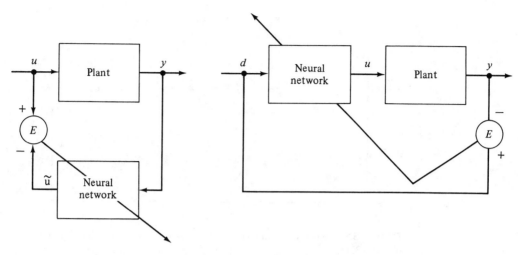

FIGURE 6.10   Alternative architectures for robot control.

Figure 6.10. The specialized architecture appears to be particularly well suited for robot control, since the neural controller is placed at the input of the controlled system, acting as a feedforward filter. In this structure the training of the system is based on comparing the desired response of the system d with the actual response y. The goal is to achieve zero error for all given inputs. Since the learning signal will track any variations in system response, this structure is suitable for on-line learning and real-time adaptation. However, such an application is useful only if the control network is near its correct operating point to insure stable and well-behaved operation. Hence, starting the training of the system of Figure 6.10(b) with random weights may not be suitable.

Psaltis et al. suggest using the structure of Figure 6.10(a), which they term a **generalized learning architecture** for off-line learning. Once convergence has been obtained, the feedback network can be placed in the forward path to provide on-line adaptive control. Another difficulty that arises with specialized learning is that backpropagation cannot be used directly, since the error arises at the output of the controlled system and not at the output of the neural network. It has been suggested that a solution to this problem is to have the errors propagate through the plant as if it were an additional layer with unmodifiable weights [Psaltis et al., 1987]. This leads back to the question of plant identification.

A complete solution to the inverse-dynamics problem has been presented by Kawato et al. [Kawato et al., 1987; Miyamoto, Kawato, et al., 1988]. Their work is based on studies of movement control in the neuromuscular system. Basically, they assume that within the central nervous system an internal neural model of the inverse dynamics of the musculoskeletal system is acquired while monitoring a desired trajectory and the associated motor commands. They simulated control and

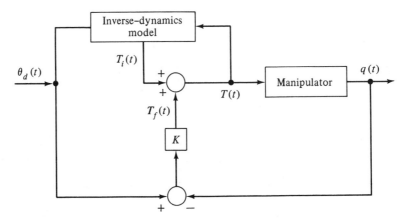

FIGURE 6.11   Block diagram of neural network for robot control, from [Kawato et al., 1987].

learning performance of a robot manipulator in order to test their hypotheses on the behavior of the biological system. A three-link direct-drive manipulator was studied, using the overall model of Figure 6.11. The terms $T(t)$, $T_i(t)$, and $T_f(t)$ denote the torque input to the manipulator, the torque computed by the inverse-dynamics model, and the feedback torque, respectively. The inverse-dynamics model receives as its input the set of joint angles representing the desired trajectory, and it monitors the total torque input to the manipulator. As learning proceeds, it would be desirable for the actual manipulator trajectory to approach the desired trajectory and hence for the feedback torque term $T_f(t)$ to approach zero. In this event the architecture of the system will approach the specialized architecture of [Psaltis et al., 1987].

The internal structure of inverse dynamics of the manipulator was obtained by representing dynamics using the Lagrangian formulation [Craig, 1986] which leads to the expression

$$\mathbf{R(q)}\ddot{\mathbf{q}} - (\sum_k \dot{q}_k \frac{\partial \mathbf{R}}{\partial \mathbf{q}_k})\dot{\mathbf{q}} - \frac{1}{2}\dot{\mathbf{q}}^T \frac{\partial \mathbf{R}}{\partial \mathbf{q}}\dot{\mathbf{q}} + \mathbf{B}\dot{\mathbf{q}} + \mathbf{G(q)} = \mathbf{T}(t) \qquad (6\text{-}14)$$

where $\mathbf{q} = (q_1, q_2, q_3)^T$ is the generalized displacement vector and $\mathbf{T} = (T_1, T_2, T_3)^T$ is the torque. $\mathbf{R(q)}$ is a 3×3 inertia matrix (which is not diagonal), $\mathbf{B}$ is a 3×3 diagonal matrix of damping coefficients, and $\mathbf{G(q)}$ represents the gravitational forces. In this equation the first term on the right-hand side represents the inertial torques, the second and third terms the centripetal and Coriolis torques, the fourth term the damping torques, and the fifth the torques due to gravity. The detailed structure of the inverse dynamics represented by Equation (6-14) is shown in Figure 6.12. The three joint-angle inputs, the three torque outputs, and the feedback torques are indicated. The blocks in this figure represent the expansion of Equation (6-14) into 26 nonlinear

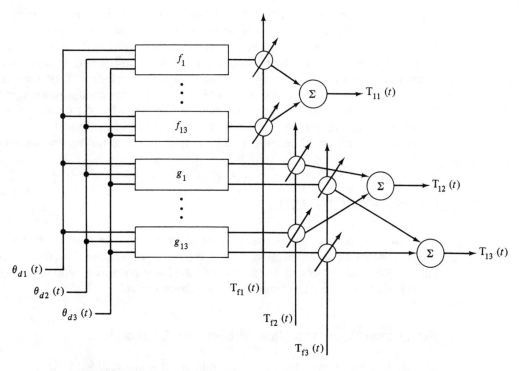

FIGURE 6.12 Detailed structure of inverse-dynamics model, from [Kawato et al., 1987].

filters $f(\cdot)$ and $g(\cdot)$. Detailed knowledge of the nature of the equations is required to generate these filters, which produce the inverse-dynamics-model output torque in the form

$$\mathbf{T}_{i1}(t) \;=\; \sum_{l=1}^{13} w_{1l} f_l(q_{d1}(t), q_{d2}(t), q_{d3}(t))$$

$$\mathbf{T}_{ik}(t) \;=\; \sum_{l=1}^{13} w_{kl} g_l(q_{d1}(t), q_{d2}(t), q_{d3}(t)), \qquad (k = 2, 3) \qquad (6\text{-}15)$$

In these expressions the terms w_{1l} and w_{kl} are the weights of synapses from a given subsystem to the output neuron. In other words, the neural network used by Kawato includes only one layer of modifiable weights. If a perfect inverse-dynamics model is found, then Equations (6-14) and (6-15) will be identical.

The performance of Kawato's system is excellent. Both the inverse- and forward-dynamics models were acquired during typical movements. As learning continued, the inverse-dynamics model gradually replaced any external feedback. The final system was able to generalize to control movements quite different from those used for training. Finally, while significant knowledge is required to construct the nonlinear filters, they need not be completely accurate. The system converged even when extraneous filters were present. Nevertheless, the structure of the filters will depend on the particular robot being controlled, and parameter values must be known or estimated. In view of the computational complexity of the implementation, this approach is probably best suited to parallel processing, when significant knowledge is available. Clearly, the method uses knowledge to reduce the number of unknown weights in the neural-network portion of the model. The trade-off between knowledge and neural-network complexity needs further investigation.

DECOMPOSITION METHODS

We now present an approach to the inverse-dynamics problem that is based on the concept of decomposition, as was the divide-and-conquer strategy discussed earlier. We begin with a decomposition of the basic equations and then consider a method that combines feedforward and feedback control.

Functional Decomposition of Dynamic Equations

It is well known that when the functional relationships to be learned by a neural network are complex and highly nonlinear, the learning time may become prohibitively long [Rummelhart et al., 1986]. Part of the difficulty arises from the size of the sample training space. In the case of robot dynamics this situation is very apparent. Consider the simple case of a 2-DOF arm. The torque depends on joint position and velocity as well as on the Cartesian acceleration. If we require, for example, ten samples in each dimension, a total of one million training samples will be required. This is clearly unrealistic. The number of required samples becomes astronomically large for 6 DOF. (It should be noted that this problem arises in the work of Kuperstein [1987], who needs training samples distributed throughout the whole space in order to learn how to move a robot arm to an arbitrary desired location.) It is apparent that the solution is to find ways to reduce the number of samples needed to learn the relationships.

The work on context-sensitive networks discussed above represents one answer to this problem, which characterizes robotic systems. The work of Kawato et al. [1987] also attempted to reduce convergence time by decomposing the dynamic equations into a large number of subsystems. The method proposed by Bassi and Bekey [1989a] is based on decomposing the dynamic equations into their basic component relations, training on these simpler relations, and then recomposing to obtain the complete input-output mapping. Thus, with reference to the general dynamics equation (6-12), the torque can be decomposed into terms that represent the Cartesian acceleration, the Coriolis and centripetal torques, the gravitational

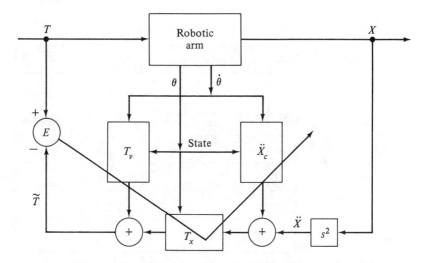

FIGURE 6.13 Generalized learning architecture using functional decomposition.

effects, and the torques due to damping. If the gravitational and damping terms are omitted for simplicity, the reduced dynamics equation becomes

$$\tau(\theta, \dot{\theta}, \ddot{\mathbf{x}}) \quad = \quad \mathbf{M}(\theta)\mathbf{J}^{-1}(\theta)[\ddot{x} - [\mathbf{H}(\theta)\dot{\theta}]\dot{\theta}] + \tau_v(\theta, \dot{\theta}) \qquad (6\text{-}16)$$

which can be decomposed into three terms as follows:

$$\tau_x(\theta, \ddot{\mathbf{x}}_0) = \mathbf{M}(\theta)\mathbf{J}^{-1}(\theta)\ddot{\mathbf{x}}_0$$

$$\tau_v(\theta, \dot{\theta}) = \tau_v(\theta, \dot{\theta}) \qquad (6\text{-}17)$$

$$\ddot{x}_c(\theta, \dot{\theta}) = -[\mathbf{H}(\theta)\dot{\theta}]\dot{\theta}$$

The implementation of these relationships by means of the generalized learning architecture (discussed in an earlier section) requires some additional computation. The behavior of the system, as seen in the above equations, depends on the entire state and not simply on the joint or Cartesian position, as provided by the network. In other words, the neural network cannot control the robot with position information alone but must be provided with velocity and acceleration information as well. Hence, we have modified the generalized architecture by adding differentiators as required by the equations. Figure 6.13 shows the modified architecture and its decomposition into the three terms of Equation (6-17).

There are clear advantages to the approach outlined above. First, it can be applied to any manipulator, since the equations are used in their most generic form. Second, since the learning is performed on simpler equations with fewer dependent variables, the number of required training samples is drastically reduced. Third, the networks themselves are simpler, requiring fewer units for implementation to achieve a given accuracy. The functional decomposition takes advantage of the natural structure of the model of a manipulator.

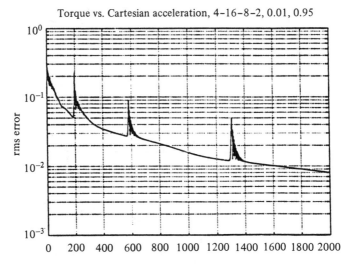

Torque vs. Cartesian acceleration, 4–16–8–2, 0.01, 0.95

FIGURE 6.14   Learning of torque-vs.-acceleration term.

The technique was applied to a model of a 2-DOF arm. The three networks designed to provide the relationships of Equation (6-17) were trained using back-propagation, with data from a simulated manipulator. Two hidden layers were used in each network, with 81 training points. The results of learning the first term of Equation (6-17), i.e., the dependence of the torque on the Cartesian acceleration, are shown in Figure 6.14. The rms error was reduced to 2.8 percent after 2000 sweeps over the training set. The "spikes" on the learning-error curve are due to a high value of the learning rate; reducing the rate eliminated the spikes but slowed down the convergence, while higher values led to instability. Similar results were obtained for the other terms in the torque equation. Further research is needed to find a suitable parallel method of adjusting all three networks simultaneously, by on-line learning, thus allowing robot control while keeping track of system variations at the same time. A block diagram of a controller showing the interconnections of the three neural networks for on-line control is shown in Figure 6.15.

Combined Feedforward/Feedback Controllers

As indicated earlier in this chapter, the application of neural-network techniques to robotics presents two major difficulties. First, the representation of strongly nonlinear mappings often results in large networks requiring large numbers of training examples and very slow convergence. Second, neural-network representations of complex functional mappings are approximate by definition, and the degree of approximation is difficult to predict. This section presents the results of a preliminary study which attempts to address both of these difficulties.

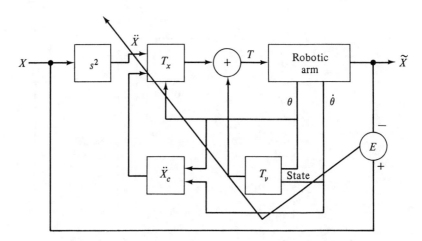

FIGURE 6.15 Robotic controller based on functional decomposition.

Functional decomposition methods, as outlined above, may lead to practical-size networks and acceptable numbers of samples in obtaining a feedforward controller. In order to reduce the error to desirable bounds, Bassi and Bekey [1989b] propose to use feedback. Specifically, they propose to use, recurrently, an optimal estimate of the Cartesian trajectory in order to keep the end effector position within predetermined bounds.

The technique basically consists of the following steps. (1) An optimum trajectory function is obtained. Optimality is used to select among the infinity of possible trajectories that connect any two given points along the trajectory, and it may be based on such criteria as minimum time, minimum acceleration, or minimum jerk, while satisfying other constraints. (2) Functional decomposition is used to learn the inverse-dynamics parameters employing a generalized learning architecture. However, since feedback is used to correct for imprecisions in the feedforward control process, only the torque/Cartesian acceleration portion of the torque equation was used. (3) The resulting network is now used as a feedforward controller (see Figure 6.15). (4) The loop is now closed with the optimal trajectory control, which calculates the acceleration required to drive the manipulator to the current optimal trajectory. A block diagram of this system is shown in Figure 6.16.

The method was applied to a 2-DOF arm performing a variety of movements. As an example, Figure 6.17 shows a start-stop movement of the arm, beginning with the end effector located $(0.5, 0)$ and ending at $(0.5, 0.5)$. This is a very large movement, equal in displacement to the total length of the arm. The goal was to achieve a straight-line trajectory. It can be seen that the trajectory deviates slightly from a straight line, possibly because only the linear terms were included in the torque equation. The final position error can be made as small as desired by a choice of control period [Bassi and Bekey, 1989b].

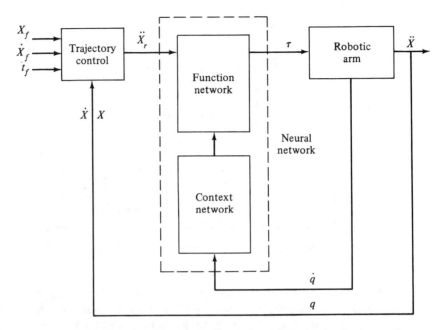

FIGURE 6.16 Connectionist feedforward and Cartesian feedback control.

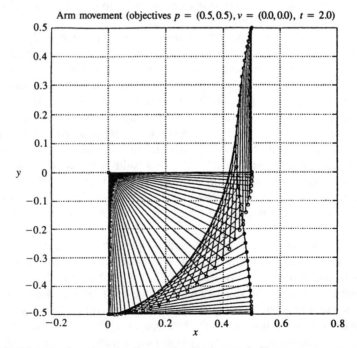

FIGURE 6.17 Combined feedforward/feedback control of large arm movement.

CONCLUSION

This chapter has presented an overview of the applications of artificial neural networks to robot control, with an emphasis on inverse kinematics and dynamics. The emphasis has been on methods developed by graduate students working with the author to overcome some of the major sources of difficulty in these applications, namely, slow convergence, large sample sizes, and lack of accuracy. While the problems of dynamics and kinematics represent a major share of this field, there are a number of other applications. For example, neural networks have been used in sensor-based robot control [Miller, 1989]. In this application there are multiple sensors and multiple command variables. The network (implemented using the CMAC architecture [Albus, 1975]) learns the nonlinear relationship between the sensor output and the command variables over particular regions of the system state space. A recent survey by Kung and Hwang [1989] lists applications in path planning, use of stereo vision in task planning, and sensor/motor control. The authors' major objective is to present systolic architectures suitable for problems in robotics.

Yet, in spite of a substantial number of publications, it is not yet clear whether neural-network methods will find substantial applications in industrial robotic systems. The idea that either kinematic or dynamic control could be achieved without a detailed knowledge of either the governing equations of robots or their parameters is extremely appealing. Yet, this appeal is tempered by the realization that training times may be prohibitively long, and that there is no current theoretical basis for selecting the number of hidden layers or the number of units in each layer to achieve a given accuracy. Furthermore, while robot control does indeed require complex computations, current algorithms allow for such computing to be done in real time. Furthermore, the increasing availability of parallel algorithms (e.g., [Fijany and Bejczy, 1989]) and processors promises to further reduce the time required to perform the computations needed for on-line control. As a consequence, at least for those situations where the robot model and its parameters are known or can be estimated, there is less need for the power of neural networks to approximate arbitrary input-output relationships.

A further problem with the acceptance of neural networks is partially related to their power. It is possible, as Kuperstein [1987] has done, to allow a network to learn eye-hand mappings for robots beginning with total ignorance. Yet, the price paid for this ability is long convergence, with large numbers of training examples obtained from the whole space. On the other hand, traditional robot-control methods require complete knowledge, and they suffer when accurate models or precise parameter values are not available. Only a few investigators, such as Handelman et al. [1989], have attempted to combine knowledge-based methods with neural-network techniques in robotics. It may be that further development of such hybrid methods, which combine knowledge, heuristics, and connectionist methods, will provide the tools for the development of new generations of intelligent, highly adaptive robotic systems.

REFERENCES

Albus, J., "A New Approach to Manipulator Control: The Cerebellar Model Articulation Controller," *J. Dynamic Systems, Measurement and Control*, vol. 97, 270–277, 1975.

Barhen, J., Gulai, S., and Zak, M., "Neural Learning of Constrained Nonlinear Transformations," *IEEE Computer*, vol. 22, 67–77, 1989.

Bassi, D. F., and Bekey, G. A., "Decomposition of Neural Network Models of Robot Dynamics: A Feasibility Study," In *Simulation and AI*, W. Webster (ed.), 8–13, Society for Computer Simulation, 1989a.

Bassi, D. F., and Bekey, G. A., "High Precision Position Control by Cartesian Trajectory Feedback and Connectionist Inverse Dynamics Feedforward," *Proc. Intern. Joint Conf. on Neural Networks*, vol. 2, 325–332, 1989b.

Brooks, R., "A Robot That Walks," *Neural Computation* vol. 1, 253–262, 1989.

Chang, P. R., and Lee, C. S. G., "Residue Arithmetic VLSI Array Architecture for Manipulator Pseudo-Inverse Jacobian Computation," *IEEE Trans. on Robotics and Automation*, vol. 5, 569–582, 1989.

Craig, J. J., *Introduction to Robotics*, Addison-Wesley Publishing Co., Reading, MA, 1986.

Elsley, R. K., "A Learning Architecture for Control Based on Back-propagation Neural Networks," *Proc. IEEE Conf. on Neural Networks*, 587–594, 1988.

Fijany, A., and Bejczy, A. K., "A Class of Parallel Algorithms for Computation of the Manipulator Inertia Matrix," *IEEE Trans. on Robotics and Automation*, vol. 5, 600–615, 1989.

Goldberg, K., and Perlmutter, B., "Using a Neural Network to Learn the Dynamics of the CMU Direct-Drive Arm II," *Report CMU-CS-88-160*, Department of Computer Science, Carnegie Mellon University, 1988.

Grossberg, S., and Kuperstein, M., *Neural Dynamics of Adaptive Sensory Motor Control*, Elsevier North-Holland, New York, 1986.

Guez, A., and Ahmad, Z., "Solution to the Inverse Problem in Robotics by Neural Networks," *Proc. Intern. Conf. on Neural Networks*, 617–624, 1988.

Handelman, D. A., Lane, S. H., and Gelfand, J. J., "Integration of Knowledge-Based System and Neural Network Techniques for Robotic Control," *Proc. IEEE Intern. Conf. on Robotics and Automation*, 1454–1460, 1989.

Hinton, G. E., "A Parallel Computation That Assigns Canonical Object-Based Frames of Reference," *Proc. Intern. Joint Conf. on Artificial Intelligence*, 683–685, 1981.

Josin, G., Charney, D., and White, D., "Robot Control Using Neural Networks," *Proc. Intern. Conf. on Neural Networks*, 625–631, 1988.

Kawato, M., Uno, Y., Isobe, M., and Suzuki, R. A., "Hierarchical Model for Voluntary Movement and Its Application to Robotics. *Proc. IEEE Conf. on Neural Networks*," 573–582, 1987.

Kung, S.-Y., and Hwang, J.-N., "Neural Network Architectures for Robotic Applications," *IEEE Trans. on Robotics and Automation*, vol. 5, 641–657, 1989.

Kuperstein, M., "Adaptive Visual-Motor Coordination in Multijoint Robots Using Parallel Architecture," *Proc. IEEE Intern. Conf. on Robotics and Automation*, 1595–1602, 1987.

Kuperstein, M., "Neural Model of Adaptive Hand-Eye Coordination," *Science*, vol. 239, 1308–1311, 1988.

Leahy, M. B., et al., "Efficient PUMA Manipulator Jacobian Calculation and Inversion," *Jour. Robotic Systems*, vol. 4, 63–75, 1987.

Miller, W. T., "Real-time Application of Neural Networks for Sensor-Based Control of Robots," *IEEE Trans. on Systems, Man, and Cybernetics*, vol. 19, 825–831, 1989.

Miyamoto, H., Kawato, M., Setoyama, T., and Suzuki, R. "Feedback Error Learning Neural Networks for Trajectory Control of a Robotic Manipulator," *Neural Networks*, vol. 1, 251–265, 1988.

Psaltis, D., Sideris, A., and Yamamura, A., "Neural Controllers," *Proc. IEEE Intern. Conf. on Neural Networks*, 551–558, 1987.

Rummelhart, D. E., McClelland, J. L., and the PDP Research Group, *"Parallel Distributed Processing,"* The M.I.T. Press, Cambridge, MA, 1986.

Winter, C. L., "BUGS: An Adaptive Critter," *Journal of Neural Network Computing*, vol. 1, 66–72, 1989.

Yeung, D.-T., and Bekey, G. A., "Using a Context-Sensitive Learning Network for Robot Arm Control," *Proc. IEEE Intern. Conf. on Robotics and Automation*, 1441–1447, 1989.

Yeung, D.-T., "Handling Dimensionality and Nonlinearity in Connectionist Learning," Ph.D. Dissertation, Computer Science Department, University of Southern California, 1989.

PROBLEMS

6.1. Verify Equations (6-8) and (6-9) for the velocity-based kinematics and inverse kinematics of the 2-DOF arm.

6.2. Consider a single-link manipulator capable of rotation about the origin and of adjusting the link length. The link with adjustable length is termed **telescoping** or **prismatic**. This is a 2-DOF system described by the "joint" variables (r, θ), where r is the link length and θ is its angle with the x-axis.

    (a) Derive the position-based forward and inverse kinematic equations for the Cartesian coordinates of the end point of the robot in terms of the joint variables.

    (b) Derive the velocity-based forward and inverse kinematic relations for this arm.

6.3. Consider the 2-DOF arm shown in Figure 6P.3. This is a variation on the arm depicted in Figure 6.4, the kinematic equations of which are given in Equation (6-7). Assume that the link length d_1 is fixed at length 1, and that its angle with the x-axis is denoted by θ. The second link forms a right angle with the first. Let the second link length be variable and denoted by r. You now have a new 2-DOF system, where the controlled "joint" variables are (r, θ).

    (a) Derive the position-based forward and inverse kinematic equations for the Cartesian coordinates of the end point of the robot in terms of the joint variables.

    (b) Derive the velocity-based forward and inverse kinematic equations for this system.

(c) Discuss the relative advantages and disadvantages of this formulation on the computation of the inverse Jacobian.

(d) Propose a context-sensitive neural network for the evaluation of inverse kinematics for this system.

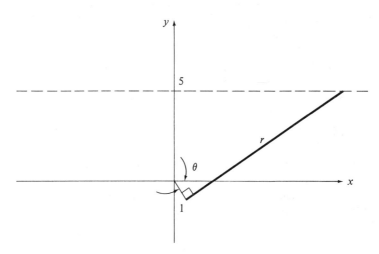

FIGURE 6P.3 A 2-DOF manipulator.

6.4. Consider the 2-DOF manipulator in Figure 6P.3. Suppose we wish to track a straight line at $y = 5$ at constant velocity, from $\theta = -50$ degrees to $+50$ degrees.

(a) Assume that the inverse kinematics for this task are unknown, and let $\theta(t)$ and $h(t)$ be constant-velocity functions. Determine the resulting points $[x(t), y(t)]$ at $t = 0, 2, 4, 6,$ and 8 seconds. Sketch the manipulator configuration at these times.

(b) Now assume that you have explicit knowledge of the inverse kinematics (see Problem 6.1). Let the manipulator end point move along the line with a velocity of 2 units/second and determine the joint positions and velocities at the same times.[1]

6.5. Consider a 3-DOF manipulator consisting of a single link with coordinates r and θ, and a third vertical axis with coordinate z. The forward positional kinematic equations are:

$$x = r \cos \theta \quad y = r \sin \theta \quad z = z$$

(a) Derive the velocity-based forward kinematic equations and write them in matrix form.

(b) Derive the velocity-based inverse kinematic equations.

---

[1]This problem is adapted from W. A. Wolovich, *Robotics: Basic Analysis and Design*, (New York: Holt, Rinehart and Winston, 1987).

    (c) Propose a context-sensitive neural network for (b), sketch it, and discuss any potential problems.

    (d) Examine the Jacobian for this sysem and find locations (if any) in joint space where it may become singular. Discuss the implications of such singularities on the use of neural networks for inverse kinematics.

6.6. Figure 6.2 shows the coupling of the context network and the function network. Show how backpropagation can be extended to the computation of associated coupling weights, and derive the required gradient expressions.

6.7. Consider the 2-DOF arm of Figure 6.4.

    (a) Derive and write the detailed vector-matrix expression for the acceleration, as in Equation (6.11).

    (b) Now assume that the masses are concentrated at the ends of the links and derive the scalar equations for the two components of the torque vector in terms of the joint variables.

    (c) Derive and write the detailed vector-matrix expression for the approximate torque expression of Equation (6-13).

6.8. A typical 6-DOF articulated manipulator has dynamics that depend on all 12 of the state variables (i.e., six positions and six velocities), as well as the desired acceleration. Thus, 18 variables are needed to relate a model output to observed Cartesian variables. Assuming that to train a neural network we select examples by using five values over the whole range of every variable, and that 1 millisecond is required to perform the network computations for one example, calculate how long it would take to examine the whole range of examples once, and how long it would take to consider 1000 iterations over the whole set of examples. Discuss ways in which this time could be shortened.

7

SUPERVISED LEARNING WITH GAUSSIAN POTENTIALS

Sukhan Lee
Center for Neural Engineering
Department of Electrical Engineering–Systems
University of Southern California

MAPPING NEURAL NETWORKS

Neural networks estimate functions. For this reason they are sometimes called "mapping neural networks" [Hecht-Nielsen, 1987b]. We can define a mapping neural network as follows:

A **mapping neural network** is a distributed parallel network performing a mapping, $\phi: I^n \rightarrow R^m$, based on the interconnection of neurons as basic nonlinear computational units, where I^n is a unit hypercube in n dimensions.

The following summarizes some current design principles used for constructing mapping networks:

1. By generating a required form of network energy function over the input space through proper interconnection among neurons, an input pattern is mapped to an output pattern as the network converges to a local minimum of its energy function. For instance, in the *autoassociative memory (AM)* [Hopfield, 1982] or the *bidirectional associative memory (BAM)* [Kosko, 1987] the symmetric connection among neurons results in stable network dynamics, ensuring the convergence of an input pattern to the corresponding local minimum of the

network energy function. The *Boltzmann machine* [Hinton et al., 1984] is based on the same principle, but in a probabilistic sense.

2. By associating individual reference patterns with output neurons, an input pattern is mapped to an output pattern through the retrieval of a reference pattern corresponding to the output neuron that wins the competition among output neurons based on the closeness between individual reference patterns and the given input pattern. For instance, in the *Hamming network* [Lippmann, 1987] the Hamming distance is used in selecting the closest reference pattern from an input pattern. This principle is the basis of the *Kohonen's self-organizing feature maps* [Kohonen, 1988], the *Carpenter/Grossberg's classification network* [Carpenter and Grossberg, 1987], and the *Hecht-Nielsen's counterpropagation network* [Hecht-Nielsen, 1987a], although these schemes include other features of their own.

3. An arbitrary input-output function or a decision boundary is approximately realized based on the multilayer feedforward connection of neurons as nonlinear computational units. For instance, in the *multilayer perceptron* [Lippmann, 1987] or the *backpropagation network* [Rummelhart et al., 1986], the input-output mapping is defined by a series of intermediate mappings between the spaces of adjacent layers. During a series of intermediate mappings, the input domain is transformed into increasingly complex nonlinear manifolds in the spaces of upper layers through the connection weights and the nonlinear activation functions of computational units. The final input-output mapping is represented by the nonlinear manifold of the input domain defined in the output space.

We are interested in investigating the class of mapping neural networks based on the third principle, since the ultimate power of a mapping neural network comes from its capability of realizing arbitrary functions. To begin with, let us introduce the *Kolmogorov-Sprecher theorem* [Kolmogorov, 1957; Sprecher, 1965], which describes the exact representation of arbitrary continuous functions defined over the n-dimensional input cube as an existence theorem for mapping neural networks [Hecht-Nielsen, 1987b].

Kolmogorov-Sprecher theorem.   For each integer $n \geq 2$, there exists a real monotonic increasing function $\psi(x)$, $\psi([0,1]) = [0,1]$, dependent on n and having the following property:

For each preassigned number $\delta > 0$, there is a rational number ϵ, $0 < \epsilon < \delta$, such that every real continuous function of n variables, $\phi(\mathbf{x})$, defined on I^n, can be exactly represented by

$$\phi(\mathbf{x}) = \sum_{j=1}^{2n+1} \chi \left[\sum_{i=1}^{n} \lambda^i \psi(x_i + \epsilon(j-1)) + j - 1 \right] \tag{7-1}$$

where χ is a real and continuous function dependent upon ϕ, and λ is a constant independent of ϕ.

As pointed out by Hecht-Nielsen [1987b], the Kolmogorov-Sprecher theorem indicates that any continuous real function can be exactly realized by a four-layer neural network composed of an input, an output, and two hidden layers with finite number of neurons. Since no constructive method for the determination of χ (which is dependent on ϕ) is currently known, a direct application of the Kolmogorov-Sprecher theorem is difficult. Irie-Miyake [1988] proved that a three-layer network with an infinite number of hidden units can represent an arbitrary function, provided that the activation functions of hidden units as well as the mapping functions are bounded and absolutely integrable. Funahashi [1989] extended the Irie-Miyake theorem to include sigmoidal activation functions, such that any continuous function is approximately realizable by three-layer networks with bounded and monotonic-increasing continuous activation functions of hidden units. A similar result is obtained by Hecht-Nielsen [1989] by showing that a subset of a backpropagation network can implement a sinusoidal function, enabling the backpropagation network to perform the Fourier-series approximation of an arbitrary function.

While the aforementioned theorems mostly pertain either to the feasibility of constructing powerful mapping neural networks with a finite number of neurons or to the capability of a backpropagation network as a universal function approximator, issues such as the ones listed below remain unsolved:

1. What are the effects of the number of layers on the realization and training of the mapping neural networks? Does an increase in the number of hidden layers render the mapping neural network more efficient either in terms of the number of neurons required for a realization or in terms of the learning speed in training ?

2. What are the effects of selecting nonsigmoidal activation functions for hidden units on the realization and training of mapping neural networks? Note that it has been shown that any absolutely integrable activation function, such as a Gaussian function, is also effective in approximating an arbitrary function. Furthermore, it can be said that a sinusoidal activation function is also effective in approximating an arbitrary function, since an arbitrary function can be synthesized by the Fourier-series expansion. Can we conjecture or prove that nonsigmoidal activation functions such as Gaussian and sinusoidal functions provide efficiency in realizing and training a mapping neural network, owing to their powerful nonlinear mapping capabilities?

To provide an insight into the above issues, a five-layer feedforward neural network is introduced in Figure 7.1, and the performance of the three different types of activation functions, i.e., sigmoidal, Gaussian, and sinusoidal functions, in generating a function $Y = f(X)$ is investigated. Figures 7.2, 7.3, and 7.4, representing the cases of sigmoidal, Gaussian, and sinusoidal activation functions, respectively, depict a successive transformation of the input domain I, $I = [0, 1]$,

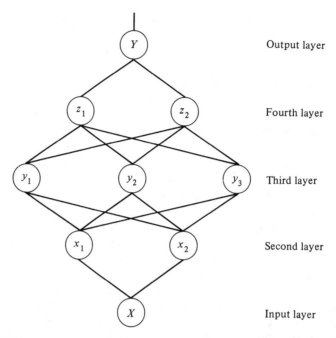

FIGURE 7.1 A neural network consisting of an input, an output, and three hidden layers is used to generate a function $Y = f(X)$ to compare the performance of three different types of activation functions: sigmoidal, Gaussian and sinusoidal.

into increasingly more complex nonlinear manifolds in the spaces of upper layers. In Figures 7.2, 7.3, and 7.4, (a) represents the output of the second layer, x_1 and x_2 in terms of the input X, (b) represents the nonlinear manifold of input domain in the $x_1 - x_2$ space, i.e., the trajectory of x_1 and x_2 in the $x_1 - x_2$ space when X varies from -1 to 1, (c) represents the output of the third layer, y_1, y_2, and y_3, in terms of X, (d) represents the output of the fourth layer, z_1 and z_2, in terms of X, (e) represents the nonlinear manifold of the input domain in the $z_1 - z_2$ space, and (f) represents the final output Y in terms of X.

The straight lines shown in (b) are based on the weights assigned to connections between the second and third layers. A point (x_1, x_2) located on a straight line parallel to the one given in the figure provides the same net input to the third layer, thus generating the same output at the third layer. In case of the Gaussian activation function, a point (x_1, x_2) located farther from the given straight line generates a lower value of y, while in case of the sigmoidal activation function, a point (x_1, x_2) generates a monotonically decreasing or increasing value of y along the direction perpendicular to the given straight line. This makes y from the Gaussian activation function more deformed and fluctuating than that from the sigmoidal activation function, thus resulting in a more complex and deformed nonlinear manifold

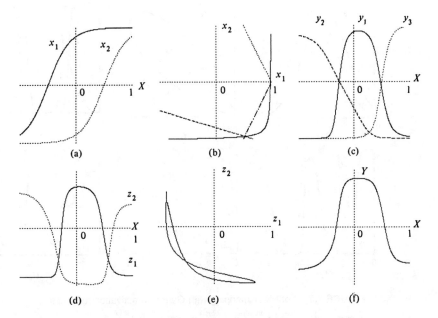

FIGURE 7.2 Nonlinear mapping with sigmoidal activation functions,
$f(\mathbf{w}^t\mathbf{x} - \theta_i) = (1 - e^{-(\sum_j w_{ij}x_j - \theta_i)/T})/(1 + e^{-(\sum_j w_{ij}x_j - \theta_i)/T})$, where $T = 0.2$.
(a) $x_1 = f(X - 0.5), x_2 = f(X - 0.5)$. (b) $x_1 - x_2$ trajectory.
(c) $y_1 = f(2x_1 - x_2 - 2)$, $y_2 = f(-0.3x_1 - x_2 - 0.8)$, $y_3 = f(2x_1 + x_2 - 2.0)$.
(d) $z_1 = f(0.5y_1 + 0.05y_2 - 0.05y_3 - 0.)$, $z_2 = f(-0.2y_1 + 0.6y_2 + 0.5y_3 + 0.1)$.
(e) $z_1 - z_2$ trajectory. (f) $Y = 0.5z_1 - 0.5z_2$.

of the input domain (as seen from the comparison between Figures 7.2(e), 7.3(e), and 7.4(e)). In general, it can be said that nonsigmoidal activation functions as well as multiple hidden layers provide the network with the capability of forming more complex nonlinear manifolds of the input domain through intermediate mappings. However, the precise mathematical analysis of the effect of nonsigmoidal activation functions and multiple hidden layers on network realization and training is a subject for further research.

This chapter presents a nonsigmoidal mapping neural network, called the **Gaussian potential function network (GPFN)** [Lee and Kil, 1988]. GPFN is capable of performing both "many-to-one" forward mappings as a pattern classifier and "one-to-many" inverse mappings as a recall processor or pattern generator [Lee and Kil, 1989], and it explores such issues as the capability of the network in realizing an arbitrary mapping and the training of the network based on supervised learning. The forward mapping of GPFN approximates a "many-to-one" continuous function by a potential field synthesized over the domain of the input space by a number of Gaussian computational units called **Gaussian potential function**

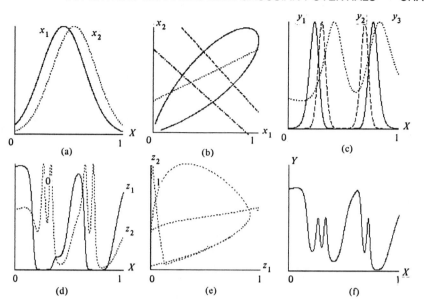

FIGURE 7.3 Nonlinear mapping with Gaussian activation functions,
$f(\mathbf{w}^t\mathbf{x} - m^i) = e^{-(\sum_j w_{ij}x_j - m_i)^2/2\sigma^2}$, where $\sigma = 0.2$.
(a) $x_1 = f(X - 0.45)$, $x_2 = f(X - 0.55)$.   (b) $x_1 - x_2$ trajectory.
(c) $y_1 = f(-0.9x_1 - x_2 + 0.8)$, $y_2 = f(-1.1x_1 - x_2 + 1.3)$, $y_3 = f(0.5x_1 - x_2 + 0.3)$.
(d) $z_1 = f(0.7y_1 + 0.5y_2 + 0.5y_3 - 0.1)$, $z_2 = f(-0.1y_1 + 0.6y_2 - 0.4y_3 - 0.1)$.
(e) $z_1 - z_2$ trajectory.   (f) $Y = 0.5z_1 + 0.5z_2$.

units (GPFUs). The synthesis of a potential field is accomplished by learning the location and shape of individual GPFUs as well as determining the minimum necessary number of GPFUs. The distinct feature of the supervised learning involved in GPFN is its capability of automatically recruiting necessary computational units, in addition to adjusting the network parameters.

The "one-to-many" inverse mapping of GPFN selects the desired input pattern which corresponds to the given output pattern and optimizes a certain performance index. The inverse mapping is carried out by an input pattern update rule based upon the **Lyapunov function**. The inverse mapping represents the specialization of a general concept, which represents great potential for the application to a recall process. A recall process is often incorporated with a pattern-recognition process to achieve selective attention [Fukushima, 1988]. In Fukushima's *Neocognitron* [Fukushima, 1980], the recall process is implemented by duplicating the forward connection in the reverse direction, and controlling the backward stream through gates. However, such a method is not only structurally complex and rigid but also functionally limited. The inverse mapping presented here based on a Lyapunov function provides a general means of achieving a recall process.

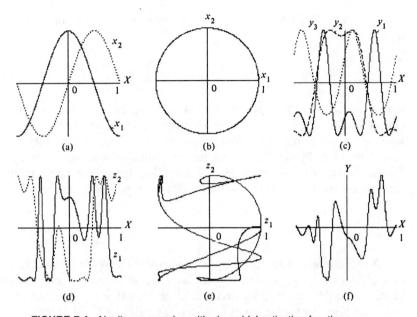

FIGURE 7.4 Nonlinear mapping with sinusoidal activation functions,
$f(\mathbf{w}^t\mathbf{x} - \phi_i) = \cos\omega(\sum_j w_{ij}x_j - \phi_i)$, where $\omega = 1$.
(a) $x_1 = f(\pi X)$, $x_2 = f(\pi X - \pi/2)$.   (b) $x_1 - x_2$ trajectory.
(c) $y_1 = f(4x_1 + x_2)$, $y_2 = f(2x_1 - 0.5x_2 - \pi/2)$, $y_3 = f(x_1 - 2x_2)$.
(d) $z_1 = f(2y_1 + y_2 - y_3)$, $z_2 = f(y_1 - 2y_2 + y_3 - \pi/2)$.
(e) $z_1 - z_2$ trajectory.   (f) $Y = 0.5z_1 - 0.5z_2$.

POTENTIAL-FUNCTION NETWORK

Design Concept

A **potential-function network** approximately realizes a "many-to-one" continuous mapping by synthesizing a potential field over the input domain by a number of potential functions. The potential field, ϕ, can be described as the weighted summation of a number of potential functions $\psi(\mathbf{x}, p_i)$, $i = 1, \ldots, M$, characterized by parameter vectors, p_i, $i = 1, \ldots, M$:

$$\phi(\mathbf{x}) \equiv \sum_{i=1}^{M} c_i \psi(\mathbf{x}, \mathbf{p}_i) \qquad (7\text{-}2)$$

where M, c_i, and $\mathbf{p}_i$, respectively, represent the number of PFUs, the summation weight, and the parameter vector of the ith potential function.

Equation (7-2) represents a general form of the following three-layer network equation:

$$\phi(\mathbf{x}) \quad = \quad \sum_{i=1}^{M} c_i \psi(\sum_{j=1}^{l} \lambda_j x_j, \mathbf{p}'_i) \tag{7-3}$$

where, instead of using the weighted summation of individual vector elements, the output vector of the input layer is directly used for the input vector to the hidden layer. In general, we can define a more general form of a multilayer feedforward neural network by directly using the multidimensional output vector from layer $i-1$ as the input vector to the layer i, assuming that neurons have multidimensional activation functions. Note that (7-2) can be represented in the form of (7-3) as follows:

$$\psi(\sum_i \lambda_i x_i, \mathbf{p}'_i) \quad = \quad \psi(\lambda^t \mathbf{x}, \mathbf{p}'_i) \quad = \quad \psi(\mathbf{x}, (\lambda, \mathbf{p}'_i)) \quad = \quad \psi(\mathbf{x}, \mathbf{p}_i) \tag{7-4}$$

As mentioned in the opening section, Irie-Miyake and Funahashi have shown that (7-2) can approximately realize an arbitrary function with sufficiently large number of hidden units, provided ψ is an absolutely integrable or a bounded monotonic function. To further investigate the capability of (7-2) in realizing an arbitrary function in relation to the number as well as the shape of PFUs, let us represent $\phi(\mathbf{x})$ based on N discrete sample points: $\phi(\mathbf{x}_1), \phi(\mathbf{x}_2), \ldots, \phi(\mathbf{x}_N)$. Then, with the following definitions,

$$\mathbf{z} \quad \equiv \quad [\phi(\mathbf{x}_1), \phi(\mathbf{x}_2), \ldots, \phi(\mathbf{x}_N)]^t \tag{7-5}$$

$$\mathbf{c} \quad \equiv \quad [c_1, c_2, \ldots, c_M]^t \tag{7-6}$$

$$\mathbf{y}_i \quad \equiv \quad [\psi(\mathbf{x}_1, \mathbf{p}_i), \psi(\mathbf{x}_2, \mathbf{p}_i), \ldots, \psi(\mathbf{x}_N, \mathbf{p}_i)]^t \qquad \text{for } i = 1, \ldots, M \tag{7-7}$$

the discrete form of (7-2) can be obtained:

$$\mathbf{z} \quad = \quad \mathbf{Y}\mathbf{c} \tag{7-8}$$

where $\mathbf{Y} \equiv [\mathbf{y}_1, \mathbf{y}_2, \ldots, \mathbf{y}_M]$: $N \times M$ matrix.

The question is, for a given $\mathbf{z}$, whether and how we can adjust $\mathbf{Y}$ to find an exact solution for $\mathbf{c}$ satisfying (7-8) or an optimal solution minimizing the error, E,

$$E \quad \equiv \quad (\mathbf{z} - \mathbf{Y}\mathbf{c})^t (\mathbf{z} - \mathbf{Y}\mathbf{c}) \tag{7-9}$$

In case $M \geq N$, there always exist one or more exact solutions for $\mathbf{c}$ that satisfy (7-8). However, the condition $M \geq N$ is unrealistic, since N is usually very large. In case $M < N$, (7-2) represents an overdetermined set of equations; thus, the existence of the exact solution for $\mathbf{c}$ depends on the special condition imposed on $\mathbf{Y}$, i.e., rank$[\mathbf{Y} : \mathbf{z}] = M$. Whether $\mathbf{Y}$ can be set to satisfy the condition, rank$[\mathbf{Y} : \mathbf{z}] = M$, by adjusting the parameters of individual PFUs, is a problem which needs to be explored.

The condition, rank$[\mathbf{Y} : \mathbf{z}] = M$, is equivalent to the condition that $\mathbf{z}$ is embedded in the subspace, $S_\mathbf{Y}$, spanned by $\mathbf{y}_1, \ldots, \mathbf{y}_M$, where $\mathbf{z}$, $\mathbf{y}_i$, $i = 1, \ldots, M$

are defined in the N dimensional sample space, S_N. Note that with fixed $\mathbf{y}_i$, $i = 1, \ldots, M$, $\mathbf{z} \notin S_{\mathbf{Y}}$ implies that no exact solution for $\mathbf{c}$ exists; instead, the optimal solution, $\mathbf{c}^*$, which minimizes the error, (7-9), can be obtained by projecting $\mathbf{z}$ onto $S_{\mathbf{Y}}$ such that

$$\mathbf{c}^* = \mathbf{Y}^+ \mathbf{z} \tag{7-10}$$

$$E_{\min} = \|(\mathbf{I} - \mathbf{P})\mathbf{z}\|^2 \tag{7-11}$$

where $\mathbf{Y}^+$ represents the generalized inverse of $\mathbf{Y}$, $\mathbf{Y}^+ \equiv (\mathbf{Y}^t \mathbf{Y})^{-1} \mathbf{Y}^t$, and $\mathbf{P}$ presents the projection matrix, $\mathbf{P} \equiv \mathbf{Y}\mathbf{Y}^+$.

The adjustment of $\mathbf{p}_i$ may provide the setting of $\mathbf{y}_i$, $i = 1, \ldots, M$, that makes $\mathbf{z}$ embed in $S_{\mathbf{Y}}$. The adjustment of $\mathbf{p}_i$ of $\psi(\mathbf{x}, \mathbf{p}_i)$ generates the trajectory or the range of $\mathbf{y}_i$, $\mathcal{R}(\mathbf{y}_i)$ in S_N, where $\mathcal{R}(\mathbf{y}_i)$ is the result of the mapping, $\mathbf{y}_i = [\psi(\mathbf{x}_1, \mathbf{p}_i), \psi(\mathbf{x}_2, \mathbf{p}_i), \ldots, \psi(\mathbf{x}_N, \mathbf{p}_i)]^t$, of the domain of $\mathbf{p}_i$, $\mathcal{D}(\mathbf{p}_i)$, with constant sample points $\mathbf{x}_k$, $k = 1, \ldots, N$. Note that all the activation functions $\psi(\mathbf{x}, \mathbf{p}_i)$, $i = 1, \ldots, M$, of the same mathematical form produce the same range, $\mathcal{R}(\mathbf{y}_i)$. With M PFUs we can arbitrarily select M points from $\mathcal{R}(\mathbf{y}_i)$ to form M vectors $\mathbf{y}_i^k$, $i = 1, \ldots, M$ of $\mathbf{Y}^k$. The linear combination of the selected M vectors defines a linear manifold, $\mathcal{L}(\mathbf{Y}^k)$, in S_N. Then the following lemma holds:

Lemma 7.1. $\mathbf{z} \equiv [\phi(\mathbf{x}_1), \phi(\mathbf{x}_2), \ldots, \phi(\mathbf{x}_N)]^t$ is exactly realizable if $\mathbf{z} \in \bigcup_{k \in K} \mathcal{L}(\mathbf{Y}^k)$, where K is a finite or infinite index set representing all the possible selections of M points from $\mathcal{R}(\mathbf{y}_i)$.

Proof. $\mathbf{z} \in \bigcup_{k \in K} \mathcal{L}(\mathbf{Y}^k)$ implies that there exists $l \in K$ such that $\mathbf{z} = \mathbf{Y}^l \mathbf{c}$. **Q.E.D.**

The implication of the above lemma is as follows:

1. $\bigcup_{k \in K} \mathcal{L}(\mathbf{Y}^k)$ provides a measure of the capability of a neural network, since it specifies the range of an exactly realizable $\mathbf{z}$, or the collection of functions corresponding to such an exactly realizable $\mathbf{z}$. $\bigcup_{k \in K} \mathcal{L}(\mathbf{Y}^k) = S_N$ implies that any arbitrary $\mathbf{z}$ can be realizable.

2. Given $\mathbf{z}$, or a range of $\mathbf{z}$, we may select a PFU or, possibly, a combination of different types of PFUs, e.g., among sigmoid, Gaussian, and sinusoidal functions, most suitable for the exact realization of $\mathbf{z}$, i.e., $\mathbf{z} \in \bigcup_{k \in K} \mathcal{L}(\mathbf{Y}^k)$.

Figure 7.5(a) illustrates a very simple example with two PFUs, $\psi(\mathbf{x}, \mathbf{p}_1)$ and $\psi(\mathbf{x}, \mathbf{p}_2)$, and three samples $\phi(\mathbf{x}_1), \phi(\mathbf{x}_2), \phi(\mathbf{x}_3)$. The example is to realize $\mathbf{z} = [\mathbf{y}_1, \mathbf{y}_2]\mathbf{c}$, where

$$\mathbf{z} = [\phi(\mathbf{x}_1), \phi(\mathbf{x}_2), \phi(\mathbf{x}_3)]^t$$

$$\mathbf{y}_1 = [\psi(\mathbf{x}_1, \mathbf{p}_1), \psi(\mathbf{x}_2, \mathbf{p}_1), \psi(\mathbf{x}_3, \mathbf{p}_1)]^t$$

$$\mathbf{y}_2 = [\psi(\mathbf{x}_1, \mathbf{p}_2), \psi(\mathbf{x}_2, \mathbf{p}_2), \psi(\mathbf{x}_3, \mathbf{p}_2)]^t$$

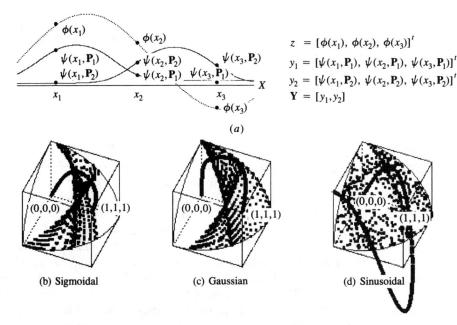

$$z = [\phi(x_1),\ \phi(x_2),\ \phi(x_3)]^t$$
$$y_1 = [\psi(x_1,P_1),\ \psi(x_2,P_1),\ \psi(x_3,P_1)]^t$$
$$y_2 = [\psi(x_1,P_2),\ \psi(x_2,P_2),\ \psi(x_3,P_2)]^t$$
$$\mathbf{Y} = [y_1, y_2]$$

(a)

(b) Sigmoidal   (c) Gaussian   (d) Sinusoidal

FIGURE 7.5 An example to illustrate $\mathcal{R}(\mathbf{y}_i)$ and $\bigcup_{k \in K} \mathcal{L}(\mathbf{Y}^k)$ for sigmoidal $((1 - e^{-x/a})/(1 + e^{-x/a}))$, Gaussian $(e^{-x^2/2a^2})$, and sinusoidal $(\sin(ax))$ PFUs. $\mathcal{R}(\mathbf{y}_i)$ is represented by a thick line contour. $\bigcup_{k \in K} \mathcal{L}(\mathbf{Y}^k)$ is represented by the dark area on the surface of the sphere fitted inside the cube. The volume defined by the dark area and the origin through a solid angle represents $\bigcup_{k \in K} \mathcal{L}(\mathbf{Y}^k)$ inside the $\frac{1}{8}$ sphere. The dark area is obtained by the trajectories of great circles formed by the intersections between all the $\mathcal{L}(\mathbf{Y}^k)$'s and the surface of the $\frac{1}{8}$ sphere.

Figures 7.5(b), (c), and (d), respectively, illustrate $\bigcup_{k \in K} \mathcal{L}(\mathbf{Y}^k)$ for sigmoidal, Gaussian, and sinusoidal PFUs with only one parameter a.

A different point of view on the realization of (7-8) can be obtained by interpreting (7-8) in the PFU space instead of sample space:

$$\begin{aligned}
\mathbf{z} &= \mathbf{Yc} \\
&= [\mathbf{r}_1, \mathbf{r}_2, \ldots, \mathbf{r}_N]^t \mathbf{c} \\
&= [\mathbf{r}_1^t \mathbf{c}, \mathbf{r}_2^t \mathbf{c}, \ldots, \mathbf{r}_N^t \mathbf{c}]^t
\end{aligned} \tag{7-12}$$

where $\mathbf{z} = [z_1, z_2, \ldots, z_N]^t$ and $\mathbf{r}_i$ is the ith row of $\mathbf{Y}$, $\mathbf{r}_i \equiv [\psi(\mathbf{x}_i, \mathbf{p}_1), \psi(\mathbf{x}_i, \mathbf{p}_2), \ldots, \psi(\mathbf{x}_i, \mathbf{p}_M)]^t$ for $i = 1, \ldots, N$. Note that $\mathbf{r}_i$, $i = 1, \ldots, N$ are $M \times 1$ vectors represented in the M-dimensional PFU space.

Equation (7-12) can be rewritten as

$$[\mathbf{r}_1^t \mathbf{c} - z_1,\ \mathbf{r}_2^t \mathbf{c} - z2,\ \ldots,\ \mathbf{r}_N^t \mathbf{c} - z_N]^t = \mathbf{0} \tag{7-13}$$

Therefore,

$$\mathbf{R}'\mathbf{c}' \equiv [\mathbf{r}_1', \mathbf{r}_2', \ldots, \mathbf{r}_N']^t \mathbf{c}' = 0 \tag{7-14}$$

where $\mathbf{r}_i' \equiv [\mathbf{r}_i^t : -\mathbf{z}_i]^t$: $(M+1) \times 1$ vector, $\mathbf{c}' \equiv [\mathbf{c}^t : 1]^t$: $(M+1) \times 1$ vector, and $\mathbf{R}' = [\mathbf{r}_1', \mathbf{r}_2', \ldots, \mathbf{r}_N']^t$: $N \times (M+1)$ matrix.

To have a solution for $\mathbf{c}'$, $\mathbf{r}_i'$, $i = 1, \ldots, N$ should reside in the M-dimensional manifold perpendicular to $\mathbf{c}'$. This can be tested by measuring the quantity Λ_p,

$$\Lambda_p \equiv \prod_{i=1}^{M+1} \lambda_i \tag{7-15}$$

where λ_i, $i = 1, \ldots, M+1$ are the eigenvalues of the cross-correlation matrix, Σ,

$$\Sigma = \frac{1}{N} \sum_{1=1}^{N} [\mathbf{r}_i' - \bar{\mathbf{r}}_i'][\mathbf{r}_i' - \bar{\mathbf{r}}_i']^t \quad \text{and} \quad \bar{\mathbf{r}}_i' = \frac{1}{N} \sum_{i=1}^{N} \mathbf{r}_i' \tag{7-16}$$

The following lemma holds:

Lemma 7.2. $\mathbf{z} = [\phi(\mathbf{x}_1), \phi(\mathbf{x}_2), \ldots, \phi(\mathbf{x}_N)]^t$ is exactly realizable if $\Lambda_p = 0$ and the eigenvectors with zero eigenvalues are not perpendicular to $[0, \ldots, 0, 1]^t$.

Proof. $\Lambda_p = 0$ implies that the $\mathbf{r}_i'$, $i = 1, \ldots, N$ are in the manifold of M or less than M dimensions. The latter condition is to guarantee that a vector perpendicular to the manifold can generate $\mathbf{c}' = [\mathbf{c}^t : 1]^t$, which has the last element of value 1. **Q.E.D.**

Lemma 2 implies that Λ_p can be used as a criterion for the adjustment of the shape of PFUs to exactly or optimally realize a function.

GAUSSIAN POTENTIAL-FUNCTION NETWORK

The (unnormalized) Gaussian potential function is selected for the construction of a **potential-function network (PFN)**, since the function is highly nonlinear but has many well-defined features, owing to its use in probability theory. A **Gaussian potential function** ψ_i is defined by

$$\psi_i = \psi(\mathbf{x}, \mathbf{p}_i) = e^{-d(\mathbf{x}, \mathbf{p}_i)/2} \tag{7-17}$$

$$d(\mathbf{x}, \mathbf{p}_i) = d(\mathbf{x}, \mathbf{m}^i, \mathbf{K}^i) = (\mathbf{x} - \mathbf{m}^i)^t \mathbf{K}^i (\mathbf{x} - \mathbf{m}^i) \tag{7-18}$$

where $\mathbf{x}$ represents an input pattern and $\mathbf{m}^i$ and $\mathbf{K}^i$ represent respectively the mean vector and the shape matrix (defined by the inverse of the covariance matrix) of the ith potential function.

We can rewrite $d(\mathbf{x}, \mathbf{m}^i, \mathbf{K}^i)$ in an expanded form:

$$d(\mathbf{x}, \mathbf{m}^i, \mathbf{K}^i) \;=\; \sum_j \sum_k k^i_{jk}(x_j - m^i_j)(x_k - m^i_k) \qquad (7\text{-}19)$$

where x_j is the jth element of $\mathbf{x}$, m^i_j is the jth element of $\mathbf{m}^i$, and k^i_{jk} is the (j,k)th element of $\mathbf{K}^i$.

Without loss of generality, k^i_{jk} can be represented based on the marginal standard deviations σ^i_j and σ^i_k, and the correlation coefficient h^i_{jk}:

$$k^i_{jk} \;=\; \frac{h^i_{jk}}{\sigma^i_j \sigma^i_k} \qquad (7\text{-}20)$$

where σ^i_j is positive real and $h^i_{jk} = 1$ if $j = k$, else $|h^i_{jk}| \leq 1$.

Instead of using the general form of k^i_{jk} given by (7-20), it is possible to use a simpler but a more restricted form of k^i_{jk} given by:

$$k^i_{jk} \;=\; \begin{cases} \frac{1}{\sigma_i^2} & \text{if } j = k \\ 0 & \text{otherwise} \end{cases} \qquad (7\text{-}21)$$

Equation (7-21) implies that the principal axes of the Gaussian potential should be aligned with the reference axes of the input space. However, the amount of flexibility lost owing to the use of (7-21) may be compensated by increasing the number of PFUs.

The network model proposed here is composed of three types of layers: the input layer, the hidden layer, and the output layer. The input and output layers are composed of linear units, and the hidden layer is composed of Gaussian potential function units (GPFUs), which produce Gaussian potential functions. The weighted output values of the GPFUs are summed by the connection between the hidden layer and the output layer in order to synthesize the required potential fields. The three-layered PFN with the GPFUs configured at the hidden layer is called the **Gaussian potential function network (GPFN)**.

Figure 7.6(a) illustrates the schematic diagram of a GPFN, including the mathematical descriptions for the functions of individual layers. Figure 7.6(b) shows a detailed structure of the ith GPFU. The calculation of (7-19) starts with the subtraction of the mean vector of the ith GPFU from the input vector at the subtraction nodes. Then the components of the vector obtained at the subtraction nodes are cross-correlated among themselves (i.e., outer product of the two same vectors) by the cross-correlator to obtain N^2 cross-correlated terms. Each cross-correlated term is multiplied by the corresponding k^i_{jk} of the shape matrix $\mathbf{K}^i$ at the multiplication nodes and summed for d_i. The output of the GPFU is then generated by exponentiating d_i.

In case the network generates as a multidimensional output vector, each component of the output vector can be independently generated by its own set of GPFUs.

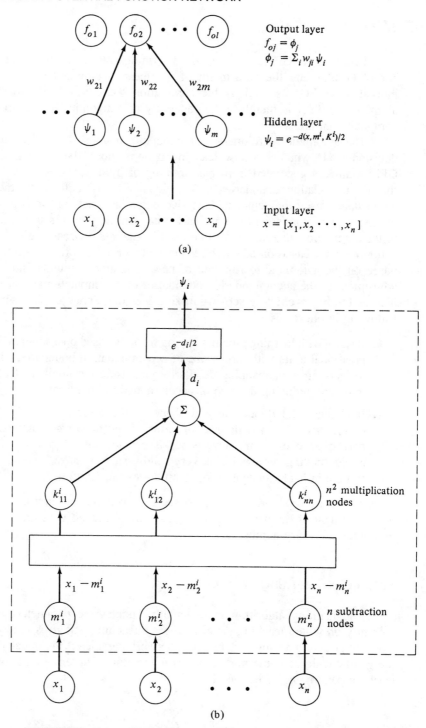

FIGURE 7.6 Schematic diagram of GPFN. (a) GPFN. (b) Connections between the Input Layer and a GPFU.

LEARNING

Learning in GPFN consists of determining the minimum necessary number of GPFUs and the adjustment of the mean vector and the shape matrix of individual GPFUs as well as the summation weights. The distinct feature of learning in GPFN is therefore the capability of automatically recruiting necessary computational units.

The automatic recruitment of computational units is based on the following decisions: (1) whether a new teaching pattern should be accommodated by the GPFUs already generated from past training or by a new GPFU, and (2) whether the accommodation boundaries of individual GPFUs, defined by the contour of equidistance from the center of Gaussian potential functions, should be readjusted to ensure error convergence as well as fast learning. The first has a similar flavor to the automatic clustering algorithm used in Carpenter/Grossberg's [1987] classification network based on adaptive resonance theory. The proposed learning scheme based on the automatic recruitment of new computational units and the automatic adjustment of the accommodation boundaries of a computational unit is referred to here as the **hierarchically self-organizing learning scheme**. This scheme has the following implications:

1. It starts with learning global mapping features based on a small number of computational units with larger size of accommodation boundaries, then proceeds to learning finer mapping details by increasing the number of computational units and reducing the size of accommodation boundaries.

2. It changes the dimension and shape of the error surface, i.e., the surface of the error function defined in terms of the network parameters, when the performance of error convergence is considerably degraded. This helps to avoid sticking on a flat or a very mildly sloping surface which might cause trouble in backpropagation or steepest-descent learning.

The learning algorithm is composed of two parts: the first is concerned with the adjustment of the network parameters and the second with the decision on the minimum necessary number of GPFUs.

Parameter Learning

The learning algorithm incrementally updates the parameters based on the currently presented teaching pattern, where a teaching pattern is randomly selected from the pool of teaching patterns. The network parameters are updated by applying the **gradient-descent method** to an error function. The error function for the pth teaching pattern, E_p, is defined by

$$E_p \equiv \frac{1}{2} \sum_{j=1}^{M} (t_{pj} - \phi_{pj}(\mathbf{n}_j))^2 \tag{7-22}$$

where n_j represents a column vector which is the collection of all parameters associated with the jth output unit, $n_j \equiv [w_j^t, m_j^t, \sigma_j^t, h_j^t]^t$, M represents the number of output units, t_{pj} represents the jth element of the desired output vector defined by the pth teaching pattern, and ϕ_{pj} represents the jth element of the actual output vector for the pth teaching pattern.

The directional vector, $\Delta n_j \equiv [\Delta w_j^t, \Delta m_j^t, \Delta \sigma_j^t, \Delta h_j^t]^t$, along which the update of the parameter vector should be made, is derived by applying the gradient-descent method to E_p.

Parameter update rule.

$$n_j^{\text{new}} = n_j^{\text{old}} + \eta \, \Delta n_j \qquad (7\text{-}23)$$

where η is the positive constant called the **learning rate**, and

- for the weight between the jth output and the ith GPFU:

$$\Delta w_{ji} = -\frac{\partial E_p}{\partial w_{ji}} = (t_j - \phi_j)\psi_i \qquad (7\text{-}24)$$

- for the jth element of the mean vector m^i:

$$\Delta m_j^i = -\frac{\partial E_p}{\partial m_j^i} = \sum_l k_{jl}^i (x_l - m_l^i)\psi_i \sum_k (t_k - \phi_k)w_{ki} \qquad (7\text{-}25)$$

- for the marginal standard deviation σ_j^i:

$$\Delta \sigma_j^i = -\frac{\partial E_p}{\partial \sigma_j^i} = \sum_l k_{jl}^i \frac{(x_j - m_j^i)(x_l - m_l^i)}{\sigma_j^i}\psi_i \sum_k (t_k - \phi_k)w_{ki}$$
$$(7\text{-}26)$$

- for the correlation coefficient h_{jk}^i for k_{jk}^i:

$$\Delta h_{jk}^i = -\frac{\partial E_p}{\partial h_{jk}^i} = -\frac{1}{2}\frac{(x_j - m_j^i)(x_k - m_k^i)}{\sigma_j^i \sigma_k^i}\psi_i \sum_k (t_k - \phi_k)w_{ki} \quad (7\text{-}27)$$

Note that, for convenience, the subscript p representing the pth teaching pattern is omitted from the notation of parameters. For more details on the derivation of the above equations see the Appendix to this chapter.

Hierarchically Self-Organizing Learning

The hierarchically self-organizing learning scheme proposed here consists of the automatic recruitment of a new GPFU and the automatic adjustment of the accommodation boundary of a GPFU. The accommodation boundary of a GPFU represents the decision boundary determining whether a new GPFU should be generated to accommodate a new teaching pattern or not. Initially, the accommodation boundary is set large for achieving rough but global learning, but gradually it is reduced for fine learning. Let us introduce an **effective radius** r_i, to describe the accommodation boundary of the ith GPFU in the form of a **hypersphere, H_i,** defined in the input space:

$$H_i(r_i) \quad = \quad \{\mathbf{x} \,|\, d(\mathbf{x}, \mathbf{m}^i, \mathbf{K}^i) \leq r_i^2\} \tag{7-28}$$

In addition, a GPFU is assigned an attribute to represent a particular class of teaching patterns. This assignment is done at the time a GPFU is generated by taking the same class represented by the teaching pattern that invoked its generation. A set of classes are predefined in case the network is used for pattern classification. However, in case the network is used for function generation, we need to define a set of classes based on the sign of the output, or based on the segmentation of the output range. The following accommodation/generation rule provides a criterion for determining when to generate a new GPFU.

Accommodation/generation rule.   If a teaching pattern is located within the hypersphere, H_i, of a GPFU, and belongs to the same class as that represented by the GPFU, then a new GPFU will not be invoked, and instead the teaching pattern is accommodated by the GPFU. If a teaching pattern is not located within the hypersphere, a new GPFU is generated at the position of the input teaching pattern.

From this rule, it can be said that r_i works as the boundary of clustering attracted by the ith GPFU. To check whether a teaching pattern falls inside the hypersphere H_i of the ith GPFU, the output value of the ith GPFU is compared with the following reference value of the ith GPFU, G_i, defined based on its effective radius, r_i:

$$G_i \quad = \quad e^{-r_i^2/2} \tag{7-29}$$

If the output of the ith GPFU is greater than G_i, it is considered that a teaching pattern falls inside the hypersphere H_i of the ith GPFU. When a new teaching pattern does not invoke the generation of a new GPFU, i.e., the new teaching pattern falls inside the hypersphere of a GPFU having the same class label, the parameters of individual GPFUs and the summation weights are adjusted according to the parameter-update rules.

The automatic adjustment of the accommodation boundary or the effective radius, r_i, can be carried out by either of two methods. The first method is based on reducing the effective radius of each GPFU gradually, starting from a large radius, and following the predetermined function. This method is simple and easily implementable but sensitive to the selected function in terms of the number of total GPFUs generated. For instance, if the effective radii of GPFUs are reduced rapidly, the network generates more GPFUs than the minimum required. This is because individual GPFUs may not have enough time to converge to their optimal shapes. On the other hand, if the effective radii of GPFUs are reduced gradually, the network consumes a large number of learning cycles, although it generates the minimum necessary number of GPFUs. Hence, the selection of a proper rate for the reduction of the effective radii is essential to successfully generate the minimum necessary number of GPFUs and achieve a desirable learning speed.

The second method is based on reducing the radii of individual GPFUs according to the progress of learning. The reduction of the radii invokes the generation of more GPFUs, and so enables the network to learn the details. Therefore, the best time for a GPFU to reduce its radii is when the network performance on learning becomes saturated with the currently available GPFUs. The progress of learning can be measured by the **performance index** P defined by

$$P \equiv e^{-E_{\text{rms}}} \tag{7-30}$$

where E_{rms} represents the **root-mean-square error** for N teaching patterns.

$$E_{\text{rms}} \equiv \sqrt{\frac{2}{MN} \sum_{p=1}^{N} E_p} \tag{7-31}$$

Note that a smaller value of E_{rms} results in a larger value of P.

Alternatively, the progress of learning can be measured by the **parameter saturation vector** s_j, defined for the jth output unit by

$$\mathbf{s}_j^{\text{new}} = \alpha \frac{\partial E_p}{\partial \mathbf{n}_j} + (1 - \alpha)\mathbf{s}_j^{\text{old}} \tag{7-32}$$

where α is a positive constant between 0 and 1.

The purpose of defining the parameter saturation vector is to monitor $\partial E_p/\partial \mathbf{n}_j$, since the saturation of the performance on learning implies the convergence of the parameters to an extremum achievable with the number of currently available GPFUs. Equation (7-32) can be interpreted as follows: (1) $\mathbf{s}_j$ moves toward $\partial E_p/\partial \mathbf{n}_j$, (2) if the network parameters remain stationary at a point or wonder around a point in the parameter space, the magnitude of $\mathbf{s}_j$ gradually decreases toward zero, and (3) if the network parameters are on the way to converge to a point in the parameter space along a certain direction, the magnitude of $\mathbf{s}_j$ gradually increases toward $\partial E_p/\partial \mathbf{n}_j$. Therefore, by monitoring the value of $\|\mathbf{s}_j\|$, the saturation of the network performance on learning can be detected.

Learning Algorithm

Initially, no GPFU is assigned to the network, and the output of the network is set to zero. The **hierarchically self-organizing learning algorithm** for the kth output unit, as shown in the following, is then applied to the network to automatically create and shape GPFUs, and adjust weight vectors.

Hierarchically self-organizing learning algorithm.

STEP 1   Set $i = 1$, $j = 0$, and $n = 0$, where i represents the number of learning cycles, j the number of GPFUs, and n the number of patterns presented to the network. Set the effective radius r_i sufficiently large enough to cover the whole input domain.

STEP 2   Invoke one learning-cycle procedure at the ith learning cycle, where one learning cycle implies the random presentation of all the teaching patterns in the pool to the network. The one-learning-cycle procedure is as follows:

1. Get the next teaching pattern.

2. Set $n = n + 1$.

3. Apply the following procedure:

   - If $|t_{pk} - \phi_{pk}| > \epsilon_m$, where t_{pk} and ϕ_{pk} respectively represent the desired and actual values of the kth output unit of the teaching pattern, and ϵ_m represents the error margin, then the following procedure is applied:

     – If there is a GPFU[1] having the same class as that of the teaching pattern presented and the teaching pattern falls inside its hypersphere, apply parameter learning.

     – If there is no such GPFU, then make a new GPFU and go to part 3 of step 2. The parameters of the GPFU are determined initially as follows:

       * Set $j = j + 1$
       * Mean vector, $\mathbf{m}^j$ = input of the teaching pattern
       * Weight value, c_j = output of the teaching pattern
       * Shape matrix, $\mathbf{K}^j = (1/\sigma_0^2)\mathbf{I}$
       * Radius, $r_j = r_0$
       * Network parameter-saturation criteria, $\rho_k = 0$

   - If $|t_{pk} - \phi_{pk}| \leq \epsilon_m$, then apply the parameter learning without testing whether the teaching pattern falls in the hypersphere of a GPFU.

   - Calculate $\|\mathbf{s}_k\|/\sqrt{n_k}$, where $\mathbf{s}_k$ represents the kth parameter-saturation vector and n_k represents the dimension of $\mathbf{s}_k$.

   - If $n > 1/\alpha$, then

   $$\rho_k^{\text{new}} = \rho_k^{\text{old}} + \beta \frac{\sqrt{n_k}}{\|\mathbf{s}_k\|}$$

   where β is a small positive constant.

   - If $\|\mathbf{s}_k\|/\sqrt{n_k} < \rho_k$, then reduce the radius of each GPFU:

   $$\text{if } r_l > r_L, \qquad \text{then } r_l^{\text{new}} = r_l^{\text{old}} * r_d, \qquad \text{for } l = 1, \ldots, j$$

   where r_L is the lower bound of radius and r_d is the radius decrement rate.

---

[1] For instance, a GPFU is classified as having the same class as that of the teaching pattern, if the sign of the weight between the GPFU and the output unit is same as the sign of the corresponding output value of the teaching pattern.

4. If all the teaching patterns are presented, go to the next step. Otherwise, go to part 1 of step 2.

STEP 3   Set $i = i + 1$.

STEP 4   If the network correctly classifies all the teaching patterns and shows satisfactory performance, then stop. If not, go to step 2.

RECALL PROCESS BY INVERSE MAPPING

The inverse mapping is to generate an input pattern **x** having association with an output pattern $\mathbf{y}^d$. Since we consider a continuous inverse mapping from the M-dimensional output space to the N-dimensional input space where $M \le N$, there may exist an infinite number of input patterns associated with the given output pattern. The problem of inverse mapping now becomes the following: Given the output pattern $\mathbf{y}^d$, generate an input pattern **x** which satisfies the forward association $\mathbf{y}^d = f(\mathbf{x})$, while optimizing the given performance index, $H(\mathbf{x})$. An example of $H(\mathbf{x})$ is $(\mathbf{x}^d - \mathbf{x})$, where $\mathbf{x}^d$ represents a particular input pattern which we desire to have **x** close to. In GPFN, $\mathbf{x}^d$ may be selected to represent a particular GPFU, so that the input pattern can possess the particular feature represented by the selected GPFU. The inverse mapping presents the following implications:

1. The specialization of a general concept, i.e., the generation of a specific example of the given concept satisfying certain constraints as well as possessing certain features. Note that the forward mapping produces a generalized concept from a set of examples. For instance, from the general concept of a "rectangle," an inverse association produces a specific rectangle which satisfies the condition of having two equal-length sides.

2. The generation of a solution for an underdetermined set of nonlinear equations to optimize a certain performance index. This is especially useful for applications in robotics, such as the inverse kinematics of a redundant arm.

The proposed approach to the solution of the inverse mapping problem using a GPFN is as follows: Given an output, let an arbitrarily selected initial input pattern converge to the desired input pattern through forward and inverse mapping, where the inverse mapping generates the input pattern correction terms based on the Lyapunov function.

Inverse Mapping Based on Lyapunov Function

Let us first select the **Lyapunov function candidate,** V, as follows:

$$V = \frac{1}{2}\tilde{\mathbf{y}}^t\tilde{\mathbf{y}} + \frac{1}{2}\tilde{\mathbf{x}}^t\tilde{\mathbf{x}} \qquad (7\text{-}33)$$

where $\tilde{\mathbf{y}} = \mathbf{y}^d - \mathbf{y}$: an $M \times 1$ output error vector, $\tilde{\mathbf{x}} = \mathbf{x}^d - \mathbf{x}$: an $N \times 1$ input error vector, $\mathbf{y}^d$ = the given output vector, and $\mathbf{x}^d$ = the input constraint vector[2] (not a solution vector, i.e., $f(\mathbf{x}^d) \neq \mathbf{y}^d$).

The time derivative of the Lyapunov function is given by

$$\dot{V} = \tilde{\mathbf{y}}^t \dot{\tilde{\mathbf{y}}} + \tilde{\mathbf{x}}^t \dot{\tilde{\mathbf{x}}} \tag{7-34}$$

$$= -\tilde{\mathbf{y}}^t \frac{\partial \mathbf{y}}{\partial \mathbf{x}} \dot{\mathbf{x}} - \tilde{\mathbf{x}}^t \dot{\mathbf{x}} \tag{7-35}$$

$$= -(\tilde{\mathbf{y}}^t \mathbf{J} + \tilde{\mathbf{x}}^t) \dot{\mathbf{x}} \tag{7-36}$$

where $\mathbf{J} \equiv \partial \mathbf{y} / \partial \mathbf{x}$: the $M \times N$ Jacobian matrix.

Equation (7-36) can be rewritten as

$$\dot{V} = -\tilde{\mathbf{y}}^t (\mathbf{J} + \mathbf{D}) \dot{\mathbf{x}} \tag{7-37}$$

with $\mathbf{D}$ satisfying $\tilde{\mathbf{y}}^t \mathbf{D} = \tilde{\mathbf{x}}^t$

Lemma 7.3.   If

$$\mathbf{D} = \frac{1}{\|\tilde{\mathbf{y}}\|^2} \tilde{\mathbf{y}} \tilde{\mathbf{x}}^t \tag{7-38}$$

then (7-37) holds.

From (7-37) and (7-38), we have

$$\dot{V} = -\tilde{\mathbf{y}}^t \left(\mathbf{J} + \frac{1}{\|\tilde{\mathbf{y}}\|^2} \tilde{\mathbf{y}} \tilde{\mathbf{x}}^t \right) \dot{\mathbf{x}} \tag{7-39}$$

Theorem 7.1.   If an arbitrarily selected initial input pattern $\mathbf{x}(0)$ is updated by

$$\mathbf{x}(t') = \mathbf{x}(0) + \int_0^{t'} \dot{\mathbf{x}} \, dt \tag{7-40}$$

where $\dot{\mathbf{x}}$ is a solution of

$$\tilde{\mathbf{y}} = (\mathbf{J} + \mathbf{D}) \dot{\mathbf{x}} = \left(\mathbf{J} + \frac{1}{\|\tilde{\mathbf{y}}\|^2} \tilde{\mathbf{y}} \tilde{\mathbf{x}}^t \right) \dot{\mathbf{x}} \tag{7-41}$$

then $\tilde{\mathbf{y}}$ converges to zero under the condition that $\dot{\mathbf{x}}$ exists along the convergence trajectory.

Proof. By applying (7-41) to (7-39), we have

$$\dot{V} = -\tilde{\mathbf{y}}^t \tilde{\mathbf{y}} = -\|\tilde{\mathbf{y}}\|^2 \leq 0 \tag{7-42}$$

where $\dot{V} < 0 \; \forall \tilde{\mathbf{y}} \neq 0$ and $\dot{V} = 0$ iff $\tilde{\mathbf{y}} = 0$.   **Q.E.D.**

---

[2] $\mathbf{x}^d$ may be the position of a particular GPFU, near which we want to have a solution.

Input-Pattern Update

The update of x based on $\dot{x}$ determined by (7-41) guarantees the convergence as long as $\dot{x}$ exists. Note, however, that the Lyapunov function V defined by (7-33) is a nonlinear function of x and may have local minima where the following equation holds:

$$\frac{\partial V}{\partial \mathbf{x}} = \tilde{\mathbf{y}}^t (\mathbf{J} + \mathbf{D}) = \mathbf{0} \tag{7-43}$$

Therefore, at or near a local minimum, (7-41) results in a large norm of $\dot{x}$. This explosion of $\dot{x}$ near a local minimum is referred to as a **jumping** phenomenon. The jumping is useful for getting out of a local minimum, but it should be controlled to curtail jumping that goes beyond the domain of the input space and to avoid jumping that wanders around the same local minimum. See the next section on jumping control for more details.

The direct calculation of $\dot{x}$ from (7-41) based on pseudoinverse or singular value decomposition techniques involves significant computation. Thus, the following theorem is introduced to provide a simpler way of computing $\dot{x}$ without violating the convergence property:

Theorem 7.2. If an arbitrarily selected initial input pattern x(0) is updated by

$$\mathbf{x}(t') = \mathbf{x}(0) + \int_0^{t'} \dot{\mathbf{x}} \, dt \tag{7-44}$$

where $\dot{x}$ is given by

$$\dot{\mathbf{x}} = \frac{\|\tilde{\mathbf{y}}\|^2}{\|(\mathbf{J} + \mathbf{D})^t \tilde{\mathbf{y}}\|^2} (\mathbf{J} + \mathbf{D})^t \, \tilde{\mathbf{y}} \tag{7-45}$$

then $\tilde{\mathbf{y}}$ converges to zero under the condition that $\dot{x}$ exists along the convergence trajectory.

Proof. By applying (7-45) to (7-37), we have

$$\dot{V} = -\|\tilde{\mathbf{y}}\|^2 \leq 0, \tag{7-46}$$

where $\dot{V} < 0 \ \forall \tilde{\mathbf{y}} \neq 0$ and $\dot{V} = 0$ iff $\tilde{\mathbf{y}} = 0$. **Q.E.D.**

Theorem 7.2 presents the following features:

1. It allows the direct calculation of $\dot{x}$ based on the quantities generated by the forward mapping,
2. At a local minimum of V, $\dot{x}$ is subject to jumping, and
3. $\dot{x} = 0$ iff $\tilde{\mathbf{y}} = 0$.

To improve the convergence property, we introduce the Lagrangian multiplier λ in the Lyapunov function:

$$V(\lambda, \mathbf{x}) \quad = \quad \frac{\lambda}{2}\,\tilde{\mathbf{y}}^t\tilde{\mathbf{y}} + \frac{1}{2}\,\tilde{\mathbf{x}}^t\tilde{\mathbf{x}} \tag{7-47}$$

The purpose of the Lagrangian multiplier is to force $\tilde{\mathbf{y}}$ to converge to zero by increasing λ exponentially with the decrease of $\tilde{\mathbf{y}}$.

Theorem 7.3. If an arbitrarily selected initial input pattern $\mathbf{x}(0)$ is updated by

$$\mathbf{x}(t^{'}) \quad = \quad \mathbf{x}(0) + \int_0^{t^{'}} \dot{\mathbf{x}}\,dt \tag{7-48}$$

and an arbitrarily selected positive Lagrangian multiplier $\lambda(0)$ is updated by

$$\lambda(t^{'}) = \lambda(0) + \int_0^{t^{'}} \dot{\lambda}\,dt \tag{7-49}$$

where $\dot{\mathbf{x}}$ and $\dot{\lambda}$ are given by

$$\dot{\mathbf{x}} \quad = \quad \frac{\frac{\lambda}{2}\,\|\,\tilde{\mathbf{y}}\,\|^2 + \frac{1}{2}\,\|\,\tilde{\mathbf{y}}\,\|\,\|\tilde{\mathbf{x}}\|}{\|(\lambda\mathbf{J} + \mathbf{D})^t\tilde{\mathbf{y}}\|^2}\,(\lambda\mathbf{J} + \mathbf{D})^t\,\tilde{\mathbf{y}} \tag{7-50}$$

$$\dot{\lambda} \quad = \quad \frac{\|\tilde{\mathbf{x}}\|}{\|\tilde{\mathbf{y}}\|} \tag{7-51}$$

then $\tilde{\mathbf{y}}$ converges to zero under the condition that $\dot{\mathbf{x}}$ exists along the convergence trajectory.

Proof. Since the time derivative of the Lyapunov function is given by

$$\dot{V} \quad = \quad \frac{\partial V}{\partial x}\dot{\mathbf{x}} + \frac{\partial V}{\partial \lambda}\dot{\lambda} \tag{7-52}$$

we have

$$\dot{V} \quad = \quad -\tilde{\mathbf{y}}^t(\lambda\mathbf{J} + \mathbf{D})\dot{\mathbf{x}} + \frac{1}{2}\,\|\,\tilde{\mathbf{y}}\,\|^2\,\dot{\lambda} \tag{7-53}$$

By applying (7-50) and (7-51), respectively, to $\dot{\mathbf{x}}$ and $\dot{\lambda}$, we have

$$\dot{V} \quad = \quad -\frac{\lambda}{2}\,\|\,\tilde{\mathbf{y}}\|^2 \leq 0 \tag{7-54}$$

where $\dot{V} < 0 \ \forall \tilde{\mathbf{y}} \neq 0$ and $\dot{V} = 0$ iff $\tilde{\mathbf{y}} = 0$. **Q.E.D.**

Note that $\dot{\lambda}$ goes to infinity when $\tilde{\mathbf{y}}$ approaches zero, forcing the input pattern to converge to the solution when $\tilde{\mathbf{y}}$ approaches zero.

The schematic diagram for the recall process based on Theorem 7.2 or 7.3 is illustrated in Figure 7.7. Note that the Jacobian $\mathbf{J} = \partial\mathbf{y}/\partial\mathbf{x}$ can be obtained directly

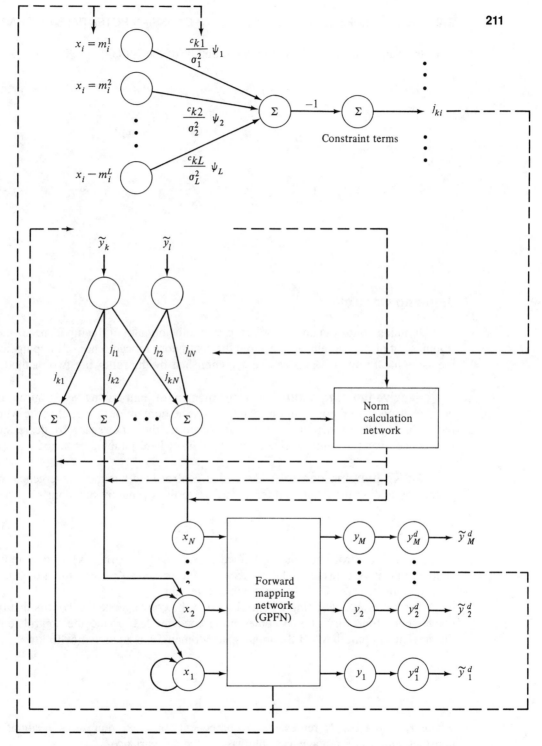

FIGURE 7.7 The inverse mapping network combined with the forward mapping network, where the inverse mapping is based on Theorem 7.2.

from the output of the GPFUs. Since the output of the ith GPFU is

$$y_i(\mathbf{x}) \;=\; \sum_{j=1}^{L} c_{ij} \psi(\mathbf{x}, \mathbf{m}^j, \sigma_j) \qquad (7\text{-}55)$$

$$\psi(\mathbf{x}, \mathbf{m}^j, \sigma_j) \;=\; e^{-(1/2\sigma_j^2) \sum_{k=1}^{N} (x_k - m_k^j)^2} \qquad (7\text{-}56)$$

we have

$$\mathbf{J} \;=\; \left[\frac{\partial y_1}{\partial \mathbf{x}}, \ldots, \frac{\partial y_i}{\partial \mathbf{x}}, \ldots, \frac{\partial y_M}{\partial \mathbf{x}} \right]^t \qquad (7\text{-}57)$$

$$= \left[\ldots, -\sum_{j=1}^{L} \frac{c_{ij}}{\sigma_j^2} (\mathbf{x} - \mathbf{m}^j) \psi(\mathbf{x}, \mathbf{m}^j, \sigma_j), \ldots \right]^t \qquad (7\text{-}58)$$

Jumping Control

Jumping control intends to select $\dot{\mathbf{x}}$ within the domain of the input space when $\dot{\mathbf{x}}$ jumps out of the domain, and to avoid the continuous reoccurrence of jumping near the same local minima. This can be accomplished by the following two methods:

Passive jumping control.   At the moment of jumping, passive control randomly selects $\mathbf{x}$ as the next initial point within the domain of the input space while redistributing the probability density function over the input space by decreasing the probability of $\mathbf{x}$ being selected near the point where jumping occurred.

Active jumping control.   An active control modifies the convergence trajectory by adding the additional term, $\frac{1}{2}\tilde{\mathbf{x}}_c^{\,t}\tilde{\mathbf{x}}_c$, to the Lyapunov function:

$$V \;=\; \frac{1}{2}\tilde{\mathbf{y}}^t\tilde{\mathbf{y}} + \frac{1}{2}\tilde{\mathbf{x}}_c^{\,t}\tilde{\mathbf{x}}_c \qquad (7\text{-}59)$$

where $\tilde{\mathbf{x}}_c$ is a control term and is defined as $\tilde{\mathbf{x}}_c = c_f \sum_{k=1}^{L}(\mathbf{m}^k - \mathbf{x})$ with c_f representing a positive constant called the **control factor** and $\mathbf{m}^k$ representing the mean vector of the selected GPFU for the kth output unit.

The net effect of adding a control term to the convergence behavior is that the convergence trajectory of $\mathbf{x}$ becomes more concentrated around the control term. To prevent jumping beyond the input space domain, $\dot{\mathbf{x}}$ is modified as follows:

$$\dot{x}_i \;=\; \begin{cases} x_L + \gamma & \text{if } \dot{x}_i > x_L \\ \dot{x}_i & \text{if } -x_L \le \dot{x}_i \le x_L \\ -x_L + \gamma & \text{if } \dot{x}_i < -x_L \end{cases} \qquad (7\text{-}60)$$

where $\dot{x}_i$, $i = 1, \ldots, N$ represents N components of $\dot{\mathbf{x}}$, x_L represents a saturation constant, and γ is a random variable having a small variance.

The term $\mathbf{m}^k$ is selected among the mean vectors of the GPFUs $\{\mathbf{m}^{ki}, i = 1,\ldots,l\}$ associated with the kth output unit as follows: First, we test whether there exists a solution between $\mathbf{m}^{ki}$ and the current $\mathbf{x}$ for $i = 1,\ldots,l$. A solution is said to exist between $\mathbf{m}^{ki}$ and $\mathbf{x}$, if the following condition holds:

$$(y_k^d - f_k(\mathbf{x})) \times (y_k^d - f_k(\mathbf{m}^{ki})) \leq 0 \qquad (7\text{-}61)$$

where y_k^d and f_k represent, respectively, the desired and the actual value of the kth output unit.

Let us denote S^k as the set of $\mathbf{m}^{ki}$s satisfying (7-61). $\mathbf{m}^{ki}$ is then selected from S^k as the one having the minimum distance from $\mathbf{x}$:

$$\mathbf{m}^k = \begin{cases} \mathbf{m}^{kj} \mid \| \mathbf{x} - \mathbf{m}^{kj} \| = \min_{\mathbf{m}^{ki} \in S^k} \| \mathbf{x} - \mathbf{m}^{ki} \| & \text{if } S^k \neq \phi \\ 0 & \text{otherwise} \end{cases} \qquad (7\text{-}62)$$

If the selected GPFUs, $\mathbf{m}^k$ $k = 1,\ldots,M$, are near the solution, a fast and stable convergence can be achieved, regardless of the initial $\mathbf{x}$. In case $\mathbf{m}^k$ $k = 1,\ldots,M$, are not selected correctly, then it is subject to the reoccurrence of jumping around the local minima. However, active control provides faster and more stable convergence than passive control.

SIMULATION

Simulation was conducted for six sets of teaching patterns, as illustrated in Figure 7.8. The first four sets of teaching patterns represent bipolar functions, while the last two sets represent continuous functions. The teaching patterns are distributed in two-dimensional input space and one-dimensional output space. At each learning cycle, all the teaching patterns in a set are presented to the network in random order. The teaching patterns of the last two sets are generated from the given continuous functions, such that at each learning cycle, ten teaching patterns are randomly selected from each of the two continuous functions and presented to the network.

It was considered that the learning reaches a satisfactory level of performance, if any of the following two conditions is met: (1) the absolute error $|t_{pk} - \phi_{pk}|$ for all teaching patterns is less than the predetermined error margin ϵ_m, and (2) the rms error E_{rms} defined by (7-31) is far less than the error margin ϵ_m.

The learning rate was chosen very carefully because (1) an excessive learning rate can cause the algorithm to fluctuate and eventually diverge, and (2) a very small learning rate can cause slow convergence, although no fluctuation occurs.

The error margin ϵ_m is set according to the range of the desired output. For instance, if the desired output has bipolar range, $[-1$ or $1]$, the error margin need not be set to a very small value, because it is satisfactory as long as the signs of the desired and the actual output values agree. After learning is completed, the desired

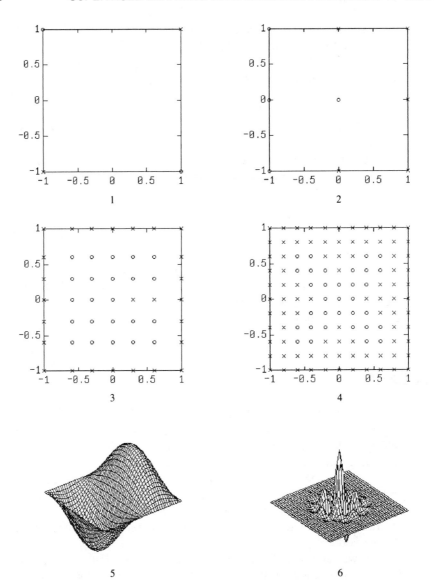

FIGURE 7.8 The six sets of teaching patterns presented to GPFN for learning. The symbols **O** and **X** indicate that the desired output values corresponding to their positions in the input space are 1 and -1, respectively. Patterns 5 and 6 represent the 3-D representation of continuous teaching patterns defined over 2-D input space, described by $\sin(\pi x_1)\cos(0.5\pi x_2)$ and $\cos(4\pi x_1)\cos(4\pi x_2)e^{-10(x_1^2+x_2^2)}$, respectively.

TABLE 7.1 LEARNING PARAMETERS GIVEN FOR EACH SET OF TEACHING PATTERNS

Teaching pattern set	1	2	3	4	5	6
Learning rate, η	0.02	0.02	0.002	0.002	0.002	0.002
Error margin, ϵ_m	1	1	1	1	0.1	0.1
Initial standard deviation, σ_0	2	2	0.2	0.2	0.1	0.1
Initial radius, r_0	3	3	30	30	60	60
Lower bound of radius, r_L	0	0	0	0	2	2
Radius decrement rate, r_d	0.9986	0.9986	0.9986	0.9986	0.9986	0.9986
α	10^{-3}	10^{-3}	10^{-3}	10^{-3}	10^{-3}	10^{-3}
β	10^{-10}	10^{-10}	10^{-10}	10^{-10}	10^{-10}	10^{-10}

TABLE 7.2 SUMMARY OF SIMULATION RESULTS

Teaching pattern set	1	2	3	4	5	6
No. of learning cycles	400	1500	4500	4500	5000	10,000
No. of GPFUs generated	2	2	5	8	2	14
E_{rms} after learning	0.0001	0.2866	0.3634	0.2916	0.1048	0.0458

output can be realized by thresholding the actual output. If the desired output has a continuous range, the error margin ϵ_m should be set to a value small enough for the network to map the given function accurately. However, the decrease of ϵ_m causes the rapid increase of the number of GPFUs to be generated. Therefore, the selection of ϵ_m should consider this trade-off.

The initial assignment of the marginal standard deviation σ_0 is another important parameter which affects the performance of learning. If σ_0 is set too high, it is difficult to learn the teaching patterns distributed densely in the input space. If σ_0 is set too low, it will take too long to learn the teaching patterns distributed coarsely in the input space. Therefore, σ_0 should be set properly according to the distribution of teaching patterns in the input space. For example, the minimum distance between the input values of the teaching patterns can be a good choice for σ_0.

The initial effective radius of a GPFU, r_0, is chosen large enough to cover most areas of the input space, so that initially the GPFN can carry out the learning with a small number of GPFUs. The lower bound of the effective radius, r_L, is defined to curtail the number of GPFUs generated for continuous mapping. Setting r_L low provides the accurate realization of a continuous function but generates a large number of GPFUs.

The parameters involved in learning are listed in Table 7.1, and the simulation results are summarized in Table 7.2 for each set of teaching patterns. The simulation results indicate the following: (1) The correct mapping for the set of teaching patterns having bipolar output values, i.e., the signs of the desired and the actual output values, agree for all the teaching patterns. (2) A good approximation (around 5 percent error or less) of continuous functions were obtained with a small

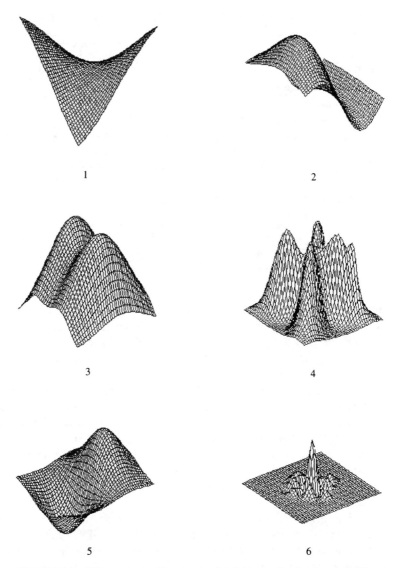

1

2

3

4

5

6

FIGURE 7.9   3-D representation of potential fields synthesized over 2-D input space, for individual sets of teaching patterns, by learning.

number of GPFUs. Figure 7.9 illustrates the 3-D representation of the potential fields synthesized over the 2-D input space by the GPFN through learning the six sets of teaching patterns. Figure 7.10 shows the decision boundaries obtained from learning the first four sets of teaching patterns having bipolar outputs.

In the simulation of the recall process, $\dot{x}$ is calculated based on Theorem 7.3,

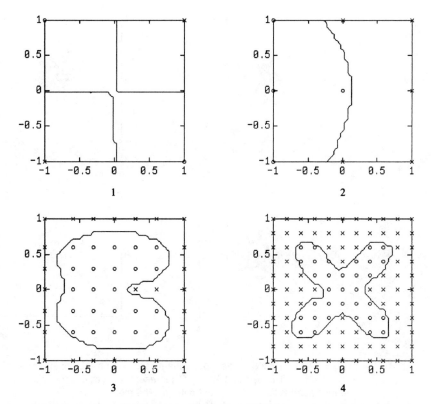

FIGURE 7.10 The decision boundaries obtained from the synthesized potential fields. The decision boundary of each set of the first four teaching patterns is obtained by thresholding each of the synthesized potential fields with the zero threshold value.

and the input pattern **x** is updated at the nth iteration by

$$\mathbf{x}(n) \quad = \quad \mathbf{x}(n-1) + \eta \dot{\mathbf{x}}(n-1) \tag{7-63}$$

where η is a small positive constant representing an **update rate**.

Two forward mapping functions are used in the simulation. The first is based on the function generated by the GPFN after learning the sixth set of teaching patterns. The second is based on the function implemented in the GPFN with 11 GPFUs, where the function has two peak points at $(-0.75, 0.75)$ and at $(0.75, -0.75)$.

The desired output values of the functions, which are the inputs to the inverse mapping, are respectively set to 0.6 and 2.0 for the first and second functions. The input patterns corresponding to the desired outputs are around $(0, 0)$ for the first function and $(-0.75, 0.75)$ or $(0.75, -0.75)$ for the second. In both cases, the

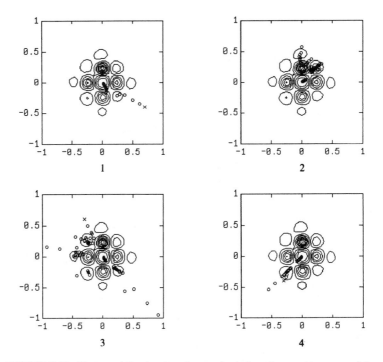

FIGURE 7.11 Traces of the input pattern recorded on the contour map of the error function. The symbols **X** and **O** represent respectively the initial and the intermediate positions of the input pattern. The mean vector-selection algorithm is applied for jumping control. All the initial positions selected arbitrarily are converged to the desired position at the center. The occurrence of jumping phenomena around the local minima can be observed.

active control of jumping is applied. The following parameters were set for the simulation:

- The saturation constant of $\dot{\mathbf{x}}$, $x_L = 10$
- The range of random variable, γ, $|\gamma| \leq 0.1$
- The update rate, $\eta = 0.2$
- The control factor, $c_f = 1$
- The initial Lagrangian multiplier, $\lambda(0) = 1$

The results of the simulation show that the arbitrarily given initial input patterns converge successfully to the correct input patterns corresponding to the desired output patterns. Figures 7.11 and 7.12 illustrate the traces of input patterns recorded on the contour map of the square error function, $e(\mathbf{x})$, $e(\mathbf{x}) = (\mathbf{y}^d - y(\mathbf{x}))^2$, to show the behavior of input-pattern convergence in the inverse mapping.

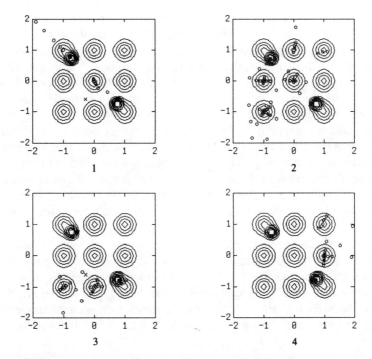

FIGURE 7.12 Traces of the input pattern recorded on the contour map of the error function. The symbols **X** and **O** represent respectively the initial and the intermediate positions of the input pattern. The control term x_c is chosen as **0** for maps 1 and 2, while the mean vector-selection algorithm is applied to maps 3 and 4 for jumping control. A higher frequency of jumpings, especially, around the center can be observed for maps 1 and 2.

CONCLUSION

This chapter has presented the following:

1. The design principle of a mapping neural network using a nonsigmoidal activation function, such as a Gaussian function.

2. A learning algorithm which explores the incremental generation of hidden units based on the self-organization of teaching patterns and the hierarchical training of teaching patterns based on the control of the clustering boundaries of individual hidden units.

3. The inverse mapping based on the Lyapunov function as a general means of achieving a recall process.

The design principle developed for a mapping neural network based on a nonsigmoidal activation function contributes to the advancement of a new methodology of designing a more general form of mapping neural network with powerful mapping capability. The learning algorithm presented, referred to as **hierarchically self-organizing learning algorithm**, is applicable to any mapping neural network by proper definition of its own clustering boundaries. The learning algorithm contributes to the development of a new learning methodology based on self-organization and hierarchical learning, which may provide a solution to the problems encountered in conventional learning techniques due to the existence of local minima, flat-surface error curvature, as well as structural inflexibility. Providing inverse mapping capability for a mapping neural network further exploits the development of a new structure of mapping neural networks capable of performing bidirectional mapping. This bidirectional mapping is useful because of the need for a recall process for selective attention. The inverse mapping based on the Lyapunov function provides a solid method to find a global solution. The research issues raised in this chapter that remain unresolved will be left for future study.

Acknowledgement.   The author wishes express his gratitude to Mr. Rhee M. Kil for his contributions to part of the theoretical development and simulation, and Mr. Jun Park for his contribution to the preparation of the manuscript. The author also wishes to express his thanks to Dr. Bart Kosko at USC and Dr. Robert Hecht-Nielsen at HNC, Inc., for their stimulation and encouragement. This work is in part supported by the USC Faculty Research and Innovation Fund.

REFERENCES

Aizerman, M. A., Braverman, E. M., and Rozonoer, L. I., "Theoretical Foundations of the Potential Function Method in Pattern Recognition Learning," *Avtomatika i Telemekhanika*, vol. 25, 917–936, 1964.

Albus, J. S., "Mechanisms of Planning and Problem Solving in the Brain," *Mathematical Biosciences*, vol. 45, 247–293, 1979.

Carpenter, G. A., and Grossberg, S., "ART2: Stable Self-Organization of Pattern Recognition Codes for Analog Input Patterns," *Applied Optics*, December 1987.

Duda, R. O., and Hart, P. E., *Pattern Classification and Scene Analysis*, 130–188, Wiley, New York, 1973.

Fukunaga, K., *Introduction to Statistical Pattern Recognition*, 89–121, Academic Press, Orlando, FL, 1972.

Fukushima, K., "Neocognitron: A Self-Organizing Neural Network Model for a Mechanism of Pattern Recognition Unaffected by Shift in Position," *Biological Cybernetics*, vol. 36, 193–202, 1980.

Fukushima, K., "A Neural Network for Visual Pattern Recognition," *IEEE Computer Magazine*, March 1988.

Funahashi, K., "On the Approximate Realization of Continuous Mappings by Neural Networks," *Neural Networks*, vol. 2, no. 3, 183–192, 1989.

Hecht-Nielsen, R., "Counterpropagation Networks," *Applied Optics*, December 1987a.

Hecht-Nielsen, R., "Kolmogorov Mapping Neural Network Existence Theorem," *IEEE ICNN*, vol. 3, 11–13, 1987b.

Hecht-Nielsen, R., "Theory of the Backpropagation Neural Network," *IEEE IJCNN*, vol. 1, 593–605, 1989.

Hinton, G. E., Sejnowski, T. J., and Ackley, D. H., *Boltzmann Machines: Constraint Satisfaction Networks That Learn*, Technical Report CMU-CS-84-119, Department of Computer Science, Carnegie-Mellon University, 1984.

Hopfield, J., "Neural Networks and Physical Systems with Emergent Collective Computational Properties," *Proc. Nat. Acad. Sci. USA*, vol. 79, 2554–2558, 1982.

Hopfield, J., "Neurons with Graded Response Have Collective Computational Properties Like Those of Two-State Neurons," *Proc. Nat. Acad. Sci. USA*, vol. 81, 3088–3092, 1984.

Irie, B., and Miyake, S., "Capabilities of Three-Layered Perceptrons," *IEEE ICNN*, vol. 1, 641–648, 1988.

Kohonen, T., *Self-Organization and Associative Memory*, 2nd ed., Springer-Verlag, New York, 1988.

Kolmogorov, A. N., "On the Representation of Continuous Functions of Many Variables by Superposition of Continuous Functions of One Variable and Addition," *Doklady Akademii Nauk SSSR*, vol. 144, 679–681, 1957.

Kosko, B., "Adaptive Bidirectional Associative Memories," *Applied Optics*, vol. 26, 4947–4960, 1987.

Kosko, B., "Feedback Stability and Unsupervised Learning," *IEEE ICNN*, vol. 1, 141–152, 1988.

Lee, S., and Kil, R. M., "Multilayer Feedforward Potential Function Network," *IEEE ICNN*, vol. 1, 161–171, 1988.

Lee, S., and Kil, R. M., "Bidirectional Continuous Associator Based On Gaussian Potential Function Network," *IEEE IJCNN*, vol. 1, 45–53, 1989.

Lippmann, R. P., "An Introduction to Computing with Neural Nets," *IEEE ASSP Magazine*, 4–22, April 1987.

Minsky, M., and Papert, S., *Perceptrons*, MIT Press, Cambridge, MA, 1969.

Rummelhart, D. E., Hinton, G. E., and Williams, R. J., *Parallel Distributed Processing*, vol. 1, 318–362, MIT Press/Bradford Books, Cambridge, MA 1986.

Slotine, J.-J. E., and Yoerger, D. R., "A Rule-Based Inverse Kinematics Algorithm for Redundant Manipulators," *International Journal of Robotics and Automation*, vol. 2, 86–89, 1987.

Sprecher, D. A., "On the Structure of Continuous Functions of Several Variables," *Translations of the American Mathematical Society*, vol. 115, 340–355, 1965.

Vidyasagar, M., *Nonlinear Systems Analysis*, 131–223, Prentice Hall, Englewood Cliffs, NJ, 1978.

Widrow, B., and Stearns, S. D., *Adaptive Signal Processing*, 15–116, Prentice Hall, Englewood Cliffs, NJ, 1985.

APPENDIX

The Derivation of Gradient-Descent Procedure

The network parameters are derived here by taking the negative gradient of the error function, (7-22). For convenience, the subscript p which represents the pth pattern is dropped in the following derivations.

1. Δw_{ji}.

$$\Delta w_{ji} \;=\; -\frac{\partial E}{\partial w_{ji}}$$

$$\frac{\partial E}{\partial w_{ji}} \;=\; \frac{\partial E}{\partial \phi_j}\,\frac{\partial \phi_j}{\partial w_{ji}}$$

$$\frac{\partial E}{\partial \phi_j} \;=\; -(t_j - \phi_j)$$

and

$$\frac{\partial \phi_j}{\partial w_{ji}} \;=\; \psi_i$$

Therefore,

$$\Delta w_{ji} \;=\; (t_j - \phi_j)\psi_i$$

2. Δm_j^i.

$$\Delta m_j^i \;=\; -\frac{\partial E}{\partial m_j^i}$$

$$\frac{\partial E}{\partial m_j^i} \;=\; \frac{\partial E}{\partial \psi_i}\,\frac{\partial \psi_i}{\partial d_i}\,\frac{\partial d_i}{\partial m_j^i}$$

$$\frac{\partial E}{\partial \psi_i} \;=\; \sum_k \frac{\partial E}{\partial \phi_k}\,\frac{\partial \phi_k}{\partial \psi_k} \;=\; -\sum_k (t_k - \phi_k)w_{ki}$$

$$\frac{\partial \psi_i}{\partial d_i} \;=\; -\frac{1}{2}\,\psi_i$$

and

$$\frac{\partial d_i}{\partial m_j^i} \;=\; -2\sum_l k_{jl}^i (x_l - m_l^i)$$

Therefore,

$$\Delta m_j^i \;=\; \sum_l k_{jl}^i (x_l - m_l^i)\psi_i \sum_k (t_k - \phi_k)w_{ki}$$

3. Δk^i_{jk}. We have two types of parameters for k^i_{jk}, i.e., σ^i_j and h^i_{jk}. Here, $\Delta\sigma^i_j$ and Δh^i_{jk} are derived separately.

- $\Delta\sigma^i_j$ for $j = k$

$$\Delta\sigma^i_j \;=\; -\frac{\partial E}{\partial\sigma^i_j} \quad\text{and}\quad \frac{\partial E}{\partial\sigma^i_j} \;=\; \frac{\partial E}{\partial\psi_i}\frac{\partial\psi_i}{\partial d_i}\frac{\partial d_i}{\partial\sigma^i_j}$$

By the same derivation as Δm^i_j,

$$\frac{\partial E}{\partial\psi_i}\frac{\partial\psi_i}{\partial d_i} \;=\; \frac{1}{2}\psi_i\sum_k (t_k - \phi_k)w_{ki}$$

and

$$\frac{\partial d_i}{\partial\sigma^i_j} \;=\; -2\sum_l h^i_{jl}\frac{(x_j - m^i_j)(x_l - m^i_l)}{(\sigma^i_j)^2\sigma^i_l}$$

Therefore,

$$\Delta\sigma^i_j \;=\; \sum_l k^i_{jl}\frac{(x_j - m^i_j)(x_l - m^i_l)}{\sigma^i_j}\,\psi_i\sum_k (t_k - \phi_k)w_{ki}$$

- Δh^i_{jk} for $j \neq k$.

$$\Delta h^i_{jk} \;=\; -\frac{\partial E}{\partial h^i_{jk}} \quad\text{and}\quad \frac{\partial E}{\partial h^i_{jk}} \;=\; \frac{\partial E}{\partial\psi_i}\frac{\partial\psi_i}{\partial d_i}\frac{\partial d_i}{\partial h^i_{jk}}$$

By the same derivation as Δm^i_j,

$$\frac{\partial E}{\partial\psi_i}\frac{\partial\psi_i}{\partial d_i} \;=\; \frac{1}{2}\psi_i\sum_k (t_k - \phi_k)w_{ki}$$

and

$$\frac{\partial d_i}{\partial h^i_{jk}} \;=\; \frac{(x_j - m^i_j)(x_k - m^i_k)}{\sigma^i_j\sigma^i_k}$$

Therefore,

$$\Delta h^i_{jk} \;=\; -\frac{1}{2}\frac{(x_j - m^i_j)(x_k - m^i_k)}{\sigma^i_j\sigma^i_k}\,\psi_i\sum_k (t_k - \phi_k)w_{ki}$$

PROBLEMS

7.1. A PFN has PFUs defined by

$$\psi(x, m, \sigma) \;=\; \sin c(\frac{x-m}{\sigma}) \;=\; \frac{\sin \pi \frac{x-m}{\sigma}}{\pi \frac{x-m}{\sigma}}$$

Prove that any one-dimensional function $f(x)$ can be implemented by this PFN, provided that an infinite number of PFUs is available. [Hint: Use the relation $\delta(x) = \lim_{N \to \infty} N \sin c(Nx)$.]

7.2. A GPFU is defined by

$$\psi \;=\; e^{-d/2}$$

$$d \;=\; \sum_{j=1}^{2} \sum_{k=1}^{2} k_{jk}(x_j - m_j)(x_k - m_k)$$

and

$$k_{jk} \;=\; \frac{h_{jk}}{\sigma^2}$$

Sketch the contour map of the GPFU on the two-dimensional input space, $[x_1, x_2]$, for the following cases of h_{jk}:

- $h_{jk} = \begin{cases} 1 & \text{if } j = k \\ 0 & \text{otherwise} \end{cases}$

- $h_{jk} = 1 \ \forall j, k$

7.3. Two functions $f_1(x_1, x_2)$ and $f_2(x_1, x_2)$ are to be implemented based on a GPFN:

x_1	x_2	f_1	x_1	x_2	f_2
1	1	$-\epsilon$	1	0	$+\epsilon$
1	-1	$+\epsilon$	-1	0	$+\epsilon$
-1	1	$+\epsilon$	0	1	$-\epsilon$
-1	-1	$-\epsilon$	0	-1	$-\epsilon$

Suppose we have three GPFNs, and each GPFN has a specific type of GPFU:

- Type 1: general shape matrix

- Type 2: all off-diagonal elements of the shape matrix are zero

- Type 3: $\mathbf{K} = (1/\sigma^2)\mathbf{I}$

Determine the least number of GPFUs in each type for the functions f_1 and f_2.

7.4. Teaching patterns are given by the set $\{(\mathbf{x}_i, t_i) \,|\, i = 1, \ldots, N\}$, where $\mathbf{x}_i$ and t_i represent the input pattern and the corresponding desired output value. A PFN has the following binary disjoint PFU:

$$\psi(\mathbf{x}_i, \mathbf{p}_j) \;=\; \begin{cases} 1 & \text{if } i \in S_j \\ 0 & \text{otherwise} \end{cases}$$

where S_j is a disjoint set of indices of input teaching patterns belonging to the area defined by the shape parameter $\mathbf{p}_j$. The error function, E is defined by

$$E = \frac{1}{2}\sum_{i=1}^{N}(t_i - \phi(\mathbf{x}_i))^2$$

where $\phi(\mathbf{x}_i) = \sum_{j=1}^{M}c_j\phi(\mathbf{x}_i, \mathbf{p}_j)$. Show that the optimum weight values c_j^* and the corresponding minimum error value E^* are given by

$$c_j^* = \bar{t}_j \quad \text{and} \quad E^* = \frac{1}{2}\sum_{j=1}^{M}n_j\sigma_j^2$$

where

$$\bar{t}_j = \frac{\left(\sum_{k\in S_j}t_k\right)}{n_j}$$

$$\sigma_j = \sqrt{\frac{\sum_{k\in S_j}(t_k - \bar{t}_j)^2}{n_j}}$$

$n_j = $ the number of teaching patterns in S_j

7.5. A PFN is represented by the following equations:

$$\phi = \sum_{i=1}^{M}w_i\psi(d_i) \qquad d_i = f(l_i) \quad \text{and} \quad l_i = \frac{1}{2\sigma^2}\|\mathbf{x} - \mathbf{m}^i\|^2$$

where $\mathbf{x}$ is an N-dimensional input pattern and $\mathbf{m}^i$ is an N-dimensional vector for the ith unit. Derive the learning rules for the network parameters w_i, σ_i, and $\mathbf{m}^i$ based on the backpropagation algorithm.

7.6. A network is represented by the following equations:

$$y = \sum_{i=1}^{L}w_i f(\text{net}_i)$$

$$f(\text{net}_i) = \frac{1}{1 + e^{-\text{net}_i}}$$

and

$$\text{net}_i = \sum_{j=1}^{N}u_{ij}x_j + \theta_i$$

For the given desired output value y^d, the input pattern is updated as follows:

$$x_j(t') = x_j(0) + \int_0^{t'} \dot{x}_j \, dt$$

and

$$\dot{x}_j = (y^d - y) \sum_{i=1}^{L} w_i f'(\text{net}_i) u_{ij} \qquad \text{for } j = 1, \ldots, N$$

Can this rule guarantee a global convergence such that the input patterns corresponding to $y = y^d$ are globally stable states in the input space? If yes, describe your reasoning. If no, find out the stable states (input patterns) corresponding to $y \neq y^d$.

7.7. A Lyapunov function candidate is defined by

$$V = \frac{1}{2}(y^d - y(x))^2$$

where y^d is the desired output value and $y(x)$ is the actual output value of x. Also, for the given desired output value y^d, the input pattern is updated as follows:

$$x(t') - x(0) + \int_0^{t'} \dot{x} \, dt$$

Determine the stable states in the input space for the following cases of $\dot{x}$:

- $\dot{x} = (y^d - y)\dfrac{\partial y}{\partial x}$

- $\dot{x} = \dfrac{y^d - y}{\dfrac{\partial y}{\partial x}}$

7.8. Consider a system that is described by the following state equations (damped Mathieu equation):

$$\dot{x}_1(t) = x_2(t)$$
$$\dot{x}_2(t) = -x_2(t) - (2 + \sin t)x_1(t)$$

Decide whether the state $\mathbf{0}$ in $[x_1, x_2]$ space is stable or not. If stable, is the state $\mathbf{0}$ globally asymptotically stable? *Hint:* Select the Lyapunov function candidate as

$$V(t, x_1, x_2) = x_1^2 + \frac{x_2^2}{2 + \sin(t)}$$

7.9. Consider a system that is described by the following state equations:

$$\dot{x}_1(t) = -x_1(t) - x_2(t)$$
$$\dot{x}_2(t) = x_1(t) - x_2(t)$$

Determine the stable state in the state space, $[x_1, x_2]$. Show that this state is globally asymptotically stable.

7.10. For a Lyapunov function candidate $V(\mathbf{x}, t)$, the input-pattern update rule is selected such that

$$\dot{V} = -V^{\alpha}$$

where α is constant. Discuss the convergence time of the input-pattern update rule for the following cases of α:

- $\alpha \geq 1$
- $0 < \alpha < 1$

PART THREE

ELECTRICAL
AND OPTICAL
NEURAL NETWORKS

DESIGN AND ANALYSIS OF ANALOG VLSI NEURAL NETWORKS

Bang W. Lee and Bing J. Sheu
Signal and Image Processing Institute
Department of Electrical Engineering–Systems
University of Southern California

Recent advances in very-large-scale-integrated (VLSI) circuit technology permit the VLSI implementation of many neural-network algorithms. VLSI neural networks process signals with massively parallel processors composed of simple amplifiers and resistive elements, instead of performing instructions sequentially in a von Neuman machine. Learning—by changing resistance values between amplifiers—can compensate for deficiencies in training data and minor changes of network component values. The immense computational power and learning capability of neural networks show excellent promise for signal and image processing and speech recognition. Several neural VLSI chips have been reported in the literature [Howard et al., 1987; Graf and Vegvar, 1987; Sage et al., 1986].

We can apply neural networks to several engineering problems: pattern recognition, image processing, prediction and noise filtering, servo control, system modeling and forecasting, and so on. Figure 8.1 shows a block diagram of a VLSI neural system. The real-world signals are converted into the discrete form (mainly digital) at the interface block. The neural signal-processing system handles the converted signals, and the outputs can be transferred to digital computing systems for further data manipulation. The interface block might function as a data con-

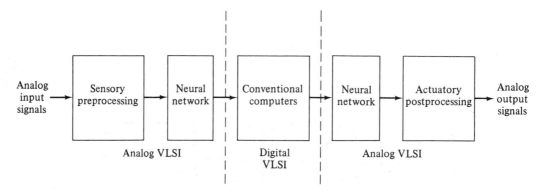

FIGURE 8.1   VLSI neural system.

verter and perform some primitive signal processing comparable to human retinas. Owing to the robustness of neural networks, outputs of the interface do not have to be completely precise. This is in sharp contrast to a conventional interfacing system. The signals inside a neural signal-processing system are distributed throughout the whole network. A small amount of damage in the system does not produce noticeable degradation of the system performance. Through learning, the interconnection weights can be modified so that the original system performance is retained.

For the VLSI implementation of neural circuits and systems, the analog approach seems to be extremely attractive in terms of hardware size, power, and speed [Tsividis, 1987]. Several promising research results have been reported, as listed in Table 8.1. Many existing VLSI neural chips can be categorized into sensory circuits and perceptual information-processing circuits. The VLSI sensory circuits have high locality, in that one neuron is connected only to the nearby neurons. Owing to the locality property, the connection problem, which is one major limitation for VLSI implementation, is no longer significant in the sensory circuits. For VLSI neural chips with low locality, the interconnections and synapses, which increase quadratically with the number of neurons, can be a fundamental limitation. So far, many neural circuits have been designed and fabricated with fixed synapse weightings. See Table 8.2.

Figure 8.2 shows the neural cells for software computation and VLSI computation. In the VLSI computation case, the neuron is realized with a simple amplifier and the synapse is realized with a resistor. In the software computation the neuron input voltage, which is a linear summation of the weighted input voltages, is amplified with a specific transfer function of the neuron. The neuron-transfer function of the software computation can be a special mathematical function, while that of the VLSI computation cannot be very flexibly defined. Notice that the network behavior can be described to be a Boltzmann machine or a Gaussian machine through the specification of neuron transfer function. In addition, the synapse weighting of

TABLE 8.1 RECENT PROGRESS IN ANALOG NEURAL CHIPS

Developer	Complexity	Technology	Applications
W. Hubbard et al. (Bell Lab., 1986)	22 neurons, 484 synapses (fixed)	CMOS amorphous-Si	Content addressable memory (CAM)
H. P. Graf et al. (Bell Lab., 1986)	256 neurons, 130K synapses (fixed)	2.5 μm CMOS amorphous-Si μm × 5700 μm)	CAM Data Compressor
M. Sivilotti et al. (Caltech, 1987)	Analog MOS circuitry, 100K transistors	2.5 μm CMOS	Retina
Y. Akiyama et al. (Keio Univ. & S. Carolina, 1988)	8 neurons, 64 synapses (variable)	2.5 μm CMOS (7900 μm × 9200 μm)	Hopfield network with adjustable R
H. P. Graf et al. (Bell Lab., 1988)	54 neurons, 2916 synapses (two fixed values)	2.5 μm CMOS (6700 μm × 6700 μm)	Hopfield network with digitally controlled R
B. Lee, B. Sheu (USC, 1988)	4 neurons, 16 synapses (fixed)	3 μm CMOS (1800 μm × 2200 μm)	Neural-based A/D converter
M. Holler et al. (Intel, 1989)	64 neurons, 8192 synapses (programmable)	1.0 μm CMOS EEPROM (5400 μm × 7350 μm)	General purpose

TABLE 8.2 COMPARISON BETWEEN SOFTWARE AND VLSI COMPUTATION

Performance	Implementation	
	Software	VLSI
Operation	Discrete fashion Serial mode	Continuous fashion Parallel mode
Neuron	Precise transfer function Required gain is independent of net size No time delay	Mismatch in gain, offset voltage Should increase w/network size Major time delay
Synapse	Perfect match Infinite dynamic range	Nonlinear Poor match Finite dynamic range
Network size	Limited by computer memory size	Limited by – I/O pads – die size – interconnection
Computational speed	Slow (∼ 10 MIPS)	Quite fast (> 2000 MIPS)

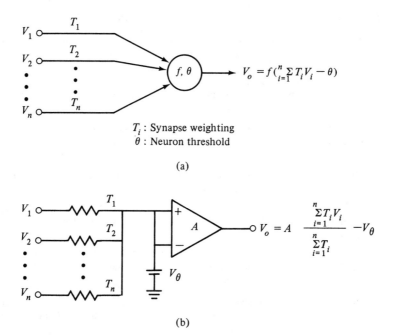

$$T_i : \text{Synapse weighting}$$
$$\theta : \text{Neuron threshold}$$

(a)

(b)

FIGURE 8.2 Neuron cells. (a) Software computation model. (b) VLSI computation model.

the software computation can be either positive or negative, while that of the VLSI computation should be only positive. Thus, a resistor and an amplifier with inverted output polarity is used to realize a negative synapse weighting.

The meaning of the neuron input voltage u in the VLSI computation with a direct-R implementation is quite different from that in the software computation. In VLSI computation, neuron input voltage u is determined by Kirchhoff's current laws,

$$u = \frac{\sum_{j=1}^{N} T_j V_j}{T_{\text{eq}}} \tag{8-1}$$

where $T_{\text{eq}} \equiv \sum_{j=1}^{N} T_j$ is the equivalent conductance at the neuron input terminal. Therefore, the neuron input voltage in the VLSI computation is effectively scaled down by a factor of T_{eq}. Notice that the $\{T_j\}$ in VLSI computation is always positive. To maintain the proper circuit operation, the amplifier gain should be increased by the same factor. The offset voltage of a neuron in software computation is added selectively, while that in a VLSI circuit is caused by device mismatches and is very difficult to control. Owing to the practical limitations in VLSI implementation of neural networks, new design techniques have to be applied.

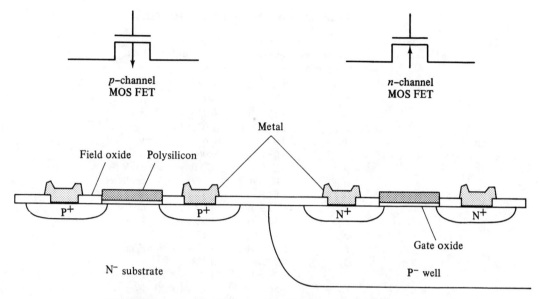

FIGURE 8.3 Cross section of n-channel and p-channel MOS transistors.

MOS DEVICES AND FUNCTIONAL BLOCKS

Devices

CMOS technologies that provide both n-channel and p-channel transistors are the mainstream for VLSI implementation, owing to their low power dissipation and high packing density properties. Figure 8.3 shows the cross section of a generic silicon-gate CMOS transistor. Typical transistor parameters are summarized in Table 8.3.

An enhancement-mode n-channel transistor is shown in Figure 8.4. When the V_{GB} increases, the amount of electrons underneath the gate oxide increases. Electrons move under the guidance of the lateral electrical field produced by the drain-to-source voltage. The transistor threshold voltage V_{th} is defined as

$$V_{th} \;=\; V_{th0} + \gamma \left(\sqrt{2\Phi_f + V_{SB}} - \sqrt{2\Phi_f} \right) \tag{8-2}$$

where the zero-biased threshold voltage V_{th0} equals

$$V_{th0} \;=\; V_{FB} + 2\Phi_f + \frac{\sqrt{2\epsilon_{Si}qN_A 2\Phi_f}}{C_{ox}} \tag{8-3}$$

and the body-effect coefficient γ for a uniform substrate is

$$\gamma \;=\; \frac{1}{C_{ox}}\sqrt{2\epsilon_{Si}qN_A} \tag{8-4}$$

TABLE 8.3 TYPICAL DEVICE PARAMETERS

Parameters	n-Channel	p-Channel	Unit
V_{tho}	0.78	-0.85	V
T_{ox}	360	360	$\overset{\circ}{A}$
X_j	0.25×10^{-6}	0.25×10^{-6}	m
N_{sub}	1.94×10^{16}	1.07×10^{16}	cm^{-3}
Φ_f	0.6	0.6	V
λ	0.038	0.060	V^{-1}
μ_0	473.7	270.0	cm/V sec
μ_{crit}	147,966	21,395	cm/V sec
Υ	0.842	0.624	V
L_d	0.27×10^{-6}	0.50×10^{-6}	m
C_j	1.34×10^{-4}	2.62×10^{-4}	F/m^2
M_j	0.48	0.49	—
C_{jsw}	5.17×10^{-10}	3.42×10^{-10}	F/m^2
M_{jsw}	0.376	0.373	—
C_{GDO}	2.56×10^{-10}	4.79×10^{-10}	F/m
C_{GSO}	2.56×10^{-10}	4.79×10^{-10}	F/m
C_{GBO}	1.00×10^{-10}	4.17×10^{-10}	F/m

*From MOSIS 2-μm p-well technology

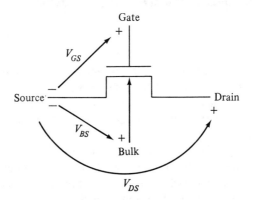

FIGURE 8.4 An NMOS transistor symbol.

Here, V_{FB} is the flat-band voltage and Φ_f is the Fermi potential.

Example 8.1

The Fermi potential Φ_f is given as $\Phi_f = \Phi_{ms} - Q_{ss}/C_{ox}$, where Φ_{ms} is the work-function difference between the gate and substrate materials and Q_{ss} is surface charge density. Owing to the existence of Q_{ss}, the threshold voltage of an n-channel MOS transistor may become negative. To achieve the balanced threshold voltages for p-channel and n-channel transistors, threshold-voltage adjustment implantation is required for the n-channel transistors.

(a) Calculate the threshold voltage of an n-channel transistor with $N_A = 10^{15}$ cm^{-3}, $Q_{ss}/q = 10^{11}$ cm^{-2}, $T_{ox} = 10$ nm, and n$^+$-doped silicon gate.

(b) With the assumption that all implanted ions will be activated, what is the required ion-implant density in order to shift V_{th} to 1.0 V?

Solution The threshold voltage is given as

$$V_{th} = \Phi_{ms} - \frac{Q_{ss}}{C_{ox}} + 2\Phi_f + \frac{\sqrt{2\epsilon_{Si}qN_A2\Phi_f}}{C_{ox}}$$

$$= -0.6 - 0.5 + 0.6 + 0.4 = -0.1 \text{ volt}$$

The required implant density N_{imp} is

$$N_{imp} = \frac{C_{ox}\Delta V_{th}}{q} = \frac{3.49 \times 10^{-8} \times 1.1}{1.6 \times 10^{-19}} = 2.4 \times 10^{11} \text{ cm}^{-2}$$

∎

When $V_{GS} < V_{th}$, the drain current is increased exponentially with V_{GS}. This operation region is called the **subthreshold** region or **weak-inversion** region. The drain-current expression is

$$I_{DS} = I_o\frac{W}{L}e^{(V_{GS}-V_{th})/nV_T}\left(1 - e^{-V_{DS}/V_T}\right) \tag{8-5}$$

where n is slope factor in weak inversion, I_o is a process-dependent scaling factor, and the thermal potential V_T equals kT/q. When $V_{GS} \geq V_{th}$, the transistor operates in the strong inversion region, which can be further divided into the triode region and the saturation region.

Triode region $[V_{GS} > V_{th} \text{ and } 0 < V_{DS} < V_{GS} - V_{th}]$:

$$I_{DS} = \mu C_{ox}\frac{W}{L}\left(V_{GS} - V_{th} - \frac{V_{DS}}{2}\right)V_{DS}(1 + \lambda V_{DS}) \tag{8-6}$$

Saturation Region $[V_{GS} > V_{th} \text{ and } V_{DS} \geq V_{GS} - V_{th}]$:

$$I_{DS} = \frac{\mu C_{ox}}{2}\frac{W}{L}(V_{GS} - V_{th})^2(1 + \lambda V_{DS}) \tag{8-7}$$

where

$$L = L_{drawn} - \Delta L \tag{8-8}$$

Here, L_{drawn} is the drawn channel length, ΔL is the channel-length reduction, and λ is the channel-length modulation coefficient.

Figure 8.5 shows the small-signal equivalent circuit of an MOS transistor.

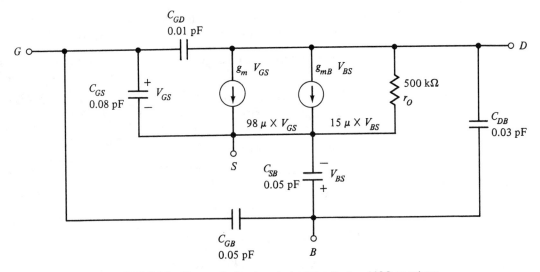

FIGURE 8.5   The small-signal equivalent circuit of an MOS transistor.

Expressions for transconductance g_m, backgate transconductance g_{mb}, and output conductance g_o in the saturation region are

$$g_m \equiv \frac{\partial I_{DS}}{\partial V_{GS}} \approx \sqrt{2\mu C_{ox} \frac{W}{L} I_{DS}} \tag{8-9}$$

$$g_{mb} \equiv \frac{\partial I_{DS}}{\partial V_{SB}} = g_m \frac{\gamma}{2\sqrt{V_{SB} + 2\Phi_f}} \tag{8-10}$$

and

$$g_o \equiv \frac{\partial I_{DS}}{\partial V_{DS}} = \lambda I_{DS} \tag{8-11}$$

Both intrinsic and extrinsic capacitances exist in an MOS transistor. The intrinsic capacitances are associated with the channel area, while the parasitic capacitances are associated with gate overlaps and source/drain junctions. Transistor intrinsic capacitance expressions in the triode region are

$$C_{GS} = C_{GD} = \frac{1}{2} C_{ox} W L$$
$$C_{GB} = 0 \tag{8-12}$$

and those in saturation region are

$$C_{GS} = \frac{2}{3} C_{ox} W L$$
$$C_{GD} = C_{GB} = 0 \tag{8-13}$$

The parasitic capacitances include overlap capacitances and junction capacitances.

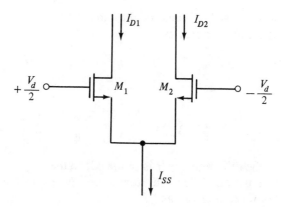

FIGURE 8.6 Circuit schematic of the input differential pairs.

Expressions for overlap capacitances between the gate and source, drain, and substrate are

$$C_{OVGS} = C_{GSO}W$$

$$C_{OVGD} = C_{GDO}W$$

$$C_{OVGB} = C_{GBO}L \qquad (8\text{-}14)$$

Here, C_{GSO}, C_{GDO}, and C_{GBO} are gate-to-source, gate-to-drain, and gate-to-substrate overlap capacitances per unit length, respectively. Junction capacitances between the source/drain diffusions and substrate are determined by the bottom area A and side-wall perimeter P as follows:

$$C_j = \frac{C_{j0}A_X}{\left(1 - \frac{V_{BX}}{\Phi_B}\right)^{MJ}} + \frac{C_{jswo}P_X}{\left(1 - \frac{V_{BX}}{\Phi_B}\right)^{MJSW}} \qquad (8\text{-}15)$$

where X denotes either S (source) or D (drain), Φ_B is the junction potential, C_{j0} and C_{jsw0} are the zero-biased capacitance per unit area and sidewall capacitance per unit length. Notice that the intrinsic capacitances can be nonsymmetric; for example C_{gs} is not always equal to C_{sg} [Sheu et al., 1988]. For switching circuits including charge-redistribution data converters and switched-capacitor circuits, more precise capacitance models should be used.

Functional Blocks

Figure 8.6 shows a differential pair which is primarily used for the input stage of an amplifier. The differential pair provides wide common-mode input range and excellent common-mode rejection ratio. If the transistors operate in the saturation region and the absolute value of the input voltage is smaller than V_{lmt}, the drain-current difference is given as

$$I_{D1} - I_{D2} = \frac{\mu C_{ox}}{2} \frac{W}{L} V_d \sqrt{\frac{4I_{ss}}{\mu C_{ox} \frac{W}{L}} - V_d^2} \tag{8-16}$$

with

$$V_{lmt} = \sqrt{\frac{2I_{ss}}{\mu C_{ox} \frac{W}{L}}} \tag{8-17}$$

At $|V_d| V_{lmt}$ the differential pair is saturated, so that the bias current I_{ss} flows through only one transistor. When the transistors operate in the subthreshold region, the current difference is given as

$$I_{D1} - I_{D2} = I_{ss} \tanh\left(\frac{V_d}{2nV_T}\right) \tag{8-18}$$

Transconductance gain G_m of the differential pair at a small differential input voltage is

$$G_m = \sqrt{\mu C_{ox} \frac{W}{L} I_{ss}} \tag{8-19}$$

in the strong inversion and

$$G_m = \frac{I_{ss}}{2nV_T} \tag{8-20}$$

in the weak inversion. The subthreshold region consumes low power and has exponential output characteristics and higher device mismatches.

The current mirror used for biasing circuitry and current arithmetic is shown in Figure 8.7. Since the transistors operating in the strong inversion are biased with the same gate voltage, the drain current ratio is given as

$$\frac{I_{D2}}{I_{D1}} = \frac{\left(\frac{W}{L}\right)_2}{\left(\frac{W}{L}\right)_1} \frac{1 + \lambda_2 V_{DS2}}{1 + \lambda_1 V_{DS1}} \tag{8-21}$$

Current addition and subtraction [Mead, 1989] can be conducted with the combination of current mirrors as also shown in Figure 8.7.

A moderate voltage gain can be obtained from a CMOS inverter circuit as shown in Figure 8.8. The maximum voltage gain is achieved when both transistors operate in the saturation region,

$$A_v = -\frac{g_{mn} + g_{mp}}{g_{on} + g_{op}} = -\frac{\sqrt{k_n} + \sqrt{k_p}}{\lambda_n + \lambda_p} \frac{1}{\sqrt{I_{Dm}}} \tag{8-22}$$

where $k \equiv \mu C_{ox}(W/L)$ and I_{Dm} is the current at the maximum voltage gain.

Example 8.2

Find the input voltage and the bias current I_D when the amplifier gain is maximum.

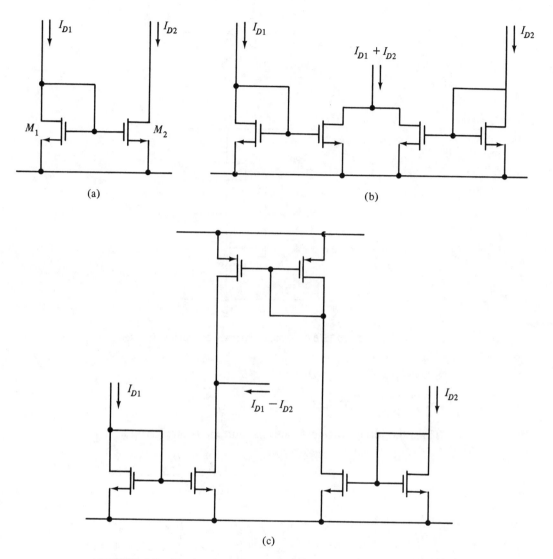

FIGURE 8.7 Circuit schematic of elementary arithmetic functions. (a) Current scaler. (b) Current adder. (c) Current subtractor.

Solution   By neglecting the finite output conductance, the drain current of an n-channel transistor I_n is

$$I_n = \frac{k_n}{2} (V_i - V_{SS} - V_{thn})^2$$

and that of a p-channel transistor I_p is

$$I_p = \frac{k_p}{2} (V_{DD} - V_i + V_{thp})^2$$

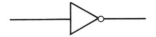

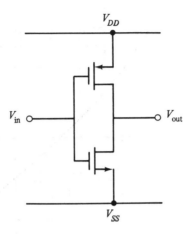

FIGURE 8.8   Circuit schematic of a CMOS inverter.

Since $I_n = I_p$,

$$V_i - V_{SS} - V_{thn} = \sqrt{\frac{k_p}{k_n}}\,(V_{DD} - V_i + V_{thp})$$

Thus, the input voltage V_i and the current I_D are given as

$$V_i = \frac{V_{SS} + V_{thn} + \sqrt{\frac{k_p}{k_n}}\,(V_{DD} + V_{thp})}{1 + \sqrt{\frac{k_p}{k_n}}}$$

and

$$I_D = \frac{k_p}{2}\left(\frac{V_{DD} + V_{thp} - V_{SS} - V_{thn}}{1 + \sqrt{\frac{k_p}{k_n}}}\right)^2$$

∎

The voltage gain for an inverter circuit is in the range of 10 to 100. To achieve a higher voltage gain, cascaded inverter structure can be used. Owing to the device mismatches, the input voltage V_i that gives the maximum voltage gain is widely distributed. The offset voltage can be cancelled out with a special switched technique [Lee et al., 1978].

The circuit schematic for a single-stage CMOS amplifier consisting of the differential-pair input stage and the CMOS inverter-type gain stage is shown in

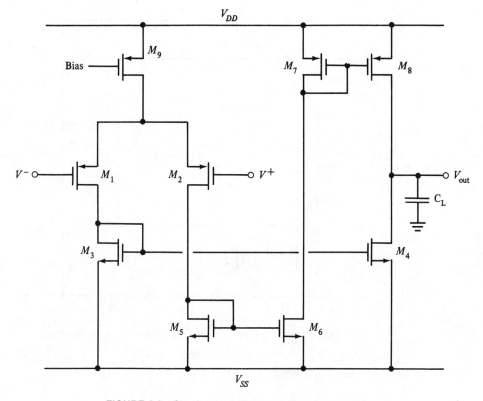

FIGURE 8.9   Circuit schematic of a single-stage amplifier.

Figure 8.9. With the use of the differential pair, the input offset is reduced. The amplifier low-frequency gain A_{vo} and unity-gain frequency f_u are given as

$$A_{vo} = G_{mi} R_o \qquad (8\text{-}23)$$

and

$$f_u = \frac{G_{mi}}{C_L} \qquad (8\text{-}24)$$

Here, G_{mi} is the transconductance of the differential pair, R_o is the output resistance, and C_L is the load capacitance. The circuit schematic for a simple two-stage CMOS amplifier is shown in Figure 8.10. The first stage consists of the differential pair and current mirror, while the second stage consists of driver transistor M_5 and current source M_6. The amplifier low-frequency gain A_{vo} is

$$A_{vo} = G_{mi} R_1 g_{m5} R_2 \qquad (8\text{-}25)$$

where $R_1 = 1/(g_{o2} + g_{o4})$ and $R_2 = 1/(g_{o5} + g_{o6})$, and g_{m5} is the transconductance

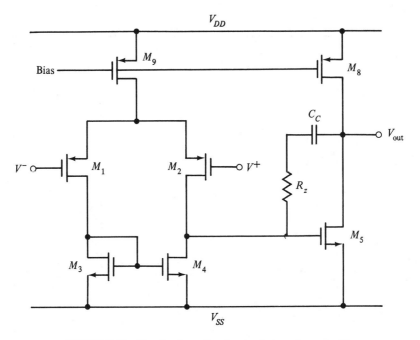

FIGURE 8.10   Circuit schematic of a simple two-stage amplifier.

of M_5. The unity frequency f_u is given as

$$f_u = \frac{1}{2\pi} \frac{G_{mi}}{C_c} \tag{8-26}$$

To achieve good amplifier stability, the nulling resistor R_z is usually set to be $1/g_{m5}$ [Gray and Meyer, 1984].

Example 8.3

Assume that all transistors have the same drain current, transconductance co-efficients $(k = \mu C_{ox}(W/L) = 100\mu A/V^2)$, and $\lambda = 0.1$ V^{-1}. Calculate the voltage gain of the following three circuits with a power dissipation of 0.05 mW and a 5-V power supply.

(a) An inverter.

(b) A one-stage amplifier.

(c) A two-stage amplifier.

Solution

(a) The voltage gain of an inverter A_{IV} is given as

$$A_{IV} = \frac{1}{\lambda} \sqrt{\frac{k}{I_D}}$$

where $I_D = 10\mu$A. Thus, $A_{IV} = 10 \times \sqrt{10} \approx 31.6$.

(b) The amplifier gain of one-stage amplifier A_{1S} is the same as that of an inverter with $I_D = 2.5\mu$A. Thus, $A_{1S} = 10 \times \sqrt{40} \approx 63.2$.

(c) The amplifier gain of a two-stage amplifier A_{2S} is given as

$$A_{2S} = \frac{1}{2}\left(\frac{\sqrt{k}}{\lambda\sqrt{I_D}}\right)^2$$

where $I_D = 3.33\mu$ A. Thus, $A_{2S} \approx 1515$.

VLSI HOPFIELD NEURAL NETWORKS

The Hopfield networks are very popular for electronic neural computing, owing to the simplicity in the network architecture and the fast-convergence property [Hopfield, 1984]. A Hopfield network composed of one-layer neurons and fully connected feedback resistors can be used to realize associative memory, pattern classifier, and optimization circuits. The network always operates along a decreasing path for the energy function, so that the final output represents one minimum in the energy function. Owing to the complexity of the energy function, there could exist several local minima. The minima in the energy function of Hopfield networks, which are decoded in the resistive network, are used for the exemplar patterns in associative-memory and pattern-classifier applications. However, the existence of local minima is not desirable for a great variety of other optimization applications.

Hopfield networks can be used as an effective interface between the real world of analog transmission media and the digital computing machines. Inputs to the Hopfield network can be analog signals. Outputs are usually discrete values, as shown in Figure 8.11. The Hopfield network not only converts analog signals into the digital format but also can conduct the first-level signal processings, which are associative recalling, signal estimation, and combinatorial optimization, in a way similar to the human retina. Because of the robustness of neural processors, output of the Hopfield neural network need not be high-precision, which is in strong contrast to conventional interface circuits. Key advantages of the VLSI neural interfaces over conventional interfaces are derived from the learning capabilities of Hopfield networks [Lippmann, 1987]. By adjusting the conductance values between the amplifiers with a learning rule, an adaptive characteristic can be made. The adaptability of a neural-based A/D converter [Tank and Hopfield, 1986], for example, will be useful not only to compensate for initial device mismatches or long-term characteristic drifts but also to provide a greater processing capability in the image- and signal-processing system.

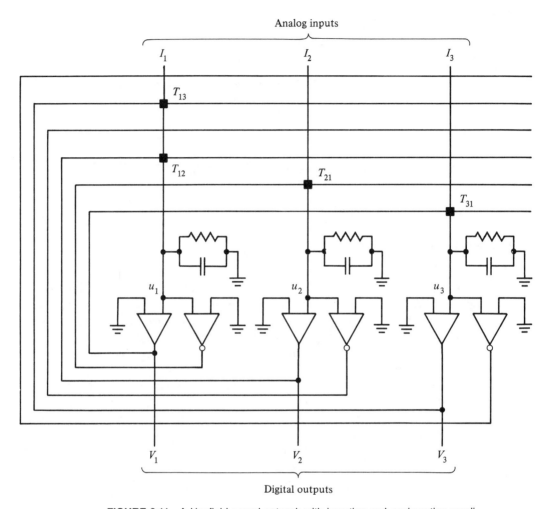

FIGURE 8.11 A Hopfield neural network with inverting and noninverting amplifiers as neurons.

Circuit Dynamics of Hopfield Networks

In a Hopfield network where the resistive network T_{ij} is symmetric and without self-feedback terms, i.e. $T_{ij} = T_{ji}$ and $T_{ii} = 0$, the energy function E can be expressed as

$$E = -\frac{1}{2}\sum_{i=1}^{N}\sum_{j=1,j\neq i}^{N}T_{ij}V_iV_j - \sum_{i=1}^{N}I_iV_i + \sum_{i=1}^{N}T_i\int_0^{V_i}g_i^{-1}(V)\,dV \qquad (8\text{-}27)$$

Here, T_{ij} is the conductance between the ith amplifier input and the jth amplifier output, V_i is the ith amplifier output voltage, I_i is the input current signal to the ith amplifier, $g(\cdot)$ is the amplifier transfer function, and N is the number of neurons. By using the energy function, the transient behavior of the Hopfield network can be explained in the following way. Input voltage of the ith amplifier u_i is governed by Kirchhoff's current law,

$$C_i \frac{du_i}{dt} = \sum_{j=1,j\neq i}^{N} T_{ij}V_j - T_i u_i + I_i \tag{8-28}$$

Here, T_i is the equivalent conductance at the ith amplifier input node,

$$T_i = \sum_{j=1,j\neq i}^{N} |T_{ij}| \tag{8-29}$$

The time derivative of the energy function can be determined as

$$\frac{dE}{dt} = -\sum_{i=1}^{N} \frac{dV_i}{dt} \left(\sum_{j=1}^{N} T_{ij}V_j - T_i u_i + I_i \right) \tag{8-30}$$

Substituting (8-28) into (8-30), we obtain

$$\frac{dE}{dt} = -\sum_{i=1}^{N} \frac{dV_i}{dt} C_i \frac{du_i}{dt}$$

$$= -\sum_{i=1}^{N} C_i g_i^{-1}(V_i) \left(\frac{dV_i}{dt} \right)^2 \tag{8-31}$$

If $g_i(\cdot)$ is monotonically increasing, dE/dt is always negative. That is to say, the network moves in the direction of decreasing the energy function. When $dV_i/dt = 0$ for all i, the steady state is reached.

Local Minima of Hopfield Network

In the VLSI-circuit realization of a Hopfield network, simple decision-making amplifiers and a resistive network are used, as shown in Figure 8.11. Each neuron includes noninverting and inverting amplifiers to handle both positive and negative synapse weightings. The output levels of a noninverting amplifier are 0 V and 1 V, while those of an inverting amplifier are 0 V and -1 V. The amplifier outputs are fed back to the amplifier inputs through the densely connected resistive network. The energy function E, which is used to describe dynamics of the network, can be expressed as

$$E = -\frac{1}{2}\sum_{i=1}^{N}\sum_{j=1,j\neq i}^{N} T_{ij}V_iV_j - \sum_{i=1}^{N} I_i V_i \tag{8-32}$$

Here, the amplifier gain is assumed to be very large. Under the condition that the resistive network T_{ij} is symmetric and without self-feedback terms, the energy function E corresponding to a given input state always decreases to settle down at one of the local minima. Owing to the nature of the energy function, the circuit output is highly dependent upon its initial state. The energy function can be used to describe the macro-property of network dynamics, while it is insufficient to describe such detailed behaviors of VLSI Hopfield circuits as the local minima, convergence speed, and the required amplifier gain for proper network operation.

Let us analyze the network in detail [Lee and Sheu, 1988]. At a local minimum, every amplifier input voltage $\{u_i\}$ satisfies the following criteria:

$$\begin{cases} u_i > 0 & \text{when} \quad V_i = 1 \\ u_i < 0 & \text{when} \quad V_i = 0 \end{cases} \tag{8-33}$$

with i being a positive integer in $[1, N]$. The ith amplifier input voltage u_i is given as

$$u_i = \frac{I_i + \sum\limits_{j=1, j \neq i}^{N} T_{ij} V_j}{T_i} \tag{8-34}$$

At the steady state, the operating range for the input current I_i is

$$\begin{cases} I_i > - \sum\limits_{j=1, j \neq i}^{N} T_{ij} V_j & \text{for } V_i = 1 \\ I_i < - \sum\limits_{j=1, j \neq i}^{N} T_{ij} V_j & \text{for } V_i = 0 \end{cases} \tag{8-35}$$

During the transient period, the voltage V_i changes in the direction that the energy function E always decreases. A local minimum is reached when all amplifiers reach the same stable condition.

A parameter GAP_i is defined as the input-current-range difference of the lower limit for $V_i = 1$ V and the upper limit for $V_i = 0$ V in (8-35),

$$GAP_i \equiv - \sum\limits_{j=1}^{N} T_{ij}(V_j^h - V_j^l) + T_{ii} \tag{8-36}$$

Here, V_j^h and V_j^l are the jth amplifier output voltages of the digital words whose ith bit from the least significant bit (LSB) have values of 1 and 0, respectively. If the parameter GAP_i is positive, there is no overlapped range of the input currents to the ith amplifier for the two digital words. On the other hand, if GAP_i is negative, both digital words can be stable at a certain input current. Therefore, the condition for the digital words not to be a local minimum of the energy function is $GAP_i \geq 0$ for all i.

Let us examine the special case of two adjacent digital words. The parameter GAP_i for the different bits between $\{V_j^h\}$ and $\{V_j^l\}$ becomes

$$GAP_i = \begin{cases} \displaystyle\sum_{j=1}^{i-1} T_{ij} & \text{if } i > 1 \\ 0 & \text{if } i = 1 \end{cases} \tag{8-37}$$

Consider two adjacent digital words with different LSB value only. If one digital word is the global minimum, then the other digital word could not be a local minimum. Notice that $GAP_i > 0$ in (8-37) is only a necessary condition to make two adjacent words not to be stable at one input current value.

The network stable output is usually the closest local minimum to the initial state. By resetting the initial condition to the ground state prior to each operation, an acceptable network result can be obtained. However, the resetting procedure greatly slows down the Hopfield network operation and cannot guarantee to achieve the global minimum on a complex energy-function surface. In VLSI neural circuits, device mismatches can be the dominant factor in deciding the convergence direction so that the resetting scheme is not sufficient.

Neural-Based A/D Converter

The function of an analog-to-digital (A/D) converter is to find a digital word $\{V_N, V_{N-1}, \ldots, V_1\}$ which is a best representation of the analog input signal. The output of an A/D converter is to achieve the minimum of the following function:

$$E_o = \left(V_S - \sum_{i=1}^{N} V_i 2^{i-1}\right)^2 \tag{8-38}$$

Here, V_S is the analog input voltage. In order to construct a Hopfield-like energy function, some modifications have to be made:

$$E = \frac{1}{2}E_o - \frac{1}{2}\sum_{i=1}^{N}(2^{i-1})^2[V_i(V_i - 1)] \tag{8-39}$$

Notice that the additional term does not affect the final correct solution. It is used to eliminate the diagonal elements in Hopfield network, i.e., $T_{ii} = 0$. By expanding (8-39), the objective function for the A/D converter can be expressed as

$$E = -\frac{1}{2}\sum_{i=1}^{N}\sum_{j=1,j\neq i}^{N}(-2^{i+j-2})V_i V_j - \sum_{i=1}^{N}(-2^{2i-3} + 2^{i-1}V_S)V_i \tag{8-40}$$

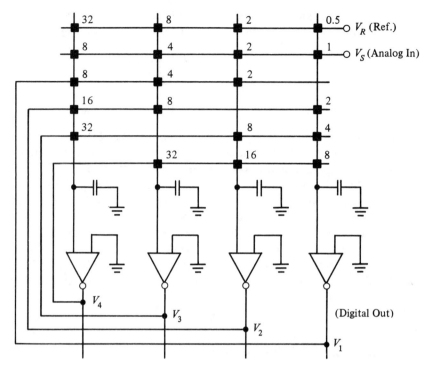

FIGURE 8.12   A 4-bit Hopfield neural-based A/D converter.

The synapse weightings T_{ij} and input current I_i can be determined from (8-32) and (8-40),

$$T_{ij} = -2^{i+j-2} \qquad (8-41)$$

and

$$I_i = -2^{2i-3} + 2^{i-1}V_S \qquad (8-42)$$

The circuit schematic of a 4-bit A/D converter is shown in Figure 8.12. The input current I_i is also implemented using the conductances (T_{iR} and T_{iS}) and the reference voltage V_R. The range for output voltage V_i in the energy function is [−1 V, 0 V], because inverting amplifiers are used in the Hopfield A/D converter. Thus, conductances $\{T_{ij}\}$ can take only positive values in VLSI implementation. The values for the conductances in the A/D converter are

$$T_{iR} = 2^{2i-3} \qquad (8-43)$$

and

$$T_{iS} = 2^{i-1} \qquad (8-44)$$

Here, T_{iR} is the conductance between the input terminal of the ith amplifier and the reference voltage V_R, and T_{iS} is the conductance between the input terminal of the ith amplifier and the analog input voltage V_S.

Example 8.4

For wider dynamic range of an A/D converter, a nonlinear A/D converter is usually utilized in speech processing applications. Design a 3-bit neural-based A/D converter with binary-weighted step size.

Solution The objective function of the nonlinear A/D converter can be described in the following equation:

$$\left(\sum_{i=1}^{3} (2^{i-1} V_i) 2^{i-1} - V_S \right)^2$$

We can obtain the energy function of a Hopfield network with following synapse weightings:

$$T_{ij} = -2^{2i+2j-4}$$
$$T_{iR} = 2^{2i-3}$$

and

$$T_{iS} = 2^{i-1}$$

∎

Since the input voltage $\{u_i\}$ is determined by the ratios of the conductances, the scaling factor to realize absolute conductance values can be used as an integrated-circuit design parameter. The normalized conductances are

$$\widehat{T}_{iS} = 1 \tag{8-45}$$
$$\widehat{T}_{ij} = 2^{j-1} \tag{8-46}$$

and

$$\widehat{T}_{iR} = 2^{i-2} \tag{8-47}$$

The maximum conductance ratio for an N-bit A/D converter has been greatly reduced from 2^{2N-2} to 2^N. If the voltage level of the amplifier is scaled to $(0 \text{ V}, -V_A)$, the reference voltage is scaled to $-V_R$, and the conversion step size is scaled to V_{step}, then the conductances are scaled to $\widehat{T}_{ij}/V_A$, $\widehat{T}_{iR}/V_R$, and $\widehat{T}_{iS}/V_{\text{step}}$, respectively.

For a specific digital output, the analog input signal V_S to the ith amplifier can be expressed as

$$V_S > -\frac{\widehat{T}_{iR}}{T_{iS}} V_R - \sum_{j=1, j\neq i}^{N} \frac{\widehat{T}_{ij}}{T_{iS}} V_j \quad \text{when } V_i = -1 \text{ V} \tag{8-48}$$

and

$$V_S < -\frac{\widehat{T}_{iR}}{T_{iS}} V_R - \sum_{j=1, j\neq i}^{N} \frac{\widehat{T}_{ij}}{T_{iS}} V_j \quad \text{when } V_i = 0 \text{ V} \tag{8-49}$$

Since

$$-\frac{\widehat{T}_{iR}}{T_{iS}} V_R - \sum_{j=1,j\neq i}^{N} \frac{\widehat{T}_{ij}}{T_{iS}} V_j = 2^{i-2} + V_O - 2^{i-1}|V_i| \tag{8-50}$$

the upper limit and lower limit of the analog input voltage always increases with i. Here, $V_R = -1$ V, and V_O is the digital output voltage which equals $\sum_{i=1}^{N} 2^{i-1}|V_i|$. To achieve a stable output, the input signal range is governed by the logic-AND operation of the range decided by each amplifier. Therefore, the lower limit of V_S at a given digital output is determined by the first logic-1 occurrence of the digital word from the least significant bit (LSB), and the upper limit is determined by the first logic-0 occurrence from the LSB. If a digital word has the first logic-0 at the ith bit from the LSB, then the next adjacent digital word has the first logic-1 at the ith bit. Thus, the ith amplifier decides the upper limit and lower limit of the analog input voltage between two adjacent digital words. That is to say, if the upper limit of the input signal corresponding to a digital word is decided by the ith amplifier, the lower limit of the upper adjacent digital word is also decided by the ith amplifier.

Example 8.5

Derive the analog input range for the word (0101).

Solution From (8-48) and (8-49), the analog voltages for each bit are given as

$$\begin{cases} V_S > 2^{-1} + 5 - 2^0 & \text{for } i = 1 \\ V_S < 2^0 + 5 & \text{for } i = 2 \\ V_S > 2^1 + 5 - 2^2 & \text{for } i = 3 \\ V_S < 2^2 + 5 & \text{for } i = 4 \end{cases}$$

Therefore, the analog voltage range determined by the LSB and the next bit is given as

$$4.5 \text{ V} < V_S < 6.0 \text{ V}$$

■

To guarantee that only one global minimum corresponding to each analog input value (i.e., without local minima) exists, only one-to-one correspondence between the digital output and analog input should exist. The indicator GAP_i, which equals the difference between the lower limit and upper limit of analog input voltage decided by the ith amplifier, can be used to understand the existence of local minima. It can be expressed as

$$GAP_i = -\sum_{j=1,j\neq i}^{N} 2^{j-1}(V_j^l - V_j^u) \tag{8-51}$$

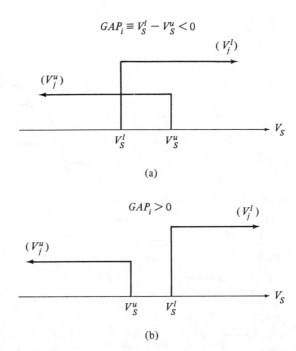

$$GAP_i \equiv V_S^l - V_S^u < 0$$

(a)

$$GAP_i > 0$$

(b)

FIGURE 8.13 Calculation of parameter GAP_i. (a) A negative GAP_i value corresponds to an overlapped signal range in two stable states. (b) A positive GAP_i value corresponds to no overlapped range.

where $\{V_j^l\}$ and $\{V_j^u\}$ are the adjacent digital words when the following conditions are satisfied:

$$\begin{cases} V_k^u = -1 \text{ V}, & V_k^l = 0 \text{ V} & \text{for } k < i \\ V_i^u = 0 \text{ V}, & V_i^l = -1 \text{ V} & \\ V_j^u = V_j^l & \text{for } j > i \end{cases} \qquad (8\text{-}52)$$

Here, the unit of GAP_i is volt. If the indicator GAP_i is negative, both the adjacent digital words can be the stable digital output at a given analog input voltage as shown in Figure 8.13. On the other hand, if the GAP_i is positive, there can be a gap of analog input voltage where no stable digital output exists. For a proper A/D conversion, the GAP_i should be zero for every i.

The indicator GAP_i becomes

$$GAP_i = -2^{i-1} + 1 \qquad (8\text{-}53)$$

because

$$\sum_{j=1}^{N} \widehat{T}_{ij}(V_j^l - V_j^h) = -1 \text{ V} \qquad (8\text{-}54)$$

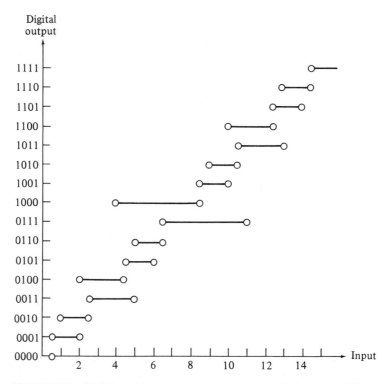

FIGURE 8.14   Digital output versus analog input characteristics for the A/D converter shown in Figure 8.12.

The above equation shows that indicator GAP is always negative except when $i = 1$. Hence, there could exist more than two digital output words corresponding to a given analog input. In addition, the overlapped length is not the same for each output word in the Hopfield A/D converter. Figure 8.14 shows the input signal range corresponding to each digital word. The overlapped digital words for a given analog input value are caused by the local minima in the energy function. The largest overlap in the analog input voltage occurs at the words (0111) and (1000), where the fourth amplifier decides the analog input range. This phenomenon is apparent because the indicator GAP_i increases with i. However, there is no overlapped input range between the adjacent digital words if these two words differ by the LSB.

The overlapped regions in Figure 8.14 indicate the existence of local minima in the Hopfield neural-based A/D converter proposed by Tank and Hopfield [1986]. For example, the words (1000), (0110), and (0101) can be the stable outputs when $V_S = 5.6$ V. The converged output in VLSI chips is determined by the initial state of the network and the device mismatches. The local minima give severe nonideal output characteristics. While nonlinearities can be remedied in software computation to some extent by resetting the network to the ground state prior to each conversion cycle [Tank and Hopfield, 1986], the circuit-transfer characteristic in VLSI chips still has strong nonlinearity due to amplifier mismatches.

Elimination of Local Minima in Neural-Based A/D Converters

A block diagram of a modified 4-bit neural-based A/D converter without local minima is shown in Figure 8.15 [Lee and Sheu, 1989]. The correction logic circuitry is added at the amplifier outputs, and the resistive network is expanded to include additional feedback elements from the correction logic circuitry. This circuitry monitors the amplifier outputs and generates the correction information to the synapse network. Notice that there is no feedback connection to the input of the first amplifier, because the digital word decided by the first amplifier does not produce a local minimum for any analog input-signal value.

To design the correction logic circuitry and the expanded resistive network, we begin with the solution for the corrected input voltage u_i using the following equation:

$$\left(T_{iR} + T_{iS} + T_{iC} + \sum_{j=1, j \neq i}^{N} T_{ij} \right) u_i$$

$$= T_{iR} V_R + T_{iS} V_S + T_{iC} F_i(V_O) + \sum_{j=1, j \neq i}^{N} T_{ij} V_j \quad (8\text{-}55)$$

where $F_i(V_O)$ is the ith correction logic output. Under the condition that V_i will take a discrete value of 0 V or -1 V and $V_R = -1$ V, the step size becomes 1 V and the analog input-voltage range becomes $[-0.5$ V, 15.5 V$]$. Let us assume that the amplifier gain is large and $T_{iC} F_i(V_O)/T_{iS}$ is monotonically increasing with i. The analog input voltage corresponding to a given digital word is bounded by the two amplifiers whose outputs are the first -1 V and 0 V from the LSB, which is guided by the same principle for the operation of the original Hopfield A/D converter.

Let us examine how to use the $F_i(V_O)$ and T_{iC} terms to eliminate the local minima in the energy function of a neural-based A/D converter. The lower limit (V_S^l) and upper limit (V_S^u) of the analog input voltage to the ith amplifier are

$$V_S^l = V_O^l - 2^{i-2} - \frac{T_{iC}}{2^{i-1}} F_i(V_O^l) \quad (8\text{-}56)$$

and

$$V_S^u = V_O^u + 2^{i-2} - \frac{T_{iC}}{2^{i-1}} F_i(V_O^u) \quad (8\text{-}57)$$

where

$$V_O^l \equiv \sum_{i=1}^{N} 2^{i-1} |V_i^l| \quad \text{and} \quad V_O^u \equiv \sum_{i=1}^{N} 2^{i-1} |V_i^u| \quad (8\text{-}58)$$

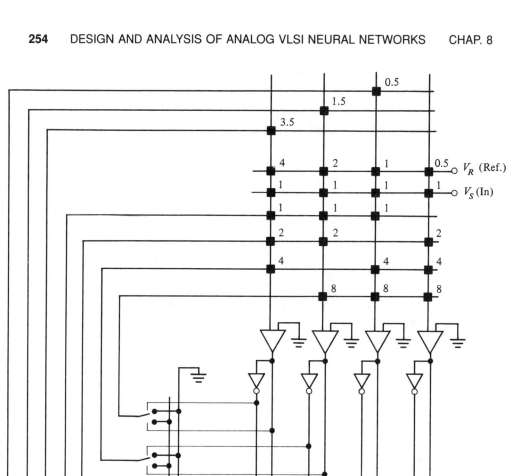

FIGURE 8.15 A modified neural-based A/D converter with self-correction circuitry.

The step size of the A/D converter is 1 V, because $V_R = -1$ V and the conductances ($\hat{T}_{ij}$, $\hat{T}_{iR}$, and $\hat{T}_{iS}$) are given in (8-45) through (8-47). The indicator GAP_i, which is the difference between V_S^l and V_S^u, should be zero when the local minima are eliminated:

$$GAP_i = -2^{i-1} + 1 - \frac{T_{iC}}{2^{i-1}}\left(F_i(V_O^l) - F_i(V_O^u)\right) = 0 \qquad (8\text{-}59)$$

In addition, V_S^l and V_S^u are related to V_O^l and V_O^u in the following way:

$$V_S^l = V_O^l - 0.5 \qquad (8\text{-}60)$$

and

$$V_S^u = V_O^u + 0.5 \qquad (8\text{-}61)$$

This is because output transitions should occur when the analog input voltage is larger than V_O by half of the step size.

From (8-59) through (8-61), nonnegative conductances T_{iC} and correction logic circuitry output can be obtained as below:

$$F_i(V_O^u) = -F_i(V_O^l) > 0 \qquad (8\text{-}62)$$

and

$$T_{iC} = \frac{2^{2i-3} - 2^{i-2}}{F_i(V_O^u)} \qquad (8\text{-}63)$$

The output of the correction logic circuitry can take a discrete value of -1 V, 0 V, or 1 V in order to be compatible with the amplifier output voltage and the reference voltage. Table 8.4 lists the information for the correction logic circuitry output of a modified neural-based A/D converter.

To perform SPICE circuit simulation [Quarles et al., 1987], amplifiers were modeled as dependent voltage sources, and the rest of the circuit was described at the transistor level. In our simulation, the normalized conductances were used. Figure 8.16 shows the simulated voltage transfer characteristics of the neural-based A/D converter. A monotonically increasing and decreasing analog input voltage was applied. The simulation results for the Hopfield A/D converter are plotted in solid lines, those for the modified A/D converter in dotted lines. The SPICE results confirm the hysteresis and nonlinearity characteristics of the Hopfield A/D converter. Simulation results of the modified A/D converter show good conversion characteristics.

VLSI Implementation

Figure 8.17 shows the die photo of the modified A/D converter fabricated by MOSIS 3-μm scalable CMOS technology [Tomovich, 1988]. The electronic synapses are realized with p-well diffusion resistors, and the electronic neurons

TABLE 8.4 LOGIC TABLE FOR THE CORRECTION LOGIC CIRCUITRY

Amplifier Output				Correction Logic Output		
D_4	D_3	D_2	D_1	C_4	C_3	C_2
0	0	0	0	0	0	0
0	0	0	1	0	0	+1
0	0	1	0	0	0	−1
0	0	1	1	0	+1	0
0	1	0	0	0	−1	0
0	1	0	1	0	0	+1
0	1	1	0	0	0	−1
0	1	1	1	+1	0	0
1	0	0	0	−1	0	0
1	0	0	1	0	0	+1
1	0	1	0	0	0	−1
1	0	1	1	0	+1	0
1	1	0	0	0	−1	0
1	1	0	1	0	0	+1
1	1	1	0	0	0	−1
1	1	1	1	0	0	0

are implemented with simple two-stage amplifiers. Since a simple CMOS amplifier has a large output impedance, it can not directly drive the feedback conductances. CMOS switches between the amplifiers and the resistors help to achieve good impedance matching. The CMOS switch size and conductance values are design parameters. In this chip, the unit resistor is chosen to be 100 kΩ, and the on-resistance of the CMOS switch with ±5-V power supplies is chosen to be 500 Ω. A significant portion of the chip area is occupied by the resistors and switches. If the resistor can be replaced by the synthesized resistors using MOS circuitry, the chip size can be greatly reduced.

The measured voltage-transfer curves for the original Hopfield A/D converter and the modified A/D converter are shown in Figure 8.18(a) and (b), respectively. The analog input-voltage range in this experiment was from 0 V to 1.5 V, because the conductances $\{T_{iS}\}$ were increased by a factor of ten. Hence, the conversion step size is reduced to 0.1 V. Experimental data agree with theoretically calculated results and SPICE simulation results very well. Figure 8.19 shows the converter response when the output changes from (0000) to (0111) and vice versa. The maximum delay time is about 5.7 μsec, and total power dissipation is 6 mW with ±5-V power supplies. Figure 8.20 shows a plot of the conversion time of the Hopfield A/D converter. The conversion time can be clearly classified into four different groups, depending on the number of iteration cycles. Since the amplifier is the major time-delay circuit, the modified A/D converter has a similar conversion speed.

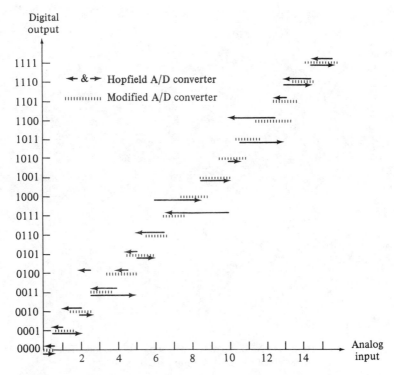

FIGURE 8.16 SPICE simulation results on the transfer characteristics of the original Hopfield A/D converter and the modified A/D converter.

Small spikes on the transfer curve are caused by device mismatches from the amplifier offset voltage, amplifier gain, and resistance. The effect of mismatches can be eliminated by the learning process if programmable synapses are available.

HARDWARE ANNEALING

Engineering optimization is an important subject in image and signal processing. A conventional searching technique for finding the global minimum is to use gradient descent, which finds the direction for the next iteration from the gradient of the objective function. For complicated problems, the gradient-descent technique often gets stuck at a local minimum where the objective function has surrounding barriers. In addition, the complexity of most combinational optimization problems increases dramatically with the problem size and makes it very difficult to obtain the global minimum in a reasonable computational time. Several methods have been reported to assist the network output to escape from the local minima [Lee and Sheu, 1988; van Laarhoven and Aarts, 1985]. The simulated annealing method

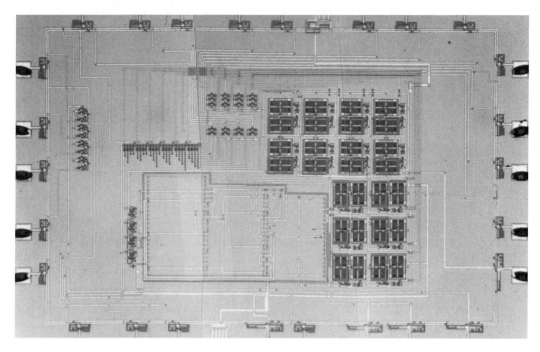

FIGURE 8.17 Die photo of the modified A/D converter. The chip size is 2.3 mm × 3.4 mm in MOSIS scalable 3-μm CMOS technology.

is one of the heuristic approaches which can be widely applied to combinational optimization problems [Kirkpatrick et al., 1983; Aarts and van Laarhoven, 1985]. The solutions by this technique are close to the global minimum within a polynomial upper bound for the computational time and are independent of the initial conditions. The simulated annealing technique has been successfully reported in VLSI layout generation [Rutenbar, 1989] and noise filtering in image processing [Geman and Geman, 1984].

Simulated annealing in software computation of neural networks can be conducted in the following way.

STEP 1. Start from a high temperature and a given reference state.

STEP 2. Compare the energy value in a new state with that in the reference state.

STEP 3. If energy value of the new state is higher than that of the reference state, weight the new state output by $e^{-\Delta E/T}$.

STEP 4. Replace the reference state with the new state.

STEP 5. Check whether all states are frozen. If yes, terminate. Otherwise, decrease temperature and go to Step 2.

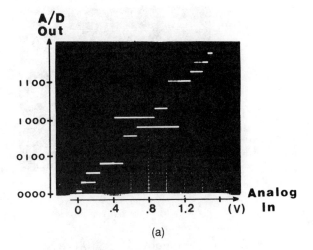

(a)

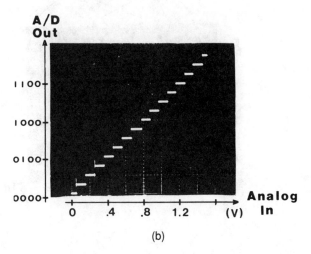

(b)

FIGURE 8.18 Measured transfer characteristics of neural-based A/D converters. (a) Original Hopfield A/D converter. (b) Modified A/D converter.

Since it usually takes a lot of time at Step 2 to compare all possible states, a specific perturbation rule is often used. The perturbation is usually called *artificial noise* in software computation.

The simulated annealing technique can help Hopfield neural networks to escape from local minima by replacing the characteristics of neurons from a sigmoid function [Rummelhart et al., 1986] to the Boltzmann distribution function. In software computation, the Hopfield network operation is described at two consecutive

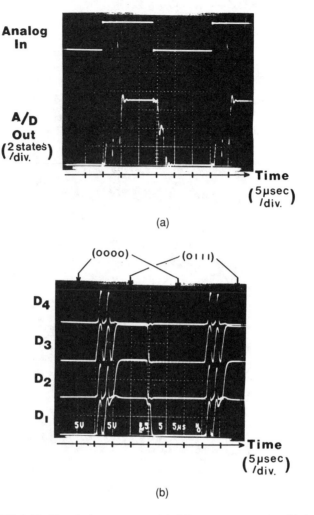

FIGURE 8.19 Transient responses. (a) A/D converter output. (b) Individual amplifier output. The A/D converter output is reconstructed with an external D/A converter.

time steps during each iteration cycle. At the first time step, input signals to the neurons are summed up; at the second, the neuron outputs are updated. The update rule for the original Hopfield networks is

$$V_i = g(u_i) \tag{8-64}$$

and that for the Boltzmann machine is

$$V_i = \frac{1}{1 + e^{-u_i/T}} \tag{8-65}$$

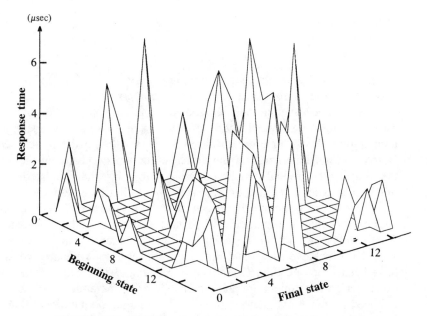

FIGURE 8.20 Response-time characteristics of the A/D converter.

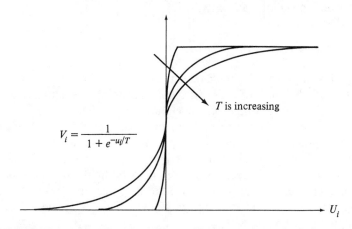

$$V_i = \frac{1}{1 + e^{-u_i/T}}$$

T is increasing

FIGURE 8.21 Analogy between the annealing temperature of a Boltzmann machine and the amplifier gain of an electronic neuron.

Here, $g(\cdot)$ is the amplifier input-output transfer function and T is the temperature of Boltzmann distribution as shown in Figure 8.21. Notice that the searching process for all possible states in simulated annealing is a part of network operation at a temperature in the Boltzmann machine. At the steady state, relative probability of state $S1$ to state $S2$ in Boltzmann distribution is determined by energy difference of the two states:

$$\frac{P_{S1}}{P_{S2}} = e^{-(E_{S1}-E_{S2})/T} \tag{8-66}$$

Here, E_{S1} and E_{S2} are the corresponding energy levels. This update rule allows the network to escape from local minima in the energy well.

Simulated annealing is analogous to metallurgical annealing. To find the lowest energy level of a metal, the best way known is to melt the metal and to reduce temperature slowly in order to allow atoms to fit into the lattice. Similarly, the Boltzmann machine can find the global minimum by changing the temperature of the update rule gradually. A good strategy to apply the simulated annealing technique in software computation is to start from a high temperature, which will make the network reach the steady state in a very short time. The ideal formulation for cooling schedule [Kirkpatrick et al., 1983] is very difficult to implement, because a large number of iterations at each temperature and a very small temperature step are required to achieve the global minimum. Several approximated cooling schedules have been proposed [van Laarhoven and Aarts, 1987]. Since the number of iterations at a given temperature and the change of temperature should be compromised to speed up the convergence process, a very large computational time is necessary in software computation. On the other hand, recent advances in VLSI technologies make possible the design of compact electronic neural networks with built-in hardware annealing capability.

Electronic Annealing

The high-speed simulated annealing technique for a Boltzmann machine is most suitable for VLSI chip design. Changing the temperature of the probability function for a Boltzmann machine is equivalent to varying the amplifier gain. Thus, the cooling process in a Boltzmann machine is equivalent to the voltage-gain-increase process in an amplifier. The amplifier gain in electronic neural circuits can be updated continuously, while the annealing temperatures in software computation are always in the discrete fashion. Hence, the final solution of the electronic neural circuits after annealing is guaranteed to be global minimum, which is in sharp contrast to the approximated convergence [van Laarhoven and Aarts, 1987] in software computation.

A systematic method to determine the initial and final temperatures for the amplifier "cooling" procedure is described below.

Initial temperature of the cooling schedule.   At a very high temperature all metal atoms lose the solid phase, so that they position themselves randomly according to statistical mechanics. An important quantity in annealing is the lowest temperature that still could provide enough energy to completely randomize the metal atoms; the equivalent is the highest amplifier gain that could make an electronic neural network escape from local minima. Figure 8.22 shows a Hopfield

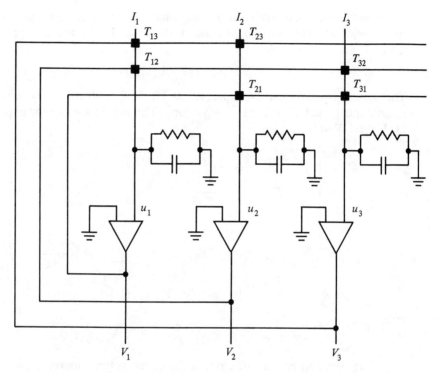

FIGURE 8.22 A Hopfield neural network with noninverting amplifiers as neurons.

neural network. Neurons are made of amplifiers, while synapses are made of resistors. If the neurons consist of high-gain amplifiers, their outputs will saturate at 0 V and 1 V, owing to the positive feedback of the network. However, given a very low amplifier gain, the network could lose the well-defined state.

By Kirchhoff's current law, the governing equation for the ith amplifier in the Hopfield network is given as

$$C_i \frac{du_i(t)}{dt} + T_i u_i(t) = \sum_{j=1, j \neq i}^{N} T_{ij} V_j(t) + I_i(t) \qquad (8\text{-}67)$$

where T_{ij} is the conductance between the ith and jth neurons and T_i and C_i are the equivalent input conductance and input capacitance at the ith amplifier. Here, $u_i(t)$ is the input voltage to the ith amplifier and $V_j(t)$ is the output voltage of the jth amplifier. By taking the Laplace transformation, (8-67) becomes

$$(sC_i + T_i)U_i(s) = \sum_{j=1, j \neq i}^{N} T_{ij} V_j(s) + I_i(s) + P_i \qquad (8\text{-}68)$$

where P_i is a constant and $U_i(s)$, $V_i(s)$, and $I_i(s)$ are transformed variables of $u_i(t)$,

$V_i(t)$, and $I_i(t)$, respectively. If all amplifiers are assumed to operate in the linear region with transfer function $A(s)$ and to have bandwidth much larger than T_i/C_i, then

$$V_i(s) = A_i(s)U_i(s) \tag{8-69}$$

The system equation can be expressed as $\mathbf{B}\underline{V} = \underline{F}$ with matrix $\mathbf{B}$ being a $N \times N$ matrix and $\underline{V}$ and $\underline{F}$ being $1 \times N$ vectors. The matrix and vector expressions for $\mathbf{B}$, $\underline{V}$, and $\underline{F}$ are

$$\mathbf{B} = \begin{pmatrix} -\dfrac{sC_1 + T_1}{A_1} & T_{12} & T_{13} & \cdots & T_{1N} \\[2ex] T_{21} & -\dfrac{sC_2 + T_2}{A_2} & T_{23} & \cdots & T_{2N} \\[2ex] \vdots & & & & \\[1ex] T_{N1} & T_{N2} & & \cdots & -\dfrac{sC_N + T_N}{A_N} \end{pmatrix} \tag{8-70}$$

$$\underline{V} = (V_1, V_2, \ldots, V_N)^T \tag{8-71}$$

and

$$\underline{F} = (-I_1 - P_1, \ldots, -I_N - P_N)^T \tag{8-72}$$

The sum and product of eigenvalues of the system matrix $\mathbf{B}$ are

$$\sum_{i=1}^{N} \lambda_i = -\sum_{i=1}^{N} \frac{(sC_i + T_i)}{A_i} \tag{8-73}$$

and

$$\prod_{i=1}^{N} \lambda_i = \det(\mathbf{B}) \tag{8-74}$$

respectively, where $\det(\mathbf{B})$ is the determinant of matrix $\mathbf{B}$. If the amplifier gain is sufficiently large, which is the condition used in Hopfield's analysis [Hopfield,1984], (8-73) and (8-74) become

$$\sum_{i=1}^{N} \lambda_i \approx 0 \tag{8-75}$$

and

$$\prod_{i=1}^{N} \lambda_i = \det(\mathbf{B}) \neq 0 \tag{8-76}$$

With the constraint that $T_{ij} = T_{ji}$, all eigenvalues will lie on the real axis of the s-plane. Thus, at least one positive real eigenvalue exists. It makes the amplifier outputs saturated at extreme values of 0 V or 1 V.

Example 8.6

For a Hopfield network with two neurons and $T_{12} = T_{21} = 1$, find the eigenvalues of the system matrix corresponding to four different amplifier-gain values of 1000, and 100, 10, and 1.

Solution   The system matrix **B** is given as

$$\mathbf{B} = \begin{pmatrix} -\frac{1}{A} & 1 \\ 1 & -\frac{1}{A} \end{pmatrix}$$

The eigenvalues are determined by

$$\left(\lambda + \frac{1}{A}\right)^2 = 1$$

Thus, the eigenvalues are

$$\lambda = \pm 1.0 - \frac{1}{A} = \begin{cases} -1.001 \ \text{ and } \ 0.999 & \text{when } A = 1000 \\ -1.01 \ \ \text{ and } \ 0.99 & \text{when } A = 100 \\ -1.1 \ \ \ \text{ and } \ 0.9 & \text{when } A = 10 \\ -2.0 \ \ \ \text{ and } \ 0.0 & \text{when } A = 1 \end{cases}$$

As the amplifier gain decreases, the positive eigenvalue decreases. and convergence speed of the system slows down. The network does not give any logical values at $A \leq 1$.   ■

Figure 8.23 shows the radius of the eigenvalues determined from the Gerschgorian theorem [Smith, 1985],

$$\left| z + \frac{sC_i + T_i}{A_i} \right| \leq \sum_{j=1,j\neq i}^{N} |T_{ij}| \qquad \text{for all } i \tag{8-77}$$

Notice that A_i and T_i are always positive. To assure that the network contains positive feedback action, there should be at least one eigenvalue whose real part is positive. The lowest amplifier gain (A_N) that satisfies the above condition can be determined from

$$A_N = \max \left\{ \frac{T_i}{\sum\limits_{j=1,j\neq i}^{N} |T_{ij}|} \qquad \text{for } 1 \leq i \leq N \right\} \tag{8-78}$$

Here, N denotes the number of amplifiers operating in the linear region. Notice that the above derivation is based on the condition that the eigenvalue lies on a circle. Since the validity of the condition depends on the maximum real value of the eigenvalues of matrix **B** determined by the resistive network $\{T_{ij}\}$, the above gain requirement is a sufficient condition that the amplifiers in the Hopfield network

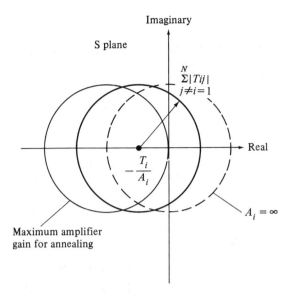

FIGURE 8.23   Radius of eigenvalues with different amplifier gains.

maintain the positive feedback action. With amplifier gain less than A_N, all output states of the Hopfield network become legal for any input signal level. Thus, A_N is the maximum amplifier gain (equivalently the lowest annealing temperature) that can still randomize the neuron outputs.

Final temperature of the cooling schedule.   The amplifiers start to be biased in the saturation region for a given input voltage if amplifier gains are increased from A_N. Let's assume that only the kth amplifier output is saturated at a value V_k. The governing equations for the new network condition are

$$C_i \frac{du_i(t)}{dt} + T_i u_i(t) = \sum_{j=1; j \neq i, k}^{N} T_{ij} V_j(t) + I_i(t) + T_{ik} V_k \quad \text{for any } i \neq k \quad (8\text{-}79)$$

The corresponding system matrix can be formed with the kth column and the kth row deleted from (8-70). Therefore, the lowest amplifier gain that makes the network maintain positive feedback is determined by

$$A_{N-1} = \max \left\{ \frac{T_i}{\sum\limits_{j=1; j \neq i, k}^{N} |T_{ij}|} \quad \text{for } 1 \leq i \leq N \right\} \quad (8\text{-}80)$$

The same T_i is used in (8-78) and (8-80). Notice that the amplifier gain for the positive-feedback state increases as the number of linear-region amplifiers decreases.

The worst case is when only two amplifiers operate in the linear region. Let's assume that the ith and kth amplifiers operate in the linear region. The system matrix $\mathbf{B_{ik}}$ can be expressed as

$$\mathbf{B_{ik}} = \begin{pmatrix} -\dfrac{sC_i + T_i}{A_i} & T_{ik} \\ T_{ki} & -\dfrac{sC_k + T_k}{A_k} \end{pmatrix} \tag{8-81}$$

Since the resistive network $\{T_{ij}\}$ is symmetrical, $T_{ik} \times T_{ki}$ is always positive. The maximum amplifier gain for two linear-region amplifiers is

$$A_2 = \max\left\{\sqrt{\dfrac{T_i T_k}{T_{ik} T_{ki}}} \quad \text{for every } i \text{ and } k \text{ with } i \neq k\right\} \tag{8-82}$$

When the amplifier gain is increased beyond A_2, only one amplifier will operate in the linear region. Even though the amplifier output is an analog value, the digital bit can be easily decided using the middle level of amplifier output swing as a reference. The logical state of the amplifier biased in the linear region can then be determined.

The amplifier gain during the hardware annealing process should start from a value smaller than A_N and stop at a value larger than A_2. In a similar way, the annealing temperature range for the Boltzmann machine using the update rule of (8-65) is

$$\frac{1}{4A_2} \leq T \leq \frac{1}{4A_N} \tag{8-83}$$

Since the updating process in electronic-network annealing can be done in a continuous fashion, its operation speed is much faster than that for the software computation.

Neural-Based A/D Converter Example

An 8-bit Hopfield-type neural-based A/D converter was used in our SPICE circuit simulation. A neuron consists of a simple CMOS operational amplifier with its gain controlled by an MOS transistor at the amplifier input. A triangular voltage waveform was applied to the gate terminal of the controlling transistor to adjust the amplifier gain. Figure 8.24 shows the simulation result with the analog input voltage being 5.0 V. The A/D converter output is reconstructed with a D/A converter. The A/D converter output starts to change when the amplifier gain is around 45 dB. In comparison, the theoretically calculated amplifier gain from (8-81) is 45.13 dB. The global minimum is always reached after one annealing cycle, as shown in Figure 8.24. Here, the initial network state is set to (00001000), which is one of the local minima corresponding to $V_{in} = 5.0$ V. Figure 8.25 shows the dynamics of the A/D converter with respect to the amplifier gain. As the

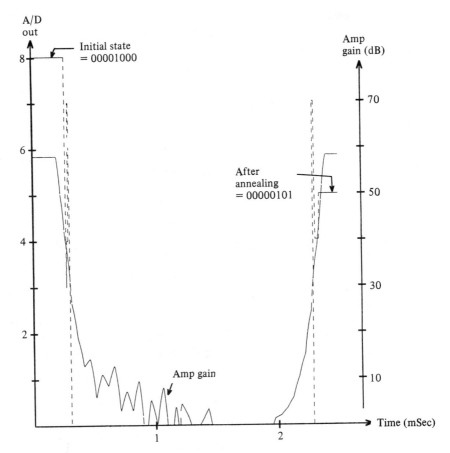

FIGURE 8.24 SPICE simulation results of an 8-bit Hopfield neural-based A/D converter in time-domain analysis with $V_{in} = 5$ V.

amplifier gain decreases, the states of amplifier outputs V_1, V_3, and V_4 are flipped. The amplifier outputs remain at these states even when the high voltage gain is restored.

Standard IC parts were used in the laboratory experiments. The amplifier gain is controlled with junction-FETs operating in the negative-feedback loop of the amplifier. Since we used p-channel depletion-mode junction-FETs, a high control-signal level makes a large amplifier gain. The 4-bit Hopfield neural-based A/D converter outputs were sampled and reconstructed by a D/A converter after every annealing cycle. Transfer characteristics of the A/D coverter are shown in Figure 8.26. The nonlinearity and hysteresis of the Hopfield A/D converter is caused by local minima in the energy function. By applying the electronic annealing technique, the global minimum is obtained.

Figure 8.27 shows the time-domain response of the A/D converter with elec-

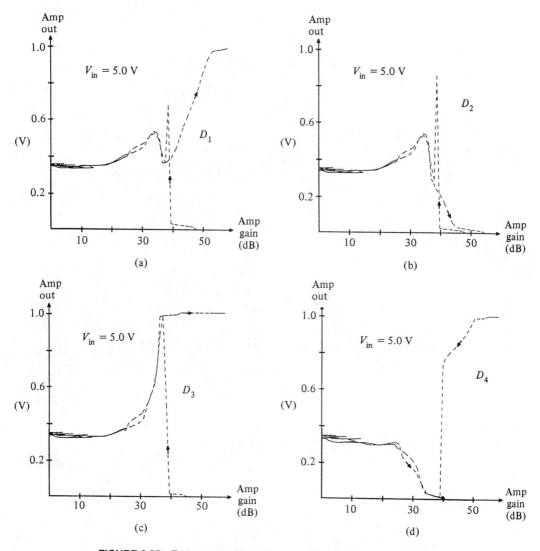

FIGURE 8.25 Trajectories of the A/D converter output versus the amplifier gain.
(a) Neuron D_1. (b) Neuron D_2. (c) Neuron D_3. (d) Neuron D_4. (e) Neuron D_5.
(f) Neuron D_6. (g) Neuron D_7. (h) Neuron D_8. The amplifier gain decreases from
60 dB to 0 dB, then increases back to 60 dB.

tronic annealing. Two analog input levels (0 V and 3.3 V) are applied. When
the amplifier gain is high and $V_{in} = 3.3$ V, the local minimum (1000) is reached.
By applying one annealing cycle, the global minimum (0011) is found as shown
in Figure 8.27(a). Other annealing styles have been investigated. With abruptly
increasing amplifier gain, the outputs could be (0011) and (0100). This phe-

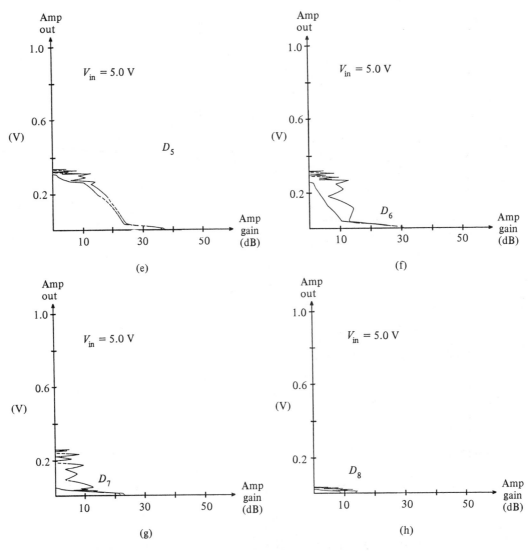

FIGURE 8.25   (contd.)

nomenon is known as the **quenching effect** in condensed-matter physics [Pollock, 1982]. When temperature of the heat bath is lowered instantaneously, particles in a solid are frozen into one of the metastable structures. This hardware experiment demonstrates that only gradual cooling is effective to reach the global minimum. The layout of an 8-bit neural-based A/D converter with hardware annealing is shown in Figure 8.28. It occupies an area of 0.48 mm^2 in the 2-μm CMOS technology.

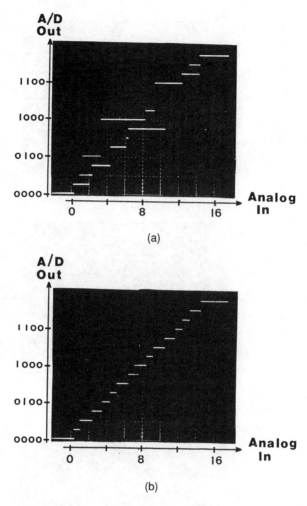

FIGURE 8.26 Transfer characteristics of a 4-bit Hopfield A/D converter. (a) Without hardware annealing. (b) With hardware annealing. The nonlinearities due to local minima were removed with hardware annealing.

GENERAL-PURPOSE NEURAL CHIPS

Most of the reported hardwares in the literature functioned as accelerators for software processing. The DARPA-supported Mark III and IV [Nielsen, 1988] general-purpose neural processors can work as peripheral devices to a VAX computer. It was reported that simulation speed of the integrated VAX-MARK machine can be improved by approximately 29 times than that of a VAX computer alone. The ANZA and Delta-1 printed-circuit boards are accelerators for IBM PC/ATs. They are composed of several VLSI chips which function as the CPU, mathematical co-

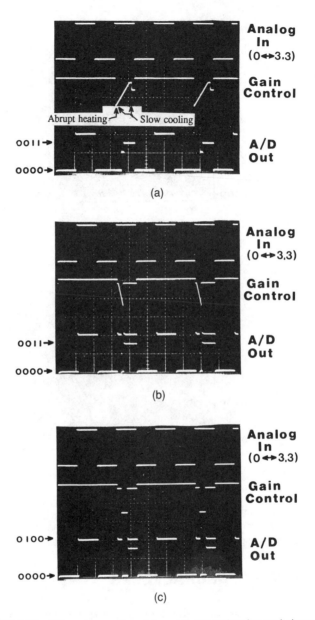

FIGURE 8.27 Different annealing styles. (a) Abrupt heating and slow cooling. (b) Slow heating and abrupt cooling. (c) Abrupt heating and abrupt cooling.

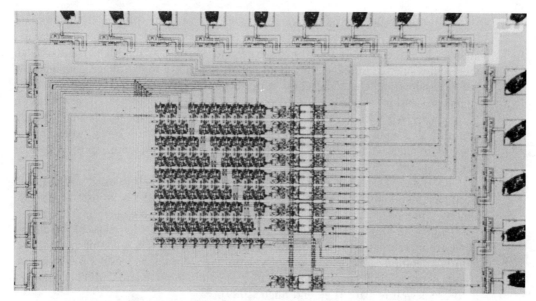

FIGURE 8.28 Die photo of an 8-bit Hopfield A/D converter with hardware annealing.

processor, and memories. These hardware accelerators basically solve difference equations of a neural network, instead of the original differential equations. This approximation using difference equations can lead to a fatal failure caused by numerical error, when the system matrix becomes very stiff [Lee and Sheu, 1990].

Example 8.7

Calculate the stiffness of Hopfield neural-based A/D converters with 4-bit, 6-bit, and 8-bit conversion accuracy.

Solution   The eigenvalues of Hopfield A/D converters are

4-bit case: -1.378, -6.482, -33.36, $+41.22$

6-bit case: -1.219, -5.191, -22.64, -104.6, -534.9, $+668.6$

8-bit case: -1.153, -4.760, -19.76, -83.40, -362.9, -1675, -8560, $+10,707$

Thus, the stiffness defined by the maximum ratio of absolute values of eigenvalues is 29.90 for 4-bit, 548.1 for 6-bit, and 9281 for 8-bit. As the stiffness increases exponentially with the number of conversion bits, it is very difficult to obtain the solutions from difference equations.   ∎

The fundamental limitation of VLSI implementation for general-purpose neural networks is the large number of interconnections and synapses. Since the number of synapses increases quadratically with that of neurons, silicon area is mainly occupied by the synapse cells and the interconnection channels.

Several research projects address the issues of novel placement and routing of neuron and synapse cells. One such activity is to design a silicon retina and cochlea in Caltech [Mead, 1989; Lazzaro and Mead, 1989]. MOS transistors in these chips operate in the subthreshold region to achieve high voltage gain and low power dissipation. The VLSI chips perform the sensory functions with preliminary signal processing similar to human organs. These electronic neural networks can be characterized with high locality, one neuron being tied to just the neighboring neurons. The input signals are processed locally and gradually spread to the whole network in a decayed format. The high-locality property is seldom explored in other neural networks.

One neural network designed for signal-processing purposes is a VLSI chip from Bell Laboratories [Graf et al., 1986]. The chip has 256 neurons and 100,000 synapses precoded during the fabrication stage. The total chip size is 5700 μm $\times$ 5700 μm in 2.5-μm CMOS technology. The weightings of synapses, which are made from amorphous Si, are defined by electron beams. The main purpose of this chip is to compress the bandwidth of video images for telephone-line transmission. Another way to obtain the high-resistivity material in the standard CMOS technology is to use a well resistor [Lee and Sheu, 1989].

When an MOS transistor operates in the triode region with strong surface inversion, the drain current can be expressed as

$$I_{DS} = \mu C_{ox} \frac{W}{L} \left((V_{GS} - V_{th})V_{DS} - \frac{V_{DS}^2}{2} \right) \tag{8-84}$$

if the channel-length modulation effect is neglected. When $V_{DS} \approx 0$, the equivalent conductance is

$$\frac{I_{DS}}{V_{DS}} \approx \mu C_{ox} \frac{W}{L}(V_{GS} - V_{th}) \tag{8-85}$$

However, the condition $V_{DS} \approx 0$ cannot be valid for a real circuit application. Figure 8.29 shows that the nonlinear conductance of a single MOS transistor can be used at special applications when only inhibitory and excitatory synapses are required [Graf et al., 1988]. The on/off switch-control data stored in the on-chip memory determine the fixed synapse weight for a content-addressable memory. The chip has 54 neurons and 2916 synapses and occupies 6700 μm $\times$ 6700 μm area in a 2.5-μm CMOS technology.

A simple way to eliminate the nonlinearity is to use both an n-channel transistor and a p-channel transistor as shown in Figure 8.30. Assuming that $V_1 > V_2$ and the transistors operate in the triode region, the drain currents are

$$I_{DSn} = \mu_n C_{oxn} \left(\frac{W}{L}\right)_n \left((V_{c1} - V_2 - V_{thn})(V_1 - V_2) - \frac{1}{2}(V_1 - V_2)^2 \right) \tag{8-86}$$

and

$$I_{DSp} = \mu_p C_{oxp} \left(\frac{W}{L}\right)_p \left((V_1 - V_{c2} + V_{thp})(V_1 - V_2) - \frac{1}{2}(V_1 - V_2)^2 \right) \tag{8-87}$$

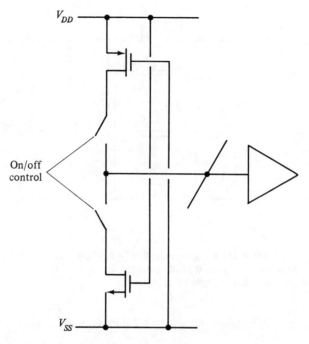

FIGURE 8.29   Circuit schematic of a fixed synapse weighting with on/off control.

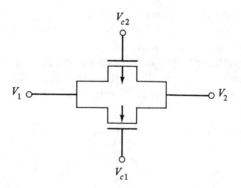

FIGURE 8.30   Circuit schematic of a CMOS transmission gate.

Here, I_{DSn} is the drain current of the n-channel transistor and I_{DSp} is that of the p-channel transistor. With the assumption of perfect matches such that $V_{thn} = -V_{thp}$, $\mu_n C_{oxn}(W/L)_n = \mu_p C_{ox}(W/L)_p (\equiv \beta)$, and $V_{c1} = -V_{c2}$, summation of the currents gives

$$I \equiv I_{DSn} + I_{DSp} = 2\beta(V_1 - V_2)V_{c1} \qquad (8\text{-}88)$$

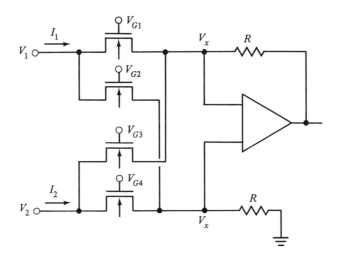

FIGURE 8.31 Circuit schematic of a synthesized resistance and a neuron. Four transistors are used to compensate the nonlinearity resulting from the channel resistance of a single MOS transistor.

Thus, the conductance T_{eq} of the CMOS switch becomes

$$T_{eq} \equiv \frac{I}{V_1 - V_2} = 2\beta V_{c1} \qquad (8\text{-}89)$$

The ideal linear conductance is seldom obtained, owing to the mismatches between two transistors. Especially, the threshold voltages are never perfectly matched, owing to the substrate bias effect.

The synthesized resistance can be obtained with the circuits originally developed for continuous-time filters [Ismail et al., 1988]. Figure 8.31 shows one such circuitry to eliminate the nonlinearity of an MOS transistor. The drain currents are

$$I_{DS1} = \mu C_{ox} \frac{W}{L} \left((V_{G1} - V_{th})(V_1 - V_x) - \frac{(V_1 - V_x)^2}{2} \right) \qquad (8\text{-}90)$$

$$I_{DS2} = \mu C_{ox} \frac{W}{L} \left((V_{G2} - V_{th})(V_1 - V_x) - \frac{(V_1 - V_x)^2}{2} \right) \qquad (8\text{-}91)$$

$$I_{DS3} = \mu C_{ox} \frac{W}{L} \left((V_{G3} - V_{th})(V_2 - V_x) - \frac{(V_1 - V_x)^2}{2} \right) \qquad (8\text{-}92)$$

and

$$I_{DS4} = \mu C_{ox} \frac{W}{L} \left((V_{G4} - V_{th})(V_2 - V_x) - \frac{(V_1 - V_x)^2}{2} \right) \qquad (8\text{-}93)$$

Here, V_x is a constant voltage. The current difference $I_1 - I_2$ is given as

$$I_1 - I_2 \equiv (I_{DS1} + I_{DS3}) - (I_{DS2} + I_{DS4})$$

$$= \mu C_{ox} \frac{W}{L} ((V_{G1} - V_{G2})V_1 + (V_{G3} - V_{G4})V_2$$

$$- (V_{G1} - V_{G2} + V_{G3} - V_{G4})V_x) \qquad (8\text{-}94)$$

With the condition that $V_{G1} + V_{G3} = V_{G2} + V_4$, the last term can be cancelled out. By setting $V_{G1} = V_{G4} = -V_{G2} = -V_{G3} (\equiv V_{sw})$, the equivalent conductance is

$$T_{eq} \equiv \frac{I_1 - I_2}{V_1 - V_2} = 2\mu C_{ox} \frac{W}{L} V_{sw} \qquad (8\text{-}95)$$

By connecting the V_x's to the input terminals of an operational amplifier, the linear conductance can be obtained.

Example 8.8

Design a 10^6-Ω resistor using both well diffusion and the synthesized-resistance structures. Compare the silicon area. The design parameters are as follows:

sheet resistance of well diffusion $= 2$ kΩ

minimum width/spacing for well diffusion $= 10$ μm

minimum width/spacing for transistors $= 2$ μm

$\mu_n C_{ox} = 50 \mu A/V^2$

Assume that the control voltage for the synthesized resistor is 5 V.

Solution In case of the well-diffused resistor, $10^6/2.0 \times 10^3 = 500$ squares are required. The resistor length is 5000 μm and the width is 10 μm. It occupies a silicon area of 5×10^4 μm^2.

In the synthesized-resistance case,

$$\frac{W}{L} = \frac{1}{10^6 \times \mu_n C_{ox} \times 5} = \frac{1}{200}$$

A transistor with channel width of 2 μm and channel length of 400 μm can be used. It occupies a silicon area of $4 \times 800\mu m^2 = 3200\mu m^2$. The synthesized resistor can greatly reduce the silicon area. $\blacksquare$

For a general-purpose VLSI neural system, programmable synapses and amplifier gain are necessary. Programmable synapses are used in the network learning process as well as in the compensation of the device mismatches. Two different approaches can be used: the digital-circuitry approach and the analog-circuitry approach. Figure 8.32 shows a digitally programmable synapse. The synapse weights are controlled by switch on time and the RC time constant. The synapse weighting stored in the memory is converted into the switching pulse width. The input voltage is converted to current and summed up at the summing capacitor C_S. With the input-voltage swing of [0 V, V_{iH}], the equivalent conductance T_{eq} is

$$T_{eq} = \frac{T_{on}}{RC} V_{iH} \qquad (8\text{-}96)$$

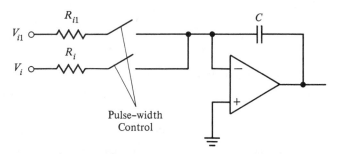

FIGURE 8.32 Circuit schematic of a switched-R synapse and neuron. By adjusting the pulse width, the charges stored in the feedback capacitor are controlled.

After each iteration, the summing capacitor should be reset. The synapse dynamic range and accuracy are totally dependent on the digital part. The digital part can be shared using the time-domain multiplexing technique.

Example 8.9

Estimate the dynamic range of the switched-R structure. Assume that $R = 10$ kΩ, $C_S = 10$ pF, power-supply voltage is $+5$ V, input voltage swing is 1 V, and the smallest pulse width is 50 nsec.

Solution   The summing voltage V_{sm} is given as

$$V_{sm} = \frac{V_{iH}}{C_S R} \times T_{sw}$$

where the maximum $T_{sw} = 50 \times 10^{-9} \times 2^n$. Here, n is the number of bits for pulse-width control. Since the maximum level of summing voltage V_{sm} is limited to the power-supply voltage, the maximum number of bits is decided by

$$n < \log_2 \left(\frac{5 \times RC_S}{V_{iH} \times 50 \times 10^{-9}} \right)$$

Therefore, $n = 3$. That is, the dynamic range is about 18 dB.   ∎

Another approach to use MOS transistors is to operate the transistors in the saturation region as shown in Figure 8.33. In the current steering circuit structure, the synapse weight is coded into current level and the current is switched by the differential pair. When the transistors operate in the saturation region, the output current I_{out} is given as

$$I_{\text{out}} = \frac{I_S + \Delta I}{2} \tag{8-97}$$

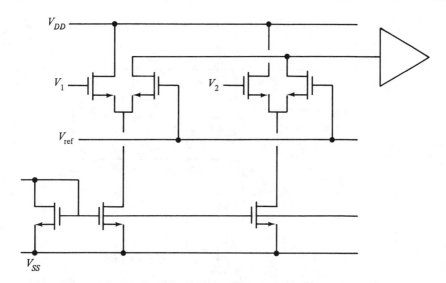

FIGURE 8.33 Current-steering synapse cell.

where

$$
\Delta I = \begin{cases}
\dfrac{\mu C_{ox}}{2} \dfrac{W}{L} \Delta V_i \sqrt{\dfrac{4I_S}{\mu C_{ox}(W/L)} - (\Delta V_i)^2} & \text{when } |\Delta V_i| \le V_{lmt} \\[3mm]
I_S & \text{when } \Delta V_i > V_{lmt} \\[2mm]
-I_S & \text{when } \Delta V_i < -V_{lmt}
\end{cases}
\tag{8-98}
$$

Here, $\Delta V_i \equiv V_1 - V_{ref}$ and $V_{lmt} = \sqrt{2I_S/\mu C_{ox}(W/L)}$. Since the synapse is nonlinear, this circuit structure cannot be used for the synapses of input layer such as T_{iS} of Hopfield neural-based A/D converters. However, this synapse can be used for the feedback components of Hopfield networks or for the hidden layers and the output layer. The synapse weights can be coded into device aspect ratios of the current mirror. A programmable synapse of limited dynamic range can be made by switching certain ratioed current mirrors [Mueller et al., 1989].

A fully programmable synapse with EEPROM cells is shown in Figure 8.34 [Holler, et al., 1989; Lee et al., ND]. The analog multiplier gives a fairly linear synapse weighting, which is decided by the device aspect ratios and the bias current. Since the EEPROM-injected charges at the floating gate can change threshold voltage of the transistor in the current mirror, bias currents of the analog multiplier are programmable. The output current I_{out} is given as

$$
\begin{aligned}
I_{out} &= I_{DS1} + I_{DS3} - (I_{DS2} + I_{DS4}) \\[2mm]
&= \frac{I_{S1} + \Delta I_1}{2} + \frac{I_{S2} - \Delta I_2}{2} - \frac{I_{S1} - \Delta I_1}{2} - \frac{I_{S2} + \Delta I_2}{2} \\[2mm]
&= \Delta I_1 - \Delta I_2
\end{aligned}
\tag{8-99}
$$

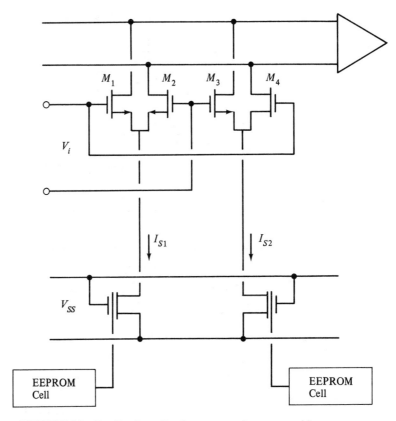

FIGURE 8.34   Circuit schematic of neurons and programmable synapses.

Here, ΔI_1 and ΔI_2 can be obtained from (8-98) with $I_S = I_{S1}$ and $I_S = I_{S2}$, respectively. Figure 8.35 shows I-V characteristics of the analog multiplier for various bias-current values. The equivalent conductance T_{eq} when $\Delta V_i \approx 0$ can be obtained as

$$T_{\text{eq}} = \sqrt{\mu C_{ox} \frac{W}{L} I_{S1}} - \sqrt{\mu C_{ox} \frac{W}{L} I_{S2}} \qquad (8\text{-}100)$$

However, voltage range V_{IR} for a linear conductance is limited by the smaller dynamic range of the two differential pairs in the following way:

$$V_{IR} = \sqrt{\frac{2\min(I_{S1}, I_{S2})}{\mu C_{ox} \dfrac{W}{L}}} \qquad (8\text{-}101)$$

Thus, the voltage range is dependent on the conductance value. For a proper input-voltage range, the device W/L ratio should be very small.

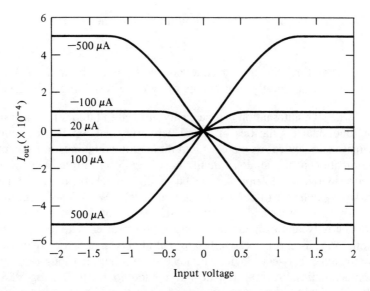

FIGURE 8.35 Simulated transfer characteristics of the synapse cell in Figure 8.34.

Example 8.10

If the neuron input voltage is $[-2 \text{ V}, 2 \text{ V}]$, power-supply voltages are ± 5 V, and the smallest programmed current difference is $1 \ \mu$A, design the device geometries for the differential pair and calculate the minimum and maximum conductance values. Assume that $\mu_n C_{ox} = 40 \mu\text{A}/\text{V}^2$.

Solution From (8-101),

$$2 = \sqrt{\frac{2 \times 10^{-6}}{40 \times 10^{-6} \times \dfrac{W}{L}}}$$

Therefore, $W/L = 1/80$. The smallest conductance T_L is

$$T_L = \sqrt{\frac{40 \times 10^{-6} \times 10^{-6}}{80}} \approx 1.414 \times 10^{-6} A/V$$

As the bias current increases, source terminal voltage of the differential pairs decreases. The lowest source voltage V_{SL} is given as

$$V_{SL} = -2 - \sqrt{\frac{I_S}{\mu C_{ox} \dfrac{W}{L}}}$$

$$\approx -2 - \sqrt{2 \times 10^6 \times I_S}$$

Since V_{SL} is -5, the maximum bias current I_{SH} is

$$I_{SH} \;=\; 4.5 \times 10^{-6} A$$

Therefore, the largest conductance T_H is approximately 3.0×10^{-6} mho. In this case, the dynamic range of synapse weighting is limited to 6.5 dB.   ∎

Design automation can be easily utilized to build VLSI neural circuits because of functional regularities in neural networks. Analog VLSI circuits in general are sensitive to device mismatches, circuit layout, and parasitic elements, so that design automation in the analog circuits is still quite primitive. However, components in neural networks do not have to be of high precision or fast switching, which are in strong contrast to conventional analog ICs. While each neuron performs simple analog processing, and the transmission speed of each synapse is very low, the rich connectivity among neurons provides powerful computational capability. In addition, the self-learning capability in neural networks can compensate not only initial mismatches between devices in a VLSI chip but also long-term drift of the device characteristics. Several new design methodologies for analog VLSI circuits, which include analog arrays, analog standard cells, parameterized cells, programmable cells, and self-reconstructive cells, are available in mixed analog-digital IC design community. Since neural networks have a high degree of modularity consisting of a small number of neuron types and synapse types, the analog standard-cell approach is very suitable to build the VLSI neural circuits.

REFERENCES

Aarts, E. H. L., and van Laarhoven, P. J. M., "A New Polynomial-time Cooling Schedule," *Proc. IEEE Int. Conf. on Computer-Aided Design*, 206–208, November 1985.

Geman, S., and Geman, D., "Stochastic Relaxation, Gibbs Distributions, and the Bayesian Restoration of Images," *IEEE Trans. on Pattern Analysis and Machine Intelligence*, vol. PAMI-6, no. 6, 721–741, November 1984.

Graf, H. P., and deVegvar, P., "A CMOS Implementation of a Neural Network Model", *Proceedings of the 1987 Stanford Conference*, 351–362, The MIT Press, Cambridge, MA.

Graf, H. P., Jackel, L. D., Howard, R. E., Straughn, B., Denker, J. S., Hubbard, W., Tennant, D. M., and Schwartz, D., "VLSI Implementation of a Neural Network Memory with Several Hundreds of Neurons," *AIP Conf. Proc. 151*, 182–187, 1986.

Graf, H. P., Jackel, L. D., and Hubbard, W. E., "VLSI Implementation of a Neural Network Model," *IEEE Computer*, vol. 21, no. 3, 41–49, March 1988.

Gray, P. R., and Meyer, R. G., *Analysis and Design of Analog Integrated Circuits*, 2nd ed., Wiley, New York, 1984.

Holler, M., Tam, S., Castro, H., Benson, R., "An Electrically Trainable Artificial Neural Network (ETANN) with 10240 'Float Gate' Synapses," *Inter. Joint Conf. on Neural Networks*, vol. 2, 191–196, June 1989.

Hopfield, J. J., "Neurons with Graded Response Have Collective Computational Properties Like Those of Two-state Neurons," *Proc. Natl. Acad. Sci. U.S.A.*, vol. 81, 3088–3092, May 1984.

Howard, R. E., Schwartz, D. B., Denker, J. S., Epworth, R. W., Graf, H. P., Hubbard, W. E., Jackel, L. D., Straughn, B. L., and Tennant, D. M., "An Associative Memory Based on an Electronic Neural Network Architecture," *IEEE Trans. on Electron Devices*, vol. ED-34, no. 7, 1553–1556, July 1987.

Ismail, M., Smith, S. V., and Beale, R. G., "A New MOSFET-C Universal Filter Structure for VLSI," *IEEE Jour. Solid-State Circuits*, vol. SC-23, 183–194, February 1988.

Kirkpatrick, S., Gelatt, C. D., Jr., and Vecchi, M. P., "Optimization by Simulated Annealing," *Science*, vol. 220, no. 4598, 671–680, May 1983.

Lazzaro, J., and Mead, C., "Circuit Models of Sensory Transduction in the Cochlea," *Analog VLSI Implementation of Neural Systems*, Kluwer Acad. Pub., 85–102, 1989.

Lee, B. W., and Sheu, B. J., "An Investigation on Local Minima of Hopfield Network for Optimization Circuits," *IEEE Inter. Conf. on Neural Networks*, vol. 1, 45–51, July 1988.

Lee, B. W., and Sheu, B. J., "Design of a Neural-based A/D Converter Using Modified Hopfield Network," *IEEE J. of Solid-State Circuits*, vol. SC-24, no. 4, 1129–1135, August 1989.

Lee, B. W., and Sheu, B. J., "Combinatorial Optimization Using Competitive-Hopfield Neural Networks," *1990 Inter. Joint Conf. on Neural Networks*, Washington DC, January 1990.

Lee, B. W., Yang, H., and Sheu, B. J., "Electrically Programmable Synapses for General-purpose VLSI Neural Systems," *IEEE Trans. on Circuits and Systems*, to be published.

Lippman, R. P., "An Introduction to Computing with Neural Nets," *IEEE ASSP Magazine*, 4–22, April 1987.

Mead, C. A., *Analog VLSI and Neural Systems*, Addison-Wesley, Reading, MA, 1989.

Mueller, P., Spiegel, J. V. D., Blackman, D., Chiu, T., Clare, T., Donham, C., Hsieh, T. P., and Loinaz, M., "Design and Fabrication of VLSI Components for a General Purpose Analog Neural Computer," *Analog VLSI Implementation of Neural Systems*, Kluwer Acad. Pub., 135–169, 1989.

Nielsen, R. H., "Neural-computing: Picking the Human Brain," *IEEE Spectrum*, vol. 25, no. 3, 36–41, March 1988.

Pollock, D. D., *Physical Properties of Materials for Engineers*, CRC Press, 14–18, 1982.

Quarles, T., Newton, A. R., Pederson, D. O., and Sangiovanni-Vincentelli, A., *SPICE3B1 User's Guide*, Department of Electrical Engineering and Computer Sciences, University of California, Berkeley, January 1987.

Rumelhart, D. E., McClelland, J. L., and the PDP Research Group, *Parallel Distributed Processing*, vol. 1, The M.I.T. Press, Cambridge, MA, 282–317, 1986.

Rutenbar, R. A., "Simulated Annealing Algorithms: An Overview," *IEEE Circuits and Devices Magazine*, vol. 5, no. 1, 19–26, January 1989.

Sage, J. P., Thompson, K., and Whithers, R. S., "An Artificial Neural Network Integrated Circuit Based on MNOS/CCD Principles," *Proc. Conf. Neural Networks for Computing*, 1986, J. S. Denker (ed.), American Institute of Physics Conf. Proc. 151, 381–385.

Sheu, B. J., Hsu, W., and Ko, P. K., "An MOS Transistor Charge Model for VLSI Design," *IEEE Trans. on Computer-Aided Design*, vol. 7, no. 4, 520–527, April 1988.

Smith, G. D., *Numerical Solution of Partial Differential Equations: Finite Difference Methods*, Oxford University Press, New York, 60–63, 1985.

Tank, D. W., and Hopfield, J. J., "Simple 'Neural' Optimization Networks: An A/D Converter, Signal Decision Circuit, and a Linear Programming Circuit," *IEEE Trans. on Circuits and Systems*, vol. CAS-33, no. 5, 533–541, May 1986.

Tomovich, C., "MOSIS-A Gateway to Silicon," *IEEE Circuits and Devices Magazine*, vol. 4, no. 2, 22–23, March 1988.

Tsividis, Y. P., "Analog MOS Integrated Circuits—Certain New Ideas, Trends, and Obstacles," *IEEE J. Solid-State Circuits*, vol. SC-22, no. 3, 317–321, June 1987.

van Laarhoven, P. J. M., and Aarts, E. H. L., *Simulated Annealing: Theory and Applications*, D. Reidel Publishing Co., Hingham, MA, 1987.

Yee, Y. S., Terman, L. M., and Heller, L. G., "A 1 mV MOS Comparator," *IEEE J. Solid-State Circuits*, vol. SC-13, no. 3, 294–298, June 1978.

PROBLEMS

8.1. Assume that the conductances and voltage ranges are equal to those of the original Hopfield A/D converter. Conduct circuit simulation of a 3-bit Hopfield neural-based A/D converter with the following conditions.

  (a) Amplifier gain is 1000.

  (b) Amplifier gain is 10.

  (c) The LSB amplifier has input offset voltage of 0.1 V.

8.2. If a 6-bit A/D converter is to be constructed using the Hopfield network, draw the circuit schematic with resistor values.

  (a) Assume that the analog voltage range to be digitized is −0.5 V to 63.5 V, the output range for the inverting amplifier is (0 V, −1 V), and the reference voltage is −1 V.

  (b) Assume that the analog voltage range to be digitized is 0 V to 10 V, the output range for the inverting amplifier is (0 V, −5 V), and the reference voltage is −1 V.

  (c) Calculate the correction resistors and tabulate the correction logic.

8.3. Conduct circuit simulation of a 4-bit Hopfield neural-based A/D converter in SPICE when the analog input voltage is 5.7 V and there are three different initial conditions. The conductances and voltage ranges are assumed to be the same as those of the original Hopfield A/D converter. The amplifier can be modeled with dependent sources and switches (MOS transistors in SPICE2 or switches in SPICE3). The capacitances are 2.0 pF, and the unit resistance is 500 kΩ.

  (a) The initial input voltages of the amplifiers are −0.1, −0.1, −0.1, −0.1 volt from the MSB to the LSB.

  (b) The initial input voltages of the amplifiers are 0.1, −0.1, −0.1, −0.1 volt from the MSB to the LSB.

(c) The initial input voltages of the amplifiers are $-0.1, -0.1, 0.1, 0.1$ volt from the MSB to the LSB.

(d) Compare the time-domain behaviors of the above three cases.

8.4. A Hopfield network can be used as a number-basis converter. Design a number converter which converts an analog signal into $a + b(\frac{\pi}{4})$ basis. The objective function is

$$\left(x - a - b\left(\frac{\pi}{4}\right) \right)^2$$

where x is the analog input, $a = \sum_{i=0}^{3} 2^i V_{ia}$, and $b = \sum_{i=0}^{1} 2^i V_{ib}$. Draw the circuit schematic with resistor values.

8.5. When the LSB amplifier in the 4-bit Hopfield A/D converter has an input offset voltage of $+0.1$ V, describe the effects on the input-output transfer curve.

8.6. Obtain the eigenvalues of the 4-bit Hopfield A/D converter with normalized conductances. Assume that all neurons operate in the high-gain region.

(a) Obtain the minimum amplifier gain which makes the A/D outputs logical values.

(b) Compare with the amplifier gain from (8-78).

8.7. Calculate the minimum amplifier gain for proper operation of the Hopfield neural-based A/D converter with original conductances.

(a) 4-bit A/D converter.

(b) 6-bit A/D converter.

(c) 8-bit A/D converter.

(d) Discuss the amplifier gain dependence as the number of conversion bits increases.

8.8. This problem is to compare the solutions of differential equations and difference equations. Construct a 4-bit Hopfield neural-based A/D converter. Assume that the analog input voltage is 5.6 V.

(a) Obtain the converted digital output using SPICE circuit simulator.

(b) Obtain the digital output using the following difference equations.

STEP 1. Calculate input voltages

$$u_i^{n+1} = u_i^n - \alpha \left(\sum_{j \neq i, j=1}^{6} T_{ij} V_j + \sum_{j=1}^{N} T_{iR} V_R + T_{iS} V_S \right)$$

where $T_{ij} = 2^{j-1}$, $T_{iR} = 2^{i-2}$, $T_{iS} = 1$, and $V_R = -1$ V. Here, α includes time constant $(1/C_i T_i)$ and integration time step.

STEP 2. Update the outputs

$$V_i^{n+1} = -\frac{1 + \tanh\left(\frac{u_i^{n+1}}{U_o}\right)}{2}$$

where U_o is assumed to be 0.05.

STEP 3. Check whether the outputs are changed or not.

- If changed, go to Step 1.
- If not changed, terminate.
- Compute the solutions for three different α values of 10^{-6}, 10^{-5}, and 10^{-4}.

(c) Compare the results from the differential method and the difference method in terms of result accuracy and computational time.

PHOTONIC IMPLEMENTATIONS OF NEURAL NETWORKS

B. Keith Jenkins
Signal and Image Processing Institute
Department of Electrical Engineering–Systems
University of Southern California

Armand R. Tanguay, Jr.
Signal and Image Processing Institute
Department of Electrical Engineering–Electrophysics
University of Southern California

TOWARD THE DEVELOPMENT OF A NEURAL-NETWORK IMPLEMENTATION TECHNOLOGY

As described in other chapters of this book, neural networks provide a different approach to solving problems as compared with more conventional algorithmic techniques, and have a wide range of potential applications. In some of these application domains the simulation performance of neural networks is comparable to that of more conventional algorithmic approaches. In many application domains, however, a realistic (and therefore large-scale) problem may overwhelm the conventional approach, in that it may be too computation intensive to be implemented on a sequential digital computer, and may not parallelize sufficiently well (if at all) for efficient computation on a parallel digital machine. On the other hand, because a neural-network algorithm is inherently parallel, it immediately suggests a parallel architecture, which may in turn be implemented using either analog or digital hardware. And for the case of large-scale problems, analog hardware will typically provide a much more efficient neural implementation than digital hardware.

In the previous chapter, fully electronic (primarily VLSI-based) neural networks were described in which the primary functionality of both the neuron units and the weighted (synaptic) interconnection matrix is incorporated on a planar microelectronic chip. An important advantage of the integrated-circuit approach to neural-network implementation is the capability for near-term technology insertion, with leverage provided by a well-established technology base characterized by a fully developed computer-aided design and computer-aided manufacturing (CAD/CAM) device and circuit repertoire. An equally important limitation is the difficulty in scaling up neural chips to incorporate large numbers of neuron units in fully (or near fully) interconnected architectures. This limitation derives from the limited pinout, off-chip communication bandwidth, and on-chip interconnection density available in both current generation and projected chip designs.

In this chapter, we consider the utilization of optical (free-space) interconnection techniques in conjunction with photonic switching and modulating devices to expand the number of neuron units and complexity of interconnection, by using the off-chip (third) dimension for synaptic communication. As we shall see, the merging of optical and photonic devices with appropriately matched electronic circuitry can provide novel features such as fully parallel weight updates and modular scalability, as well as both short- and long-term synaptic plasticity.

Many approaches to the incorporation of photonic and optical technology in the implementation of neural networks are currently being pursued in the research community. The intent of this chapter is not to present a review of these various approaches, the details of which can be obtained from several of the references suggested as further reading at the end of this chapter. Instead, our focus herein is directed toward a description of key photonic devices and techniques based on fundamental optical phenomena, as well as toward a unique and generalizable approach to their potential use in the implementation of large-scale, highly parallel neural-network architectures. The unusual nature of some of these techniques has interesting implications for the design of naturally mapped architectures and associated learning/computing algorithms. We will address a number of these unique features in the context of a description of the basic optical phenomena that can be used to advantage, and of the array of photonic devices that comprise the system designer's palette. Because the incorporation of optical and photonic hardware casts the subject of neural-network implementations in a somewhat unfamiliar light, we first discuss a set of desirable and requisite characteristics for neural-network implementation technologies.

An important feature of any implementation technology is that of generality: a "building-block" approach. The growth and synthesis of material structures, and their incorporation into devices, must be well characterized, understood, and repeatable, for a *small number* of specific material combinations and device structures. These devices are then assembled into circuits or architectures for the implementation of specific computational models. This provides leverage in two ways: (1) the small number of useful and well understood components are used repeatedly in different structures for different applications, and (2) architecture- and system-level designers need not be experts in the properties of the material and device structures used to configure the components, saving many man-hours in the design of computational systems over a completely custom approach. Such a purely custom approach could preclude the widespread use of these architectures and systems, as has been characteristic, for example, of optical information-processing and optical signal-processing systems over the past two decades.

It is not only important for the implementation *technology* to be of a building-block nature, but also for the *models* underlying the computational architectures to support such an approach, and in fact to be of a building-block nature themselves. Ideally the models would comprise a set of common components and operations at the functional level, such as specific types of neuron units, weighted interconnections, weight updates, and comparisons with desired target values. Then the mapping from model and functional architecture to hardware architecture, layout, and implementation can proceed efficiently as well. This building-block approach at both the model and hardware levels has certainly been characteristic of the development of digital electronics, and has been largely responsible for its success.

Assuming that appropriate neural-network models and a corresponding technology base can be merged within a compatible building-block approach, neural-network systems potentially provide a unique capability for large-scale *analog, nonlinear* computation. As such, the neural-network paradigm potentially alleviates two critical bottlenecks that have impeded the widespread implementation of large-scale analog, nonlinear computing systems based on nonneural architectures: the lack of appropriate generic hardware components and of the sufficiently leveraged manpower required for their economical design and manufacture, as well as difficulty in establishing efficient techniques for mapping from the application and model domain onto compatible hardware. With regard to the former bottleneck, neural-network architectures are generally forgiving with respect to device nonuniformities and imperfections, creating much-needed latitude for the device designer. With regard to the latter bottleneck, the neural-network paradigm inherently provides a mapping from the problem domain onto a highly parallel architecture, which immediately yields a starting point for its layout in analog hardware.

In the case of photonics for neural-network applications, the hardware technology is being developed *simultaneously* with the neural computation model(s). This implies at least two things. First, it is crucial to retain *flexibility* in the functionality of each component, so that as the neural computation models evolve, the hardware can evolve along with it. The development of an entirely new technology base typically takes at least a decade; such a delay between model development and hardware realization is generally unacceptable. Thus, the generic technology base *must* provide sufficient flexibility. Second, not only should the neural computation model steer the technology development, but the reverse can, and indeed *must*, also occur. This assures a mutual compatibility in outcome.

The basic requisite functions for a neural-network technology base appear to be: neuron unit response, weighted interconnections (fixed and variable), input/output, learning computation and weight update, and duplication capability (i.e., the capability of making a copy of a network structure). In addition, other features are desirable, such as higher-order connection capability. The neuron unit response, at the most common and basic level, is a sum-of-inputs followed by a monotonic nonlinearity. The nonlinearity should have the flexibility of providing different amounts of gain; for example, it is useful to have a high gain to implement a binary threshold, and a low gain to implement a nearly linear response. The neuron unit should be bipolar in that it permits both positive and negative inputs, so that inhibitory and excitatory connections can be realized. This we consider to be the minimal requisite functionality of a neuron unit. In addition, a very desirable feature is the capability for bipolar outputs. Note that biologically this is not necessarily the case, but useful neural computation models will likely deviate substantially from biological reality and may require this capability. Other capabilities are also desirable, such as leaky integrator effects [Mead, 1989] and more complex behavior such as that required in shunting networks [Carpenter, 1987].

Each weighted interconnection must store a learned or initialized value, and perform a multiplication operation on the signals passing through. An analog multiplication is generally much more efficient than a digital one for reasons of speed and device area or volume. For this reason, it is worth some effort to provide analog storage for the weights. Note that the very large number of weights used in many networks implies that minimization of the incorporated hardware complexity of the requisite storage and multiplication operations is crucial for physical realizability. Input/output is often ignored at the higher levels, but can critically affect the physical architecture and can be a major factor in determining the overall throughput. The input/output function includes the input of signals, the output of results, and the input of weights if necessary.

It is important at the outset to distinguish among systems that have fixed weights; systems that have programmable weights (that are externally computed but loaded into the network); and systems that have full learning capability, in which the learning algorithm is implemented as part of the parallel system. The associated hardware complexity can be quite different in each of these cases. Finally, duplication capability is useful, for example, for replicating a prelearned network when multiple copies of the network are to be produced and subsequently used with fixed connections. Probing the weight values in a hardware implementation may at first sound straightforward, but implementing very large numbers of weights in a small volume can in some cases preclude such capability.

Applications of hardware implementations of neural networks could include sensor signal processing and fusion, pattern recognition, associative memory, and robotic control. These applications imply a wide range of hardware requirements. For example, most vision processing is characterized by moderately large numbers of neuron units, with small to moderate connectivity and primarily local interconnections. Associative memory, on the other hand, typically requires a very high connectivity.

Semiconductor-based VLSI technology has proven to be very capable for the implementation of most, if not all, of the above functions. It also has the capability for integration of control circuitry and/or arbitrary digital or logical operations on the same chip as the neural processing circuitry. However, an important issue in neural implementations is that of *scalability*, since many neural-network applications are likely to require very large numbers of neuron units and connections. As pointed out above, it is primarily the consideration of scalability that leads us to the conclusion that purely electronic VLSI circuits will work well for certain applications, but can benefit greatly from the incorporation of photonics for other applications.

Two important considerations in VLSI implementations are area complexity and pinout requirements. A fully connected network of N neuron units requires area $O(N^2)$. One can think of this as having only a single linear dimension available for the neuron units themselves, in order to leave room for the connections. This, of course, limits the size of fully connected networks that can be accommodated on a single chip. For example, chips have been fabricated with 54 neuron units and 2916 ternary (three-level) synapses, and it is estimated that approximately 700 neurons, fully connected with (10^5 to 10^6) similar synapses, could be implemented on a CMOS chip using 0.5 μm design rules [Jackel, 1988]. Learning capability with analog synapses may require substantially more area per synapse. On the other hand, networks with low connectivity and only local connections between neuron units permit a much larger number of neuron units to be implemented on a chip. For example, the silicon retina of Mead et al. comprises a 48 $\times$ 48 array of neuron-like units, each connected to its 6 nearest neighbors on a hexagonal grid [Mead, 1988]. A much larger number of neuron units, of order 10^5, could be implemented with such a locally connected array, since the neuron units and the connections each require area only $O(N)$. So we see that a critical limiting factor in the VLSI implementation of neural networks is the area required for on-chip interconnections, and that the area required for neuron units is relatively inconsequential.

The number of pinouts that can be provided on a chip is proportional to its linear dimension, not to its area. This degree of pinout capacity is well matched to fully connected networks in which the weights do not need to be input or output frequently, and to locally connected networks of low to moderate bandwidth. An example of the latter is a vision network that operates at video frame rates; in this case the signal can be easily time multiplexed onto a relatively small number of lines for communication onto and off the chip.

On the other hand, other application areas will require a higher input/output (I/O) bandwidth and/or a large number of neuron units with high connectivity. For example, if the weights are to be fed onto and off a chip frequently, substantial multiplexing would be required for reasonably large networks (e.g., up to 200 pinouts can generally be accommodated, but as described above, as many as 10^5 to 10^6 synaptic weights can be incorporated on the chip). Wafer scale integration with bump-bonding techniques can help by providing large, multiwafer structures, but the number of I/O lines is still likely to be modest due to practical and physical constraints. So we see that a second critical limiting factor in the VLSI (and wafer scale integration) implementation of neural networks is the number of I/O lines that can be practically incorporated. Neural applications utilizing large fully connected networks such as associative memory would benefit greatly from implementations of 10^5 to 10^6 fully connected neuron units, implying the need for 10^{10} to 10^{12} synaptic weights. In addition, the intermediate realm of large networks with partial but moderate-to-large connectivity will likely also prove beneficial to a wide range of applications.

In this chapter, we discuss a variety of issues that impact the development of photonic technology as applied to hardware implementations of neural networks with enhanced capabilities. Photonics has the potential for the implementation of networks with large numbers of neurons (10^5 to 10^6) and high connectivity (approximately 10^{10} analog-weighted interconnections) in one "module." The approach taken here is to use electronics to implement the internal function of each neuron unit, and to use optics to implement the connections, weights, and I/O. With this technique most of the area of a two-dimensional (2-D) "chip" can be used to implement the neuron units themselves, and optical free-space propagation and volume holograms can be used to implement the interconnections. Thus the interconnections actually occupy a three-dimensional (3-D) *volume*, which improves scalability dramatically.

The next section of this chapter describes the fundamental optical principles and key photonic technology concepts that are needed for neural-network implementations, and covers photonic analog arithmetic, switching, interconnections, sources, and detectors. Architectural considerations are discussed in the subsequent section, including the use of volume interconnections, signal representation, and desired architectural features. The next section then presents a photonic implementation strategy that satisfies most of the desired criteria. In the two concluding sections we investigate the ultimate limitations of photonic implementations of neural networks, and consider the future of such implementations.

FUNDAMENTAL PRINCIPLES OF PHOTONIC TECHNOLOGY

In order to effectively appreciate the potential advantages as well as the limitations of extending the VLSI (electronic) repertoire to include photonic components and optically inspired functionality, we will first identify and then explain a few truly fundamental principles of the optical and photonic technologies on which such hybrid neural-network implementations are based. In this section, therefore, we discuss the basic features of optical analog computation with both coherent and incoherent illumination sources, photonic switching devices and their various neuron-like functions, the characteristics of photonic interconnections that are essential to the implementation of synapse-like interneuron wiring, and the principal features of sources (photonic power supplies) and detectors (photonic-to-electronic signal converters).

Optical Analog Computation

At the present time, most proposed photonic implementations of neural networks are based on analog operations, both in the representation of neuron outputs and in the incorporation of interconnection weights. This emphasis of *analog* computation over perhaps more familiar *digital* computation derives principally from several distinct advantages that accrue to analog optical systems designed to handle the switching and interconnection of very large numbers of inputs and outputs at each circuit node (neuron unit). These advantages include a significant reduction in the number of switching components required to sum multiple inputs [Abu-Mostafa, 1989], an increase in the degree of fan-in and fan-out allowable from each circuit node, the elimination of analog-to-digital and digital-to-analog converters, a significant decrease in signal routing and interconnection complexity, the potential utilization of natural physical phenomena within certain photonic devices to accomplish difficult computational functions directly, and the possibility of higher computational throughput per unit dissipated energy in operations characterized by high computational complexity. Additionally, two notable disadvantages of analog systems, error accumulation and lack of precision in representation, may prove to be relatively unimportant in the neural-network environment, due in part to the self-organizing and error-correcting nature of many neural learning algorithms [von der Malsburg, 1987]. We will return to a number of these issues throughout the remainder of this chapter.

The computational operations necessary for the implementation of a wide range of neural and neural-like networks are surprisingly simple, consisting primarily of addition, subtraction, multiplication, and nonlinear thresholding. The operation of addition usually must be performed over a very large number of inputs at a given neuron unit, representing weighted excitatory signals from other interconnected neuron units; subtraction is utilized to differentiate excitatory inputs from inhibitory inputs to a given neuron unit, as is common, for example, in models of the visual process and of associative memories. Multiplication is necessary for the provision of linear interconnections with signal-independent weights, which in turn store learned (or preprogrammed) information, and hence form an important constituent of the neural paradigm. Finally, nonlinear thresholding operations are performed in order to provide the appropriate transfer function between the neuron activation potential (sum of all inputs, both positive and negative, to a given neuron unit), and the output each neuron unit generates in response. It is this nonlinearity in particular that gives multilayer neural networks their computational power and allows recurrent networks to iteratively approach one of several stable states of the system. The detailed nature of the nonlinearity itself can affect a number of critical system properties, including the number of iterations (or equivalently the time) required to achieve steady state, and the stability of the network in the presence of noise, inaccuracy, and nonuniformities among both the neuron units and the interconnections. In some envisioned neural-network implementations, it is also important to be able to alter the nature of the nonlinear thresholding function dynamically during the computational phase of operation.

In addition to these elementary operations (and combinations thereof), it is necessary to accommodate operationally for both the learning function (which includes input-dependent interconnection weight updates) and the computational function (which in general requires iterative feedback and the implementation of nonlinear thresholding, usually with fixed interconnection weights). The only additional fundamental operation required by these features, that of input-dependent interconnection weight updates, can usually be reduced to at most a combination or sequence of the previously described fundamental operations of addition, subtraction, multiplication, and nonlinear thresholding. It is important to note, however, that in this case the operations pertain directly to the implementation of interconnection weights, rather than to functions performed by the neuron units; hence, the physical processes involved may in fact be considerably different in nature, and thus subject to a quite different set of constraints. This differentiation between the two different "types" of basic operations (those pertaining to the neuron units and those pertaining to the interconnection pathways and weights) is discussed in more detail below, as well as in the section describing the fundamental physical and technological limitations of neuro-optical computing.

At the outset, we must further differentiate between those fundamental photonic operations that are intended for "optical" implementation and those that are envisioned for "optoelectronic" implementation. In the first category, we place those types of physical processes in which one or more beams of light interact either *directly* (as in coherent interference) or through an intermediate physical medium (as in the summation of two incoherent beams of light on a single detector). In the second category, we place operations that involve one or more photon-to-electron or electron-to-photon conversion processes prior to the actual implementation of the desired function, which is then assumed to be accomplished using intermediate (primarily analog, but perhaps digital) circuitry. An example of this latter category might be the subtraction of two optical signals by independent but simultaneous photodetection of each signal, followed by the use of an analog electronic differential amplifier to execute the functional subtraction. Most proposed neuro-optical processors rely to some degree on both types of physical implementation mechanisms (refer to the sections "Architectural Considerations for Photonic Neural-Network Implementations" and "An Implementation Strategy," below). In fact, the eventual degree of success achievable by neuro-optical computing techniques rests heavily on an appropriate balance of these mechanisms within a given system, optimized to yield the greatest computational advantage within the allowable physical and system constraints.

Optoelectronic implementations of neural functions for the most part rely on optical signals as inputs and outputs to and from the neuron units in order to allow for both high bandwidth and high interconnection multiplexing capacity, and on electronic signal combination and processing locally within each neuron unit. As such, optoelectronic functions are characterized primarily by the *optical* characteristics of interconnection and by the *electronic* characteristics of computation. The former will be described below, while the latter have been discussed both by Bang Lee and Bing Sheu elsewhere in this volume [Lee, 1992] as well as by Carver Mead in a recent elegant monograph [Mead, 1989]. On the other hand, *optical* implementations of these functions rely on communication by, as well as the interaction of, two or more optical signals in order to accomplish the relevant computation, which is often (but not always) followed by a photon-to-electron conversion process in some form of single channel or array detector. It is to the fundamental principles of such optical computational interactions that we next turn our attention.

In order to adequately consider even so basic a process as optical addition, it is essential to differentiate between two basic types of optical interactions (as determined by the nature of the optical signals involved): *incoherent* and *coherent*. Incoherent interactions occur whenever the light wavefronts representing the input signals temporally dephase (do not oscillate in unison) over the relevant time of observation (detector temporal integration window), in that they are either both temporally incoherent at the outset, or are *each* temporally coherent but separated in optical frequency by more than the inverse of the observation time. Interactions in which the input optical signals spatially dephase over the aperture of the relevant detector wherever the output is utilized (detector spatial integration window) are also incoherent for all practical purposes, and will obey incoherent summation rules as given below. Coherent interactions occur, on the other hand, whenever the light wavefronts representing the input signals simultaneously maintain a constant phase relationship over the detector spatial and temporal integration windows.

From these remarks, it can be seen that it is quite important to understand the distinction between coherent (or incoherent) *light* and coherent (or incoherent) *interactions* as defined by the eventual detector configuration and operational parameters. For example, it is perfectly acceptable to consider a situation in which two mutually coherent optical beams interact to produce an interference pattern with a spatial scale that is small compared with the relevant detector aperture. In such cases, the interaction will in fact follow *incoherent* summation rules, as the detector effectively *integrates* the space-variant interference pattern over the full detector aperture to produce exactly the same result as the interaction of two mutually incoherent (temporally) optical beams.

Given these preconditions, then, the actual rules for the basic operations are quite straightforward. Consider first the case of addition of two incoherent optical signal beams in a *collinear* geometry, in which the two distinct input beams (of identical cross sections) with intensities I_1 and I_2 are assumed to emerge from a beam-combining optical system (as yet undetermined) such that the two output beams are collinear. If the beams are combined, for example, by a nondispersive (wavelength-insensitive) 50/50 (50 percent transmission, 50 percent reflection) beamsplitter as shown in Figure 9.1(a), two possible output beams I_out and I'_out are created, each with an intensity given by:

$$I_\text{out} = I'_\text{out} = \frac{1}{2}(I_1 + I_2) \tag{9-1}$$

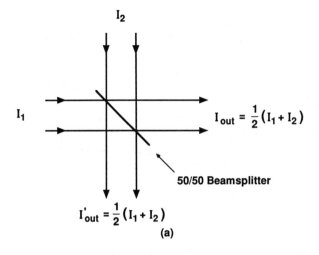

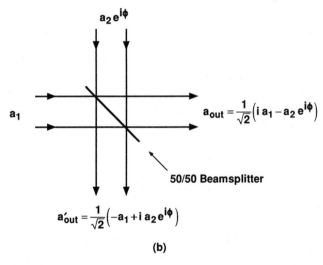

FIGURE 9.1 Illustration of optical addition utilizing a 50/50 beamsplitter. (a) Collinear *incoherent* beam geometry. (b) Collinear *coherent* beam geometry, showing input and output *amplitudes*. (c) Collinear *coherent* beam geometry, showing input and output *intensities*.

The output intensity is thus linearly proportional to the sum of the input intensities. Note that this operation cannot be accomplished without an inherent loss, in the case shown above equal to 0.5 or about 3 dB. In fact, if we wish to combine N beams collinearly by this technique (using a linear chain of nondispersive beamsplitters), $N - 1$ beamsplitters are required with transmissivities given by

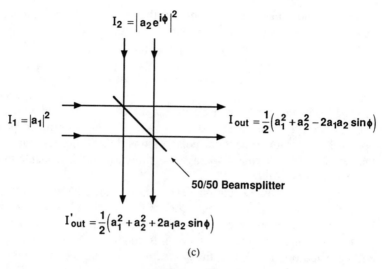

$$I_2 = \left| a_2 e^{i\phi} \right|^2$$

$$I_1 = |a_1|^2$$

$$I_{out} = \frac{1}{2}\left(a_1^2 + a_2^2 - 2a_1a_2 \sin\phi\right)$$

50/50 Beamsplitter

$$I'_{out} = \frac{1}{2}\left(a_1^2 + a_2^2 + 2a_1a_2 \sin\phi\right)$$

(c)

FIGURE 9.1 (contd.)

$1/2$, $2/3$, $3/4$, ..., $(N-1)/N$, representing a total loss of $(N-1)/N$ with an overall throughput of $1/N$:

$$I_{out} = \frac{1}{N}\left(I_1 + I_2 + I_3 + \cdots + I_N\right) \tag{9-2}$$

Instead of using a linear chain of beamsplitters with different transmissivities, we could alternatively construct a binary tree structure by pairing the inputs that again requires $N-1$ beamsplitters, but in this case with *equal* transmissivities of $1/2$. This system of beamsplitters also exhibits an overall throughput of $1/N$ (for even values of N). Although beam combination of a large number of inputs by the multiple-beamsplitter method is impractical, we will utilize this result a little later in order to understand the essential features of holographic beam combiners, which are subject to many of the same constraints.

It should be noted in passing that the overall throughput loss implied by Equation (9-2) can be circumvented *if* the beams to be summed incoherently are sufficiently distinct in wavelength that a *dichroic mirror* can be used to combine them. A dichroic mirror reflects light within a given wavelength range and transmits light outside of that range. Multiple dichroic mirrors can be used to collinearly sum multiple beams through appropriate choice of the input wavelengths in each arm, and of the characteristic wavelengths of each succeeding dichroic mirror.

Consider next the case of addition of two *coherent* optical signal beams in a collinear geometry. An example, again using a beamsplitter, is shown schematically in Figure 9.1(b). The presence of the beamsplitter generates a $\pi/2$ phase shift for each transmitted beam, and a π phase shift for each reflected beam [Haus, 1984]. In this case, due to the coherent nature of the two input signal beams, the output intensity is no longer given simply by the sum of the input intensities. In fact, the output *amplitude* is proportional to the sum of the input signal *amplitudes* (provided that the two beams have identical polarizations):

$$a_{\text{out}} \quad = \quad \frac{1}{\sqrt{2}} \left(ia_1 - a_2 e^{i\phi} \right) \tag{9-3}$$

in which ϕ is the relative phase between the two wavefronts (here assumed constant over the detector aperture) and $i = \sqrt{-1}$. It should be noted parenthetically that optical beams with orthogonal polarizations do not interfere, and hence follow the incoherent addition rule. We assume throughout this chapter that all beams are polarized identically.

From this simple equation, several important principles can be seen to emerge. First, the representation we must choose for simple addition to occur with coherent light is different than in the case of incoherent light: in the coherent case, we must use the *amplitudes* (containing phase information), whereas in the previous (incoherent) case addition is linear in the *intensities*. Second, the input-output transformation represented by Equation (9-3) reveals an easy method for implementing both addition and subtraction: we merely set the phase difference to $-\pi/2$ for addition, and to $\pi/2$ for subtraction. This can be accomplished either by adjusting the relative path lengths of the two input beams, or by inserting an appropriately oriented wave plate in one of the two beams. In the incoherent case treated above, no such algorithm exists, since we are adding intensities (which are positive definite quantities), and direct subtraction is not possible without intermediate intervention by an active optical or optoelectronic device. Third, note that the second output beam is now not symmetric with the first:

$$a'_{\text{out}} \quad = \quad \frac{1}{\sqrt{2}} \left(-a_1 + ia_2 e^{i\phi} \right) \tag{9-4}$$

This asymmetry in output amplitudes directly results from the asymmetry between the phases of the reflected and transmitted components in a partially transmitting mirror [Haus, 1984].

Since the intensity of an optical beam is related to its amplitude (within a proportionality constant, here taken to be unity) by the expression:

$$I_m \quad = \quad (\mathbf{a}_m^*)^T \cdot \mathbf{a}_m \tag{9-5}$$

in which $\mathbf{a}_m$ is the vector amplitude of the wave representing its polarization, $*$ represents the complex conjugation operation, and T represents the transpose of the vector, the output intensities in the two coherently summed channels are given by:

$$I_{\text{out}} \quad = \quad \frac{1}{2} \left[a_1^2 + a_2^2 - 2a_1 a_2 \sin \phi \right] \tag{9-6}$$

and

$$I'_{\text{out}} \quad = \quad \frac{1}{2} \left[a_1^2 + a_2^2 + 2a_1 a_2 \sin \phi \right] \tag{9-7}$$

as shown in Figure 9.1(c). From these two equations it can be seen that for arbitrary values of the phase shift ϕ, the output intensity is not simply related to the sum of the input intensities, but instead has a seemingly undesirable cross term. We can use this cross term to advantage by noting that for phase shifts of 0 or any integer multiple of π, both output intensities are equal, and reduce to the expression previously noted for the incoherent case [Equation (9-1)]. Thus for coherent illumination, we can perform addition either directly with the amplitudes, or with the intensities if we are careful about proper phasing of the input signals. One difficulty with the former approach is that most detectors are linear in intensity but not in amplitude, as will be discussed in further detail below.

In direct analogy with the analysis presented for the case of incoherent multiple-signal-beam summation, we can extend the above equations to include the case of multiple collinear coherent inputs using appropriate combinations of beamsplitters. For N coherent input beams summed optimally, the output amplitude is given by:

$$a_{\text{out}} \quad = \quad \frac{i^{N-1}}{\sqrt{N}} \, [a_1 + a_2 + a_3 + \cdots + a_N] \tag{9-8}$$

In order to achieve this result, one must again use $N-1$ beamsplitters with (intensity) transmissivities identical to those employed in the incoherent case, and in addition the relative phases must be arranged such that the phase difference between a_2 and a_1 is $-\pi/2$, and each successive beam is *increased* in phase by $\pi/2$.

In all of the cases described above, we have constrained the problem by requiring that the output beams all be *collinear*, and in fact many proposed neuro-optical architectures implicitly demand such a constraint. We will show in later sections, however, that this is perhaps an unnecessary and in many cases undesirable constraint. Hence we consider here also the case of optical addition with *noncollinear* output beams, requiring instead only that the summed beams fill the same detector aperture. There are a number of interesting variants of these two constraints, but we will limit the discussion to the two principal cases only. One possible configuration is shown in Figure 9.2(a), in which two incoherent signal beams are summed within the detector aperture by using two 100 percent reflecting mirrors, producing an output intensity given by:

$$I_{\text{out}} \quad = \quad I_1 + I_2 \tag{9-9}$$

in which we have neglected an obliquity factor that is dependent on the angle of incidence of each beam with respect to the detector, and that is nearly unity for small angles of incidence. This output intensity is uniform across the detector aperture, as shown schematically in the figure. In addition, relaxation of the requirement for collinearity can be seen to now allow for the use of mirrors instead of beamsplitters, eliminating the loss we found in the previous (collinear, incoherent) case at the expense of increased *angular* multiplexing.

Up to this point in the discussion, we have had to consider the *phase* of the optical wavefronts only for the case of collinear, coherent addition. In that

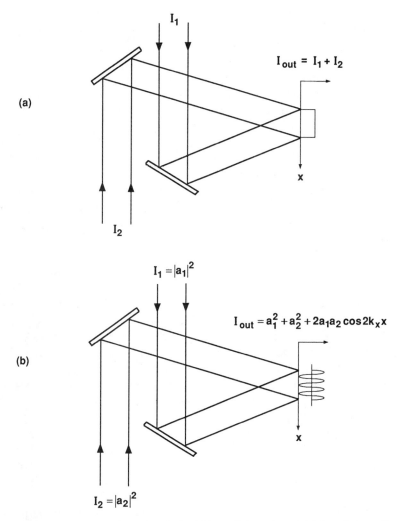

FIGURE 9.2 Illustration of optical addition utilizing mirrors. (a) Angularly multiplexed *incoherent* beam geometry. (b) Angularly multiplexed *coherent* beam geometry.

case, we only needed to use the *relative* phase shift between the two beams to derive Equations (9-6) and (9-7), since the phase shift is constant in both space and time over the detector spatial and temporal integration windows. In order to consider the case of *noncollinear, coherent* addition, however, we must allow for the space-variant phase shifts that naturally result when two coherent wavefronts cross at a nonzero angle. These effects are automatically taken into account if we express each wave (beam) amplitude in a form that incorporates both its *magnitude* and its *phase* everywhere in space at a given instant of time. For a plane wave (in which the planes of constant phase are oriented normal to the direction of propagation), it proves convenient to use the form $\mathbf{a} \exp(i\mathbf{k} \cdot \mathbf{r})$, in which $\mathbf{a}$ is a vector representing the polarization of the optical wave (its amplitude in each of the principal coordinate directions), $\mathbf{k}$ is the *wave vector* of the optical wave (defined as a vector with direction normal to the planes of constant phase, and with magnitude $|k| = 2\pi n/\lambda$, in which n is the refractive index of the propagation medium and λ is the wavelength of the light wave in vacuum), and $\mathbf{r}$ is a position vector defined from an arbitrary origin in space ($\mathbf{r} \equiv x\hat{x} + y\hat{y} + z\hat{z}$, in which $\hat{x}, \hat{y}$, and $\hat{z}$ are unit vectors along the Cartesian coordinate axes).

For the case of coherent illumination, then, the result of noncollinear summation is as shown schematically in Figure 9.2(b). In this case, the phase of each input wave varies across the detector aperture (assumed to lie in the plane $z = 0$) at a rate that is a function of the angular separation of the incident beams, as well as of the angular deviation of the bisector from normal incidence. This condition can be represented by writing the wave amplitudes with a space-variant phase, which is in turn dependent on the x-component of the wave vector k_x in the form $a_1 \exp(ik_x x)$. The two waves will thus interfere in the plane of the detector, forming essentially a new wave with a local amplitude given by the sum of the incident amplitudes. The resulting intensity pattern has both a space-invariant (uniform) and a space-variant (sinusoidal) component:

$$I_{\text{out}} = a_1^2 + a_2^2 + 2a_1 a_2 \cos 2k_x x \qquad (9\text{-}10)$$

in which we have once again neglected a constant obliquity factor. If we assume that the detector is linear in intensity over the dynamic range represented by this equation, and furthermore that the detector is uniform in responsivity over its aperture, then the output from the detector will be the *spatial average* of this interference pattern, resulting in an output intensity that is in fact a sum of the input intensities, as represented by Equation (9-9). In this case, the result is independent of the relative phase shift (difference) between the two beams at their points of entry into the beam-combiner system, since such a phase shift will merely result in a translation of the interference pattern without altering its integrated value. This result also can be extended to the case of multiple input signal beams, with the stipulation that mirrors cannot be allowed to occlude each other; hence, for a given beam width, only a certain number of beams can be combined without loss by means of this method without overcrowding the available angular spectrum.

The operation of optical multiplication is fundamentally different in a number of ways from those of addition and subtraction. Perhaps the most important difference is that the multiplication of either beam amplitudes or intensities cannot be accomplished directly, but must instead utilize a nonlinear medium of some form within which the beams can interact. There are two principal types of interactions to consider: those in which the two beams must be present *simultaneously* in order to form the desired product, and those in which the two beams are utilized *sequentially* in time. In general, the former interactions tend to operate on the amplitudes and hence require mutual coherency, whereas the latter interactions typically form products of (incoherent or coherent) intensities, which are therefore more straightforward to detect with currently available intensity-sensitive detectors.

Simultaneous multiplication of two optical beams is suggested by Figure 9.2(b), in which two coherent signal beams are angularly multiplexed to form the interference pattern given by Equation (9-10). Note that the space-variant part of the output intensity in the plane of the "detector" is proportional to the product of the amplitudes, i.e., is of the form $2a_1a_2 \cos 2k_x x$. If instead of employing a uniform (spatially averaging) detector as before, we were now to employ a space-variant detector sensitive to the local intensity, it is possible to record this modulation term along with the unmodulated (uniform) bias represented by the squares of the two amplitudes. If in addition the "detector," for example, is assumed to generate a change in either its absorption coefficient or its refractive index as a function of the recorded intensity pattern (for a given exposure), a diffraction grating will be formed. The resulting diffraction grating can be characterized by an amplitude that is proportional to the product of the input signal beam amplitudes, and that can be probed by a third so-called "readout" beam. This is at once the basic principle of holographic recording (as explained in more detail below in the subsection on "Photonic Interconnections") and at the same time allows the implementation of the multiplicative operation for coherent inputs. It should be noted that although this process produces a useful result for the case of two inputs, extension to larger numbers of inputs is not trivial, and requires the utilization of higher-order terms in the susceptibility tensor (representing the complex dielectric constant) for implementation. The one exception to this rule is the use of the probe (readout) beam intensity I_p as a third effective input, in which case output intensities proportional to either $I_p a_1 a_2$ or $I_p I_1 I_2$ can be detected, depending on the operational parameters of the recording medium and readout configuration.

If the simultaneity requirement is relaxed to allow for sequential interactions in an intervening photosensitive medium, then it is possible to multiply two incoherent input signals by means of the simple generic scheme shown in Figure 9.3. The medium again acts as an effective detector for beam 1, generating a transmittance (in its range of linearity) proportional to the intensity of beam 1. This transmittance can be generated either directly by the incident intesity, or through the exposure given by the product of the intensity and the exposure time as in the familiar case of photographic film. Beam 2 is effectively employed as a probe beam, such that the output intensity is given by:

$$I_{\text{out}} \; = \; c I_1 I_2 \qquad\qquad (9\text{-}11)$$

as desired, in which c is a proportionality constant subject to the constraint that:

$$c I_1 \; \leq \; 1 \qquad\qquad (9\text{-}12)$$

This process, as in the previous case, is extendable to accommodate an arbitrary number of inputs by iteration, unfortunately resulting both in a lengthy generation

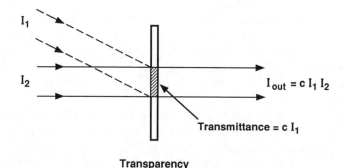

I_1

I_2

$I_{out} = c\, I_1\, I_2$

Transmittance = c I$_1$

Transparency

FIGURE 9.3 Illustration of optical multiplication utilizing a medium with variable transparency.

sequence for a large number of inputs, and in the potential for significant nonlinear effects with a heavily constrained overall dynamic range. For the case of N input beams, we can utilize $N-1$ exposure steps in combination with $N-1$ intermediate readout steps and a final readout step with beam N to generate an output intensity of the form:

$$I_{out} = c^{N-1}I_1I_2I_3\cdots I_{N-1}I_N, \qquad \text{with } c^{N-1}I_1I_2I_3\cdots I_{N-1} \leq 1 \qquad (9\text{-}13)$$

In direct analogy to the case of summation, we could instead utilize a binary tree structure, which requires only $\log_2 N$ time steps but uses the same *number* of devices.

Finally, it should be noted that this latter process of incoherent beam multiplication through an intervening medium by sequential illumination is suggestive of the process of *spatial light modulation*, in which the same basic concept is extended to cover a two-dimensional array of multiplication elements. In fact, this process is an essential component of the general area of photonic switching, to which we will turn our attention below.

Before turning to the topics of photonic switching and photonic interconnections, we conclude this section with a discussion of the fourth principal computational process that can be performed optically (as opposed to optoelectronically, as discussed below): that of the incorporation of functional nonlinearity. Although many types of functional nonlinearities are of interest in a generalized analog computational system, those of primary utility in the neural-network environment are for the most part threshold-like in nature. A threshold function $f_T(x)$ of some input variable x (such as the input intensity, for example) can be described in general by:

$$\begin{aligned}
f_T(x) &\cong T_{min}, & -\infty \leq x < x_1 \\
f_T(x) &= m(x), & x_1 \leq x < x_2 \\
f_T(x) &\cong T_{max}, & x_2 \leq x \leq \infty
\end{aligned} \qquad (9\text{-}14)$$

in which the function $m(x)$ is a monotonic function with a minimum value of T_{min}

and a maximum value of T_{max}. For a step-function response, the function $m(x)$ can be eliminated by setting $x_1 = x_2$. In many cases, a smoother transition between the two extreme states has been found to generate enhanced network stability and faster settling times. In such cases, the function $m(x)$ may be taken, for example, as a sigmoid with an exponential onset and an asymptotic approach to the saturation level.

The incorporation of such nonlinear functionality by direct optical means can be achieved through the use of a number of different types of nonlinear materials; such materials typically exhibit a change in their refractive index or absorption coefficient proportional to the first- and higher-order powers of the local optical intensity. One example of such a material is photographic film, which after development exhibits a (negative) sigmoid-like exposure characteristic, with a saturation value determined by the maximum optical density achievable within a given film thickness. [The optical density (OD) of a medium is given by the negative of the decadic logarithm of its transmittance; for example, a film that transmits 1 percent of the incident illumination has an optical density of two (OD2).] Another common example of an optical nonlinearity is the photoconductive saturation behavior of certain semiconductor materials such as cadmium sulfide, zinc selenide, and silicon. In this latter case, the distinction between an "all-optical" nonlinearity and an optoelectronic nonlinearity becomes somewhat blurred, as the photoconductor can be thought of as a light-sensitive electronic device.

Such optical techniques for the generation of functional nonlinearities at present suffer several inherent disadvantages, in that they often require either an off-line post-exposure development step (which is unsuitable for real-time operation at high frame rates), long response times, or very high optical intensities to achieve saturation. In addition, such materials have not yet proven to be readily programmable, which is often a desirable feature from the systems perspective in order to accommodate variable threshold functions, gain, saturation values, and offsets. As we will see in the next section, the incorporation of electronic circuitry with optical detectors and modulators to achieve *optoelectronic* nonlinearities can greatly increase the threshold sensitivity and operational bandwidth of nonlinear switching elements, while simultaneously providing flexible programming capabilities.

Photonic Switching

The switching function, that of providing an output that is (perhaps nonlinearly) dependent on one or more inputs, is a principal distinguishing characteristic of neuron units. Electronic circuit elements (particularly as configured by very large scale integration techniques) are quite well suited to the switching task, as long as the number of inputs (representing the fan-in) and the number of outputs (representing the fan-out) are both kept relatively small (less than a few hundred or so for the case of analog fan-in and fan-out). However, for neural-network implementations that demand a high degree of connectivity (with a concomitantly large number of neuron units), the required gate count as well as the *area* required for interconnection routing in purely electronic implementations rapidly gets out of hand.

The fundamental aspects of the fan-in and fan-out components of the switching function are quite distinct, and lead to different types of demands on the chosen implementation technology. The *fan-in* of a number of inputs requires that a particular functional relationship be established between the generated output, on the one hand, and the set of inputs, on the other. In the case of a neural network, the output typically depends on both sums and differences of various combinations of the inputs. Therefore, a given implementation technology must properly generate the requisite logical or functional relationship, as well as provide for an appropriate physical input mechanism (e.g., the input leads in the case of an electronic implementation). For electronic circuits, the network area required for the provision of input leads and functional circuitry typically scales directly with the number of inputs, which is an unfortunate dependence when the number of inputs is large. *Fan-out*, on the other hand, usually implies the broadcast of a single output value to a number of (input) locations or nodes. In electronics, the output power required to drive the inputs to a large number of nodes scales directly with the number of these nodes, which again does not scale favorably (but turns out to be an unavoidable penalty in any case). Significant (N-fold) fan-out often involves the incorporation of high-power driver circuitry, which may have to be duplicated M times ($M < N$) in order to avoid unacceptable loading of the output stages.

The combination of both fan-in and fan-out components of the switching function reveals a further demand on the real estate required for the establishment of weighted *interconnections*. In a fully connected neural network with N neurons, for example, area must be provided for the incorporation (storage and programming) of N^2 independent weights as well as N^2 independent signal pathways. Hence, the chip area required in a VLSI circuit implementation of such a fully connected neural network will scale at least as the square of the number of neuron units $[O(N^2)]$. Network segmentation into a number of interconnected chips can help somewhat to expand the network size beyond the limitation imposed by applying this constraint to a single chip. However, the limiting factor in the multiple-chip case rapidly becomes interchip communication (I/O), as pinouts from VLSI chips of greater than two hundred or so are not technologically feasible at present.

Photonic implementations of neural networks take advantage of the simple beam-combining mechanisms outlined above to multiplex inputs and outputs, and as such exhibit much higher capacity for fan-in and fan-out than do typical electronic implementations. The utilization of *optical* rather than electronic interconnections for the fan-in and fan-out functions provides for completely different scaling laws at large numbers of inputs and outputs to a given neuron unit, as described in more detail in the next subsection ("Photonic Interconnections").

Even given photonic interconnections with a high degree of fan-in and fan-out capability, the nonlinear functional (switching) relationship between the output and combinations of the inputs must still be provided for. For purposes of neural-network implementation, the primary photonic switching component is the *spatial light modulator*, a device that alters either the amplitude or phase across an expanded probe beam in response to the local intensity (or exposure) across an input (writing or recording) beam.

The simplest example of a spatial light modulator, albeit one that cannot operate at real-time frame rates, is photographic film. Following exposure to an information-bearing optical field, in which an image of a given scene is brought into focus on the two-dimensional plane of the film, a "latent" (undeveloped) image is formed within the photographic emulsion on the surface of the film. Chemical development is used to transform the latent image into a measurable change in the optical transparency (transmissivity) of the film, which can then be "read out" or probed by secondary illumination to reveal features of the recorded scene. In this context, slide projection is in fact the equivalent of *amplified* readout with a probe beam, in the sense that the reconstruction of the image is accomplished at a much higher level of intensity (for a longer period of time) than the original exposure.

As can be seen from this example, the basic functions performed by a spatial light modulator are those of *detection, functional transformation*, and *optical modulation*, as shown schematically in Figure 9.4(a). In the case of photographic film, the detection process occurs at photosensitive centers during exposure, the functional transformation (the transfer function that relates the output transparency to the input exposure) is incorporated during development and fixing, and the optical modulation process is accessed during readout. This division of the spatial light modulation function into three key elements is particularly useful in the discussion of optoelectronic spatial light modulators, which typically consist of separately identifiable detectors, control circuitry, and modulation elements, as shown schematically in Figure 9.4(b)–(d). This functional division also allows extensive use to be made of sophisticated electronic circuitry deployed locally within each pixel, both to generate programmable nonlinear control functions and to compensate to a certain degree for the nonidealities inherent in the optical detection and optical modulation elements.

Up to this point in the discussion, we have focused on *optically addressed* spatial light modulators (OASLMs) that respond locally to the incident light intensity, as this light-detection function is common to most envisioned photonic neural-network architectures. Another way of controlling the modulation within an array on a pixel-by-pixel basis is to configure the spatial light modulator such that it can accept a serial or parallel electronic input signal, which can be decoded (or demultiplexed) to drive each individual modulator element. Such *electrically addressed* spatial light modulators (EASLMs) can be driven, for example, by the output of a television camera to again combine the functions of detection, functional transformation (which may be accomplished in an external circuit), and modulation. One advantage of such a combination is the current advanced state of the art in closed-circuit television cameras (CCTVs), which exhibit exceedingly high performance at relatively low cost. One notable disadvantage, however, is the implied limitation on the frame rate of the combined device, since most high-resolution TV cameras are designed to operate at less than one hundred frames per second.

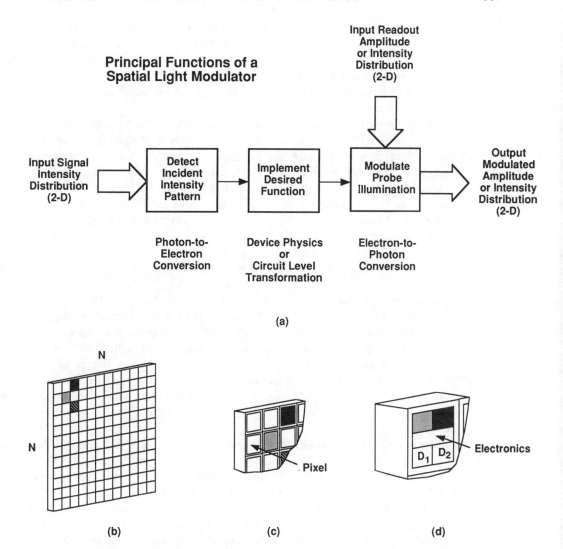

FIGURE 9.4 Fundamental principles of spatial light modulator function. (a) Block diagram of the principal functions of an optically addressed spatial light modulator, including the detection, functional implementation, and modulation functions. (b) Schematic diagram of an $N \times N$ array of spatial light modulator pixels, in which three pixels are shown in different transmission states. (c) Expanded view of the pixel array, showing an incomplete fill factor within each pixel. (d) Expanded view of a single pixel within the array, illustrating one possible pixel configuration that incorporates two detector elements D_1 and D_2, control electronics for impedance matching and functional implementation, and two modulator elements. shown here in different transmittance states.

Over the past two decades, a wide range of physical modulation mechanisms have been investigated for use in various types of spatial light modulators. Such mechanisms include the modulation of the index of refraction or birefringence in single-crystal materials by means of an applied electric field (the *electrooptic* effect), the reorientation of liquid crystal molecules (producing in turn a change in the index of refraction or birefringence) by either an applied electric field or by local optically induced heating, changes in coloration produced by optical absorption (the *photochromic* effect), modulation of the polarization of reflected light by application of local magnetic fields (the *magnetooptic* effect), surface deformations in a thin film or membrane induced by either applied electric fields or local optically induced heating, changes in the local refractive index induced by the application of pressure or by the transmission of an acoustic wave (the *acoustooptic* effect), and electric-field modulation of the absorption or dispersion properties of semiconductor device structures. The utilization of these physical modulation mechanisms in various spatial light modulator configurations has been addressed in a number of review articles [Tanguay, 1985; Warde, 1987], journal special issues [e.g., *Spatial Light Modulators for Optical Information Processing*, 1989], and topical conference proceedings [e.g., *Spatial Light Modulators and Applications*, 1990].

The principal configurational and operational characteristics of spatial light modulators that are of interest for application to neural networks include optical sensitivity, write (input) wavelength, read (output) wavelength, input-output transfer function, functional programmability, operational bandwidth, degree of integration, pixel size, total number of pixels per chip, output modulation contrast ratio, dynamic range, and dissipated power density. In many cases, these characteristics are interdependent, and thus impose at times contradictory design constraints that must be optimized in the overall systems context. The fundamental and technological limitations that affect device design and performance are discussed further below and in a succeeding section.

As is the case for electronic circuitry, both monolithic and hybrid approaches to the development of optoelectronic spatial light modulators with suitable functionality have been employed. In the *monolithic* approach, the detectors, control circuitry, and modulation elements within each individual picture element (pixel) are integrated within a single class of materials on a supporting substrate, as shown schematically in Figure 9.5. An example of such an approach is the integration of p-n or p-i-n junction photodiodes with metal-semiconductor field-effect transistors (MESFETs) [Sze, 1981a] to drive multiple-quantum-well (MQW) optical modulators based on the quantum-confined Stark effect (QCSE) [Miller, 1990], all fabricated by means of photolithographic processing with multiple mask levels on gallium arsenide (GaAs) substrates. In Figure 9.5, two distinct approaches to the monolithic integration of spatial light modulators are illustrated, differentiated primarily by the method employed to physically or electrically isolate (pixelate) the modulator elements.

Two particularly critical parameters of spatial light modulators used in neural-network implementations are the contrast ratio and dynamic range of the modulator. Their values can in certain cases be increased by incorporating the active modu-

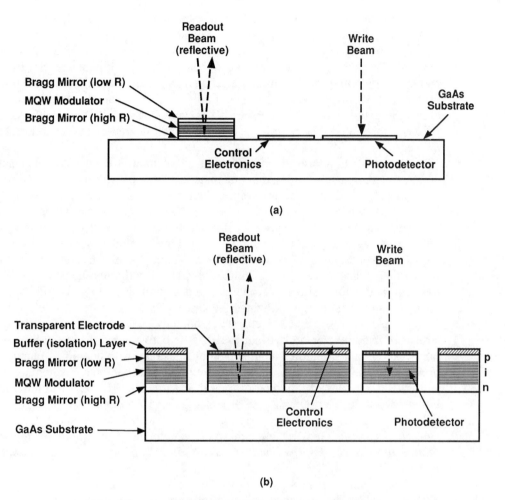

FIGURE 9.5 Examples of monolithically integrated spatial light modulators. The chosen examples incorporate photodetectors, control circuitry, and multiple-quantum-well modulators within each pixel on a single gallium arsenide (GaAs) substrate. In (a), the control electronics and photodetector elements are fabricated following the photolithographic definition and physical isolation of the modulator elements, while in (b) a buffer (isolation) layer is used to allow fabrication and interconnection of all of the elements without chemical or ion beam etching beneath the control electronics. Passivation layers required for interconnection isolation are not shown.

lation layer (for example, a multiple-quantum-well structure) within a symmetric or asymmetric optical (Fabry-Perot) cavity [Whitehead, 1989a; Whitehead, 1989b; Whitehead, 1989c; Yan, 1989]. The asymmetric case is shown schematically in Figure 9.5(a), in which two multilayer Bragg mirrors are used to form a reflective cavity with a high reflectivity (R) on the substrate side, and a lower reflectivity on the air-incident side. One of several advantages of monolithic integration is the potential for utilizing common components for multiple purposes. For example, the basic MQW modulator structure can also be used as a p-i-n photodetector by application of appropriate bias voltages, as shown in Figure 9.5(b). To date, significant progress in such monolithically integrated optical modulators has been achieved, although spatial light modulators with large numbers ($> 10^4$) of pixels have not yet been fabricated that exhibit the relatively high degree of integration described above.

In the *hybrid* approach, on the other hand, certain of the device functions may be integrated on a substrate within one materials system (with its associated process technology) in order to optimize either their performance characteristics or manufacturability, while others are integrated on a separate substrate within a different materials system (with a necessarily distinct process technology). Following separate processing sequences for each individual component, the two substrates are then interconnected (bonded together) such that the mating pixels on each substrate are in pairwise electrical contact. For example, several currently investigated types of spatial light modulators (SLMs) incorporate the detection elements and control circuitry on a silicon (Si) substrate utilizing standard VLSI design rules, while the modulation elements are based in a separate technology (such as multiple-quantum-well structures integrated on a GaAs substrate). Alternatively, hybrid spatial light modulators can be fabricated on a single common substrate, with additional functionality provided by the growth, deposition, or coating of a second active material onto the substrate. Examples of this type of hybrid SLM include silicon VLSI/ferroelectric liquid crystal devices [Drabik, 1990] and silicon/PLZT devices [Lin, 1990]. Such hybrid SLMs are also in the early stages of advanced development and are the subject of current intensive research and development efforts [*Spatial Light Modulators for Optical Information Processing*, 1989; *Spatial Light Modulators and Applications*, 1990].

Using either of these two approaches to spatial light modulator fabrication, devices based on both transmissive and reflective readout can be constructed, with different implications on the overall systems design in each case. In particular, the reflective mode can be used to advantage in configuring a hybrid-integrated SLM to mate the detection and control circuitry functions of the device with the optical modulation function. Use of the reflective readout configuration allows the detection and control circuitry to be integrated on a substrate that is opaque to the readout illumination wavelength [Kyriakakis, 1990], as shown schematically in Figure 9.6.

As an example of the degree of functional integration currently envisioned for spatial light modulators that are specifically designed for photonic implementations of neural networks, a silicon-based CMOS chip has recently been designed and fabricated [Asthana, 1990a; Asthana, 1990b] that incorporates two input detectors, control circuitry, and two (optical modulator) output drivers within each 100×100 μm pixel as shown schematically in Figure 9.7(a). It should be noted that these current dimensions do not in any sense represent a lower limit, but rather

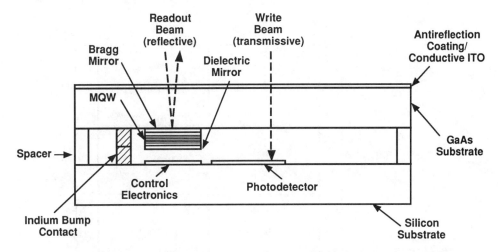

FIGURE 9.6 Example of a hybrid spatial light modulator, in which the photodetectors and control electronics are fabricated on a silicon substrate, and the multiple-quantum-well modulator elements are fabricated on a gallium arsenide (GaAs) substrate. The two sets of devices are bump contacted on a pixel-by-pixel basis to provide parallel electrical continuity.

a practical size for laboratory demonstrations and experiments, as well as a useful size from the perspective of neural-network applications. The pixel layout allows for two 30×50 μm detectors, followed by a 15-transistor dual-input, dual-output differential amplifier that implements a sigmoid-like transfer function, with externally programmable saturation characteristics. Output pads are also provided for hybrid bonding (by bump-contact techniques [Shirouzu, 1986]) to an InGaAs/GaAs multiple-quantum-well modulator structure fabricated on a GaAs substrate [Kyriakakis, 1990]. Utilizing $2\,\mu$m CMOS design rules, the control circuitry easily fits within 25×100 μm, leaving adequate space for the modulator output pads as shown in Figure 9.7(b)–(c). This currently allows for the integration of 10^4 pixels per cm^2, or 6×10^4 pixels per square inch. The functional operation of this circuit will be discussed in the section, "An Implementation Strategy," below.

Before leaving the subject of photonic switching, we should note that the general principles outlined above can be used to design a wide variety of mutually compatible devices with different functionalities, as well as with different tradeoffs among the set of configurational and operational parameters. For example, it is relatively straightforward to design time-integrating and time-differentiating circuits; sharp (step-like) thresholds; level slices; sigmoid-like functions, their complements, and their derivatives; inverters; and logarithmic amplifiers. Many such functions can be implemented with only a few integrated components, such as capacitors, diodes, transistors employed as current amplifiers, and biased transistors employed as resistors [Mead, 1989]. Therefore, these functions can easily be incorporated within each pixel (neuron unit) of a two-dimensional spatial light modulator, as

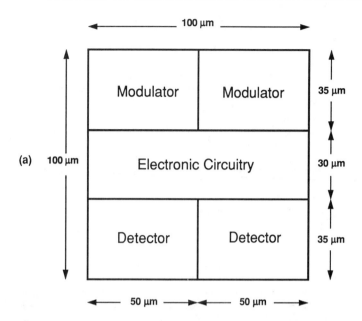

FIGURE 9.7 VLSI layout of a generalizable silicon-based spatial light modulator structure. (a) Neuron pixel layout. (b) Photograph of a single neuron unit in VLSI implementation, with probe pads substituted for the two detectors (bottom) and for contact to the two modulation elements (top). (c) Photograph of a 6 × 6 array of neuron units on a VLSI chip that incorporates additional test circuitry.

well as in some cases between pixels for the implementation of nonlocal (other than pointwise) operations such as automatic gain control and nearest-neighbor inhibition.

Photonic Interconnections

Given that the neuron units are to be represented by individual pixels within a two-dimensional spatial light modulator, interconnections must now be established between each individual neuron unit (pixel) and many (if not all) other neuron units. As such, the chosen interconnection scheme must be capable of the appropriate degree of fan-in and fan-out, be characterized by sufficient transmission bandwidth in each channel, and be scalable to relatively large numbers of neuron units. In addition, the neural-network paradigm presents the additional requirement that the interconnections be *weighted*, such that the output from a given point-to-point interconnection is proportional to the product of the input and a stored constant or weight. This requirement eliminates from consideration a large number of possible switching networks that provide full reconfigurability in a nonblocking manner (such as a crossbar or shuffle-exchange network), but without the capacity to incorporate weights within each interconnection pathway. In adaptive networks (those that incorporate learning algorithms), these interconnection weights must have the

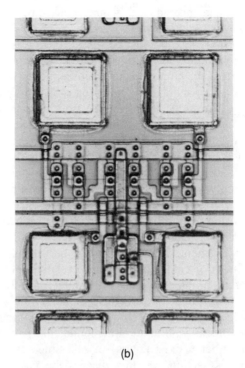

(b)

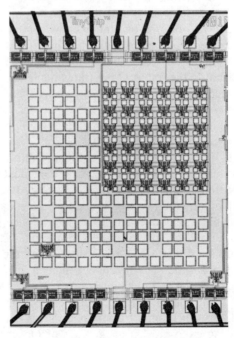

(c)

FIGURE 9.7 (contd.)

capability of being updated in a manner determined by the particular learning algorithm employed. A nontrivial consequence of these last two requirements is that the interconnection weights must be *stored* for at least as long as the average iterative computation, if not *much* longer; yet, they must simultaneously exhibit dynamic programmability if the network is to exhibit either short-term or long-term plasticity.

For very small numbers of neurons with a low degree of connectivity, one possible way of forming the interconnection network would be to use fiber optic transmission lines with modulated semiconductor laser diodes as sources and optical receivers as detectors, much like a fiber optic local area network. The weights could be incorporated by means of a variable-gain amplifier at either end of each fiber optic link, with weight storage in local dynamic random-access memory (RAM) or static read-only memory (ROM) circuits. Unfortunately, the sheer bulk of each transmitter, receiver, and fiber optic link precludes scalability to large neural-network systems. For example, a fully connected 20-neuron network would involve 400 sets of sources, transmission lines, and detectors, which would currently represent a prohibitive requirement. The same would be true of a 50-neuron network with a fan-out and fan-in of eight, representing a relatively low degree of connectivity.

In order to be able to satisfy the interconnection requirements for a large number of neuron units that are fully or nearly fully interconnected, the appropriate photonic technology to employ is that of *holographic* interconnections, in which the weights as well as the interconnection patterns themselves are stored as holograms in either a fixed (static) or real-time (dynamic) holographic recording material. In this section, we first discuss the basic principles that apply to the utilization of holographic recording for point-to-point interconnections. Next, we describe the physical origins of a number of complexities with holographic interconnection schemes that lead to both interchannel crosstalk and throughput losses. An architecture that lends itself to the minimization of such complications will be described in detail in the section, "An Implementation Strategy," below. Finally, the potential for incorporation of real-time volume holographic recording media such as photorefractive materials in holographic interconnection networks is addressed.

The essential principle of holographic recording, that of the space-variant interference of two mutually coherent wavefronts, was discussed briefly in reference to Equation (9-10) and is illustrated in Figure 9.2(b). In this figure, two angularly separated (noncollinear) collimated beams are incident on a photosensitive material, such that their mutual interference locally exposes the material to the intensity distribution given by Equation (9-10). In Figure 9.2(b), the photosensitive material was assumed to spatially integrate across the interference pattern, producing an output that depends on only the spatial *average* of the intensity distribution. Suppose now that we use instead a photosensitive material with the property that its *local* index of refraction or absorption coefficient depends on the *local* incident intensity (exposure), which allows the complete interference pattern to be *recorded*. The resulting change in the local optical properties of the medium may either be immediate (as in the case of a photochromic transformation, for example), or may require development following exposure (as in the case of bleached photographic negatives or

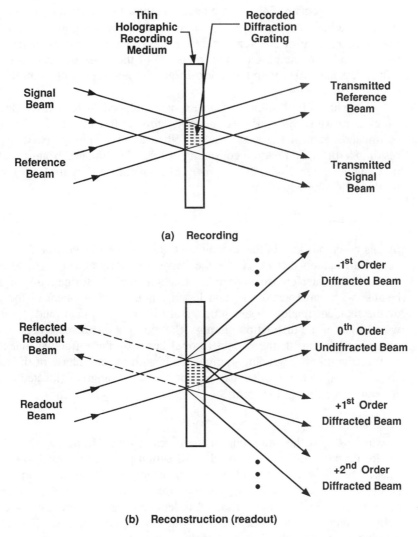

FIGURE 9.8 A simplified holographic recording configuration: case of plane wave signal and reference beams, and a *thin* holographic recording medium. (a) Recording. (b) Reconstruction with a plane-wave readout beam.

dichromated gelatin thin films). Figure 9.8(a) shows such a detection or recording geometry in which a thin semi-transparent layer of photosensitive material acts as a quasi-planar holographic recording medium. The interference pattern produced by the mutually coherent signal and reference beams within the holographic recording medium is recorded to form a diffraction grating within the volume accessed by both beams simultaneously, as shown in the figure. For simplicity in Figure 9.8 (as well as in subsequent figures), we have not shown the refraction of the incident and transmitted beams at the input and output faces of the holographic recording medium that occurs due to a difference between the refractive indices of the medium and its surround. The amplitude (and intensity) of the reflected beam shown in Figure 9.8(b) depends directly on the index difference, and represents a throughput loss on readout.

Consider first the case of an exposure-dependent refractive index variation. Illumination of such a space-variant modulation of the refractive index by a coherent collimated beam of the same wavelength λ as the exposure (writing) beams will result in a diffraction pattern consisting of several collimated beams, each emanating in a characteristic direction as shown schematically in Figure 9.8(b), and as given by the following equation:

$$\mathbf{k}_{mx} = \mathbf{k}_{rx} + m\mathbf{K}_G; \qquad |\mathbf{K}_G| = \frac{2\pi}{\Lambda_G} = |\mathbf{k}_2 - \mathbf{k}_1|; \qquad m = 0, \pm 1, \pm 2, \ldots \quad (9\text{-}15)$$

In this equation, $\mathbf{k}_{mx}$ is the x-component of the wave vector of the mth diffracted beam (diffraction *order*), $\mathbf{K}_G$ is the wave vector (assumed oriented along the x-axis) of the interference pattern (diffraction grating) formed by the two writing beams (with wave vectors $\mathbf{k}_1$ and $\mathbf{k}_2$), $\mathbf{k}_{rx}$ is the x-component of the wave vector of the incident readout beam propagating in the x-z plane, and Λ_G is the spatial wavelength of the diffraction grating. The multiple diffracted orders result from the phase modulation of the readout (probe) beam by the refractive index modulation $n(x)$ of the thin holographic grating; the magnitude and phase of the readout beam amplitude immediately after passing through the hologram (located at the position z_0) can be written in the form:

$$A_{\text{diff}} \quad = \quad a_r e^{i(k_{rx}x + k_{rz}z_0)} e^{i\phi_G(x)} \qquad\qquad (9\text{-}16)$$

in which A_{diff} is the amplitude of the diffracted wavefront, $\phi_G(x) = 2\pi n(x)d/\lambda$ is the local phase shift induced by the diffraction grating (assumed to be of thickness d), $a_r e^{i(k_{rx}x + k_{rz}z_0)}$ is the incident readout beam amplitude at the exit plane of the hologram (z_0), and k_{rx} and k_{rz} are the x and z components of the wave vector $\mathbf{k}_r$, respectively. Each of the diffracted orders can then be directly associated with a corresponding Fourier component of the modulated amplitude [Goodman, 1968], which can be expanded in terms of the form:

$$A_m e^{imK_G x} \qquad\qquad (9\text{-}17)$$

In order to assess the effectiveness with which the holographic grating diffracts the incident beam into a particular diffraction order, it is convenient to define the *diffraction efficiency* η of each order as:

$$\eta \quad \equiv \quad \frac{|A_m|^2}{|a_r|^2} \qquad\qquad (9\text{-}18)$$

The essential diffraction properties of thin absorption gratings (in which the modulation occurs in the local absorption coefficient) are the same as for the case of thin

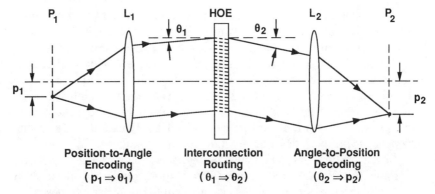

FIGURE 9.9 A point-to-point interconnection system, using a holographic optical element (HOE) for interconnection routing, and lenses as position-to-angle and angle-to-position encoders. In this example, the holographic optical element effectively performs an input angle to output angle transformation, such that light emitted (or transmitted) at point p_1 in the input plane (P_1) is detected at point p_2 in the output plane (P_2).

pure phase gratings, with two principal exceptions: (1) for sinusoidal absorption gratings, the diffracted orders are limited to $m = -1, 0$, and 1; and (2) the presence of absorption significantly decreases the maximum first-order diffraction efficiency that can be achieved.

In order to illustrate how such holographic gratings can be employed to generate weighted point-to-point interconnections, we need to introduce two additional concepts: the lens as an angle-to-position encoder, and the superposition of holographic gratings recorded with different diffraction efficiencies. The first concept can be understood with reference to Figure 9.9, in which a simple lens is placed one focal length away from a point source in the input plane of a photonic interconnection, and a second simple lens is placed one focal length away from the output plane. What is normally thought of as the focal property of a lens results in the generation of a collimated beam (a beam comprising both parallel rays and planar wavefronts) following the first lens, with an *angle* (both in and out of the plane of the page) that depends on the *position* of the point source in the focal (input) plane. In this sense, the first lens acts as a position-to-angle encoder, providing a one-to-one correspondence between the input location and the output collimated beam angle. Depending on the nature of the grating stored within the holographic optical element, the collimated beam will be diffracted into a new direction characterized by a *different* angle. The second lens will then focus the diffracted beam to a point in the output plane that depends on this angle, thus acting as an angle-to-position encoder. The utilization of different orientations of gratings within the holographic optical element allows for the interconnection of any arbitrary point in the input plane to any other point in the output plane.

Suppose now that we choose to superimpose a number of planar gratings within the holographic medium, each with a different wave vector (orientation and grating period) and grating modulation (variation of the refractive index or the absorption coefficient). Assuming for the moment that the diffraction process is linear, each input point will be interconnected with a number of output points as determined by the set of recorded gratings. Likewise, each output point will be interconnected with a specified number of input points. Each interconnection will be weighted by its diffraction efficiency as determined by Equation (9-18), which is in turn dependent on the index of refraction (or absorption coefficient) variation recorded for each grating. As such, the holographic optical element acts as a multiport variable beamsplitter, redirecting (diffracting) a given fraction of each input beam to a specified set of output beams. By employing lenses as described above, this feature allows the construction of a point-to-point interconnection with weights and arbitrary fan-out/fan-in (delimited only by the number of gratings recorded).

There is at least one obvious problem with the interconnection scheme outlined above, however, in that any *given* grating will connect *any* of the input points to specific output points pairwise, as shown by Equation (9-15). This particular feature occurs because each input point generates a collimated beam with a distinct wave vector k_r corresponding to a particular direction (angle) of propagation, each of which satisfies Equation (9-15) with a different diffracted wave vector (for each diffracted order) k_m. The result of this degeneracy is that any recorded hologram that is designed to connect a single input point to one or more output points will in fact also connect *every* other input point to corresponding sets of output points, using the same relative interconnection pattern for each input point. This effect can be utilized to advantage, for example, in parallel digital optical computing systems with interconnection symmetry or regularity, since one simple hologram can in effect implement a very large number of point-to-point interconnections (the equivalent of wires in the case of an electronic implementations) [Jenkins, 1984]. For neural networks, however, the common requirement of nearly arbitrary (highly irregular) interconnections makes this feature undesirable.

A second problem with the proposed interconnection scheme is the presence of a multiplicity of diffracted *orders* for each diffraction grating, as shown in Figure 9.8, which occasions the connection of each input point to a number of geometrically related output points even for the case of a single stored grating.

The solution to this seeming dilemma is to extend the holographic medium into the third dimension (the direction of light propagation), creating a *volume* holographic optical element (VHOE) to take the place of the thin planar element discussed above. Two essential properties of VHOEs bear directly on the utilization of such elements in photonic interconnections. The first is that diffraction is limited to the first order only and all higher diffracted orders are suppressed if the holographic medium is thick enough, as defined below and shown schematically in Figure 9.10. This occurs because each additional "layer" in the thickness direction of the holographic medium provides an additional constraint on the diffraction phenomenon; these constraints act collectively to enhance the amplitude diffracted into

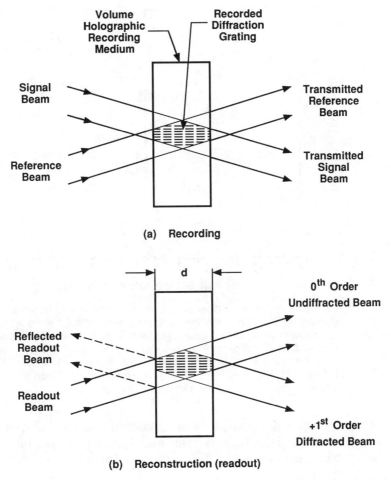

FIGURE 9.10 Volume holographic recording with plane-wave signal and reference beams. (a) Recording. (b) Reconstruction, showing the elimination of the higher diffracted orders.

the zeroth and first orders by means of constructive interference, at the expense of the other diffracted orders.

The second important property of a volume holographic optical element is that of *angular selectivity*. Specifically, the range of input angles that can diffract from a given grating decreases as the thickness of the grating is increased. The central angles that are allowed in the case of a thick grating are the same angles that define the two beams that initially *created* the holographic grating. This property therefore eliminates the inadvertent connection of all input points pairwise to a matching set of output points, and allows for the generation of *independent, weighted* interconnections as are desired for neural-network applications.

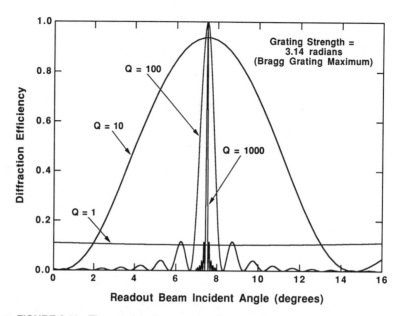

FIGURE 9.11 The angular alignment sensitivity of a volume holographic optical element, as a function of the dimensionless Q-parameter defined in the text. The grating strength for all of the curves (3.14 radians) is optimized to produce 100 percent diffraction efficiency in the limit of large Q (Bragg diffraction regime), and is not optimized for low-Q gratings. Note that the diffraction efficiency is essentially independent of angle for low-Q gratings, and is very strongly peaked at the Bragg angle (7.5 degrees in this case) for high-Q gratings.

In order to differentiate "thin" grating diffraction behavior (the so-called Raman-Nath diffraction regime) from "thick" grating behavior (the so-called Bragg diffraction regime), it is convenient to define a dimensionless "thickness" parameter Q such that:

$$Q = \frac{2\pi\lambda d}{n\Lambda_G^2} \qquad (9\text{-}19)$$

in which n is the average refractive index of the holographic recording medium, and the remaining parameters are as specified previously. In general, gratings for which $Q \geq 10$ operate well within the Bragg regime, while gratings with Q parameters less than unity exhibit unacceptable degrees of Raman-Nath character for truly independent multiplexed interconnection applications. The angular response characteristics of both planar and volume diffraction gratings are shown as a function of the Q parameter in Figure 9.11, in which the transition from pure Raman-Nath to pure Bragg behavior for increasing values of Q can be seen. Note that the number of input points that can be independently connected to an equally sized array of output points is a decreasing function of the width of the angular response.

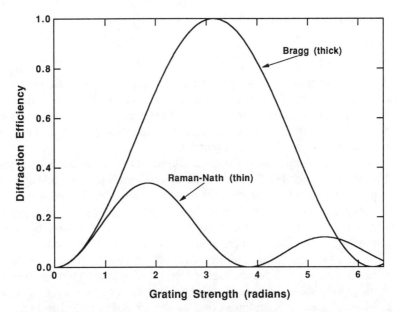

FIGURE 9.12 The first-order diffraction efficiency of thin (Raman-Nath diffraction regime) and thick (Bragg diffraction regime) holographic gratings as a function of the grating strength.

The throughput efficiency of a volume holographic optical element as used in an interconnection application is determined to first order by the diffraction efficiency of each individual interconnection grating, in direct analogy to the definition of the diffraction efficiency for the planar hologram case in Equation (9-18). For example, for the case of an unslanted pure phase grating with equiphase fronts (i.e., planes of constant phase) parallel to the bisector of the recording beams with wave vector k and perpendicular to the entrance face of the volume holographic recording medium, the diffraction efficiency at the Bragg (optimum readout) angle is given by [Kogelnik, 1969]:

$$\eta = e^{-\alpha d / \cos \theta_B} \sin^2 \left(\frac{\pi \Delta n d}{\lambda \cos \theta_B} \right) \tag{9-20}$$

in which α is the absorption coefficient of the holographic recording medium of thickness d at the optical readout wavelength λ, Δn is the amplitude of the refractive index modulation, and θ_B is the Bragg angle defined by $2k \sin \theta_B = K_G$. As can be seen from Equation (9-20), the diffraction efficiency of the first order for a single grating can approach 100 percent if the absorption coefficient satisfies the requirement $\alpha d \ll 1$, provided sufficient index modulation Δn can be produced by the exposure process. The dependence of the first-order diffraction efficiency on the grating strength is shown in Figure 9.12 for both thin (Raman-Nath) and thick (Bragg) pure phase diffraction gratings. The grating strength v is defined as the integrated peak phase modulation of the grating in each case, and is given by:

$$v = \frac{2\pi \Delta n d}{\lambda \cos \theta_B} \tag{9-21}$$

The maximum first-order diffraction efficiency of the thin diffraction grating is about 34 percent, which occurs at a grating strength of 1.8 radians. Thick diffraction gratings achieve 100 percent diffraction efficiency at a grating strength of π radians, at which point the diffraction efficiency of the thin grating has peaked and is nearly at its first zero, as shown in Figure 9.12.

The extremely narrow angular alignment characteristics of volume diffraction gratings in principle allow the simultaneous multiplexing of large numbers of independent, weighted interconnections to be recorded between the input plane and the output plane (refer to Figure 9.9). In addition, the use of angular multiplexing allows for both fan-out from a given input point to a number of output points, and fan-in from a number of input points to a single output point.

The holographic implementation of the fan-out from a single input point to a number of output points uses several multiplexed (superimposed) holographic gratings to achieve the desired weighted fan-out, one for each output point. Consider a 4-input, 4-output interconnection as shown in Figure 9.13. For each input point x_j that we wish to interconnect to an output point y_i', the recording process requires the pairwise coherent interference within the holographic recording medium of x_j with a second beam y_i corresponding to y_i'. The interconnection of x_1 to $y_1', y_2', y_3',$ and y_4' therefore requires the pairwise coherent interference of x_1 with y_1, x_1 with y_2, and so on. This process results in the fourfold fan-out of x_1 to all of the outputs.

The fan-out from a single reference beam to a number of output beams is directly analogous to the readout of a traditional hologram (of, for example, a two-dimensional or three-dimensional image), provided that the full set of beams $\{y_i\}$ is coherently recorded with the given reference beam x_j. Although up to this point we have formulated the point-to-point holographic interconnection problem in terms of collimated (plane-wave) input and output beams that record individual diffraction gratings (characterized by a single grating wave vector) within the holographic recording medium, many alternative recording and reconstruction geometries can be envisioned that produce equivalent results. In the case of traditional holography, for example, the input transparency bearing the image to be recorded is illuminated with a collimated beam, resulting in a complex diffraction pattern at the front entrance plane of the holographic recording medium. Collimated, converging, or diverging reference beams can be utilized to produce reconstructed images with a wide variety of optical imaging characteristics. Likewise, various input- and output-beam geometries can be used in a point-to-point interconnection system to optimize the overall system characteristics, such as freedom from interchannel crosstalk, optimum use of the spatial frequency recording characteristics of the holographic recording medium, optical system complexity, and convenience of the optical layout (particularly when viewed in conjunction with associated optical subsystems).

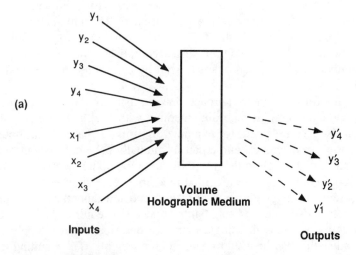

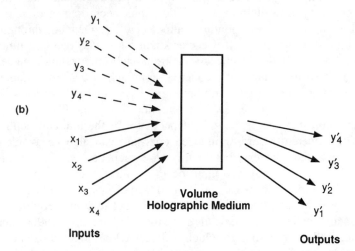

FIGURE 9.13 Schematic representation of a 4-input, 4-output holographic interconnection, showing 4 coherent input beams x_1-x_4 and 4 coherent recording beams y_1-y_4, each of which corresponds to a desired output $y_1'-y_4'$. In (a), the sets $\{x_j\}$ and $\{y_i\}$ interfere within the volume holographic medium, recording the desired interconnection diffraction gratings. In (b), a new set of input beams $\{x_j\}$ illuminates the volume holographic medium, reading out the weighted interconnection pattern and forming appropriately weighted sums at each of the outputs $\{y_i'\}$.

The fourfold fan-in of inputs x_1, x_2, x_3, and x_4 to y_1' can likewise be accomplished by recording each of the necessary interconnections pairwise, as before for the fan-out case. The recording process for the fully implemented 4-to-4 interconnection therefore involves the generation of 16 individually weighted diffraction gratings that connect the full set of inputs $\{x_j\}$ to the full set of outputs $\{y_i'\}$. The multiplexed hologram that accomplishes this function can be recorded in a number of ways, each characterized by certain advantages and disadvantages [Psaltis, 1988].

In the fully coherent approach, the requisite gratings can be recorded by illuminating the holographic recording medium with $\{x_j\}$ and with $\{y_i\}$ simultaneously. This can be accomplished, for example, by using a spatial light modulator to store each of the sets of values, and a pair of mutually coherent readout beams to encode these values and interfere them within the holographic element. In this manner, all of the required gratings are recorded in a single exposure; however, two difficulties are inherent in this single-exposure, fully coherent approach. The first problem is that a fully independent N-to-M interconnection requires NM stored interconnection weights, whereas the single exposure described above supplies only $N + M$ input values that can be used to generate the weights. The resulting interconnection matrix can in fact connect all of the input points to all of the output points, but the relative fan-out weights from each input point will be degenerate. One way to avoid this degeneracy is to illuminate the holographic recording medium with each input x_j and a full set of corresponding outputs $\{y_i\}$, sequencing through all N of the inputs (and changing the set of corresponding outputs) one at a time. This procedure generates an independent fan-out from each input point. The second problem with the single-exposure, fully coherent approach is that undesirable gratings will be recorded among the $\{x_j\}$ and among the $\{y_i\}$ that can lead to considerable coherent crosstalk among the *desired* interconnection pairs. This coherent interference process diminishes the degree of independence of the interconnections.

This coherent-recording-induced crosstalk can also be avoided by sequencing the recording process, but in this case each desired grating pair is recorded separately such that only one input beam x_j interferes with one output beam generator y_i (recording beam for the desired output beam y_i') at a time. This scheme effectively eliminates the coherent crosstalk, but does not eliminate another form of crosstalk (called *beam degeneracy* crosstalk [Jenkins, 1990a; Jenkins, 1990b; Asthana, 1990c], the origin of which is described below) that can be equally severe. In addition, the complication imposed by the incorporation of such a sequential recording schedule can be a serious constraint for large $N \times M$ (N input points to M output points) interconnections, as NM independent recording steps are required for full programming of the interconnection. This proves to be particularly problematic for the rapid generation of weight updates in a large-scale neural interconnection network that incorporates synaptic plasticity. Furthermore, sequential recording of holographic exposures can cause partial erasure of previously recorded interconnection weights in certain types of holographic recording materials, necessitating the use of recording schedules that attempt to balance the weights recorded at the beginning of the sequence (and hence partially erased by all subsequent exposures) with the weights recorded at the end of the sequence [Psaltis, 1988]. The use of such recording schedules usually implies an overall decrease in both the exposure efficiency and throughput efficiency of the resulting holographically recorded interconnection matrix, as well as the buildup of noise resulting from the series of space-variant erasures.

One potential scheme for reducing coherent-recording-induced crosstalk, beam degeneracy crosstalk, and sequential recording schedules involves the use of an array of coherent but mutually incoherent sources to simultaneously expose the holographic recording medium to only the desired sets of gratings [Jenkins, 1990a; Jenkins, 1990b; Asthana, 1990c]. This scheme will be discussed in detail in a later section.

The fan-out process is illustrated in Figure 9.14, in which implementations using both beamsplitters and volume holographic optical elements are shown. The case of fan-out utilizing beamsplitters is shown schematically in Figure 9.14(a). As can be seen in the figure, the input beam can be divided among the output beams with arbitrary weights set by the transmissivities of the beamsplitting elements BS_i. If the final beamsplitter is a mirror, the fan-out process can be accomplished with essentially zero throughput loss. By analogy to the beamsplitter case, as well as by direct analysis, it can be proven that the holographic fan-out process shown in Figure 9.14(b) can also be accomplished with essentially arbitrary weights, with no optical throughput loss inherent in the fan-out process itself. It is interesting to note that these two implementations differ in at least one essential feature, in that the beams fanned out from the holographic implementation originate within the same volume, while the beams fanned out from the beamsplitter implementation originate from vertically displaced beamsplitters. If we were to extend the fanned-out beams in the latter case backward toward the left-hand side of Figure 9.14(a), we could imagine replacing the three discrete, vertically displaced beamsplitters with a single, multiplexed "virtual" beamsplitter that generates the same set of output beams. One physical realization of such a "virtual" beamsplitter component is in fact the multiplexed volume hologram shown in Figure 9.14(b).

The collinear fan-in process is illustrated in Figure 9.15 for both types of implementations. As discussed above, for the beamsplitter implementation an intrinsic fan-in loss is encountered for the case of collinear fan-in with incoherent inputs, while the intrinsic loss can be circumvented by resorting to mirrors and employing angular multiplexing. The use of mutually coherent inputs can allow for collinear fan-in without loss, but only for *specific* combinations of input beam amplitudes and phases determined by the transmissivities of the beamsplitters. All other combinations of input beam amplitudes and phases will result in a throughput loss, and for certain configurations can generate sufficient crosstalk to violate the desired independence of the interconnection system. For the case of volume holographic optical elements, the situation is identical, such that collinear fan-in is grossly inefficient for large numbers of fan-in interconnections to the same node. On the other hand, appropriate use of angular multiplexing can eliminate this seemingly inherent fan-in

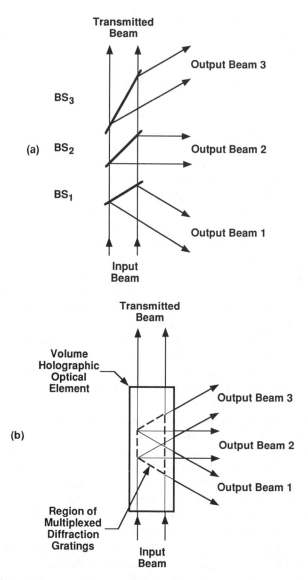

FIGURE 9.14 Schematic representation of the fan-out process for optical beams, for the case of one input and three outputs. (a) With beamsplitters (BS_1–BS_3). (b) With a single holographic optical element containing three multiplexed (spatially superimposed) diffraction gratings.

loss, giving rise to a highly multiplexed, efficient interconnection element [Jenkins, 1990a; Jenkins, 1990b; Asthana, 1990c] as described in a later section.

The physical origin of this intrinsic optical throughput loss in the case of

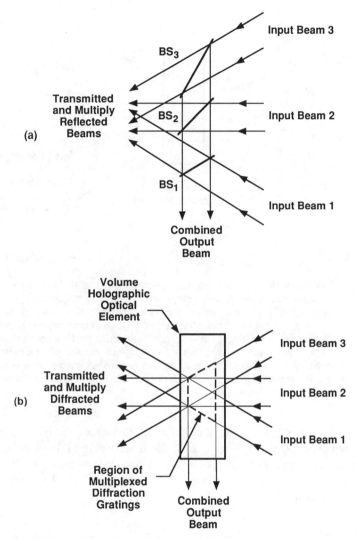

FIGURE 9.15 Schematic representation of the fan-in process for optical beams, for the case of three angulalry distinct inputs and one combined collinear output beam. (a) With beamsplitters, showing the unavoidability of a throughput loss (for incoherent input beams) associated with the set of transmitted (and multiply reflected) beams. (b) With a single holographic optical element containing three multiplexed (spatially superimposed) diffraction gratings, showing an analogous throughput loss.

collinear fan-in is directly related to the mechanism that gives rise to beam degeneracy crosstalk. In Figure 9.16 we show a 4-to-4 holographic interconnection that is assumed to have been recorded by the sequential-exposure technique described

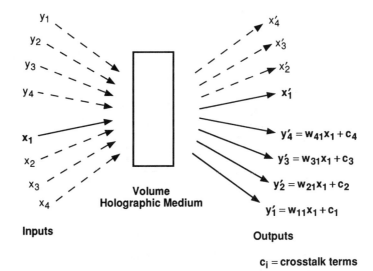

FIGURE 9.16 Illustration of the generation of crosstalk in holographic optical interconnections due to beam degeneracy: recording/readout configuration. The input beams $\{x_j\}$ are assumed to have interfered within the volume holographic medium with the set of recording beams $\{y_i\}$, producing only the desired set of interconnection gratings with weights w_{ij}. Illumination of the volume holographic medium with beam x_1 produces a 1-to-4 fan-out into the output beams $\{y_i'\}$, as well as the zeroth-order beam x_1'. Due to the effects of beam degeneracy, power is also coupled into the zeroth-order beams x_2'–x_4', and crosstalk terms $\{c_i\}$ are introduced into the outputs.

above in reference to Figure 9.13, in order to include all 16 individually weighted interconnection gratings but none of the undesirable gratings that can give rise to coherent-recording-induced crosstalk. In this case, readout by the input beam x_1 generates the four output beams y_1' through y_4', with values given by the stored interconnection weights w_{ij}:

$$y_i' \;=\; w_{i1}x_1 \tag{9-22}$$

Within the holographic medium, however, each of the four output beams can in turn act as an *input* beam, generating undesired output beams in the directions $x_2', x_3',$ and x_4'. These undesired output beams are a result of diffraction from the gratings recorded between each output generating beam y_i and the full set of input beams $\{x_j\}$. Each output beam is automatically Bragg matched (at the correct Bragg angle) to the full set of input beams due to the collinear recording geometry employed. We refer to the fan-in as *collinear* in this case because each input beam x_j that is fanned in to a given output y_i' produces an output beam in the *same* direction. The generation of diffracted intensity in the directions x_2'–x_4' from readout with x_1 results in a throughput loss for the interconnections between x_1 and the set of output beams $\{y_i'\}$. In addition, the throughput losses of the individual output beams $\{y_i'\}$

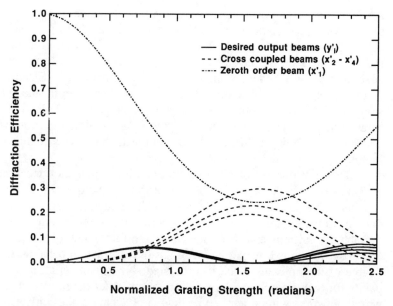

FIGURE 9.17 Illustration of the generation of crosstalk in holographic optical interconnections due to beam degeneracy: diffraction efficiency as a function of grating strength for the readout configuration of Figure 9.16. Shown are the depletion of the zeroth-order beam x'_1 and the rise of the desired output beams y'_i, accompanied by a strong buildup of the cross-coupled beams x'_2–x'_4.

will not be equal in general. Furthermore, the undesired diffracted beams x'_2–x'_4 can *also* act as input beams, generating additional output beams in the directions $\{y'_i\}$ that coherently interfere with the beams directly diffracted in those directions by the input beam x_1. The combination of interconnection-dependent losses from the output beams $\{y'_i\}$ into the "cross-coupled" beams $\{x'_j\}$, and of interconnection-dependent coupling from $\{x'_j\}$ into $\{y'_i\}$, gives rise to an undesired redistribution of the intensities of the output beams. This phenomenon is referred to as *beam degeneracy* crosstalk, as it arises from the beam direction degeneracy (collinearity) of the output beams fanned into a single output point.

Both the throughput loss and the beam degeneracy crosstalk that characterize holographic interconnection geometries with collinear fan-in can be estimated by numerical simulation of the diffraction process from a multiplexed grating [Asthana, 1990c]. By using the optical beam propagation method [Johnson, 1986] to simulate the diffraction process, we can analyze the 4-to-4 interconnection described above for the case of a single beam readout, as shown in Figure 9.16. The results of such an analysis are presented in Figure 9.17, which shows the diffraction efficiency of each of the four beams fanned out from the single input point, as well as the three cross-coupled beams in the directions $\{x'_j\}$ and the zeroth-order (undiffracted) beam. For this illustration, all 16 interconnection weights are equal in magnitude.

As the grating strength is increased, a significant amount of intensity is coupled into the cross-coupled components, robbing the designated fan-out beams of the desired diffracted intensities. In addition, the *relative* diffraction efficiencies observed in the designated fan-out beams are no longer independent of the grating strength, as desired in a fully independent weighted interconnection. Extensive modeling of N-to-N holographic interconnections with collinear fan-in and incoherent inputs suggests that the throughput decreases approximately as $1/N$, which is potentially catastrophic for large interconnection networks. In a later section, we will describe an alternative holographic recording approach that obviates this $1/N$ throughput factor.

The development of a viable photonic interconnection technology is based in no small part on the availability of appropriate photosensitive recording materials [Psaltis, 1988; Smith, 1977; Gunter, 1988; Gunter, 1989]. Many interconnection demonstration experiments have been performed in the laboratory on bleached photographic emulsions and dichromated gelatin films, both of which are thick enough (10 to 30 μm) to exhibit sufficient Bragg-like diffraction behavior to allow a limited degree of multiplexing to be incorporated. Neither material, however, exhibits capacity for real-time operation, which is essential for the implementation of photonic neural networks with at least some degree of synaptic plasticity. On the other hand, one principal advantage of photographic film and dichromated gelatin is their essentially infinite read-write asymmetry, which is highly desirable in many applications as described below.

By *real-time operation*, we mean that the holographic interconnections can be programmed (exposed) and used (read out) on roughly the same time scale (perhaps at kHz frame rates), without the necessity of chemical development processes or the like. By *read-write asymmetry*, we mean that the readout of a programmed interconnection should not erase the stored weights at an accumulated readout exposure equal to that of the recording exposure. Ideally, we would like to have the capability of exposing the holographic interconnection to the recording beams with essentially instantaneous "development" of the stored gratings, with the recording process characterized by very high sensitivity during the "learning" process. At the same time, we would like to be able to initiate readout of the stored interconnection pattern without altering the stored weights for a length of time equal to the desired "computation" time. Although in many applications the learning and computation times may differ by only an order of magnitude, in other cases it is desirable to compute for very long times compared with the learning phase, and yet still maintain the capacity for (slowly varying) weight updates.

The class of photosensitive recording materials that has been most extensively investigated for photonic interconnection applications does in fact have the capacity for sensitive holographic recording, is available in "thick" samples that allow for the formation of Bragg-regime diffraction gratings, exhibits a high multiplexing capacity, and allows for the inclusion of modest read-write asymmetries. This class is that of the so-called "photorefractive" materials [Gunter, 1988; Gunter, 1989], which includes single crystals of semi-insulating optical materials such as bismuth silicon oxide ($Bi_{12}SiO_{20}$), bismuth germanium oxide ($Bi_{12}GeO_{20}$), lithium niobate ($LiNbO_3$), strontium barium niobate ($Sr_{1-x}Ba_xNb_2O_6$), potassium niobate ($KNbO_3$) and barium titanate ($BaTiO_3$), as well as semi-insulating semiconductors such as gallium arsenide (GaAs), indium phosphide (InP) and cadmium telluride (CdTe). The use of the term "photorefractive" to describe these materials exclusively is somewhat misleading, in that many other classes of materials are known to undergo a refractive index change following illumination as well as those traditionally included in the class described above. But at least the term is descriptive of the basic phenomenon involved, as outlined below.

In photorefractive materials such as bismuth silicon oxide, exposure to an interference pattern at an appropriate wavelength (characterized by significant photosensitivity) generates free charge carriers (electrons or holes) liberated from deep traps. The number of photogenerated carriers is in general proportional to the local intensity absorbed by the crystal; as such, the photogenerated carrier population mimics the exposure pattern in both amplitude and phase. The photogenerated carriers are free to diffuse to regions of lower intensity, or they can be assisted out of the brightest regions by application of a bias electric field to produce carrier drift. In either case, they tend to be retrapped, in turn creating a space charge distribution that has the same spatial frequency as the interference pattern. This space-variant space charge distribution produces a locally modulated electric field with the same spatial frequency (as determined by the grating period or grating wavelength), which in turn induces a local change in the refractive index of the photorefractive material through the linear (Pockels) or quadratic (Kerr) electrooptic effect [Kaminow, 1974]. The refractive index grating can then be probed by a readout beam to generate a diffracted beam, just as in the case of the pure phase gratings described previously.

An excellent set of review articles on the physical properties and applications of photorefractive materials has been assembled by Gunter and Huignard [Gunter, 1988; Gunter, 1989]. The state of the art is such that 1 cm^3 crystals of many of these materials have been grown, and shown to exhibit a very high degree of optical quality. Exposure sensitivities vary widely, but several crystals require of order 500 $\mu J/cm^3$ for full exposure to saturation (the highest grating strength that can be achieved in that particular crystal). This corresponds to the absorption of about 50 mW/cm^2 of optical intensity throughout 1 cm^3 of material for an exposure period of 10 msec. The range of spatial frequencies that can be supported in these materials ranges from a few lines/mm to over 2000 lines/mm. Diffraction efficiencies close to 100 percent have been observed in several types of crystals, while others saturate nearer to 10 percent for thicknesses of order 1 cm.

Optimization of photorefractive materials for interconnection device applications is under way, including the development of growth processes for large photorefractive crystal boules with a high degree of optical uniformity; the characterization of both unintentionally incorporated impurities and intentionally incorporated dopants that alter the holographic recording, readout, and storage characteristics; the use of applied d.c. and a.c. bias electric fields to enhance the holographic recording sensitivity; the use of polarization effects to enhance the reconstructed image signal-to-noise ratio; and the antireflection coating of the (typically high index) front and rear crystal surfaces to increase the diffraction efficiency and avoid the presence of unwanted gratings due to multiple reflections [Karim, 1988; Karim, 1989a; Karim, 1989b]. In addition, the origin of electric-field nonuniformities that occur within photorefractive crystals during grating recording is under active investigation, and several methods of eliminating the field collapse have been discovered [Herbulock, 1988]. Use of these methods increases both the saturation diffraction efficiency and the grating response time, resulting in more efficient interconnection devices that operate at higher recording sensitivities.

Sources and Source Arrays

In reviewing a large fraction of the journal articles published over the past decade on optical information processing and computing, including the most recent coverage of photonic implementations of neural networks, you will be inspired perhaps by the cleverness of a particular proposed architecture, or intrigued by the novel features of a particular device structure. But you will also be amazed at the apparent lack of emphasis on certainly one of the most fundamental components in any proposed photonic computational system: the source of the light! This oversight may be caused in part by direct analogy to the situation in VLSI electronics, in which it is a bit unglamorous (and probably also to a certain extent unnecessary) to concentrate on the battery or the power supply. After all, electrical power is relatively inexpensive, widely available, well characterized, and reasonably abundant. At peak usage, your home probably uses about 10 kW, most of which is dissipated in the air conditioner.

However, the situation in photonic technology is quite different. Sources of coherent optical radiation that can produce average output powers in the 10 kW range exist in only a few laboratories, are very large (about 15 m^3), usually emit in the far infrared (10.6 μm), and are far from inexpensive. Incoherent sources in the range of 100 to 1000 W are available [xenon-mercury (Xe-Hg) gas discharge lamps, for example], but this type of source is typically noisy (exhibits large intensity fluctuations), difficult to collimate, and characterized by a very short lifetime (from the systems perspective). In addition, gas discharge lamps are broadband sources, and as such usually require wavelength filtering in order to provide compatibility with wavelength-sensitive devices such as volume holographic optical elements and spatial light modulators. A broadband source that has been suitably filtered to allow readout of a typical volume holographic optical element (within the allowable spectral bandwidth of the stored diffraction gratings) might generate only about 10^{-5} to 10^{-6} of its total rated power in the wavelength region of interest. For the 1000 W Xe-Hg lamp, this results in only about 1 to 10 mW of quasi-monochromatic optical power.

Coherent, monochromatic optical power can be provided by an array of different types of laser sources [Milonni, 1988], including the argon-ion (Ar$^+$) laser, the neodymium-YAG (Nd-YAG) laser, the helium neon (He-Ne) laser, the helium cadmium (He-Cd) laser, dye lasers, excimer lasers, and semiconductor laser diodes. Typical monochromatic (single laser line) power outputs from the first two types range from about 500 mW to 25 W. Helium neon and helium cadmium lasers are readily available as well as relatively inexpensive, but have output powers that are typically in the range 1 to 5 mW, peaking out at about 50 mW. Dye lasers are often optically pumped by argon-ion lasers, and hence exhibit power outputs slightly lower than that of the pump laser. Excimer lasers are typically operated in the pulsed mode of operation at repetition rates of 10 to 1000 pulses per second, and emit average powers in the 10 to 100 W range. Finally, semiconductor laser diodes are available with very long lifetimes at output powers of 1 to 20 mW, and much shorter lifetimes in the 100 mW to 1 W range.

Of these six different types of coherent sources, the first five are still relatively bulky (about 0.1 m^3), consume considerable electrical power, generate significant amounts of heat (many must be water cooled to ensure stable operation and practical lifetimes), and are very expensive (especially when compared with a comparable electronic power supply!). Although these sources can be (and indeed are) employed in current systems-level demonstrations, their collective liabilities do not augur well for their eventual incorporation in commercially viable computational systems in general, and perhaps neural-network applications in particular. This leaves the last category, that of semiconductor-diode lasers (including, possibly, miniaturized diode-pumped Nd-YAG lasers), for further consideration.

Before discussing the properties of semiconductor-diode lasers as optical power sources any further, we should at least note that the range of output powers available from these sources (1 to 100 mW for single element devices) is rather limited. Taking an upper bound (with continued research and development) of about a watt per device gives us a realistic estimate of the amount of average coherent source power available for at least circuit-level implementation of photonic neural networks, though certainly at the systems level phased arrays of stripe laser diodes and/or multiple sources could conceivably be employed.

Semiconductor-diode lasers [Kressel, 1977; Casey, 1978a; Casey, 1978b] have been extensively investigated and developed over the past two decades for a broad range of commercial applications, including compact-disk player recording and read-out, fiber optical communications systems [Jones, 1988], merchandise optical scanners, and laser printers. The physical size of these lasers is small enough (about $0.3 \times 1 \times 5$ mm) to fit in a standard transistor (or IC) package, as long as external cooling is not required. Lasers with power outputs of 1 to 10 mW are relatively inexpensive, costing a few tens of dollars in quantity on the average. Higher-output power lasers are considerably more expensive, however, as are lasers with very narrow spectral linewidths (so-called *single-longitudinal-mode* lasers). For the higher-power lasers (as well as for the intermediate-power lasers that are required to maintain a high degree of center-wavelength accuracy), external cooling (e.g., by means of a thermoelectric cooler) must be provided in order to maintain thermal stability in both wavelength and output power.

The wavelength ranges spanned by semiconductor-diode lasers are dictated by the direct bandgap materials used to fabricate the coherent light emitting diode (semiconductor p-n junction). Aluminum gallium arsenide/gallium arsenide (AlGaAs/GaAs) lasers grown on single-crystal gallium arsenide substrates emit at wavelengths in the range 780 to 900 nm, while lasers based in the quaternary indium gallium arsenide phosphide (InGaAsP) compound semiconductor system (and grown on indium phosphide substrates) emit at wavelengths further into the infrared (1.2 to 1.6 μm). The aluminum gallium arsenide/gallium arsenide lasers in particular are nearly wavelength matched to the peak sensitivity of both silicon and gallium arsenide photodetectors, as might be employed for photonic switching in spatial light modulator arrays, or for detection of computed results in a system diagnostic or output plane.

Within these ranges, a typical multimode semiconductor-diode laser has a spectral bandwidth of 0.5 to 2 nm; a single longitudinal mode laser has a much narrower spectral bandwidth of order 10^{-4} nm (about 50 MHz centered at an optical frequency of 3.5×10^{14} Hz). Both multimode and single-longitudinal-mode diode lasers can be used to write and read holographic optical interconnection elements, as long as the coherence length of the laser is larger than the thickness of the holographic recording medium. The coherence length of a laser is essentially the maximum path difference over which two beams derived from the same laser can maintain the stable phase relationship necessary to exhibit an interference pattern. In applications requiring high multiplexing capacity within the holographic interconnection medium (or significant path differences among beams that must coherently interfere), the narrower linewidths of the single-longitudinal-mode lasers are often preferable, since their coherence lengths are several orders of magnitude longer. For example, typical multimode semiconductor-diode lasers operated above threshold exhibit coherence lengths in the range 0.1 to 10 mm, while stabilized single-longitudinal-mode diode lasers can have coherence lengths exceeding 1 m.

Employing a single, high-intensity optical power source in a typical neural-network application carries with it a potential penalty: an inherent tradeoff between energy efficiency on the one hand, and the need for array generation optics on the other. This tradeoff arises from the fact that most optoelectronic implementations of neuron unit arrays have either photodetectors or modulation windows (in some cases both) that are smaller in size than each individual pixel, as was shown schematically in Figures 9.4 and 9.7. The ratio of the area of a given photosensitive element to the entire pixel area is referred to as the *fill factor* of the pixel (with respect to that particular element). Typical fill factors for the photodetectors and modulation windows may range from less than 0.1 in the case of monolithic integration to about 0.5 for hybrid integrated devices. Light that falls outside the appropriate areas within a given pixel will at best contribute to the overall system throughput loss, and at worst may adversely affect the function of adjacent devices that exhibit photosensitivity.

In order to efficiently channel the optical illumination to the correct photosensitive regions, we need to (a) *expand* the source illumination uniformly to fill the entire aperture of the device in question (a spatial light modulator or volume holographic optical element, for example), (b) in many cases *collimate* (or recollimate) the light source to produce a planar wavefront with a beam of constant width, (c) *spatially filter* the beam to enhance its uniformity by eliminating significant fixed-pattern noise, (d) *focus* the light within each individual pixel to a size compatible with the relevant photosensitive area (in effect thereby generating a two-dimensional array of focused beamlets), and (e) *align* the resulting array of focused beamlets with each succeeding device in the optical path.

The procedures and optical elements required for beam expansion, collimation, and spatial filtering are well understood among the optical community for the case in which the source beam is initially *axially symmetric*, as is typical of gas and excimer laser systems. In typical semiconductor laser diodes, however, the planar nature of the light emitting heterojunction region often gives rise to a diffraction-induced beam divergence *parallel* to the junction of 3 to 10 degrees, and a corresponding beam divergence *perpendicular* to the junction of 20 to 60 degrees. Comparable procedures and optical elements for such *anamorphic* (non-axially symmetric) beams are more complex, and are currently under development. Also under development are a number of types of semiconductor-diode lasers that emit approximately axially symmetric beams suitable for standard collimation and filtering systems.

The optical source array generation problem has received considerable attention recently, due primarily to significant interest in optical interconnection systems. In one promising approach, a two-dimensional array of computer-generated and photographically reduced amplitude-encoded Fresnel zone plates has been used to form an 8×8 grid of microlenses that function by means of *diffraction* (from what is, practically speaking, a computer-generated hologram (CGH)) rather than *refraction* [Marrakchi, 1990]. In another well-developed approach, computer-generated binary phase holograms (so-called *Dammann* gratings [Dammann, 1971]) have been configured to form large grid patterns of regularly spaced illuminated spots with predetermined locations and fill factors [Morrison, 1989]. Using this latter technique, 32×32 arrays have been generated with both high throughput efficiencies and low scattered light by crossing two fabricated 1×32 grating arrays. In addition, an 81×81 array has been experimentally demonstrated by using two pairs of crossed 1×9 grating arrays in an optical arrangement that generates multiple images by means of a convolution operation [McCormick, 1989a]. In both of these techniques, all of the resulting light beamlets are mutually coherent, as they derive from the same source. This mutual coherence has an impact on the utilization of such source arrays for the generation of independent holographic interconnection networks, as described in the subsection on "Photonic Interconnections" above.

An interesting alternative to the generation of pixelated optical sources by modification of the properties of a *single* source is that of direct fabrication of *multiple source arrays*. One striking example is the recent successful fabrication of over one million independent surface-emitting semiconductor-diode lasers on a single gallium arsenide chip [Jewell, 1990]. Both cylindrical and square cross-section

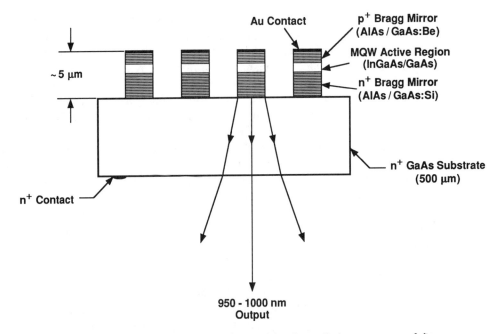

FIGURE 9.18   Illustration of a surface-emitting laser diode source array [after Jewell, 1990]. In this example, the individual semiconductor laser diodes are isolated by chemically assisted ion beam etching techniques, must be individually contacted, and emit *through* the GaAs substrate.

microlasers have been fabricated with diameters and edge dimensions in the range 1 to 5 μm, with heights above the surface of the wafer of about 5.5 μm as shown schematically in Figure 9.18. In the fabrication process employed, the laser mirrors are arranged to generate laser emission *through* the 500 μm thick gallium arsenide substrate, as shown in the figure. In order to accomplish this without significant absorption in the substrate, the active (lasing) medium is composed of InGaAs quantum wells with GaAs barriers, giving rise to an emitted infrared wavelength ($\approx$ 950 nm) that lies in a region of substrate transparency.

In the present configuration, the lasers are essentially optically isolated, and hence are not designed to be mutually coherent (phase locked). In fact, over time constants typical of holographic recording in currently available photorefractive crystals (milliseconds), it is likely that such arrays are for all practical purposes *mutually incoherent*, due both to the optical isolation and to process-induced variations in device parameters that alter the wavelength emitted from each individual laser. Arrays of surface-emitting semiconductor lasers that have been specifically *designed* to have uniformly separated wavelengths have also been demonstrated [Chang-Hasnain, 1990]. We shall return to this characteristic in a succeeding section that addresses a particular strategy for photonic neural-network implementation.

At present, each laser within the array operates at a threshold voltage of about 10 volts and a threshold current of a few milliamperes, resulting in a power dissipation of 10 to 50 milliwatts per device at threshold, and higher for power outputs significantly above threshold. In order to keep the overall power density within established limits (1 to 10 W/cm^2) and thus to keep from overheating the substrate (resulting in potentially deleterious effects on wavelength stability and/or catastrophic failure), the lasers must either be spaced appropriately, operated in a pulsed (on/off) mode at less than unity duty cycle, or temporally multiplexed (turning on only a few lasers at a time) by resorting to individual rather than parallel addressing. Given the current rate of progress in the development of these and other types of surface-emitting laser arrays, it is reasonable to expect demonstration of continuous operation of up to 10^4 microlasers per square centimeter within the near future.

It should be noted that the array shown in Figure 9.18 is not currently configured for parallel operation of all of the sources simultaneously, which would require electrical contact to the tops of each selectively etched microcavity. This feature could likely be provided by an additional surface passivation and metallization step. Matrix-addressable surface-emitting laser arrays have recently been fabricated by forming columns of lasers separated by etched isolation grooves, and interconnected across the grooves by striped row contacts [Orenstein, 1990a]. Application of an appropriate bias voltage across a given pair of electrodes (column and row) activates the laser diode at the intersection, allowing for raster-scanned operational modes as well as fully parallel operation [Von Lehmen, 1990].

Other currently investigated approaches to surface-emitting laser array fabrication use various techniques to form the microlaser cavities *within* the planar substrate without the need for deep etched isolation grooves, such as by the use of ion implantation to form electrically insulating isolation layers between the laser cavities [Tai, 1989a; Orenstein, 1990b] or by the current confinement that results from photolithographic definition of one of the two laser mirrors and its associated electrical contact [Tai, 1989b]. Fabrication processes that yield planar or quasi-planar device structures allow for direct parallel contact if desired without the complications of depositing contacts on vertical sidewalls.

Before leaving the subject of semiconductor laser diodes and surface-emitting laser arrays, it is worthwhile to note a very useful feature of such devices: their capacity for *high-bandwidth direct modulation*. By this we mean that the output intensity of the semiconductor laser source can be modulated (at full modulation depth, i.e., from well below the threshold for lasing to peak output power) at frequencies up to a few gigahertz by direct variation of the voltage applied across the device. This attribute can be used to advantage in many neuro-optical implementation architectures by eliminating the need for mechanical or electro-optical shutters, as well as by offering temporal multiplexing as an additional degree of freedom for the systems designer.

One additional type of solid state device that is capable of both single-source and source-array fabrication is the light emitting diode (LED). Closely related to the semiconductor laser diode, the LED is also a p-n junction device that can be fabricated with considerably less processing complexity by elimination of the high-reflectivity mirrors that form the semiconductor laser cavity. An additional advantage is the lack of a threshold for operation, allowing the LED to emit over a much wider dynamic range of applied voltages. One drawback of light emitting diodes is that they are relatively broadband (incoherent) sources, and as such are not usable as sources for holographic recording applications (and in many cases for readout of multiplexed holographic optical elements as well). In addition, they are relatively inefficient emitters with typical electrical-to-optical conversion efficiencies of a few percent. This feature tends to make LEDs rather power consumptive for a given amount of usable output intensity.

Detectors and Detector Arrays

Detectors are optoelectronic components that act as photon-to-electron converters, in that they transform incident optical intensity into electronic form, usually a voltage or a current. Detectors therefore allow the optical representation of neuron unit outputs, for example, to be converted into an electronic representation for further processing. As such, they are important components for the photonic implementation of neural networks in at least two functional areas: (a) as input transducers for the necessary optical detection function of optically addressed spatial light modulators, and (b) as output transducers for the translation of optically generated intermediate and final results to an appropriate electronic format. After all, once you've gone to all of the trouble of learning and computing with a neural network, it might prove worthwhile occasionally to actually get the answer out and use it to initiate some other useful process!

In both of these functional areas, we can further categorize detectors as (a) single-pixel detectors, and (b) interconnected detector arrays. In the first category, we include both single-element detectors that have one optical input aperture and one output channel, as well as the single-pixel detectors employed as part of an array in two-dimensional spatial light modulators. This latter assignment is made because, even though detectors used in spatial light modulators are perhaps *configured* in an array, their outputs are used only within one or at most a few local pixels. In the second category, we include arrays of detector elements that are interconnected in such a way that the *entire* parallel (one- or two-dimensional) array can be read out electronically through one or more output channels. An example of a detector array in this category might be the light-sensitive element in the CCD (charge-coupled-device) camera, now commonplace in many solid state cameras and video cassette recorders.

This distinction between single-pixel detectors and detector arrays is important, because the technologies that are commonly employed in these two cases differ in a number of respects, and as a result can exhibit wide differences in performance characteristics such as bandwidth, sensitivity, linearity, and dynamic range. In the case of single-pixel detectors, for example, it proves easier to jointly optimize performance parameters because of the larger number of degrees of freedom available to the device designer in a single-input, single-output system. The detector array designer, on the other hand, often must make additional tradeoffs dictated by the nature of the charge storage and readout process employed over the full set of integrated pixels.

In the context of photonic neural-network implementations, single-pixel detectors have two primary functions. The first is to act as optical signal to electronic signal converters within optically addressed spatial light modulators, to translate a pixel's worth of incident light intensity (representing, for example, the weighted sum of signals from the output of a plane of neuron units) into a voltage or current. The resultant electronic signal can then be processed by local intrapixel circuitry to produce the desired neural threshold function for subsequent optical encoding (modulation). This process could be accomplished either onboard a monolithic or hybrid integrated optically addressed spatial light modulator (OASLM), or on a separate detector chip that interfaces with an electrically addressed spatial light modulator (EASLM). In this latter case, the detector will most likely fall under the *detector array* category discussed further below, since a parallel-to-serial conversion is typically required to extract the array of data (e.g., an image) from the detector chip (followed by a serial-to-parallel conversion to load the signal into the EASLM). It should be noted that even in the case of monolithic spatial light modulators that do not feature discrete detectors, electronic control circuitry, and modulators, converting a two-dimensional optical input distribution into a modified two-dimensional output distribution *necessarily* involves a local detection function, even if it is not particularly easy to separate the detection process from the modulation process.

The second important single-pixel detector function is to provide for single-point monitoring functions within the system, such as the output power from a given laser source, the average power emitted from a laser source array, or a particular system output that activates a desired process or function (for example, the identification of a specific defect pattern on a manufactured part within the input image field of a neural image processor, that in turn results in rejection of the part).

Perhaps the simplest type of detection element that can be incorporated in a single pixel is the *photoconductor*, which typically consists of a thin film of material that alters its resistance to electrical current in response to the intensity of incident illumination. The most commonly used single-pixel photodetectors, however, are based in some way or other on the *semiconductor p-n junction diode*. Under reverse bias in a p-n junction diode, photocarriers created by light absorbed within the region of the junction between n-type and p-type semiconductor layers are swept *out* of the junction region by the internal electric field across the junction, and collected in the external circuit. If the internal electric field is high enough, each photocarrier can acquire enough energy during sweepout to generate an avalanche of additional carriers, leading to significant gain in the class of so-called *avalanche photodiodes*.

The inclusion of an intrinsic (undoped or compensated) layer of semiconductor material between the n-type and p-type layers allows for a significant reduction in the junction capacitance of the device, with a corresponding improvement in signal

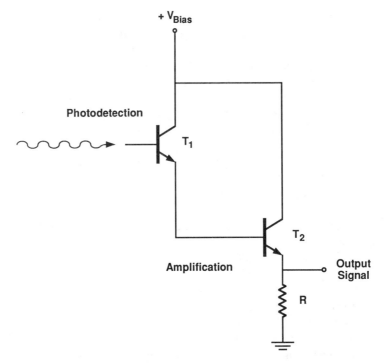

FIGURE 9.19   Schematic diagram of a photo-Darlington pair utilized as a high-gain detector/amplifier combination.

bandwidth. Such devices are commonly referred to as p-i-n photodiodes, packaged versions of which are commercially available for a wide variety of photosensor functions. Typical p-i-n photodiodes exhibit risetimes of a few nanoseconds, are linear in output over seven orders of magnitude of input intensity, and are sensitive to very low light-intensity levels. For silicon p-i-n photodiodes, sensitivities of about 0.4 milliamperes of output current per milliwatt of optical input power at a wavelength of 830 nm are common, which represents a conversion efficiency from photons to electrons of approximately 60 percent.

Phototransistors are light-sensitive devices that exhibit current gain in exactly the same manner as a transistor, with the exception that the controlling base current is injected *optically* rather than through the base lead. In fact, most VLSI transistors (both bipolar and MOS) are photosensitive (though perhaps not optimized for the photodetector role), and must be protected from stray light in order not to compromise their performance characteristics. The principal advantage of a phototransistor is its inherent current gain of order 100 to 1000, which often makes the interface of the photodetector to following circuitry more straightforward. In cases requiring exceptionally high gain in the front (photodetection) end, two transistors can be paired as shown in Figure 9.19 so that one acts as a phototransistor and the other as a current amplifier. Such a two-transistor combination has achieved widespread use and is referred to as a *photo-Darlington pair* [Sze, 1981b]. The tradeoffs for increased gain in both of these cases are risetime (which translates directly into signal bandwidth) and area required for integration. Typical risetimes for phototransistors are almost three orders of magnitude higher (a few microseconds) than those characteristic of p-i-n photodiodes. Photo-Darlingtons are yet another factor of ten or so slower in response time. Optimized phototransistors and photo-Darlingtons require relatively large collector-base junctions in order to provide an appropriately sized photosensitive region that can be accessed by optical imaging techniques.

In many if not most cases, the type of photodetector chosen for use as a single-pixel detector in a spatial light modulator application depends on its integrability with associated control electronics and modulation elements. This, in turn, depends on whether the particular spatial light modulator in question is monolithically or hybrid integrated, as discussed in the section on photonic switching above, and on which semiconductor substrate the photodetection element itself is to be fabricated. In some cases, the desire for integration of a high density of neuron units may place strict bounds on the area allocated to each separate function in general, and on the photodetection and requisite amplification function in particular.

In traditional applications of photodetector technology, for example in spectroscopy and optical metrology, linearity of response (output voltage or current as a function of the input intensity) is prized, as is a wide dynamic range over which linearity is assured. In neural-network applications, however, linearity is typically less of an issue. In fact, it is often convenient to *use* the inherent nonlinearity of the input-output characteristic of a particular photodetector device to generate part or all of the nonlinearity required of the overall neural unit function. This can result in a lower overall expenditure of real estate for each neuron unit, increasing the neuron array density, as well as in a reduction of circuit complexity within each pixel. One such example is the output-current saturation characteristic of phototransistors at high input intensities, which can be used to emulate the upper saturation regime of the sigmoidal neuron response function.

Detector arrays are employed whenever the intensity distribution of a one- or two-dimensional image field requires conversion to electronic form for interface with succeeding computational or output stages of the system. In a very real sense, a two-dimensional detector array is nothing more than the business end of an optoelectronic *camera* that can be positioned anywhere within the optical system that the local intensity distribution represents a desired result. In fact, low-reflectivity beamsplitters can be used to merely "sample" the local intensity distribution of a given beam of light, allowing most of the incident light to propagate in a further computational arm of the optical train for use elsewhere.

Detector arrays are inherently different in at least one key respect from the single-pixel photodetectors (as well as arrays of photodetectors used in optically addressed spatial light modulators) discussed previously: the need to provide for some form of output channel multiplexing, in order to avoid the requirement for a one-to-one correspondence between pixels in the array and output pins. For example, in a 1000×1000 element detector array, fully parallel readout requires one *million* output channels or pinouts. As a result, detector arrays are usually

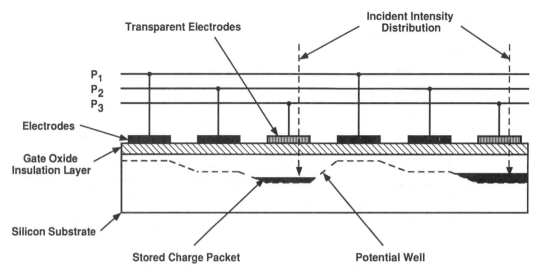

FIGURE 9.20 Schematic diagram of a charge-coupled-device (CCD) photo-detector array fabricated on a silicon substrate. Electrostatic potential wells are created by application of appropriate voltages to the three-phase bias electrode structure, with electrical isolation provided by the gate oxide layer. Light incident through the transparent electrodes creates stored charge that can be transferred to an output signal terminal by proper sequential phasing of the bias voltages (P_1 to P_3).

configured to perform some form of parallel-to-serial conversion of the data into a single high-bandwidth serial channel prior to the readout of each frame (though multiple output channels can also be used). This can either add significant circuit complexity to the area surrounding each pixel in order to accommodate for the parallel-to-serial conversion and interpixel communication function, or be directly incorporated into the design of the photodetection elements themselves, as in the case of the CCD arrays discussed below.

The state of the art of detector arrays has advanced tremendously even over the past decade, to the point where solid state detector arrays with quite spectacular performance are used everywhere from astronomical applications (as detectors for even the largest telescopes), to earth observation satellites (infrared focal plane arrays), to photomicroscopy (in place of the traditional film-based photographic camera), to consumer products (electronic still photography and video cameras).

One of the most successful and generally available types of solid state detector array is the *charge-coupled-device* (or CCD) array [Sze, 1981c; *Optical Engineering*, 1987a; *Optical Engineering*, 1987b]. In this technology, usually based on MOS fabrication techniques in silicon (but adaptable to compound semiconductor substrates as well), incident illumination within a given pixel causes the accumulation of photogenerated charge in an electrostatic potential well formed by the application of bias voltages on a set of electrodes, as shown schematically in Figure 9.20. In operation, the CCD array is illuminated for a given exposure time (slightly less than one full frame interval), during which time the charge generated by the incident illumination is integrated within each primary well. Subsequently, appropriate voltages are applied by means of multiphased electrode structures to *spill* the accumulated charge packet into the neighboring well, while simultaneously moving the charges in the neighboring well to *its* neighboring well, and so on throughout the array.

The overall operation resembles the function of an array of one-dimensional shift registers. At one edge of the structure, the charge packets from each row are collected into a single column that is read out by a very high speed shift register (a linear, usually buried channel CCD array) to form the single output channel. Full readout of the array must occur before the next frame is exposed (except in specifically designed cases such as the time-delay-and-integrate or TDI mode of operation, in which only *one* shift is interposed between successive exposures).

One-dimensional arrays of CCD elements have been successfully fabricated in sizes of 1×2048, while special purpose two-dimensional CCD imaging arrays 2048×2048 in size are commercially available [Blouke, 1987]. This represents a parallel detector with 4,194,304 individual pixels! In one particular 2048×2048 CCD array, the imaging area is 5.5×5.5 centimeters, with a pixel size of 27×27 microns. This array exhibited a dark (unilluminated) noise buildup in each pixel of only 6 to 12 electrons when read out at a rate of 50,000 pixels per second, which allows for detection of extremely low-level signals with excellent signal-to-noise ratio. Given a well capacity of about 700,000 electrons, this very low noise figure suggests a dynamic range in excess of 70,000, nearly five orders of magnitude! For well charge densities less than 200,000 per pixel, the linearity is better than 0.5 percent over this portion of the full dynamic range. Finally, this array exhibited an extraordinarily high charge transfer efficiency of 0.999992, representing the fraction of charge within a given pixel that is routinely transferred to an adjacent pixel without loss.

The integration of large-scale detector arrays by means of VLSI techniques provides the prospect of special-purpose arrays that perform part of the computational function *within* the confines of the array. One example of such special-purpose chips is the incorporation in a CCD array of charge-coupled analog circuitry to perform arithmetic operations such as addition, subtraction, and magnitude comparison [Fossum, 1987]. Such an array could allow for detection of parallel differential outputs, with both positive (excitatory) and negative (inhibitory) weighted sums as dual optical inputs in a (positive-definite) intensity representation.

ARCHITECTURAL CONSIDERATIONS FOR PHOTONIC NEURAL-NETWORK IMPLEMENTATIONS

We now turn our attention to the *use* of the photonic components and fundamental principles described above in the implementation of highly parallel neural-network *architectures*. The focus in this section is on a general framework that emphasizes characteristics common to different approaches to photonic and optical neural-network implementations, as well as on illuminating some of the key fundamental differences among the various implementation approaches. A review of recent and ongoing research in photonic and optical neural-network implementations is beyond the scope of this chapter; sources of such information can be found in the "Suggested Further Reading" section at the end of this chapter.

Photonic neural-network implementations can be adaptive or nonadaptive, can represent the signal using different physical quantities, and can be built using one-dimensional (1-D) or two-dimensional (2-D) arrays of neuron units with two-dimensional or three-dimensional (3-D) interconnection elements. These issues, in addition to other features that are desirable in any photonic implementation of a neural network, are discussed in this section. Throughout, one should keep in mind the distinctions that exist among systems with fixed interconnections, programmable systems, and truly adaptive systems. We will initially concentrate on the implementation of a single layer of a network, and subsequently show how this generalizes to multiple layers.

The computation process of any one layer of a neural network can be represented by:

$$ y_i = f\left[\sum_j w_{ij} x_j\right] \tag{9-23} $$

in which neuron unit j is situated at the input to the layer of interconnections, neuron unit i is situated at the output of the layer of interconnections, y_i is the output of neuron unit i, x_j is the output of neuron unit j, w_{ij} is the weight associated with the interconnection between them, and the function f represents the neuron unit nonlinearity. The term inside the brackets, the activation potential, will be denoted by ρ_i. Note that the term in brackets is a matrix-vector product between an interconnection weight matrix and an input vector. The function f then operates independently on each element of the resulting vector; this is called a *point nonlinearity*, and as such lends itself to implementation with a spatial light modulator (SLM).

Most current learning algorithms fall into one of a small number of classes. For example, one such class can be specified by:

$$ \Delta w_{ij} = \alpha \delta_i x_j - \beta w_{ij} \tag{9-24} $$

in which $\Delta w_{ij} = w_{ij}(k+1) - w_{ij}(k)$ is the weight update, k represents the iteration index, α is the learning gain constant, and β is a decay constant that is included primarily for hardware convenience; β can be set to 0 when so desired. Suitable choices of the training term δ_i give different learning algorithms, such as Hebbian, Widrow-Hoff, single-layer least minimum squares (LMS), and for the case of multilayer networks, backward error propagation. (For example, an optical architecture that potentially implements backward error propagation in a multilayer neural network is described by Wagner and Psaltis [Wagner, 1987]). In this chapter we will restrict our attention to this particular class of algorithms for illustrative purposes. Although other classes of learning algorithms can likely also be implemented using photonic hardware, research to date has focused primarily on the class represented

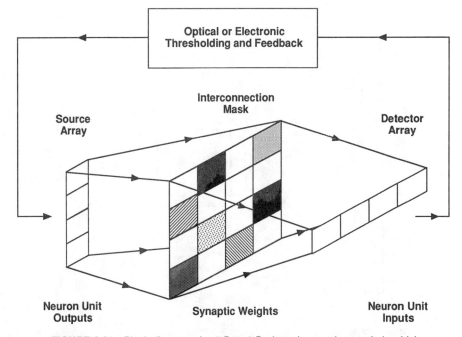

FIGURE 9.21   Block diagram of a 1-D to 1-D photonic neural network, in which a one-dimensional neuron unit array is fully interconnected to a one-dimensional detector array by means of a two-dimensional interconnection mask.

by Equation (9-24). An important aspect of Equation (9-24) for implementation is the outer product between the training vector δ and the input vector x for the weight matrix update.

An example of a photonic neural system is shown in block-diagram form in Figure 9.21. This system utilizes a 1-D array of neuron units at the input and output, and a 2-D interconnection mask. Each pixel in the input is expanded optically (using cylindrical lenses) and illuminates the corresponding row of the interconnection mask. The mask stores the analog weights and provides a pointwise multiplication before the beam is contracted so that one column from the mask is incident onto one corresponding output pixel. The optical system in effect provides a fully parallel analog optical matrix-vector multiplication as represented by the bracketed term in Equation (9-23), performed over all i. Threshold functions and feedback connections are provided by means of either photonics or electronics. The first experimental demonstration of such a system applied to neural-network implementations used an array of light emitting diodes (LEDs) as inputs to, and a linear detector array as the output from, the optical interconnection [Psaltis, 1985; Farhat, 1985]. This particular system utilized electronics to provide the threshold functions and feedback connections.

It should be noted that many variants of Figure 9.21 are possible; some are

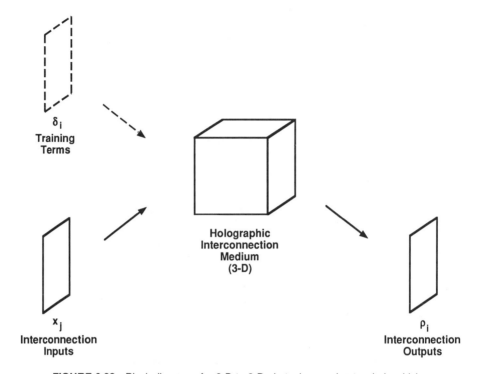

δ_i
**Training
Terms**

**Holographic
Interconnection
Medium
(3-D)**

x_j
**Interconnection
Inputs**

ρ_i
**Interconnection
Outputs**

FIGURE 9.22   Block diagram of a 2-D to 2-D photonic neural network, in which
a two-dimensional neuron array is interconnected to a two-dimensional output
array by means of a three-dimensional volume holographic optical interconnection
mask. The input plane, output plane, and optional training plane are shown. Many
variants of this geometry with similar properties are possible.

more compact than others, though all of them share essentially the same basic
characteristics. The interconnection mask can be fixed (e.g., photographic film) or
variable (e.g., an SLM). In the latter case the SLM can be electronically or optically
addressed. Electronic addressing is appropriate for straightforward interfacing to
an electronic machine that supplies the (updated) interconnection weights, whereas
for a maximum adaptation rate an optical addressing technique would ultimately be
optimal. Currently available SLMs with large numbers of pixels tend to be slow
(500×500 analog pixels with 1-ms to 100-ms frame times) [Tanguay, 1985]; much
faster technologies are being developed for future use [see, for example, Lentine,
1988; Lentine, 1991; McCormick, 1989b]. Such a system, with 1-D inputs, 1-D
outputs, and 2-D interconnections, will likely scale up to between 100 and 1000
fully connected neuron units.

A photonic system that can implement larger numbers of neuron units and interconnections is shown in Figure 9.22. All neuron unit planes are now 2-D arrays,
and the interconnection medium is a 3-D structure, implemented in a volume holo-

graphic material. In effect, there is a separate volume grating connecting each input neuron unit j to each output neuron unit i. The diffraction efficiency of each grating is proportional to the weight, w_{ij}, of the corresponding interconnection. Note that each such grating is analogous to a beamsplitter, as discussed in the previous section, with the primary difference that the volume gratings are direction (and wavelength) selective. Thus, beams incident on such a "beamsplitter" at other than the correct angle are not affected by the presence of the holographic beamsplitter. Properly recorded, then, the grating w_{ij} is situated in angular orientation and grating period so that it affects only the inputs at the angle corresponding to x_j, and will direct the corresponding output $w_{ij}x_j$ to the correct summation node ρ_i. The achievable numbers of neuron units and interconnections are currently subjects of considerable debate, but would likely be 10^4 to 10^6 neuron units per plane and of order 10^{10} independent interconnections with weights, assuming continued research unveils no impassable boundaries.

For the case of an adaptive network, we use a variable (typically photore-fractive) holographic material for recording and implementing the interconnections. To incorporate learning, a training plane comprising a 2-D array of nodes generates the δ_i terms (Figure 9.22). During a weight update, an exposure is made of the interference pattern between beams emanating from the two left-hand planes in the figure. Each of the two left-hand planes could be implemented using, for example, a 2-D spatial light modulator illuminated by an expanded beam. This results in a change in the refractive index modulation representing the current weight that is dependent on the product $\delta_i x_j$, so that with appropriate choices of parameters, the increment in diffraction efficiency can be made proportional to $\delta_i x_j$. Ideally, this records changes (updates) in the interconnection weights within the hologram given by Equation (9-24), above, in the form of gratings situated with appropriate angular orientation and grating period. It should be noted that generating and recording these weight updates is not a simple matter, and care must be taken to insure that the appropriate interference terms are recorded and that not too much crosstalk is inadvertently created. Recording and recall of the correct values is primarily a number representation issue and is discussed below; undesirable crosstalk depends on the recording and reconstruction technique, as previously discussed in the subsection on "Photonic Interconnections."

An example of one source of holographically induced interconnection crosstalk is an inadvertent degeneracy of gratings. Even though each volume grating affects only the beams incident at a particular angle with respect to the grating, it affects *all* of the beams at that particular angle. Because of this, an entire cone of beams (with its axis of symmetry aligned with the grating wave vector) can be affected by a single diffraction grating. This degeneracy creates an undesired coupling between different interconnections in a fully connected network. For neuron unit sources on an ideal, rectangular grid, this coupling can be eliminated by removing neuron units from certain locations in the array, leaving sparsely distributed neuron units arranged in a degeneracy-breaking pattern. This eliminates the undesired coupling, at the expense of a reduction in the number of neuron units from N^2 (for an $N \times N$ array) to $N^{1.5}$ [Psaltis, 1989].

The case of a nonadaptive network is likely to be an important one as well. In this case the interconnection hologram does not have to be recorded in accordance with a specific learning algorithm. If the weights are known a priori, then any applicable recording technique will suffice. In many cases, however, the weights may not be known. A common scenario may involve the training of a "master" network; once it has been trained, copies of the network could be produced in a production environment. If the network is large, and particularly if it utilizes volume holographic optical interconnections, then probing the values of all of the weights could be impractical. The most efficient production means in this case would be to make direct copies of the volume hologram. Thus, the capability of rapidly copying a multiplexed volume interconnection hologram is important.

The physical representation of the signal directly impacts the operation of a photonic neural network. The physical quantities available for optical representation of a signal level are field amplitude, phase, intensity, polarization, spatial position or frequency, and wavelength. We will consider only the most likely candidates: field *amplitude* (with phase) and *intensity*. For the case of an amplitude (with phase) representation, the signals may in general be complex valued; bipolar signals, of course, represent a subset of these numbers, and thus can be represented. Given that x and y are represented as (electric or magnetic) field amplitudes, the resulting detected activation potential of neuron unit i, ρ_i, is given by

$$\rho_i^{(\text{coh})} = \left| \sum_j w_{ij} x_j \right|^2 \qquad (9\text{-}25)$$

for the case of a coherent sum, and by

$$\rho_i^{(\text{incoh})} = \sum_j |w_{ij} x_i|^2 \qquad (9\text{-}26)$$

for the case of an incoherent sum (refer to the preceeding section on "Fundamental Principles of Photonic Technology"). In both Equations (9-25) and (9-26) the weight w_{ij} is represented physically by the *amplitude* diffraction efficiency. The coherent sum given by Equation (9-25) has the advantage of allowing for the addition of both positive and negative numbers in computation of the neuron unit potential, as desired for the incorporation of both excitatory and inhibitory neuron unit inputs. Clearly, Equations (9-25) and (9-26) deviate from conventional neural-network models. The effects on different neural-network models of such deviations in the summation before thresholding are not currently well understood.

If we instead encode the signal levels as intensities, the activation potential becomes

$$\rho_i^{(\text{int})} = \sum_j w_{ij} x_j \qquad (9\text{-}27)$$

which is the desired activation potential, but at the expense of all terms in the summation being nonnegative. In this case the weight w_{ij} is represented physically by the *intensity* diffraction efficiency. A technique for effectively achieving bipolar signals in this case will be discussed in the section describing "An Implementation Strategy."

The signal representation used also impacts the nature of the weight updates. The physical weight updates can be derived using common models of photorefractive (or other) recording materials. Such a derivation requires a number of approximations and assumptions to be made regarding the chosen operational mode. By appropriate choice of the operational mode, the ideal weight update rule given by Equation (9-24) can be approximately obtained for both intensity representation and amplitude representation cases. The operational mode may not prove to be the same in each case, and may differ in such parameters as the size of the weight updates, the size of the existing weights before the update, and the exact characteristics of the holographic material used. The "second-order" terms that deviate from the precise form of Equation (9-24) are also different in the two cases; the effect of such terms on learning algorithm performance is not well characterized or understood, and is currently an active area of research.

So far we have discussed only a single interconnection layer with neuron units for inputs and outputs. If such a physical network includes feedback, it can be generalized to functionally implement an arbitrary multilayer feedforward or recurrent network. Figure 9.23 illustrates this principle, showing one *physical* layer of neuron units, one layer of interconnections from the neuron units to a set of fan-in nodes, and feedback from each fan-in node to the corresponding neuron unit. These neuron units can be conceptually divided into groups corresponding to different *functional* layers. Some of the physical interconnections then represent functionally feedforward connections (represented by solid lines and boxes in Figure 9.23), and some represent functionally lateral connections within a layer (represented by broken lines and boxes in Figure 9.23). Feedback connections to previous layers, and feedforward connections that bypass the next subsequent layer, can also be incorporated in a similar manner, but are not shown in the figure. This technique for implementing multilayer networks using a single physical layer has been discussed by Farhat for the case of 1-D neuron unit arrays interconnected by a 2-D mask, and used in the implementation of parallel optoelectronic simulated annealing [Farhat, 1987]. Thus any photonic (single physical layer) architectures discussed herein generalize to multilayer networks, provided that they have capability for arbitrary connections and feedback.

In summary, the desirable characteristics of photonic implementation of neural networks include: (1) modularity, so that multiple "modules" can be cascaded; (2) capability for lateral, feedforward, and feedback interconnections, which can be achieved physically by use of a single-layer network with feedback and arbitrary interconnection capability; (3) analog, weighted connections with analog signals; (4) bipolar signals and weights; (5) scalability to large numbers of neuron units with high connectivity; (6) generality, so that different neuron models, network models, and learning algorithms can be implemented within the same basic technology; (7)

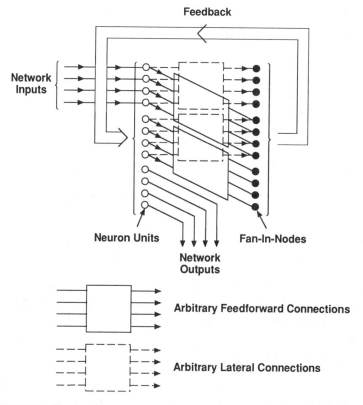

FIGURE 9.23 A single-layer physical neural network with feedback, used to implement a multilayer recurrent functional network. The solid boxes indicate feedforward connections, the broken boxes lateral connections.

compatibility of different components within a given architecture; and (8) overall feasibility of the proposed combination of algorithm, architecture, devices, and materials. In addition, the optical/photonic hardware would ideally incorporate the following features: (1) simultaneous, parallel updates of all interconnection weights at each iteration; (2) high optical throughput; (3) low interconnection crosstalk; and (4) flexible functionality for the neuron unit response, so that different neuron models and learning algorithms can be accommodated.

AN IMPLEMENTATION STRATEGY

In this section a photonic technique for the implementation of neural networks is described that potentially satisfies the aforementioned desirable characteristics and features [Jenkins, 1990a; Asthana, 1990a; Jenkins, 1990b; Asthana,

1990b; Jenkins, 1990c]. This photonic neural-network implementation technique utilizes optoelectronic spatial light modulators (SLMs) for the 2-D neuron unit and training term planes. Each neuron unit incorporates dual channel encoding to allow for the representation of bipolar input and output signals, and comprises two integrated detectors, two modulators, and integrated electronics. The neuron unit input and output signals are represented in the optical system by intensity. The interconnections are based on a 3-D holographic material with a novel incoherent/coherent recording and reconstruction technique that permits simultaneous updates of all weights during each iteration. In addition, the interconnections utilize a unique double angular multiplexing arrangement to minimize interchannel crosstalk and throughput losses, in which each pixel of the object beam SLM is illuminated by a set of mutually incoherent beams, each at a different angle. This implementation technique is explained in the remainder of this section.

A key feature of this implementation strategy is the use of an array of individually coherent sources that are mutually incoherent to generate an array of coherent beam pairs used for holographic recording and reconstruction in the interconnection network. Consider the problem of recording two holograms, object A recorded with reference beam x_j and object B recorded with reference beam $x_{j'}$, as shown in Figure 9.24(a). The objects A and B could each be a 2-D array of data. In order to write both holograms simultaneously, A and x_j originate from the same coherent source and are mutually coherent; similarly for B and $x_{j'}$. However, B and $x_{j'}$ originate from a different source than A and x_j, so that each pair is incoherent with respect to the other pair. In this way, there are no extra (crosstalk) holograms written, such as that between A and $x_{j'}$, or between x_j and $x_{j'}$. This technique can be used for more than two multiplexed holograms, in which case a separate source is assumed for each hologram written.

During reconstruction, the holograms are illuminated by the same set of reference beams x_j and $x_{j'}$. This simultaneously reconstructs the arrays A and B [Figure 9.24(b)]. If the arrays are in registry upon reconstruction, a pixel-by-pixel incoherent sum will be achieved in the output array. If we now consider each reference beam x_j to be the output of a neuron unit at the input to an interconnection layer, then each reconstructed hologram corresponds to the fan-out from one neuron unit, with a contribution to each pixel in the output array proportional to the weight of the corresponding interconnection. This is depicted in Figure 9.24(b) and (c), in which the two signals fanning in to a given neuron unit are derived from separate, mutually incoherent optical sources. Note that this technique provides an incoherent sum for the potential of each neuron unit [Equation (9-26) or Equation (9-27), depending on the chosen representation], as desired.

Another critical as well as unique feature of the photonic architecture described herein is a "double angular multiplexing" technique in which one input node or pixel in the object beam path has multiple beams passing through it at different angles. Thus, a set of angularly multiplexed beams is introduced for each object beam node δ_i, as shown in Figure 9.25. A threefold angularly multiplexed fan-in from $x_1, x_2,$

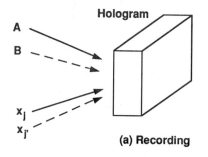

(a) Recording

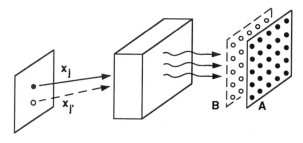

(b) Reconstruction

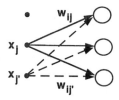

(c) Fan-out/Fan-in Interconnections

FIGURE 9.24 Incoherent/coherent technique for recording and reconstructing multiple holograms simultaneously, in which all solid lines represent mutually coherent beams, and all broken lines represent a separate set of mutually coherent beams. (a) Recording. (b) Reconstruction. (c) Holographic representation, in which each hologram represents the fan-out from a given neuron unit.

and x_3 to yield neuron unit potential ρ_1 is depicted in this figure; solid lines represent mutually coherent beams (all dashed lines represent a mutually coherent set as well; similarly for mixed dashed lines). Note that this multiplexing technique eliminates the fan-in beam degeneracy characteristic of collinear geometries referred to above in the subsection "Photonic Interconnections." Thus, the ensuing cross-coupling

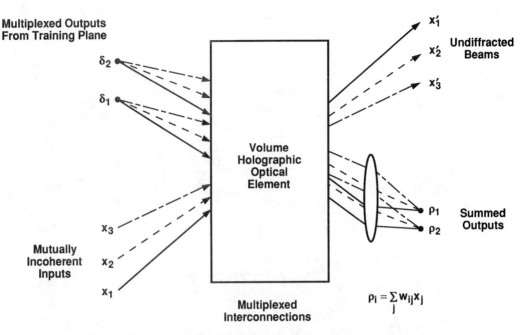

FIGURE 9.25 Double-angularly multiplexed volume holographic optical interconnection, designed to circumvent the effects of beam degeneracy. The mutually incoherent input beams ($\{x_j\}$) are angularly multiplexed over j, as are the corresponding sets of output beams from the training plane ($\{\delta_i^{(j)}\}$) generated by the coherent sources S_j, to produce an angularly multiplexed fan-in at each summed output, thus yielding the neuron activation potentials $\{\rho_i\}$.

terms are absent, and a much more accurate set of weights can be recorded and reconstructed at each iteration.

A photonic architecture for neural-network implementation that utilizes these principles is shown in Figure 9.26, for the case of Hebbian learning ($\delta_i = y_i$). The components shown in the figure comprise one module; inputs and outputs refer to this particular module. Only feedforward connections are shown. The upper spatial light modulator, SLM_1, generates the training terms δ_i that also represent neuron unit outputs in this case. The lower spatial light modulator, SLM_2, is the array of input neuron units. An array of individually coherent but mutually incoherent sources is used to illuminate the system; they are provided by a mutually incoherent laser diode array or by a coherent beam passing through an SLM that temporally modulates the phase of each pixel independently. (It can be shown that the latter method is equivalent to the former for the particular type of holographic recording and reconstruction used herein.) A volume holographic material stores the requisite weighted interconnections, and can implement either fixed or adaptive interconnections depending on the material used.

Both spatial light modulators in Figure 9.26 consist of an array of pixels. Each

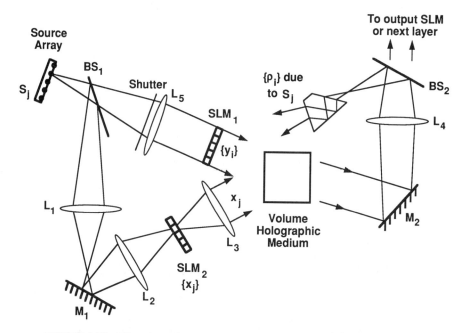

FIGURE 9.26 Photonic architecture for neural-network implementation that incorporates a parallel source array, double angular multiplexing, and incoherent/coherent recording and reconstruction; the Hebbian case is depicted.

pixel within a given array comprises three types of elements: (1) two integrated detectors for input of positive and negative parts of the neuron unit activation potential, (2) integrated electronic circuitry to provide the neuron unit (sigmoid or hard threshold) nonlinearity, and (3) two hybrid or monolithically integrated modulators for separate optical readout of the positive and negative neuron unit outputs. The SLMs, as shown, are read out in transmission, and have detectors situated so as to receive optical inputs on the right face of the SLM.

In the learning phase, the shutter is open as shown schematically in Figure 9.27. Light from each source S_j is approximately collimated so that it illuminates the entire array on SLM_1, at an angle dependent on the position of the jth source. Thus, for an N-by-N array of sources, there are N^2 beams reading out the contents of SLM_1 simultaneously, each at a different angle; the entire array of terms $\{y_i\}$ is encoded onto each of these beams. Each such beam then interferes only with its corresponding reference beam x_j, derived from the *same* source and encoded by SLM_2, in the holographic medium. This writes the set of desired weight update terms $\alpha x_j y_i$.

During the computation phase the shutter is closed to prevent learning, as shown schematically in Figure 9.28. The array of sources is imaged onto SLM_2 as a set of readout beams, so that each individual source corresponds to one pixel

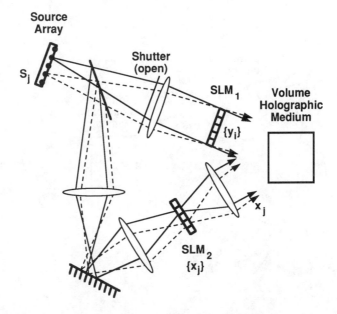

FIGURE 9.27   Photonic architecture for neural-network implementation: recording configuration. This configuration implements the learning function in the photonic architecture of Figure 9.26. The sets of beams emitted from the source array (two are shown) interfere in the volume holographic medium to update the weights stored in the interconnection holograms.

(neuron unit) on the SLM. The SLM modulates each beam so that the transmitted beam has an intensity proportional to the output value of the corresponding neuron unit. Thus, the jth source illuminates the jth pixel of this SLM, providing the signal x_j that becomes a reference beam to read out the jth hologram. This hologram reconstructs an array of spots, similar to that depicted in Figure 9.24, that contribute to the input of each neuron unit in the output plane. The optics is set up so that this array is imaged onto the detector array. In the complete neural-network architecture of Figure 9.26, additional optical elements (mirror M_2, lens L_4, and beamsplitter BS_2) are used to displace the detector array plane to the detector side of SLM_1, providing the neuron unit activation potentials. In addition, this beam is sent through beamsplitter BS_2 to a subsequent layer in the next module or to the output layer.

A generalized architecture that incorporates learning algorithms of the form of Equation (9-24) is shown in Figure 9.29. Instead of SLM_1, as in Figure 9.26, this architecture utilizes a training-term (δ_i) generator that is implemented via one or more optoelectronic SLMs. In general, target values t_i, actual neuron unit outputs y_i, or possibly activation potentials ρ_i may be provided as inputs to the training-term generator. The physical arrangement of optical beams passing through the training-term generator (from left to right) is the same as that shown passing through SLM_1 in Figure 9.26. Lateral and feedback connections can be incorporated by including

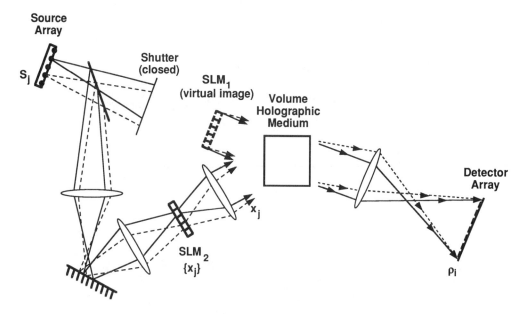

FIGURE 9.28 Photonic architecture for neural-network implementation: reconstruction configuration. This configuration implements a single forward pass of
the computing function in the photonic architecture of Figure 9.26. The lower
set of beams acts as a set of reference beams and generates a set of weighted
output arrays that are imaged onto the detector array. Each stored hologram is
reconstructed by a single neuron unit x_j, and fans out with appropriate weights to
illuminate the detector array. The full set of reconstructed holograms sums within
each pixel to yield the neuron activation potentials $\{\rho_i\}$.

an optical feedback path from the output of the hologram to the input side of
SLM_2.

For many applications, both SLM_1 and SLM_2 can be fabricated using the
same technology. Let's consider the case of a sigmoidal response with bipolar
inputs and bipolar outputs. The electronics within each neuron unit can take the
difference between the two detector inputs to yield the (bipolar) neuron potential.
It can then perform the sigmoidal nonlinearity and send the result to appropriate
(positive-channel or negative-channel) modulator(s). For example, we have fabricated a number of silicon chips that integrate the necessary control electronics
with appropriate detectors. One possible circuit that has been designed to incorporate the necessary functionality is shown schematically in Figure 9.30. Outputs
from the two photodetection stages (V_{in1} and V_{in2}) are differentially amplified using two pairs of CMOS transistors (M_1–M_3, M_2–M_4), generating two separate
and complementary outputs. The differential amplifier has been designed to saturate for large values of the input signal difference, producing the upper asymptotic limit behavior characteristic of the sigmoid function. Each output signal is

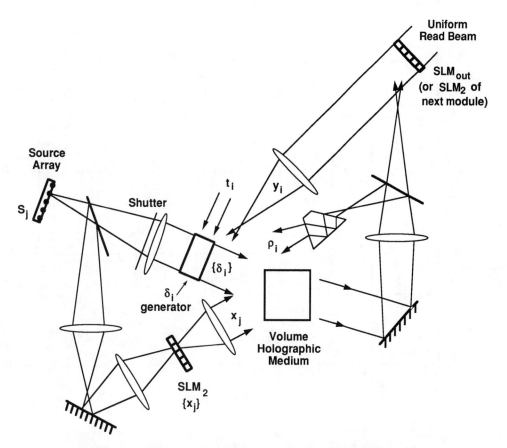

FIGURE 9.29 Generalized photonic architecture for neural-network implementation, including provision for the generation of arbitrary training terms (δ_i).

then inverted and clipped by another CMOS transistor pair (M_{21}–M_{22}, M_{11}–M_{12}), which asymmetrizes the transfer curve and adds the lower asymptotic limit of the sigmoid function. Finally, each output signal is inverted yet again and shifted in level by a dual-transistor subunity-gain amplifier stage (M_{23}–M_{24}, M_{13}–M_{14}), producing complementary output signals (V_{out1} and V_{out2}) that control the dual-channel modulation elements. External provision is made in each pixel (neuron unit) for the adjustment of the gain (slope) and saturation level of each characteristic curve. This external bias adjustment allows for postfabrication fine tuning of the overall response of the circuit, given process-induced variations in device characteristics.

A sample set of characteristic curves measured from one of these chips is shown in Figure 9.31, with the voltage on the second detector input channel as the parameter. These curves show the differential function of the dual-channel circuit,

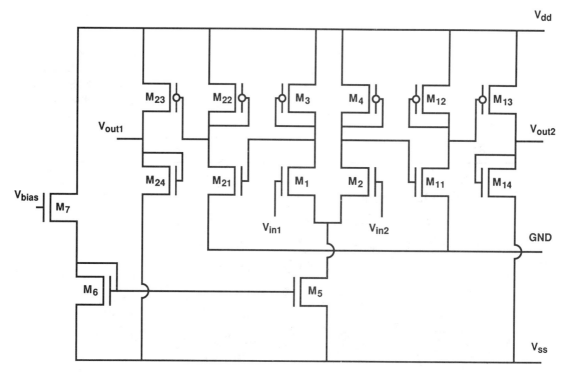

FIGURE 9.30 Schematic diagram of a dual-input, dual-output differential amplifier that effects a sigmoidal transfer characteristic.

as well as the desired sigmoidal response characteristic. A 6×6 array of these $100 \times 100 \ \mu$m neuron units has also been fabricated with excellent uniformity.

The modular nature of this photonic neural-net architecture can be inferred from Figure 9.29; the upper right SLM is SLM_2 of the subsequent module. Feedback paths from one module back to previous modules can be added, if desired, in a relatively straightforward manner. Bipolar signals are incorporated by the dual-channel nature of the SLMs, with positive and negative channels for each neuron unit. Since each neuron unit has two physical outputs and two physical inputs, each interconnection between two neuron units physically consists of four separate weighted connections (positive modulator to positive detector, positive modulator to negative detector, etc.). Thus, even though each physical weight is nonnegative in value, their combination permits effective implementation of bipolar functional weights. In fact, the extra degrees of freedom provided by four independent weights can require revised weight-update rules to ensure convergence of the learning process [Petrisor, 1990].

With the current spatial light modulator design at $100 \ \mu$m $\times 100 \ \mu$m per neuron unit, 10^4 neuron units per cm^2 can be implemented on each SLM. By constructing

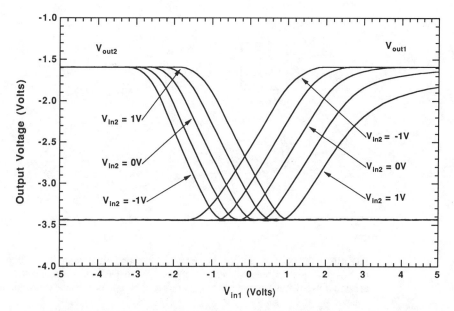

FIGURE 9.31 Experimentally obtained transfer characteristics from the circuit shown in Figure 9.30, showing the output voltage in both channels (V_{out1} and V_{out2}) as a function of one input voltage (V_{in1}), with the other input voltage (V_{in2}) as a parameter.

an SLM as a mosaic of such arrays, a 7.5 cm × 7.5 cm SLM could implement approximately 5×10^5 neuron units. Each "tile" or small array within such a mosaic need not be carefully aligned with respect to the other tiles, as the optical system just images the array back onto itself; in the case of multiple modules or lateral/feedback connections, however, all SLMs must be similarly tiled, within an appropriate tolerance figure. Note that the current design utilizes only 2 μm feature sizes in CMOS; this could eventually be scaled down by a factor of 4 in each dimension, yielding more than an order of magnitude increase in the number of neuron units implementable per unit chip area (or an equivalent reduction in the overall size with the same number of neuron units).

It should now be clear that this architecture can be generalized to implement certain other neural models. The use of electronic circuitry for the neuron unit function and training-term generation provides significant inherent flexibility. For example, we have completed preliminary designs of units for forward and backward propagating signals in a backpropagation-style multilayer neural network. Although the optical weight updates in the holographic medium are restricted to outer-product terms [Equation (9-24)] in the architecture as shown, variants of the architecture may permit other learning scenarios.

Finally, we consider the important question of making duplicates of a network that has already been trained. Since a volume hologram may store of order 10^{10}

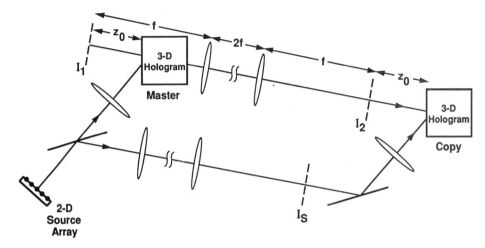

FIGURE 9.32 Optical layout for copying the entire contents of a three-dimensional volume holographic optical element (VHOE) into a second VHOE, utilizing a two-dimensional array of individually coherent, but mutually incoherent sources.

independent weighted interconnections, probing the value of each interconnection weight, and writing these values into each duplicate hologram, would yield a very inefficient duplication process. A preferable technique is to make direct copies of the multiplexed volume hologram. Here we describe a technique for copying such a multiplexed volume hologram in one step [Jenkins, 1990c]. To our knowledge this has never previously been achieved, but the use of incoherent/coherent holographic recording and reconstruction makes it in principle quite straightforward. Figure 9.32 shows an optical setup for duplicating the hologram. The master hologram is illuminated with the same set of reference beams as those employed during exposure; all of the mutually incoherent reference beams illuminate the master volume hologram simultaneously, recalling all of the stored holograms in parallel. The source array is imaged so that it generates an identical set of reference beams on the secondary (copy) holographic medium. Similarly, the reconstructed object beams are also imaged so that they are incident on the secondary holographic medium with amplitude and phase identical to that during recording of the master hologram. The appropriate pairs of beams interfere in the secondary holographic medium, making a complete copy of the original hologram. (As shown in Figure 9.32, the copy will actually be a spatially inverted version of the original. A slight variant of the optical system depicted in the figure can produce a copy that is identical to the original.) Thus it is conceivable to mass produce copies of a previously trained interconnection pattern, without ever knowing exactly what the interconnection weights are.

We conclude this section with a brief summary of the current implementation status of this particular photonic approach to neural-network fabrication. For the neuron unit arrays, 6×6 arrays of dual-channel detectors integrated with neuron function electronics have been fabricated in silicon and operate correctly. Individual multiple-quantum-well (InGaAs/GaAs) modulators have been successfully fabricated and tested, and exhibit drive voltages compatible with the electronics. The novel double-angularly multiplexed incoherent/coherent interconnection technique has been tested experimentally at the level of two inputs/two outputs and simulated at the level of four inputs/four outputs, all with very favorable results [Jenkins, 1990c; Asthana, 1990b; Asthana, 1990c]. In addition, several learning algorithms that incorporate some of the unique features of the optical hardware have been successfully designed and simulated. Large 2-D arrays of laser diodes that are not mutually coherent have been fabricated recently [Jewell, 1990; Orenstein, 1990a; Von Lehmen, 1990]. Photorefractive crystals are routinely grown commercially and can be purchased from vendors for use at visible as well as infrared wavelengths. In addition, the basic requisite features of the double angularly multiplexed incoherent/coherent holographic recording techniques have been demonstrated in single crystals of bismuth silicon oxide ($Bi_{12}SiO_{20}$), though not as yet at infrared wavelengths compatible with both the laser diode source array and the multiple-quantum-well spatial light modulators. All of the other components in the architecture (lenses, beamsplitters, etc.) are essentially available off the shelf.

As with any research project in progress, several questions pertaining to the photonic approach outlined herein remain partially unanswered. Consider, for example, the incoherent/coherent source array. Given the current state of the art of laser diode arrays, the total power dissipation will limit the number, maximum optical power, and spacing of the individual sources. Cross-coherence among the sources can cause undesirable crosstalk among corresponding interconnections, although in some neural-network models a small to moderate degree of interconnection crosstalk is not likely to cause intolerable degradation in performance. Fortunately, a larger spacing of sources implies that each laser can output a higher power, and also assures a higher degree of mutual incoherence. Other remaining questions include the achievable contrast ratio and uniformity of the spatial light modulators; suitable monolithic or hybrid techniques for integrating detectors, electronics, and modulators; optimization of the learning algorithm relative to the chosen holographic material's storage and erasure time constants; and linearity and limitations of the hologram copying process. The next section discusses fundamental and technological limitations of the photonic hardware and their impact on the performance of photonic neural-network architectures.

FUNDAMENTAL PHYSICAL AND TECHNOLOGICAL LIMITATIONS OF NEURO-OPTICAL COMPUTATION

Even though we are relatively early on in the development of viable neuro-optical computing systems, it is not too early to begin asking questions about the ultimate boundaries that may impact our future achievements. This line of inquiry can have a twofold impact. First, discovery of inherently *fundamental physical limitations* that affect all forms of computation can, if correctly applied to the neural computational paradigm, both provide us with an ultimate goal worthy of achievement, and perhaps warn us in advance of architectural choices that will prove unworthy of technological implementation. Second, careful analysis of the *technological limitations* (device performance boundaries within a given technological implementation) that affect system performance can provide us with necessary guidance in choosing among many possible implementation strategies. The goal, of course, is to come up with the right combination of implementation strategy and technological choices to achieve the highest computational throughput (or perhaps learning rate) based on any one of a number of metrics. In this section, then, we discuss both the fundamental physical and technological limitations that impact the future performance of neuro-optical computational systems.

The Energy Metric

Your brain is truly a remarkable instrument from a computational point of view (as well as from many other points of view!). Although estimates (as well as individuals!) vary, it is thought that the human brain consists of about 10^{11} neurons, each interconnected (in certain regions of the brain) to 10^3 to 10^4 other neurons [Changeux, 1985; Dowling, 1987; Hubel, 1979]. The human brain exhibits both short- and long-term memory, performs sophisticated image analysis in fractions of a second, operates as an effective associative memory integrated over a whole lifetime of learning, and yet operates on a power budget that is only a fraction of the power dissipated by the average light bulb in your home [Iversen, 1979]. In order to accomplish this, the active switching elements, the neurons, operate at an average power level about seven orders of magnitude lower than that characteristic of VLSI logic circuits [Mead, 1989b]. If this were not possible, it's likely that you'd be running a temperature even *without* the flu!

This discussion points to one of many possible metrics by which computational systems can be judged: energy (or power) dissipation. In fact, many modern supercomputers are limited in performance *precisely* because of power-dissipation boundaries, or the ability to extract the heat generated by the computational process from the volume used to perform the work. We can perhaps think of computation as broken down into three fundamental parts: *representation of information, implementation of computational complexity*, and *detection of the results*. From the energy metric point of view, *everything* costs energy: what goes in costs energy, what comes out costs energy, and what goes on in between costs energy too. The trick in building the computational engines of the future (neural or otherwise) will be to maximize the overall performance with a minimum expenditure of energy.

Some Quantum Limitations

By *representation of information*, we mean the choice of data representation on which computations are performed. Some examples might include the binary representation, M-ary representations, an analog representation, or the residue representation [Huang, 1979]. This choice has implications at the fundamental level for the energy cost to represent a number within a given probability of error. For example, if we detect an optical signal bit that is binary encoded with a so-called "ideal" detector that can tell the difference between receiving exactly zero photons and one or more photons, it only takes ten photons on the average to guarantee that the signal is received with a probability of error of one part in a billion, or a "bit error rate (BER)" of 10^{-9}. The average photon at a typical optical communications wavelength of 1300 nm has an energy of only 1.5×10^{-19} joules, so the total energy cost per bit is 1.5 attojoules (1.5×10^{-18} joules). For a communications channel operating at 10 gigabytes (8×10^9 bits) per second, this implies a power dissipation due to representation cost alone (without worrying yet about the *transmission* or *detection* of the information) of only 0.12 microwatts. For currently available detectors, about a thousand photons are required to achieve the same BER, so the necessary representation cost increases to 12 microwatts. In most currently envisioned communications systems, this cost is overwhelmed by other factors.

But what if we chose to represent numbers in an *analog* representation instead? If we were to follow the same kinds of quantum statistical rules, we would find that to represent the number "1000", say, with an effective bit error rate of 10^{-9} requires about 150 *million* photons [Tanguay, 1988]. This is about 15 million times larger than the representation cost of a single binary bit, and about 1.5 million times larger than the binary representation cost of the number 1000.

If we assume that the analog representation need only cover numbers between 0 and 1000, then the dependence of the probability of error on the number of photons used to represent the highest number (1000) is given in Figure 9.33. Interestingly, even if we are willing to give up on a couple of orders of magnitude of error probability, our energy cost isn't reduced very much. In fact, it costs about 27 million photons to represent 1000 with 1 percent error, and about 11 million photons to represent it with as much as 10 percent error. These numbers can all be reduced by about two orders of magnitude if we are willing to give up a factor of ten in dynamic range, limiting the highest representable number to 100 instead of 1000, as shown in the figure.

These errors arise fundamentally from the quantum-statistical nature of light, and from the fact that we just can't guarantee the number of photons in a packet of light (without resorting to exotic things like "squeezed states," which have their own practical limitations as well as other costs). In the brain, of course, it is currently thought that many (but not *all*) of the quantities involved in signal transmission, both electrical and chemical, are analog in nature.

The Incorporation of Computational Complexity

Given the fact that it is considerably more expensive to represent quantities in analog as opposed to binary form, why don't we always choose to compute in the binary representation? The answer is that many operations are less energy

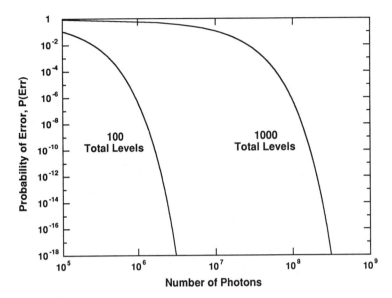

FIGURE 9.33 The single-pixel probability of error $P(\mathrm{Err})$ as a function of the number of photons detected within each pixel, for the cases of 100 and 1000 analog grey levels.

consumptive to perform in the binary representation, but others are not. The difference lies in the degree of computational complexity that can be implemented on a given representation for a particular computational operation within a chosen technological implementation. For our purposes here, we may define the computational complexity of a given operation as the minimum number of irreducible binary bit operations (over all possible computational algorithms and machine architectures) required to complete the calculation assuming that the data is represented in binary throughout.

For operations of low computational complexity such as transferring data from the CPU to memory or logic and control operations, computation in the binary representation tends to have a significant energy-consumption advantage at the fundamental limits (as well as at the current technological limits for both electronic and photonic processors). On the other hand, for operations of high computational complexity such as the two-dimensional Fourier transform that require a very large number of irreducible binary operations to perform (for the optimum algorithm), computation in the analog representation tends to exhibit lower overall energy consumption, particularly in photonic implementations.

The Hybrid Representation Concept

In the case of neural networks, a number of characteristic types of computational operations are typically employed, including for example the calculation of weight updates and storage of updated weights, the fan-out of neuron unit outputs, the multiplication of fanned-out outputs by weights, the communication of weighted signals, the fan-in and summation (or differencing) of weighted inputs, and the thresholding of summed inputs to form neuron unit outputs. These operations span a wide gamut of computational as well as physical complexity. As such, we suggest that optimum neural-network performance from an energy-metric viewpoint may turn out to be best achieved with a hybrid representation, in which the signal representation is essentially binary for certain functions, and essentially analog for others.

An example of the use of this hybrid representation concept is the use of a hard threshold function within each neuron unit to create a two-state output (*on* and *off*), and the use of analog holographic storage for all interconnection weights, as described in a previous section. In this case, the *inputs* to each neuron unit are analog, while the *outputs* from each neuron unit are binary. Multiplications are performed in a fully hybridized representation (multiplicands are analog while multipliers are binary), but summations are fully analog (the superposition of fanned-in input intensities). Given a particular choice of implementation technology, then, the overall power budget for a given hybrid representation can be established and compared with similar power budgets for fully analog and fully binary representations.

The Inherent Costs of Interconnections

Regardless of the representation chosen, it is clear that any computational energy budget must take into account the nonnegligible cost of the interconnections themselves. Interconnections characteristic of neural networks are merely a form of weighted communication channels, characterized by a high degree of fan-out and fan-in. For both electronic and photonic implementations that have adaptive weights, it takes energy to calculate the weight updates, it takes energy to store the resultant updated weights, it takes energy to perform the multiplications implied by the weighting of the output signals, and it takes energy to communicate the various signals between layers.

In the electronics case, these energy costs derive from charging up the capacitances of switching devices in the various forms of memory, flipping switches in the various arithmetic operations (both addition and multiplication) for binary representations, operating linear and nonlinear devices for analog representations, and charging and discharging the capacitance associated with output line drivers as well as the capacitance associated with the physical interconnections (wires) among the various parts of the circuit. In the photonics case, the comparable energy costs derive from the generation of light by coherent optical sources, the holographic recording of weights and weight updates, the throughput losses engendered by readout of the holographically stored (and multiplexed) interconnection matrix, any throughput losses associated with the fan-out and fan-in processes, and the inter- and intralayer communication costs.

The bottom line is that in most cases, complex, highly multiplexed interconnection networks with a high degree of fan-in and fan-out are very energy consumptive, and for the neural-network case may prove to be the largest energy sink.

The Inherent Cost of Detection (Switching)

No useful computational system can avoid the costs of detection, both of intermediate results that are essential to following calculations, and of the sought-after answers or output states that initiate subsequent actions or analysis. And this is the cost above all costs that we are certainly willing to pay, as answers or outputs validate the usefulness of the system and its design. As pointed out earlier, there are three primary areas in which detections are essential: in the generation of summed inputs prior to functional transformation into individual neuron unit outputs (usually on the input side of an optically addressed spatial light modulator), in the generation of specific system outputs, and in the holographic recording of interconnection weights.

The physical process of detection *inherently* involves the dissipation of finite energy (if accomplished in finite time within prescribed uncertainties, as is appropriate for computation), since it necessarily involves the irreversible switching of the state of a physical component, as well as the guarantee that the switched state will be maintained over the time period of measurement without fluctuations due, for example, to thermally induced statistical variations. This is particularly true in highly distributed computing systems such as neural networks that depend on a certain degree of predictability and synchronization of communicated results for progressive computation. As such this is not really a fundamental physical limitation, but rather a technological limitation imposed by the system designer, who would really like to see some intelligible output from the system in the near future.

Optimization of the Computational Architecture

The design of a computational architecture in many ways fixes the fundamental performance limitations of the system, as choices must be made about the representation of data within the architecture, the methods employed for the implementation of computational complexity, and the frequency and nature of the detections required for both intermediate and final results. For neural networks capable of sophisticated operations, optimization of the computational architecture against one or more metrics (such as total energy cost for a given computation, or total power at a given operating frequency) will necessitate an appropriate balance among the various representations employed, as well as among the physical mechanisms employed to accomplish the necessary computations. A further balance must be struck between the fraction of the computational burden that is assigned to interconnections, and the fraction that is accomplished by switching (whether logic, arithmetic, or detection of results).

For many classes of computational problems, the neural-network paradigm may prove to be nearly optimal even in the regime in which all of the individual components are assumed to be operating at their respective fundamental physical performance boundaries. Relative to a modern digital supercomputer, certainly, neural networks seemingly offer an unusual mix of hybrid representations (primarily analog), interconnections (highly multiplexed as well as weighted), and switching (infrequent relative to the rate at which interconnections are utilized). It is at the very least intriguing to imagine whether or not our biological heritage has stored within it a useful clue about highly efficient computation for truly sophisticated problems.

Technological Limitations

The choice of a technological base (or bases) within which to design a neural network with a large number of neuron units and a high degree of connectivity implies yet another set of performance constraints above and beyond the fundamental physical boundaries referred to above. These *technological limitations* may not yet have been reached within the development of a given technology, but can at least be estimated given what we know about the physics of operation of the devices in question. One such technological limitation, for example, governs the total energy-dissipation density that can be tolerated on a given semiconductor substrate without either an unacceptable temperature rise that affects device performance, or resort to extraordinary cooling measures (that may prove to be unfeasible in an optical path). As a second example, the energy required to represent a single bit using current digital logic circuits integrated in silicon is about seven orders of magnitude *above* the thermal fluctuation limit [Tanguay, 1988].

In a previous section of this chapter, we discussed a particular photonic implementation strategy for neural networks that involved specific technological choices for the various types of components required by the architecture. At the present state of development of photonic computational systems, we do not have the luxury of designing everything within a single technological base, as is the case perhaps for computational subsystems based on VLSI chips. "Optical silicon" has not yet emerged, or at the very least has not yet been identified and recognized as such, even though numerous candidates have been intensively investigated.

Perhaps the leading candidate at the current time is the compound semiconductor system based on gallium arsenide (GaAs) and including related ternary compounds such as indium gallium arsenide ($In_xGa_{1-x}As$) and aluminum gallium arsenide ($Al_xGa_{1-x}As$). Within this system, at least, sources, source arrays, spatial light modulators, integrated electronic circuitry, volume holographic optical elements, detectors, and detector arrays have all been fabricated and evaluated with varying degrees of success. What has *not* been established to date is the mutual compatibility of all of these elements operating within a given systems context. This demonstration of mutual compatibility in all relevant performance specifications is essential, because in a highly interconnected system the overall performance achieved is often most strongly influenced by the component with the *least* desirable characteristics. An obvious example is that of a single-channel optical communications link, for which the transmission bandwidth will be delimited by the lowest-bandwidth component among the source/modulator, transmission medium, and detector/amplifier.

In the remainder of this section, we briefly discuss a number of the types of technological limitations that will impact the performance of currently envisioned photonic implementations of neural networks.

With regard to sources and source arrays, the principal technological issues are the minimization of laser thresholds to allow for parallel operation of a large number of sources on a single chip, the coherence length achievable with ultrashort-cavity surface-emitting lasers when fabricated in an array (which impacts the holographic recording process), the uniformity of wavelength across the array (particularly for parallel readout of wavelength-sensitive devices such as multiple-quantum-well spatial light modulators), and both the short-term (process-determined) yield and the long-term reliability of individual sources within a large-scale array.

For the case of spatial light modulators, key technological issues include the maximum density of neuron units that can be integrated on a monolithic or hybrid chip with appropriate detectors, control circuitry, and modulators within each pixel; the sensitivity to input intensity; the neural unit functionality (and perhaps programmability) that can be achieved at the minimum cost in real estate and energy dissipation; the contrast ratio and uniformity of the contrast ratio across the array of pixels (neuron units); the achievable dynamic range of the input/output transfer function; and the operational bandwidth that can be reached assuming a 50 percent duty cycle for each neuron unit (which determines the total power dissipation of the chip).

The high degree of interconnectivity envisioned for photonic implementations of neural networks hinges primarily on the achievement of appropriate functionality in the volume holographic optical elements used to record and store interconnection weights, produce fan-in and fan-out from each neuron unit, and allow for highly parallel readout of the weighted interconnection network. Key technological limitations for currently investigated photorefractive materials include the optical quality routinely achievable in large (1 cubic inch) single-crystal samples, the storage capacity of the medium as determined by the highest spatial frequency gratings that can be recorded, the sensitivity for recording of updated weights [Johnson, 1989] at the source wavelength (which in turn determines the source power necessary to initiate weight updates during the learning phase), the potential for "fixing" of the stored interconnection weights to allow for nondestructive readout during computation, and the capability for copying the contents of the stored interconnection matrix into another holographic medium (in order to provide the capacity for mass production of fixed-pattern interconnections following a training sequence executed with a dynamic medium). Perhaps the most important technological limitation of a given holographic recording medium will prove to be the total number of weight-update cycles that can be initiated without complete erasure of the weight updates recorded during the very first training cycle. This number in effect sets an upper bound on the learning capacity of the photonic neural network.

The primary technological limitations of importance to single-pixel detectors, as used, for example, on the input side of optically adressed spatial light modulators, include the sensitivity of the detector/amplifier combination (which together with the spatial light modulator gain determines the overall loop gain for a single computational iteration), the modulation bandwidth in conjunction with following circuitry, and the chip area required to achieve the desired sensitivity and bandwidth tradeoff. Depending on the technological base within which the spatial light modulator is fabricated, the potential for integration with control circuitry and in some cases the modulation elements themselves provides an additional constraint.

For detector arrays, many of the same issues apply with the additional constraints of uniformity of each performance parameter across the array, and the reliability of the full array of pixels. Another important technological issue is the frame rate for readout of the entire array at a given pixel density, which is determined both by the technological base within which the array is fabricated, and by the physical structure of the array and its readout configuration. As discussed in an earlier section, charge-coupled-device (CCD) arrays are typically read out by temporally multiplexing the contents of a full frame onto one or a few high-bandwidth serial outputs. The contents of each row of stored charge packets generated during the exposure cycle are shifted out to a high-speed serial readout buffer, which reads out one entire column of pixels in between each lateral shift of the rows as shown schematically in Figure 9.34.

This parallel-to-serial conversion limits the frame readout rate to the maximum serial transfer rate achievable in the readout buffer, divided by the number of pixels in the array. For example, if the array is 2048×2048 pixels in size with a readout buffer operating at 200 MHz, the frame rate will be limited to about 60 frames per second. For many neural-network applications, this frame rate may be more than sufficient for access to the desired outputs (including the time required for temporal demultiplexing of the output). In cases that demand higher frame rates, the array can be segmented so that multiple readout buffers can be used, each accessing a fraction of the total number of rows in the array.

An unusual feature of identifying the technological constraints that bound *any* neural-network implementation, whether it be electronic, photonic, chemical, mechanical, or all of the above, is the fact that we just don't know enough yet about the operation of highly interconnected nonlinear systems of large dimension to fully assess the impact of a *particular* constraint on the overall system operation. One example is the degree to which nonuniformities in the neuron units themselves (e.g., in their sensitivity, contrast ratio, or overall response function) or in the interconnection medium can be tolerated by an architecture that is to a large extent self-organizing. A second example is the necessity within a certain neural-network paradigm of implementing precisely the right nonlinearity that translates summed neuron inputs to neuron outputs (or, for that matter, the very existence of nonlin-

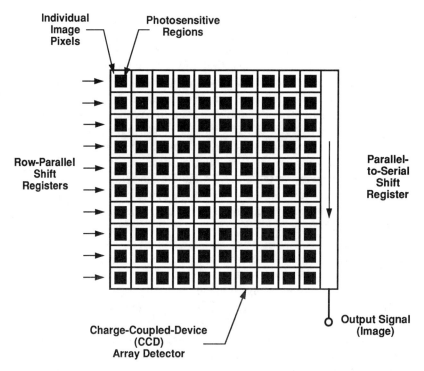

FIGURE 9.34 Illustration of parallel-to-serial conversion in two-dimensional detector arrays such as the charge-coupled-device (CCD) array. Charge accumulated within each photosensitive region during exposure is transferred laterally by a set of row-parallel shift registers to a high-speed parallel-to-serial shift register, which reads out the entire array one column at a time.

earities in the recording and storage of weight updates, and in the readout of the full weighted interconnection pattern). Some of these types of questions may be amenable to simulation, but in other cases we may have to await the results from actual implementations to refine our understanding of the technological requirements.

THE FUTURE OF NEURO-OPTICAL COMPUTATION

A wide variety of photonic architectures and components are currently under intensive investigation for neural-network applications. A thorough discussion of these alternative strategies and their strengths and weaknesses is unfortunately beyond the scope of this chapter. In this final section, we address the future prospects of neuro-optical computation from the point of view of those critical issues that are common to all such proposed implementation strategies.

The Critical Issues

As with any emerging technological breakthrough, successful advanced development of photonic neural networks will require that the technology prove to be *manufacturable*, in the sense that it is amenable to mass-production techniques at reasonable cost; *flexible in design*, in that the technological base provides significant degrees of freedom for architectural and functional variations; and *leveraged* as much as possible by developments in related technologies that can offload a significant fraction of the development time and costs. Implicit in these three key features is the issue of the component uniformity that can be achieved over large array sizes, and the related issue of the scalability of the technology to large-scale systems either by increases in the basic array sizes or by the incorporation of a modular design from the outset.

In all useful computational systems, the bottom line is to a large extent determined by the maximum amount of computational throughput capacity that can be squeezed into the smallest system volume within a tolerable energy-dissipation constraint or power budget. In the case of photonic neural networks that utilize the implementation strategy outlined in a previous section of this chapter, the two most important factors that influence the computational throughput capacity are the storage capacity of the volume holographic optical element, and the operational bandwidth of the neuron units (nonlinear spatial light modulators).

The storage capacity of a holographic interconnection medium is in turn determined by the maximum number of independent weighted interconnections that can be recorded and retrieved per unit volume. Although we discussed this issue in an earlier section from a theoretical viewpoint (and in yet another section from an architectural viewpoint), we have not addressed herein the even more important question of the *actual* density of independent interconnections achievable with photorefractive (or other photosensitive real-time materials) that contain a considerable number of scattering centers and exhibit diffraction efficiencies that depend strongly on the spatial frequency of the recorded grating. Demonstration of a high density of weighted interconnections with low interchannel crosstalk in a real-time holographic recording medium will provide a benchmark of achievement for photonic implementation strategies, as well as a metric by which one can more appropriately estimate eventual system performance. Demonstration of parallel weight updates at high sensitivity (requiring tolerable optical source intensities) during a complete training cycle is also necessary for a convincing proof of system feasibility.

The operational bandwidth of two-dimensional spatial light modulators that can be used as neuron unit arrays will prove to be orders of magnitude larger than the bandwidth characteristic of biological systems. Feasibility analyses, as well as preliminary device characterization studies, indicate no fundamental or technological barriers to operation of individual neuron units at bandwidths exceeding 100 MHz [Asthana, 1990b]. For a 100×100 element neuron unit to switch at 100 MHz with a 50 percent duty cycle, however, generates a watt of power dissipation for every 2 picojoules of switching energy required by an individual neuron unit, including the detector, amplifier, control circuitry, and modulator. Although the neuron unit arrays in most neural-network architectures will not approach 50 percent duty cycles from full *off* to full *on* in actual operation, this still gives us a very tight energy-dissipation budget, and may eventually force a lowering of the design bandwidth.

For photonic implementations of neural networks that use optical imaging and holographic interconnection systems extensively to increase the computational throughput capacity, an important question will continue to be the fraction of "un-filled" system volume dedicated to wavefront and beam propagation. Miniatur-ization of many sophisticated optical signal-processing systems has been a focus of effort only recently, and can be expected to produce significant system volume reductions through clever (as well as careful) opto-mechanical engineering. For example, gradient-index (GRIN) techniques have been used in conjunction with photolithographic planar processing to produce regular two-dimensional arrays of diffraction-limited microlenses that can be incorporated in stacked planar optical modules with greatly reduced unfilled system volume [Iga, 1984]. There are, how-ever, several inherent limits (both fundamental as well as technological) that provide lower bounds on the physical volume required to implement a high degree of inter-connectivity among planes of neuron units.

When all is said and done, it is certainly a fair question to ask whether the physical volume of a neuro-optical computer module would be better off densely packed with silicon chips that emulate the same functionality. All of the prelimi-nary evidence gathered to date suggests that the answer to this question shifts rather dramatically from an emphatic "Yes" in the limit of small numbers of neurons and required interconnections, to a more tenuous "No" as the number of neurons and density of required interconnections continues to increase. Perhaps the most inter-esting question for the future of neuro-optical computation is the clear identification of this performance boundary.

The Incorporation of Neural Paradigms

In concluding this chapter on neuro-optical computation, we assert that al-though the majority of preliminary demonstrations of photonic neural-network ar-chitectures have seemingly focused on associative memories in general, and on variations of the Hopfield-Amari [Hopfield, 1982; Amari, 1972] network in particu-lar, it is essential that photonic implementations have the capacity for incorporation of a wide variety of neural-network architectures, computational algorithms, and learning rules. This is particularly important in view of the early stage of devel-opment that characterizes our current understanding of the operational performance of even the most fashionable neural-network models, when scaled up to large num-bers of densely interconnected neuron units with realistic stochastic variations in individual neuron unit performance.

Furthermore, it is likely that useful neural networks incorporated in a systems framework may require either a number of layers with different characteristics, or considerable preprocessing and postprocessing to achieve sophisticated functionality. One example of a neural paradigm that requires such additonal sophistication is the Dynamic Link Architecture of von der Malsburg discussed in Chapter 11 [Buhmann, 1991] as applied to pattern-recognition problems by means of graph-matching techniques. A photonic implementation of this architecture will likely require several interacting modules for complete functionality.

Currently investigated photonic architectures and components for neural-network implementation do not yet enjoy the flexibility of full-fledged computer-aided design and computer-aided manufacturing that is the hallmark of the silicon VLSI circuit industry. On the other hand, tremendous strides have been made in just the past few years in the simulation of even complex optical systems including the effects of both refractive and diffractive components. The next step, from extensive simulation capabilities to design automation, is under active investigation and may, when taken, herald the beginnings of a viable photonic-based neural-network implementation technology.

SUGGESTED FURTHER READING

Abu-Mostafa, Y. S., and Psaltis, D., "Optical Neural Computers," *Scientific American*, vol. 256, no. 3, 88-95, 1987.

Applied Optics, Special Issue on Neural Networks, vol. 26, no. 23, 1 December, 1987.

Arsenault, H., Szoplik, T., and Macukow, B. (eds.), *Optical Processing and Computing*, Academic Press, New York, 1989.

Collier, R. J., Burckhardt, C. B., and Lin, L. H., *Optical Holography*, Academic Press, New York, 1971.

Feitelson, D. G., *Optical Computing: A Survey for Computer Scientists*, M.I.T. Press, Cambridge, MA, 1988.

Goodman, J. W., *Introduction to Fourier Optics*, McGraw-Hill, New York, 1968.

Gunter, P., and Huignard, J.-P., *Photorefractive Materials and Their Applications I*, vol. 61 in Topics in Applied Physics Series, Springer-Verlag, New York, 1988; also Gunter, P., and Huignard, J.-P., *Photorefractive Materials and Their Applications II*, vol. 62 in Topics in Applied Physics Series, Springer-Verlag, New York, 1989.

Haus, H. A., *Waves and Fields in Optoelectronics*, Prentice Hall, Englewood Cliffs, NJ, 1984.

Ishihara, S. (ed.), *Optical Computing in Japan*, Nova Science Publishers, Commack, NY, 1990.

Nussbaum, A., and Phillips, R. A., *Contemporary Optics for Scientists and Engineers*, Prentice Hall, Englewood Cliffs, NJ, 1976.

Optical Computing, vol. 9 of the 1989 OSA Technical Digest Series, Optical Society of America, Washington, DC, 1989.

Pankove, J. I., *Optical Processes in Semiconductors*, Prentice Hall, Englewood Cliffs, NJ, 1971.

Proceedings of the IEEE International Conference on Neural Networks, vol. III, San Diego, 1987, 549-648; *Proceedings of the IEEE International Conference of Neural Networks*, vol. II, San Diego, 1988, 357-442; *Proceedings of the International Joint Conference on Neural Networks*, vol. II, Washington, DC, 1989, 457-494 (The Institute of Electrical and Electronics Engineers, Piscataway, NJ).

Smith, H. M., *Holographic Recording Materials*, vol. 20 in Topics in Applied Physics Series, Springer-Verlag, New York, 1977.

Sze, S. M., *Physics of Semiconductor Devices*, 2nd ed., Wiley, New York, 1981.

REFERENCES

Abu-Mostafa, Y., "Complexity in Neural Systems," app. D in Mead, C. A., *Analog VLSI and Neural Systems*, Addison-Wesley, Reading, MA, 1989, 353-358.

Amari, S.-I., "Learning Patterns and Pattern Sequences by Self-Organizing Nets of Threshold Elements," *IEEE Transactions on Computers*, vol. C-21, 1197-1206, 1972.

Asthana, P., Chin, H., Nordin, G., Tanguay, A. R., Jr., Piazzolla, S., Jenkins, B. K., and Madhukar, A., "Photonic Components for Neural Net Implementations Using Incoherent/Coherent Holographic Interconnections," *OC'90 Technical Digest, International Commission for Optics*, Kobe, Japan, 1990a.

Asthana, P., Chin, H., Nordin, G., Tanguay, A. R., Jr., Petrisor, G. C., Jenkins, B. K., and Madhukar, A., "Photonic Components for Neural Net Implementations Using Incoherent/Coherent Holographic Interconnections," in *OSA Annual Meeting Technical Digest 1990*, vol. 15 of the 1990 OSA Technical Digest Series, Optical Society of America, Washington, DC, 1990b, 57.

Asthana, P., Nordin, G., Piazzolla, S., Tanguay, A. R., Jr., and Jenkins, B. K., "Analysis of Interchannel Crosstalk and Throughput Efficiency in Highly Multiplexed Fan-Out/Fan-In Holographic Interconnections," in *OSA Annual Meeting Technical Digest 1990*, vol. 15 of the 1990 OSA Technical Digest Series, Optical Society of America, Washington, DC, 1990c, 242.

Blouke, M. M., Corrie, B., Heidtmann, D. L., Yang, F. H., Winzenread, M., Lust, M. L., Marsh IV, H. H., and Janesick, J. R., "Large Format, High Resolution Image Sensors," *Optical Engineering*, vol. 26, no. 9, 837-843, 1987.

Buhmann, J., Lange, J., von der Malsburg, C., Vorbrüggen, J. C., and Würtz, R. P., "Object-Recognition with Gabor Functions in the Dynamic Link Architecture—Parallel Implementation on a Transputer Network," in *Neural Networks for Signal Processing*, B. Kosko (ed.), Prentice Hall, Englewood Cliffs, NJ, 1992; chap. 5 (this volume).

Carpenter, G. A. and Grossberg, S., "ART 2: Self-Organization of Stable Category Recognition Codes for Analog Input Patterns," *Applied Optics*, vol. 26, no. 23, 4919-4930, 1987.

Casey, H. C., Jr., and Panish, M. B., *Heterostructure Lasers. Part A: Fundamental Principles*, in Quantum Electronics—Principles and Applications Monograph Series, P. F. Liao and P. Kelley (eds.), Academic Press, New York, 1978a.

Casey, H. C., Jr., and Panish, M. B., *Heterostructure Lasers. Part B: Materials and Operating Characteristics*, in Quantum Electronics—Principles and Applications Monograph Series, P. F. Liao and P. Kelley (eds.), Academic Press, New York, 1978b.

Chang-Hasnain, C. J., Maeda, M. W., Stoffel, N. G., Harbison, J. P., and Florez, L. T., "Surface Emitting Laser Arrays with Uniformly Separated Wavelengths," *Electronics Letters*, vol. 26, no. 13, 940-942, 1990.

Changeux, J.-P., *Neuronal Man: The Biology of Mind*, Pantheon Books, New York, 1985.

Dammann, M., and Gortler, K., "High-Efficiency In-Line Multiple Imaging by Means of Multiple Phase Holograms," *Optics Communications*, vol. 3, no. 5, 312-315, 1971.

Drabik, T. J., and Handschy, M. A., "Silicon VLSI/Ferroelectric Liquid Crystal Technology for Micropower Optoelectronic Computing Devices," *Applied Optics*, vol. 29, no. 35, 5220-5223, 1990.

Dowling, J. E., *The Retina: An Approachable Part of the Brain*, The Belknap Press of Harvard University Press, Cambridge, MA, 1987.

Farhat, N. H., "Optoelectronic Analogs of Self-Programming Neural Nets: Architecture and Methodologies for Implementing Fast Stochastic Learning by Simulated Annealing," *Applied Optics*, vol. 26, no. 23, 5093-5103, 1987.

Farhat, N. H., Psaltis, D., Prata, A., and Paek, E., "Optical Implementation of the Hopfield Model," *Applied Optics*, vol. 24, no. 10, 1469-1475, 1985.

Fossum, E. R., "Charge-Coupled Computing for Focal Plane Image Preprocessing," *Optical Engineering*, vol. 26, no. 9, 916-922, 1987.

Goodman, J. W., *Introduction to Fourier Optics*, McGraw-Hill, New York, 1968, chap. 4.

Gunter, P., and Huignard, J.-P., *Photorefractive Materials and Their Applications I*, vol. 61 in Topics in Applied Physics Series, Springer-Verlag, New York, 1988.

Gunter, P., and Huignard, J.-P., *Photorefractive Materials and Their Applications II*, vol. 62 in Topics in Applied Physics Series, Springer-Verlag, New York, 1989.

Haus, H. A., *Waves and Fields in Optoelectronics*, Prentice Hall, Englewood Cliffs, NJ, 1984, 63-72.

Herbulock, E. J., Garrett, M. H., and Tanguay, A. R., Jr., "Electric Field Profile Effects on Photorefractive Grating Formation in Bismuth Silicon Oxide," *OSA Annual Meeting Technical Digest 1988*, vol. 11 of the 1988 OSA Technical Digest Series, Optical Society of America, Washington, DC, 1988, 143.

Hopfield, J. J., "Neural Networks and Physical Systems with Emergent Collective Computational Activity," *Proceedings of the National Academy of Sciences, USA*, vol. 79, 2554-2558, 1982.

Huang, A., Tsunoda, Y., Goodman, J. W., and Ishihara, S., "Optical Computation Using Residue Arithmetic," *Applied Optics*, vol. 18, no. 2, 149-162, 1979.

Hubel, D. H., "The Brain," *Scientific American*, vol. 241, no. 3, 44-53, 1979.

Iga, K., Kokubun, Y., and Oikawa, M., *Fundamentals of Microoptics: Distributed-Index, Microlens, and Stacked Planar Optics*, Academic Press, Tokyo, 1984.

Iversen, L. L., "The Chemistry of the Brain," *Scientific American*, vol. 241, no. 3, 134-149, 1979.

Jackel, L. D., "Electronic Neural Networks," in *OSA Annual Meeting Technical Digest, 1988*, vol. 11 of the 1988 OSA Technical Digest Series, Optical Society of America, Washington, DC, 1988, 146.

Jenkins, B. K., Chavel, P., Forchheimer, R., Sawchuk, A. A., and Strand, T. C., "Architectural Implications of a Digital Optical Processor," *Applied Optics*, vol. 23, no. 19, 3465-3474, 1984.

Jenkins, B. K., Petrisor, G. C., Piazzolla, S., Asthana, P., and Tanguay, A. R., Jr., "Photonic Architecture for Neural Nets Using Incoherent/Coherent Holographic Interconnections," in *OC'90 Technical Digest, International Commission for Optics*, Kobe, Japan, 1990a.

Jenkins, B. K., Tanguay, A. R., Jr., Piazzolla, S., Petrisor, G. C., and Asthana, P., "Photonic Neural Network Architecture Based on Incoherent/Coherent Holographic Interconnections," in *OSA Annual Meeting Technical Digest 1990*, vol. 15 of the 1990 OSA Technical Digest Series, Optical Society of America, Washington, DC, 1990b, 56.

Jenkins, B. K. and Tanguay, A. R., Jr., "Incoherent/Coherent Multiplexed Holographic Recording for Photonic Interconnections and Holographic Optical Elements," United States Patent Application USC-2254, University of Southern California, Los Angeles, CA, 1990c.

Jewell, J. L., Lee, Y. H., Scherer, A., McCall, S. L., Olsson, N. A., Harbison, J. P., and Florez, L. T., "Surface-Emitting Microlasers for Photonic Switching and Interchip Connections," *Optical Engineering*, vol. 29, no. 3, 210-214, 1990.

Johnson, R. V., and Tanguay, A. R., Jr., "Optical Beam Propagation Method for Birefringent Phase Grating Diffraction," *Optical Engineering*, vol. 25, no. 2, 235-249, 1986.

Johnson, R. V., and Tanguay, A. R., Jr., "Fundamental Physical Limitations of the Photorefractive Grating Recording Sensitivity," chap. 3 in *Optical Processing and Computing*, H. Arsenault, T. Szoplik, and B. Macukow (eds.), Academic Press, New York, 59–102, 1989.

Jones, W. B., Jr., *Introduction to Optical Fiber Communication Systems*, Holt, Rinehart and Winston, New York, 1988.

Kaminow, I. P., *An Introduction to Electrooptic Devices*, Academic Press, New York, 1974.

Karim, Z., Garrett, M. H., and Tanguay, A. R., Jr., "Bandpass AR Coating Design for Bismuth Silicon Oxide," in *OSA Annual Meeting Technical Digest 1988*, vol. 11 of the 1988 OSA Technical Digest Series, Optical Society of America, Washington, DC, 1988, 125.

Karim, Z., and Tanguay, A. R., Jr., "Bandpass AR Coating for the Photorefractive Materials $LiNbO_3$, $BaTiO_3$, CdTe, and PLZT," in *OSA Annual Meeting Technical Digest 1989*, vol. 18 of the 1989 OSA Technical Digest Series, Optical Society of America, Washington, DC, 1989a, 78.

Karim, Z., Kyriakakis, C., and Tanguay, A. R., Jr., "Improved Two Beam Coupling Gain and Diffraction Efficiency in Bismuth Silicon Oxide Crystals Using a Bandpass AR Coating," in *OSA Annual Meeting Technical Digest 1989*, vol. 18 of the 1989 OSA Technical Digest Series, Optical Society of America, Washington, DC, 1989b, 29.

Kogelnik, H., "Coupled Wave Theory for Thick Hologram Gratings," *Bell System Technical Journal*, vol. 48, no. 9, 2909-2947, 1969.

Kressel, H., and Butler, J. K., *Semiconductor Lasers and Heterojunction LEDs*, in Quantum Electronics—Principles and Applications Monograph Series, Y.-H. Pao and P. Kelley (eds.), Academic Press, New York, 1977.

Kyriakakis, C., Karim, Z., Jung, J. J., Tanguay, A. R., Jr., and Madhukar, A., "Fundamental and Technological Limitations of Asymmetric Cavity MQW InGaAs/GaAs Spatial Light

Modulators," in *Proceedings of the Optical Society of America Topical Conference on Spatial Light Modulators, Incline Village, Nevada*, Optical Society of America, Washington, DC, 1990.

Lee, B. W., and Sheu, B. J., "Design and Analysis of VLSI Neural Networks," in *Neural Networks for Signal Processing*, Bart Kosko (ed.), Prentice Hall, Englewood Cliffs, NJ, 1992; chap. 8 (this volume).

Lentine, A. L., Hinton, H. S., Miller, D. A. B., Henry, J. E., Cunningham, J. E., and Chirovsky, L. M. F., "Symmetric Self-Electro-Optic Effect Device: Optical Set-Reset Latch," *Applied Physics Letters*, vol. 52, 1419-1421, 1988.

Lentine, A. L., Chirovsky, L. M. F., and D'Asaro, L. A., "Photonic Ring Counter Using Batch-Fabricated Symmetric Self-Electro-Optic-Effect Devices," *Optics Letters*, vol. 16, no. 1, 36-38, 1991.

Marrakchi, A., Hubbard, W. M., Habiby, S. F., and Patel, J. S., "Dynamic Holographic Interconnects with Analog Weights in Photorefractive Crystals," *Optical Engineering*, vol. 29, no. 3, 215-224, 1990.

McCormick, F. B., "Generation of Large Spot Arrays from a Single Laser Beam by Multiple Imaging with Binary Phase Gratings," *Optical Engineering*, vol. 28, no. 4, 299-304, 1989a.

McCormick, F. B., Lentine, A. L., Morrison, R. L., Walker, S. L., Chirovsky, L. M. F., and D'Asaro, L. A., "Simultaneous Parallel Operation of an Array of Symmetric Self-Electrooptic Effect Devices," in *OSA Annual Meeting Technical Digest 1989*, vol. 18 of the 1989 OSA Technical Digest Series, Optical Society of America, Washington, DC, 1989b, 60-61.

Mead, C. A., *Analog VLSI and Neural Systems*, Addison-Wesley, Reading, MA, 1989.

Mead, C. A., *op. cit.*, 1989b, 3.

Mead, C. A. and Mahowald, M. A., "A Silicon Model of Early Visual Processing," *Neural Networks*, vol. 1, 91-97, 1988.

Miller, D. A. B., "Quantum-Well Self-Electro-Optic Effect Devices," *Optical and Quantum Electronics*, vol. 22, S61-S98, 1990.

Milonni, P. W., and Eberly, J. H., "Specific Lasers and Pumping Mechanisms," chap. 13 in *Lasers*, Wiley, New York, 1988, 411-468.

Morrison, R. L., and Walker, S. L., "Binary Phase Gratings Generating Even Numbered Spot Arrays," in *OSA Annual Meeting Technical Digest 1989*, vol. 18 of the 1989 OSA Technical Digest Series, Optical Society of America, Washington, DC, 1989, 111.

Optical Engineering, Special Issue on Charge-Coupled-Device Manufacture and Application, vol. 26, no. 9, 827-943, 1987a.

Optical Engineering, Special Issue on Charge-Coupled-Device and Charge-Injection-Device Theory and Application, vol. 26, no. 10, 963-1076, 1987b.

Orenstein, M., von Lehmen, A. C., Chang-Hasnain, C., Stoffel, N. G., Harbison, J. P., Florez, L. T., Wullert, J. R., and Scherer, A., "Matrix Addressable Surface Emitting Laser Array," in *Proceedings of the 1990 Conference on Lasers and Electro-Optics*, vol. 7 of the 1990 Technical Digest Series, Optical Society of America, Washington, DC, 1990a, 88.

Orenstein, M., von Lehmen, A. C., Stoffel, N. G., Chang-Hasnain, C., Harbison, J. P., Florez, L. T., Clausen, E., and Jewell, J. L., "Lateral Definition of High Performance Surface Emitting Lasers by Planarity Preserving Ion Implantation Processes," in *Proceedings of the 1990 Conference on Lasers and Electro-Optics*, vol. 7 of the 1990 Technical Digest Series, Optical Society of America, Washington, DC, 1990b, 504.

Petrisor, G. C., Jenkins, B. K., Chin, H., and Tanguay, A. R., Jr., "Dual Function Adaptive Neural Networks for Photonic Implementation," in *OSA Annual Meeting Technical Digest 1990*, vol. 15 of the 1990 OSA Technical Digest Series, Optical Society of America, Washington, DC, 1990, 56.

Psaltis, D., and Farhat, N. H., "Optical Information Processing Based on an Associative-Memory Model of Neural Nets with Thresholding and Feedback," *Optics Letters*, vol. 10, no. 2, 98-100, 1985.

Psaltis, D., Brady, D., and Wagner, K., "Adaptive Optical Networks Using Photorefractive Crystals," *Applied Optics*, vol. 27, no. 9, 1752-1759, 1988.

Psaltis, D., Brady, D., Gu, X.-G., and Hsu, K., "Optical Implementation of Neural Computers," in *Optical Processing and Computing*, H. H. Arsenault, T. Szoplik, and B. Macukow (eds.), Academic Press, Orlando, FL, 1989, 251-276.

Shirouzu, S., Tsuji, T., Harada, N., Sado, T., Aihara, S., Tsunoda, R., and Kanno, T., "64 × 64 InSb Focal Plane Array with Improved Two Layer Structure," *Proceedings of the SPIE*, vol. 661, Society of Photo-Optical Instrumentation Engineers, Bellingham, WA, 1986.

Smith, H. M., *Holographic Recording Materials*, vol. 20 in Topics in Applied Physics Series, Springer-Verlag, New York, 1977.

Spatial Light Modulators and Applications, vol. 14 of the 1990 OSA Technical Digest Series, Optical Society of America, Washington, DC, 1990.

Spatial Light Modulators for Optical Information Processing, Special Issue of *Applied Optics*, vol. 28, no. 22, 1989, 4739-4913.

Streetman, B. G., *Solid State Electronic Devices*, 2nd ed., Prentice Hall, Englewood Cliffs, NJ, 1980.

Sze, S. M., *Physics of Semiconductor Devices*, 2nd ed., Wiley, New York, 1981a, 312-361.

Sze, S. M., *op. cit.*, 1981b, 783-784.

Sze, S. M., *op. cit.*, 1981c, 407-427.

Tai, K., Fischer, R. J., Wang, K. W., Chu, S. N. G., and Cho, A. Y., "Use of Implant Isolation for Fabrication of Vertical Cavity Surface-Emitting Laser Diodes," *Electronics Letters*, vol. 25, no. 24, 1644-1645, 1989a.

Tai, K., Fischer, R. J., Seabury, C. W., Olsson, N. A., Huo, T.-C. D., Ota, Y., and Cho, A. Y., "Room-Temperature Continuous-Wave Vertical-Cavity Surface-Emitting GaAs Injection Lasers," *Applied Physics Letters*, vol. 55, no. 24, 2473-2475, 1989b.

Tanguay, A. R., Jr., "Physical and Technological Limitations of Optical Information Processing and Computing," *Materials Research Society Bulletin*, Special Issue on Photonic Materials, vol. XIII, no. 8, 36-40, 1988.

Tanguay, A. R., Jr., "Materials Requirements for Optical Processing and Computing Devices," *Optical Engineering*, vol. 24, no. 1, 2-18, 1985.

von der Malsburg, C., "Goal and Architecture of Neural Computers," in *Neural Computers*, R. Eckmiller and C. von der Malsburg (eds.), vol. 41 of NATO Advanced Science Institutes Series F: Computer and Systems Sciences, Springer-Verlag, New York, 1987.

von Lehmen, A., Orenstein, M., Chang-Hasnain, C., Banwell, T., Wullert, J., Stoffel, N., Florez, L., and Harbison, J., "Rastered Operation of Row-Column Addressed Vertical-

Cavity Surface-Emitting Laser Array," in *OSA Annual Meeting Technical Digest 1990*, vol. 15 of the 1990 OSA Technical Digest Series, Optical Society of America, Washington, DC, 1990, 15.

Wagner, K., and Psaltis, D., "Multilayer Optical Learning Networks," *Applied Optics*, vol. 26, no. 23, 5061-5076, 1987.

Warde, C., and Fisher, A. D., "Spatial Light Modulators: Applications and Functional Capabilities," chap. 7.2 in *Optical Signal Processing*, J. L. Horner (ed.), Academic Press, New York, 477-523, 1987.

Whitehead, M., and Parry, G., "High-Contrast Reflection Modulation at Normal Incidence in Asymmetric Multiple Quantum Well Fabry-Perot Structure," *Electronics Letters*, vol. 25, 566-568, 1989a.

Whitehead, M., Parry, G., and Wheatley, P., "Investigation of Etalon Effects in GaAs-AlGaAs Multiple Quantum Well Modulators," *IEE Proceedings*, vol. 136, pt. J, no. 1, 52-58, 1989b.

Whitehead, M., Rivers, A., Parry, G., Roberts, J. S., and Button, C., "Low-Voltage Multiple Quantum Well Reflection Modulator with On:Off Ratio > 100:1," *Electronics Letters*, vol. 25, no. 15, 984-985, 1989c.

Yan, R. H., Simes, R. J., and Coldren, L. A., "Wide-Bandwidth, High-Efficiency Reflection Modulators Using an Unbalanced Fabry-Perot Structure," *Applied Physics Letters*, vol. 55, no. 19, 1946-1948, 1989.

ACKNOWLEDGMENTS

We gratefully acknowledge the contributions to this effort provided by our faculty colleagues Christoph von der Malsburg, Joachim Buhmann, and Anupam Madhukar, and by our graduate research assistants Greg Nordin, Praveen Asthana, Howard Chin, Sabino Piazzolla, Greg Petrisor, Chris Kyriakakis, Zaheed Karim, John Rilum, and Ed Herbulock. Special thanks are also due to Gloria Bullock and Delsa Tan for their help in the preparation of this manuscript. Funding for the materials, device, and systems aspects of our research program on photonic implementations of neural networks has been provided by the Defense Advanced Research Projects Agency, the University Research Initiative "Center for the Integration of Optical Computing" (sponsored by the Air Force Office of Scientific Research), the National Center for Integrated Photonic Technology (sponsored by the Defense Advanced Research Projects Agency), the Joint Services Electronics Program, and NTT Corporation.

PROBLEMS

9.1. Consider a system of beamsplitters arranged to combine a set of N input beams to form a single, collinear output beam with an intensity proportional to an equally weighted

sum of all of the inputs. Choose a particular architecture for the beamsplitter arrangement, and justify it in terms of efficiency, simplicity, or minimization of component
count. For the case of incoherent illumination, derive the optimal transmissivities of
the beamsplitters in your arrangement, and prove that the chosen architecture generates an input-output relationship in the form of Equation (9-2). Repeat the analysis
for the case of coherent illumination, and derive the equivalent of Equation (9-8) that
characterizes the chosen architecture.

9.2. Two mutually coherent beams of intensities $|a|^2$ and $|b|^2$ are incident on a detector.
The coherent superposition of the beams is given by, in one dimension,

$$A(x) = ae^{jk_1x} + be^{jk_2x}$$

(a) Plot the resulting intensity, $|A(x)|^2$, as a function of x.

(b) Show that the integral of $|A(x)|^2$ over an integral number of its periods is equal
to $|a|^2 + |b|^2$, thus proving that the detector's response is equal to the *incoherent*
sum of the individual beams.

9.3. For the case of a thin phase grating with a sinusoidal index modulation given by
$n(x) = n_0 + n_1 \sin k_G x$ with $n_1 < n_0$, calculate the value of $n_1 d$ that maximizes
the diffraction efficiency into the first diffracted order, and the maximum diffraction
efficiency achievable. Assume that the grating is read out by a semiconductor laser
with a wavelength of 850 nm. For a given incident intensity of the optical readout
beam, calculate the ratio of the intensity diffracted into the zeroth, second, and third
diffracted orders to that diffracted into the first order.

9.4. Consider the process of diffraction from a thin *amplitude* grating with a spatially varying transmissivity and negligible phase modulation. For a sinusoidal transmittance
modulation given by $t(x) = t_0 + t_1 \sin k_G x$ with $t_1 < t_0$, calculate the value of t_1 that
maximizes the diffraction efficiency into the first diffracted order, and the maximum
diffraction efficiency achievable. Assume that the grating is read out by a semiconductor laser with a wavelength of 850 nm. For a given incident intensity of the optical
readout beam, calculate the ratio of the intensity diffracted into the zeroth, second,
and third diffracted orders to that diffracted into the first order. Discuss the essential
differences observed between the amplitude and phase grating cases.

9.5. Consider the process of holographic grating recording in a thick holographic recording
medium. Assume that the grating is recorded and read out by a semiconductor laser
with a wavelength of 850 nm, and that the angle included between the two recording
beams is 30 degrees. What is the spatial frequency of the recorded grating? How
thick must the hologram be in order to generate a grating parameter Q (as defined in
the text) of 1000? What is the approximate angular width of this recorded grating (as
measured, for example, by varying the angle of incidence of the readout beam)?

9.6. For the thick holographic grating described in Problem 9.4, calculate the amplitude
of the refractive index modulation that is necessary to achieve 100 percent diffraction
efficiency on readout. How large an absorption coefficient can be tolerated in the
holographic recording medium at the readout wavelength if the absorption loss in
diffraction efficiency is to be kept below 5 percent?

9.7. Consider the holographic interconnection scheme depicted in Figure 9.9. First, derive the basic relationship for a lens that associates a given point p_1 in the input plane with a resulting beam angle θ_1. Given a focal length of 5 centimeters for lenses L_1 and L_2, what is the minimum spacing required between nearest neighbor points in the input plane for a grating Q of 1000? What Q will be required to accommodate of order 10^4 input positions?

9.8. Design a differentiating circuit for incorporation in an optically addressed spatial light modulator, using the principles of Chapters 8 and 9. Assume that the detector is a $p\text{-}i\text{-}n$ photodiode, and that the modulator can be treated as a purely capacitive load. If the modulator can be modeled as a parallel-plate capacitor of dimensions 30×50 μm, with a thickness of 1 μm and a relative dielectric constant typical of gallium arsenide multiple-quantum-well devices ($\varepsilon = 13$), estimate the bandwidth over which the differentiator is operational.

9.9. If storage of one synaptic weight in VLSI requires a memory element 15 μm $\times$ 15 μm in size, what is the maximum number of synaptic weights that can be implemented on a 1 cm $\times$ 1 cm chip? If a VLSI neural network is fully connected using one such memory element for each synapse, how many pins are required for input to, and output from, the set of neuron units? How many pins would be required for parallel input of the weights? If an optical synaptic weight can be implemented in an effective volume of 5 μm $\times$ 5 μm $\times$ 5 μm, what is the maximum number of synaptic weights that can be implemented in a volume 1 cm $\times$ 1 cm $\times$ 1 cm?

9.10. (a) If a neural network is simulated on a digital, sequential machine, how many multiply operations and add operations are required to simulate the computational process of a single-layer feedforward network with N neuron units and a connectivity (number of connections per neuron unit) of M? If a multiply operation can be performed in 100 ns and an add operation in 25 ns, what is the minimum time it will take for one pass through the network if $N = 10^6$ and $M = 10^4$?

   (b) For the outer-product learning of Equation (9-24), neglecting the decay term, how many multiply operations and add operations are required for one iteration of weight updates, in terms of M and N? For a two-layer network (one hidden layer), with each layer having $N = 10^6$ and $M = 10^4$, and assuming 10^4 different patterns presented 1000 times each, how long will the network take to be trained (assuming one forward pass and one update of all weights per presentation, 100 ns per multiply operation and 25 ns per add operation)?

   (c) For the same numbers as in (b), assuming each layer of a photonic system can perform a forward pass in 100 ns and a set of parallel weight updates in 1 μs, how long will it take to be trained?

9.11. (a) Design an algorithm that uses only nonnegative signals outside of each neuron unit, nonnegative weights, and allows two separate inputs to and two separate outputs from each neuron unit. It should be able to perform neural computation and weight updates for learning. Your answer should be in the form of a flow chart. You may perform subtraction and division only within each neuron unit; only addition, multiplication, interconnection, and storage can be performed external to the neuron units. (No need to simulate.)

(b) After many iterations during learning, might there be a problem with weights saturating or going out of bounds? If not, why not? If so, conjecture as to how this problem might be avoided.

9.12. In regard to Equation (9-24), find an expression for δ_i for the following algorithms:

(a) Perceptron.

(b) Widrow-Hoff.

(c) Backward error propagation, for a multilayer net for

(i) output layer.

(ii) hidden layers.

Assume that $\beta = 0$ for this problem. (*Note:* This problem requires familiarity with neural networks not discussed in this chapter.)

9.13. Referring to the system of Figure 9.21, if the interconnection mask SLM were electronically addressed with a serial line, capable of transmitting analog values at 50 MHz, and there are 10^6 pixels (analog weights), what is the maximum frame rate? If there are 10^3 parallel lines addressing? If the SLM is optically addressed, what limits the frame rate?

9.14. (a) Referring to Figure 9.23, show how the following network can be drawn as a single-layer network with feedback.

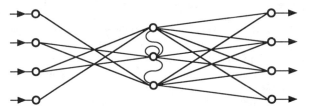

(b) How can the architecture shown in Figure 9.26 be modified to include feedback connections within the module? Sketch the resulting architecture.

9.15. Consider a charge-coupled-device array as shown schematically in Figure 9.34, of dimension 1000×1000 pixels with a serial readout buffer that operates at a clock frequency of 100 MHz. Calculate the maximum frame rate achievable, and the speed required of the row shift registers. Calculate the ratio between the total storage time required of the first pixel read out to that of the last in each frame.

INDEX

Note: Italicized page numbers locate references.

A

Aarts, E. H. L., 257, 258, 262, *282*, *284*
Absolutely summable sequence, 6
Abu-Mostafa, Y., 293, *374*
Accelerators, hardware, 271–73
Accommodation boundaries, automatic
    adjustment of, 202, 203–5
Accuracy method, 134–35
Ackley, D. H., 190, *221*
Acoustooptic effect, 308
Activation functions, 191–93, 194, 195
    See also Gaussian potential function
        network (GPFN)
Activations, 21
Active jumping control, 212
Adaptive K-means clustering, 19
Adaptive networks, 313

Adaptive vector quantization (AVQ), 22
    competitive algorithms, 19
  networks, 18
  for phoneme recognition, 1–4, 29–31
Addition, photonic, 293, 295–301
Additive noise, 95
Ahmad, Z., 164, *184*
Aihara, S., 310, *378*
Aizerman, M. A., *220*
Akiyama, Y., 231
Albus, J. S., 163–64, 183, *184*, *220*
Algorithm(s)
  backpropagation, 164, 166, 175
  competitive-learning, 18–25
    competitive AVQ, 19
    differential (DCL), 21–31
    supervised (SCL1), 20–21, 25–28
    supervised (SCL2), 20, 21, 25–28
    unsupervised (UCL), 19–20